THE
COLOR
OF THE
LAW

The

JOHN HOPE FRANKLIN

Series in African American History
and Culture

Waldo E. Martin Jr. & Patricia Sullivan, editors

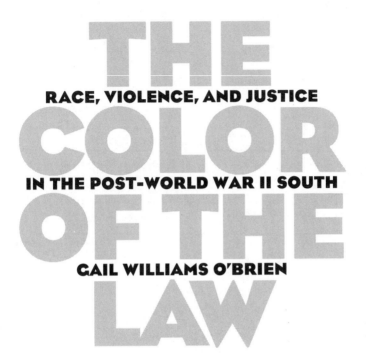

THE
RACE, VIOLENCE, AND JUSTICE
COLOR
IN THE POST-WORLD WAR II SOUTH
OF THE
GAIL WILLIAMS O'BRIEN
LAW

THE UNIVERSITY OF NORTH CAROLINA PRESS

Chapel Hill & London

*Publication of this work was aided by a generous
grant from the Z. Smith Reynolds Foundation.*

The paper in this book meets the guidelines for permanence and durability of the Committee
on Production Guidelines for Book Longevity of the Council on Library Resources.
Library of Congress Cataloging-in-Publication Data
O'Brien, Gail Williams.
The color of the law : race, violence, and justice in the post–World War II South /
by Gail Williams O'Brien.
p.   cm. — (The John Hope Franklin series in African American history and culture)
Includes bibliographical references and index.
ISBN 0-8078-2475-5 (cloth: alk. paper)
ISBN 0-8078-4802-6 (pbk.: alk. paper)
1. Discrimination in criminal justice administration—Southern States—History—
20th century.   2. Afro-Americans—Southern States—History—20th century.
3. Mobs—Southern States—History—20th century.
4. Southern States—Race relations—History—
20th century.   I. Title.   II. Series.
HV9955.S63027   1999
364'.089'96073075—DC21   98-30827
CIP

03 02 01 00 99   5 4 3 2 1

To

Kelly *and* Tony,

with love

CONTENTS

ILLUSTRATIONS

ACKNOWLEDGMENTS

My gratitude is deep and wide. I appreciate the leadership of John W. Cell and the advice and support of the participants, including the late Betty Shabazz, in a National Endowment for the Humanities (NEH) Summer Seminar in the mid-1980s, when I began to shift the focus of my work from the nineteenth century to the twentieth. I am grateful to the Woodrow Wilson International Center for Scholars for a year-long fellowship that greatly facilitated the formation of this study, and to NEH, the Virginia Center for the Humanities and Public Policy, and North Carolina State University (NC State) for providing time away from my university duties at critical stages in the manuscript's development. Thanks, too, to the American Historical Association, the College of Humanities and Social Sciences (CHASS) at NC State, NEH, and the Harry S. Truman Library for travel and research support. Special thanks to Sarah Smith in the CHASS Dean's Office at NC State for all of her assistance as I sought research support.

Professor Jacquelyn Dowd Hall played an important role in my early efforts to secure institutional support for the project, while Professors James O. Horton and Leon Litwack provided critical assistance every step of the way. I remain extremely grateful for their willingness to take time from their own busy schedules to fulfill my requests.

I very much appreciate the interest and hard work of Attorney Patti A. Goldman of the Public Citizen Litigation Group in Washington, D.C., in getting the federal grand jury records unsealed, and the efforts in my behalf of William M. Cohen, chief of Criminal Justice, and Pamela S. Jackson, senior paralegal specialist, of the U.S. Attorney's Office in the Middle District of Tennessee in Nashville. Attorney Cohen played a key role in the government's taking no position in regard to my petition to have the grand jury records unsealed, and Ms. Jackson enthusiastically assisted me in getting access to the grand jury material whenever I needed it. Bonnie Gay, assistant director of the Freedom-of-Information and Privacy Staff of the U.S. Justice Department in Washington, has also been very supportive, especially in my acquisition of photographs for the book. Additionally, I wish to thank the Crisis Publishing Co., Inc., publisher of the magazine of the National Association for the Advancement of Colored People, for authorizing the use of photographs from *The Crisis*.

The late Paul F. Bumpus, former district attorney general of Tennessee, widened the possibilities of the study by loaning me the Lawrenceburg trial transcript, and I remain indebted to him. Every archivist and librarian that I encountered was extraordinarily helpful. In particular, I should like to thank archivist Wayne Moore and librarian Genella Olker of the Tennessee State Library and Archives. Thanks, too, to Mrs. Haroldine Helm of Independence, Missouri, who supplied the most wonderful "home away from home" that I have ever experienced. Peter Ammirati provided refreshing honesty, wry humor, and marvelous research assistance during my year at the Wilson Center; I also greatly appreciate the research assistance of Debbie Blackwell, Chris Dawes, and Seth Maskett.

Attorney Richard Dinkins, a senior partner in Z. Alexander Looby's law firm, put me in touch with invaluable sources in Columbia who, in turn, made my interviews there possible. These crucial contacts included the late Tennessee attorney general William M. Leech Jr. as well as human resources coordinator Ophelia Tisby and elder specialist Walter "Pete" Frierson of Legal Services of South Central Tennessee. All of those whom I interviewed in Columbia and elsewhere freely shared time, information, and opinions, and I remain exceedingly grateful. The Reverend Raymond Lockridge kindly met with me every time I traveled to Columbia.

Many thanks to those who read and commented on portions of the manuscript or on papers and drafts of articles that became part of the manuscript. They include Janaina Amado, Ray Arsenault, W. Fitzhugh Brundage, Jane Censer, Spencer Crew, Pete Daniel, Raymond Gavins, Jacquelyn Dowd Hall, James Horton, Robin Kelly, Robert Korstad, Leon Litwack, and Joe W. Trotter, along with several of my colleagues at North Carolina State University—Holly Brewer, David Gilmartin, William C. Harris, Joseph Hobbs, Walter Jackson, Mimi Kim, Linda McMurry, Nancy Mitchell, John David Smith, Pamela Tyler, and Kenneth Vickery. I should like to extend a very special word of thanks to my colleague, Alex De Grand, who read and commented on a much longer version of the entire manuscript, as well as on the shorter one.

Thanks, too, to Lewis Bateman, executive editor; Katherine Malin, editor, and all of those associated with the UNC Press. One could not ask for a more positive, professional group with whom to work. Additionally, I appreciate the strong support and suggestions of the two readers of the manuscript, W. Fitzhugh Brundage and Joe W. Trotter.

Last, but by no means least, I should like to thank my daughter, Kelly O'Brien, and my husband and colleague, Tony La Vopa. Without their help, suggestions, and encouragement, this book would never have become a reality. During my darkest days—and there were more than a few—they invariably saw the light at the end of the tunnel and persuaded me that a book was in the making. For all of these reasons, and more, I lovingly dedicate this book to them.

THE
COLOR
OF THE
LAW

INTRODUCTION

With its incessant demand for labor and its clarion call for democracy, World War II penetrated the remotest corners of American society. Most notably in the South, it affected race relations more powerfully than any event since the Civil War almost one hundred years earlier. Changes occurred as blacks, as well as whites, fought in the armed forces, migrated in large numbers within and outside the region, switched jobs, joined unions, and sometimes improved their living standard. African Americans also heard a national rhetoric intoning freedom and equality, while their own press called for a Double-V, victory at home as well as abroad.

As these alterations transpired, blacks and whites developed very different expectations about postwar society. More than ever, African Americans determined that they should have fair and equitable treatment, and even cautious southern black leaders expressed opposition to segregation and demanded an end to discrimination in all phases of American life. In contrast, as members of the dominant group, most whites remained oblivious to problems faced by black Americans in a segregated society and blithely assumed that the postwar world would look much like the prewar world.

Some whites were adamant that this would happen. Determined to put blacks, especially returning veterans and civilians whose material circumstances had improved, "in their place," white racists mounted a postwar campaign of terror. The year 1946 saw an increase in lynchings, an attempted revival of the Ku Klux Klan, and two race "riots" in which black people and property were attacked.

Yet despite this initial surge in violent activity, which was preceded by a wave of riots throughout the country in 1943, extralegal violence in the aftermath of World War II never reached the high levels that it had attained after the Civil War and World War I. Ku Klux Klan revitalization efforts sputtered despite avid recruitment drives in 1946 and 1949, while 1952, 1953, and 1954 represented the first lynching-free years since recordkeeping had begun in 1882. In addition, no race riots occurred in the South until the 1960s, beyond an alleged one in Columbia, Tennessee, in February 1946 and another in Athens, Alabama, in August of that year. Moreover, the sixties riots were strikingly different from the forties riots, with blacks rather than whites taking the initiative, and with property rather than persons representing the target.

This study asks why the violent proclivities of some whites erupted at the war's end and, even more important, why extralegal violence did not have the scope and duration that many feared it would following the conflict. It then explores the implications of limited white lawlessness for black Americans and the criminal justice system. Did diminished white violence in the wake of the war mean that public officials were protecting African Americans better than they had in the past? Or did authorities assume a greater responsibility for social control as crowd violence lessened, with the result that unequal enforcement of the law worsened?

The vehicle used for exploring these issues is an averted lynching, known in the parlance of the times as the "Columbia, Tennessee, Race Riot," and the subsequent state actions and legal proceedings that flowed from it. The actions and proceedings included the stationing of the Tennessee Highway Patrol and State Guard in Columbia; a federal grand jury hearing involving alleged civil rights violations by state law officers while in Columbia; and two state trials of African Americans on charges of shooting local and state police.

In this study, I attempt to marry "the concreteness and contingency" of a historical case study with "the analytic explicitness and comparative grounding of sociological analyses." As historian Larry J. Griffin and his associates at Vanderbilt University explain so well: "Events, finally, are analytic composites that fuse the historically particular and the theoretically general so thoroughly that the distinction between the two is largely moot."[1]

In keeping with this perspective, the first chapter of this book narrates the averted lynching and the actions and proceedings that emanated from it, while the remaining chapters unpack the various stages of the episode. The chapters disassembling the event roam widely, from the streets of Columbia across the nation and around the globe. In time, they stretch backward to the Civil War and forward to the present. Throughout, the Columbia affair serves as an anchor, guiding the analysis and, hopefully, rendering it concrete and accessible, but its exposition is not the end in itself. Instead, this work at its most fundamental level focuses on historical processes at work in

American—and especially southern—society, processes for which the Columbia episode represents a clarifying moment.

In explaining the eruption of extralegal violence at the war's end, my study points toward long-held traditions in the South that bound together local authorities and perpetrators of mob actions. Whites also felt threatened as blacks experienced an expanded sense of personal efficacy and entitlement during the conflict, and a number of white servicemen in particular found intolerable the greater latitude that black soldiers enjoyed abroad or that whites thought they enjoyed.

The failure of mob violence to reach the levels that it had formerly achieved was due in part to the changing role of black businessmen in their communities and in relation to whites during the first half of the twentieth century. Ironically, though not accidentally, it also derived from the growing sense of personal efficacy and entitlement among black citizens, which whites found so intimidating. Too, the war's conclusion saw the climax of momentum among liberal and leftist forces that had been building since the New Deal and, in some southern communities, increased black voting power. Finally, and most significantly, underlying structural changes, including the exodus of both whites and blacks from the rural South, made mob violence less likely to occur.

My exploration in the second half of the book of the relationship between African Americans and the criminal justice system makes manifest the intrinsic link between political arrangements and criminal justice components. Specifically, it demonstrates the way politics affected the police and the courts in the South at a time when disfranchisement and legal segregation had been in place for fifty years. Inferentially my study suggests that because politics cannot be eliminated from criminal justice machinery, the relationship between the two must be understood if greater equity for all is to be achieved.

In exploring this relationship, this book provides a concrete example of the way institutional racism operates in American society. For many whites, this phenomenon is difficult to grasp. Dominant in the society and bred on notions of rugged individualism, equal opportunity, and equity before the law, many white Americans simply find it impossible to envision any institution being saturated with racial bias. Yet this is the inevitable outcome of a society that evolved for centuries as separate and unequal. Even arrangements that are designed without race in mind can have racial implications if they are created in circumstances where whites are insiders and blacks are outsiders.

A fine-grained contextual analysis of the Columbia episode was feasible because an extraordinary array of written and oral sources became available. Fearing that racial violence would explode in the wake of World War II as it had following World War I, liberal and leftist organizations were poised at the war's conclusion to monitor and publicize disorders. Thus, when they heard about racial trouble in Columbia, they rushed investigators to that Middle Tennessee town. I began my inquiry with investigative reports and published materials produced by the National Association for the Advancement of Colored People (NAACP), the Southern Regional Council (SRC), the Southern Conference on Human Welfare (SCHW), Tuskegee Institute (now Tuskegee University), and the American Communist Party.

These were accompanied by detailed documentation by the NAACP of its considerable involvement on behalf of African Americans in the criminal cases stemming from the Columbia affair. Similar documentation of the involvement of the SCHW, and of its relations with the NAACP, also appeared in its organizational records. Apart from but closely related to the Columbia experience, the files of Communist Party leader Robert Minor contained a plethora of detailed reports regarding a lynching that occurred in Maury County in 1933. (Columbia is the county seat of Maury.)

In addition to the materials generated by private organizations and individuals, the Tennessee State Archives yielded a journal and active duty reports maintained by the brigadier general of the Tennessee State Guard during the week following the averted lynching, when the Guard was stationed in Columbia. The state archives also contained an extraordinary transcript of the examination of black suspects by state and local officials during the two days following the Columbia "riot." This transcript included the questioning of two men who were later killed in jail. Their interrogations took place just a couple of hours before their deaths.

State supreme court documents included the transcripts of two hearings: a plea of abatement and a change of venue from a trial in which twenty-five African Americans were indicted for shooting a Columbia policeman. The same files contained a two-volume transcript of the trial of two black Columbians charged with shooting a highway patrolman.

Beyond these materials, documents produced by public agencies initially proved elusive. This situation altered drastically in the fall of 1989 when the district attorney who prosecuted the twenty-five African Americans for shooting the Columbia policeman unexpectedly mailed me a ten-volume transcript of that trial. Then in the spring of 1990, as a result of a legal action that I initiated in conjunction with a public service law firm in Washington, D.C., a federal judge in Nashville granted me access to transcripts from a grand jury hearing concerned with alleged excesses of law officers. Taken over the course of eleven days, these transcripts totaled more than 2,000 pages. I supplemented them with detailed Federal Bureau of Investigation (FBI) reports and a Justice Department file that I obtained through Freedom of Information requests.

Because my purpose was to use the Columbia episode as a bridge to wider issues, I also acquired relevant primary materials on topics such as the extensive efforts of the International Union of Mine, Mill, and Smelter Workers (Mine Mill) to organize the Tennessee phosphate mines in the 1930s and 1940s; the treatment of black soldiers during World War II; the racial attitudes of black and white servicemen; and the views of a number of individuals who testified before President Truman's Committee on Civil Rights on matters related to minority rights and law enforcement.

While written materials provided detailed information about the Columbia episode and related topics, interviews were extremely important in helping me both to acquire additional insights into the participants' lives and relationships and to see them in their full, human dimension. Fortunately, oral sources proved as rich as written ones. A visit to the Legal Defense Fund in New York, formerly the legal arm of the NAACP, led me to the Nashville law firm that in 1946 had worked with Thurgood Marshall in defending those charged in the Columbia cases. A senior partner in this organization placed me in touch with invaluable sources in Columbia, both black and white.

As a result of these contacts, I interviewed, among others, the brother of an African American who was killed while in jail; a woman who was the wife of one and daughter-in-law of another of the community's most prominent black businessmen and leaders in 1946; the son of the local sheriff; a policeman who was shot during the conflict; three highway patrolmen; the daughter of the brigadier general of the State Guard; and the FBI agent in charge of its investigation.

I have also spoken with three of the twenty-five black defendants in the first and most important trial stemming from the shooting of the policeman; with the partner of one of the defense lawyers and the law school roommate of another; with the prosecuting attorney and the wife of his assistant; and with two jurors. Always in conducting these interviews, I have approached blacks through blacks and whites through whites, with the exception of my initial contact with the African American attorney in Nashville, who put me in touch with both black and white sources in Columbia.

Beyond Columbia, I have interviewed, among others, the authors of the SCHW and SRC reports and the first black attorney to join the Civil Rights Section (CRS) of the U.S. Justice Department. The late Maceo Hubbard became a CRS lawyer late in 1946 just as the Columbia cases were coming to a close.

While one usually thinks of the South as the spawning ground for racially motivated mob actions, recent events such as the Rodney King affair and the O. J. Simpson trial serve as sharp reminders that continuing difficulties between the police and black citizens and deeply divergent assessments of the criminal justice system by blacks and whites are national in scope. They are not, however, *new* phenomena. Instead, they are the results of processes that stretch deep into the recesses of American history. Because the Columbia "riot" constitutes a revealing episode on this continuum of development, it is to that story that we now turn.

1

THE COLUMBIA STORY

CONFRONTATION

For Gladys Stephenson, getting the children's radio repaired was a trying experience. A 37-year-old domestic worker and mother of four, Stephenson lived in a black working-class neighborhood in the West End in Columbia, a small Middle Tennessee town located about forty-three miles south of Nashville. She had sent the radio in for repairs in early January 1946. Her eldest son James would soon be home from the Navy, and she may have wanted it in working condition for his return; certainly, the other children were clamoring for it. When Stephenson's 17-year-old son, John Robert, carried the radio to the repair shop at Caster-Knott, a department store situated on the southeast corner of the Columbia square, he was told by LaVal LaPointe, the service shop manager, that repairs would cost between $8 and $10.[1]

About a month later when John Stephenson returned to the store to pick up the radio, he learned that it had been sold to a farmer who worked for John Calhoun Fleming Sr. Fleming was the father of William "Billy" Fleming, a 28-year-old Army veteran who began apprenticing in radio repair under the GI Bill at Caster-Knott around December 1, 1945, just a few months after his discharge from service. Although the store had a policy that permitted the sale of an item brought in for repair and not picked up within thirty days, radios were scarce, the younger Fleming later admitted, and none other than Stephenson's had ever been sold. Upon learning of the sale of her children's radio, Gladys Stephenson made her first trip to Caster-Knott, where she conversed with LaPointe. Rather than the $8 to $10 orig-

James Stephenson (Courtesy of NAACP)

inally estimated for repairing it, the shop manager now said charges would be $13.75, with batteries needed to make it play bringing the cost to $17.50. Stephenson informed LaPointe that she could not pay the latter amount but would pay the former. He promised to retrieve the radio.

A week or so later John Stephenson, accompanied by his 19-year-old brother James who was now home from service, returned to the store. According to LaPointe, he "went into considerable detail" to explain to James the work that had been done on the radio. The older Stephenson responded that he felt the charges were too high and that because he was "a radio man in the Navy," he could make the necessary repairs. Stephenson then asked LaPointe to remove the new tubes and to charge him only for the labor involved. LaPointe refused, saying that this would require the removal of some additional parts and would "take all of the profit out of the repair job." James at that point paid LaPointe the $13.75 and left the store without comment.[2]

When Gladys arrived home from work that afternoon and discovered that the radio still would not play and that it had no electric cord, she was quite upset. The next day, Friday, February 22nd, she informed her employer Evelyn Watkins Sowell, a Columbia widow, of her difficulties. Sowell called Caster-Knott and spoke with someone who said that Gladys should return to the store and an adjustment would be made. On Saturday, the 23rd, Gladys returned, only to be told that the manager was in Nashville and she would have to come back another time to see him.

On February 25, 1946, between 9:30 and 10:00 A.M., Gladys Stephenson and her son James made a final, fateful trip to the radio repair shop at Caster-Knott. Exasperated, Gladys announced upon their arrival, "Here I am with the same radio." LaPointe then commented that he had "had quite a bit of trouble with that radio," and Gladys responded, "Yes, you have, because it has not given satisfaction."[3] Gladys Stephenson and LaVal LaPointe then engaged in what one store clerk termed "a loud argumentative conversation" in which Stephenson insisted that the radio had always played on electric current; LaPointe informed her that it would not do so now without additional parts, and she responded that she felt as if she had already paid for those parts. She also added that she did not wish him to do any further work on the radio beyond the reattachment of the electric cord.[4] Throughout the discussion, James Stephenson and Billy Fleming remained silent.

As Stephenson and his mother descended from the third floor of Caster-Knott where the repair shop was located, an elderly white man entered the store with a broken radio. Although Gladys Stephenson insisted that she did not speak to this individual but to her son, she was obviously aggravated, and she burst out as they passed the man, "I will take my radio some place else and have it fixed, all they did here was tear it up."[5] Infuriated, Fleming told her to leave the store. When Gladys communicated this remark to her son, James handed her the radio and placed himself between her and the assistant repairman.

As mother and son exited, James Stephenson allegedly looked back through the window of the closed door "in what Fleming considered to be a threatening manner." The young Army vet then raced through the door, hitting the former Navy man in the back of the head with his fist. Stephenson, a welterweight boxer in the Navy, immediately spun around and punched Fleming, who fell through a small window located between the sidewalk and the entry to the store (not the large plate glass window at the front of the store, as everyone later believed). Losing his balance, Stephenson fell in after him, and both men came up fighting. "Once the fight got underway," LaPointe recollected, "neither Fleming nor James Stephenson made an effort to retreat."[6]

Apparently LaPointe tried to assist Fleming, but Gladys Stephenson grabbed him from behind. She claimed that the repair shop manager slapped her; LaPointe insisted he attempted to hold and quiet her. "When we stepped out the door, one of the men slapped me and the other man, Mr. Flemming [sic], hit my boy and we was fighting, we was fighting mad," she later recalled. LaPointe himself admitted, "Things were a little confused, it happened so fast."[7]

Wrenching herself free from LaPointe, Gladys grabbed a piece of glass from the broken window, and lunged at Billy Fleming's back, rendering a glancing blow to his shoulder.[8] At that point, another white man wearing a khaki soldier's jacket, who was probably Elmer H. Rogers, a veteran and an employee at a nearby hosiery mill, raced across the street from the courthouse and threw Gladys to the ground, blacking her eye, tearing her coat, and hitting her on the arm.

As Fleming and Stephenson fell across an automobile parked in front of a store on the square, both LaPointe and Rogers assisted Fleming, and the Navy vet was "subdued without further blows."[9] Although a white man (possibly LaPointe) who was holding Stephenson's mother told Stephenson that he "had better go ahead and run and get out of there," James stayed to assist Gladys.[10] Both were held at the front of the store for three or four minutes until the police arrived. Bleeding profusely from a cut in his leg, Fleming was taken to the back of the store for first aid. Later, he was carried in an ambulance to the hospital where he spent the night. Though not seriously injured, he was treated for the cut and for shock.

As the police approached, LaPointe and Rogers "walked upon the sidewalk." Ignoring them, police chief Walter Griffin demanded from James Stephenson his knife, a weapon the young man did not carry. As Griffin drew back his billy club to strike the former soldier, his mother screamed: "Don't you hit that boy, you ought to investigate before you start hitting." The police chief lowered his arm, but the other officer, W. E. "Clyde" Frazier, a radio operator at the Columbia police station, struck Gladys two or three times as Griffin again asked if James Stephenson had a knife, and Gladys excitedly yelled "That boy don't carry a knife."[11]

During the fight, a largely white crowd of fifty to sixty people had gathered. Many directed angry remarks toward James Stephenson. Both he and his mother were placed in a police car and taken to the Columbia jail. There they were held in adjacent cells for half an hour to an hour. Then they were taken to a small side room where they were asked if they were guilty of fighting on the street. Each said yes; each was fined $50, the maximum penalty in such cases. No further questions ensued.

Rather than being freed, however, the Stephensons were led back to their cells. They remained there until early in the afternoon when Police Chief Griffin removed them to the county jail. Unbeknownst to either Gladys or James, John Fleming Sr. had obtained a warrant for attempted murder against the pair for their alleged attack upon his son. At the county jail, Sheriff James J. Underwood Sr. "patted us down to see what we had," James recalled, and he inquired of the young man if he were hurt. Only his

BEALUM, EARLINE V

Tue Mar 19, 2019

(Estimated hold expiration date)

Transit Date: Sat Mar 09 2019

The color of the law : race,

33029040727422

Hold note:

*
*
*
*
*
*
*

POC

BEALUM, EARLINE V

Tue Mar 19, 2019

(Estimated hold expiration date)

thumb, he answered, and the sheriff then asked about the weapon he had used in his fight with Fleming. When Stephenson said his fist, Underwood noted that Fleming was "cut pretty bad." It must have happened when he fell through the window, the Navy vet responded, and the sheriff said "Okay," though he added, "The people up town are talking." When Stephenson was asked later what the sheriff had meant, he said Underwood had told him people were talking "about a mob."[12]

By early afternoon on the 25th, cars filled with white men from the Culleoka vicinity in eastern Maury County, the home of the Flemings, began arriving on the square in downtown Columbia. They were joined by phosphate and hosiery mill workers and by an assortment of others, including auto mechanics, filling station attendants, and taxicab drivers. Many, though not all, were in their late teens and early twenties. World War II veterans comprised the most volatile element in the crowd. Among those appearing on the square was Billy Fleming's father, John Sr. Inebriated, the elder Fleming urged the lynching of Stephenson, but he "fainted" and had to be taken away. He had breathed too many ether fumes when he visited his son in the hospital, he later claimed to the FBI![13]

While the crowd milled, Hannah Peppers proceeded to the county jail where Sheriff Underwood permitted a visit with her daughter and grandson. As she crossed the town square, Peppers saw "some white people there, quite a few there." They were "kind of bunched off in bunches," and from one cluster of two or three men, Peppers heard the remark: "We are going to take them two 'niggers,' the Stephenson 'niggers' out of the jail and hang them."[14] For black Maury Countians, such threats held ominous overtones, for within the previous two decades, two lynchings had occurred in the community, one in the Culleoka vicinity itself.

Yet rather than mention this conversation to the sheriff, Peppers raced immediately after her jail visit to the first block of East Eighth Street, an area known among many blacks as the "Bottom" and among whites as "Mink Slide." There she pleaded with James Morton, a third-generation funeral home owner, and with Julius Blair, East Eighth Street's 76-year-old patriarch and soda "fount" proprietor, to get her daughter and grandson out of jail. Quite familiar with such proceedings, both men promised their assistance.

Shortly thereafter, they made their way, along with Blair's eldest son Saul (often spelled Sol), and another local resident, John Dudley, to the office of Magistrate C. Hayes Denton. For the first time, they learned that the Stephensons had been charged with attempted murder, and they began to perceive the extent of white restiveness. Denton in fact urged them to leave mother and son in jail for their own safety. Well aware that Henry Choate had been removed from jail and lynched in 1927, and that Denton's automobile had been used in the 1933 abduction and subsequent lynching of Cordie Cheek, Blair responded resolutely: "Let us have them, Squire. . . . We are not going to have any more social lynchings in Maury County."[15]

Concerned about potential trouble, James Morton telephoned the sheriff following this visit, and he endeavored to locate him at the courthouse. Underwood, who had already heard reports of disturbances throughout town as he left the court, had driven to the Bottom, where he was conversing with Julius and Saul Blair when Morton approached. Clearly, mob violence was on the sheriff's mind, for he had "commenced telling off a tale" as soon as he encountered the Blairs about how his father had prevented the lynching of a white man in Arkansas, and he promised there would be no trouble in Columbia.[16]

Next the conversation had shifted to politics. In October, Underwood had lost the Democratic primary to Billy Fleming's younger brother Flo by a mere thirteen votes, and the Blairs were trying to convince the sheriff to run himself or his son for the office on an independent ticket.[17] Upon encountering the trio, Morton expressed his concern about the anger of whites toward James Stephenson, and he and the Blairs agreed to meet the sheriff at the jail at 5:00 so that mother and son could be released into their custody. Later as Underwood turned the pair over to the East Eighth Street proprietors, he urged: "Take care of them."[18] Gladys Stephenson was driven to her home "out on West End," but James was taken to the Bottom "where we could see after him better than at home," Julius explained.[19]

Just as word of Stephenson's alleged attack on Billy Fleming spread rapidly among whites in Maury County, rumors that rope had been purchased and that young Stephenson's life was in danger circulated among African Americans. Soon armed black Maury Countians were pouring into the Bottom. By early evening, when Sheriff Underwood and his first deputy Claude Goad traveled to East Eighth Street, the sheriff found "probably one hundred fifty negroes . . . forty to fifty or maybe more [with] guns in their hands, shotguns, rifles of different types and calibers."[20]

In their trips to the Bottom, law officers encountered anger and frustration among many in the assemblage. When Columbia authorities entered the area, "a lot of negroes jumped on the police car," and one on the rear bumper yelled, "Let's turn the car over." "A colored boy, a 'nigger,'" as one police officer termed him, declared that "he had fought for freedom overseas and he was going to fight for it here." Another, in reference to Sheriff

Underwood, told crowd members that "if they would get out of the way he would kill the son-of-a-bitch now."[21]

In contrast, black leaders remained respectful toward the sheriff and the police but nevertheless firm in their commitment to keep whites out of the area. Saul Blair told the group as they jumped on the car, "You all are the craziest bunch I have ever seen. Get off the Law's car," while Calvin Lockridge, a carpenter and Missionary Baptist minister, "gently" took the Sheriff by the arm and "kept nudging . . . [him] out of the crowd" when he heard the threat against his life. Either Saul Blair or James Morton also urged: " 'Keep quiet, lets hear what he has to say,' " as Underwood tried to speak to the crowd.[22]

Lockridge, however, had in his possession "an Army paratrooper's [semi-automatic machine] gun and several clips of ammunition," while James Morton, restaurant-poolroom owner Meade Johnson, and possibly Julius Blair carried double-barreled shotguns. Morton told police officer George Reeves "he didn't want any white people in the area," including "white taxis." "Get rid of the white people on the square," he maintained, "and the negroes would be all right."[23]

Before leaving, Deputy Goad spoke privately with Saul Blair. "It is getting pretty hot uptown, get the boy out," he suggested. When Blair relayed this information to "Pappa," Julius made his decision. "Get him out," he declared. "Go out the dirt road to East End Street, come in on the Bear Creek Pike, and come in to the Nashville Pike," he instructed his 55-year-old son as he described a circuitous and hopefully safe route out of Columbia. Thomas William "Tommy" Neely, who was in Saul's barbershop "getting a shine," agreed to drive. Robert Frierson and James "Popeye" Bellanfante volunteered to accompany him. Meanwhile James Stephenson, who had observed armed whites on the square when he took his girlfriend home about 6:30 that evening, had obtained a gun and shells from Blair's Barbershop on his return to East Eighth Street. He then climbed on top of a building with about twenty-five other armed men, at least a couple of whom were still "in uniform." Stephenson left the area, because Blair and Neely suggested that if he departed "maybe they [whites] would quiet down."[24]

The trip seemed star-crossed from the beginning. As the five men set out in Neely's 1941 Ford Coupe, the engine sputtered and died. Transmission problems! Backing up, Neely got the car started and hurried to his nearby home, where they switched to his 1938 Dodge. Armed with two shotguns, three or four pistols, and Bellanfante's submachine gun, they sped away again. This time, just after they entered the Nashville highway near Haynes

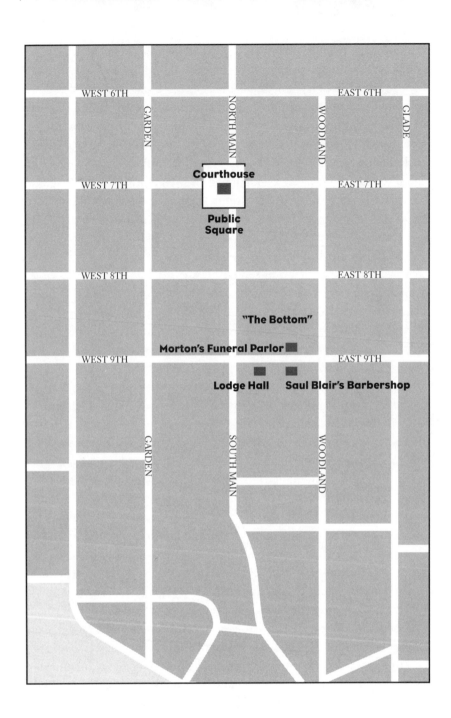

WEST 6TH   EAST 6TH

GARDEN   NORTH MAIN   WOODLAND   GLADE

Courthouse

WEST 7TH   EAST 7TH

Public Square

WEST 8TH   EAST 8TH

"The Bottom"

Morton's Funeral Parlor

WEST 9TH   EAST 9TH

Lodge Hall   Saul Blair's Barbershop

GARDEN   SOUTH MAIN   WOODLAND

Map of downtown Columbia, Tennessee

Haven farm, a tire blew out and Neely had no spare! Quickly the men pushed the car alongside the gate at Haynes Haven, while Neely rushed inside to ask a Mr. Chapman, whom he knew, to phone Blair's barbershop and request that bootblack George Nicholson come to their rescue.[25]

Joined by Nicholson in his car, the men, now six in number, advanced rapidly toward Spring Hill on their way to Nashville. Then came an awful scraping sound; the fender of Nicholson's car was rubbing against the tire. Ever resourceful, the occupants "picked us up a plank and knocked the fender out some."[26] They then moved en masse to the side of the car opposite the problem so that the fender lifted enough from the tire to allow them to proceed to Spring Hill.

Once there, Neely and Stephenson stealthily made their way through the village on foot, while the others sought assistance. "A big white fellow" tried to help them pry the fender away from the wheel to no avail.[27] They next took the tire off and proceeded to a nearby restaurant where they encountered none other than James Stephenson's uncle, who loaned them a hammer and assisted them in making the necessary repairs. After retrieving Stephenson and Neely on the outskirts of town, they sped toward Nashville and Union Station. There Saul Blair bought a ticket, the men whiled away a few hours in "George Gordon's Cafe," and at 2:10 in the morning, James Stephenson boarded a train for Chicago and the safety of his father.[28]

Once Saul Blair left town with Stephenson and the other members of their party, Julius Blair called the sheriff's office to report that the young man was gone, and he asked the sheriff's son, who answered the phone, to get word of Stephenson's departure to his father and the other white people on the square.[29] The senior Blair then proceeded to a meeting at the home of teaching supervisor and former College Hill High School instructor Johnnie B. Fulton. Several community leaders, including Mary Morton who served as the secretary of the group, had assembled there to raise money for the acquisition of land for a school the county had agreed to build once black residents purchased the site.

Meanwhile, whites continued to mill around on the town square, conversing and drinking beer from nearby establishments or liquor that they had brought with them. Although his efforts came to no avail, John Fleming Jr.—in marked contrast to his father—showed up that evening to urge them to go home.

As Sheriff Underwood described the scene after his visit to the Bottom: "small groups of two to four white men . . . were along the sidewalk on South Main Street near the Mink Slide Area and the Square immediately adjacent."[30] Columbia Mayor Eldridge Denham also witnessed "several

Taken on the night of February 25, 1946, at the corner of South Main and East Eighth Streets. The Highway Patrol officer with stripes on his sleeve looking toward the first block of East Eighth (the Bottom) is J. J. Jackson. Note the intermingling of highway patrolmen and armed white civilians and the sailor's uniform under the jacket of the civilian facing the camera. (Courtesy of United States Attorney's Office, Middle District of Tennessee)

little bunches of white people," though he discerned their loose coalescence into two groups: one in front of a restaurant and, ominously from Julius Blair's perspective, another in front of "the Fair Store," a department store above which Culleoka resident and Magistrate C. Hayes Denton had his office.[31] Although the mayor later claimed, as did other local and state officials, that most in the crowd were "juveniles," the town's presiding officer commented that the gathering included "a few service men and quite a number of ex-service men, quite a few soldiers gathered in the evening."[32]

Shortly after Underwood returned to his office, "a big bunch" of about fifty men approached the jail and "began to kick in this side door." Quickly the sheriff, armed with a machine gun, opened the door and "told them I would lock every damned one up." "Where's the Negro," Carl Kelly, a soldier, called out from the crowd. "It wasn't any of their damned business," the sheriff retorted, though he added that "they [the Stephensons] were not here." He then arrested two of the men who appeared to be leaders of the group on charges of public drunkenness and profanity, and the crowd began to disperse, its members reverting once more to milling around the courthouse.[33]

In the Bottom, fear and apprehension persisted. Armed men remained on rooftops and in the street, talking, watching, and consuming beer. After taking his wife to the school meeting at Fulton's house, James Morton returned to East Eighth where he heard "two or three" shots from the whites' vicinity at Ninth and South Main Streets. Briefly he conversed with E. B. Noles, a highway patrolman based in neighboring Marshall County who had driven to the Bottom. "James," Noles cautioned him, "you tell those colored people to break up and scatter down here." "Mr. Noles, I will do that," Morton replied, though he continued: "In the meantime you go up town and get those fellows to scatter. . . ." Another sound like a shot erupted; Noles sped away. Morton hurried back to Fulton's. "There is a mob forming down town. It is liable to cause trouble. I think you all ought to go home," he excitedly informed the group.[34]

As Morton and his wife raced back to their funeral home on the first block of East Eighth Street, Julius Blair too "jumped in [his] car and rushed to [his] place of business" where he quickly ushered people out, turned off the lights, and headed home. Those gathered on the street urged others to darken their establishments, and in an attempt to shroud the area completely, they shot out streetlights.[35]

When Columbia's police chief heard shots emanating from the Bottom, he decided to proceed into the area, although whites on the square warned him that "the darkies" there were armed "with shotguns, rifles, and pistols."[36] On Griffin's order, all six of the town's policemen left their location near the Fair Store' and headed on foot toward East Eighth Street, with a crowd of whites trailing along behind them. At the corner of South Main and East Eighth, Officers Frank Collins and George Reeves were told to stay behind to keep whites out of the area. Next, with 70-year-old Griffin and 66-year-old Will Wilsford leading the way, and with their guns still in their holsters, Columbia's other four policemen proceeded diagonally across East Eighth and into the Bottom.

As they made their way down the street, a voice called out from the crowd bunched together in the darkness below, "Here they come," and another, "Halt!" The police paused as Griffin yelled back: "Boys, we just want to come down to talk to you." Confusion appeared to reign as members of the group "began to talk a right smart . . . and were hollering." Suddenly the command to "Fire!" sounded. Shots rang out and continued to ring out as the police scurried back up the street and into cars. All four of the officers were hit, with Wilsford, struck with "buck shot" "in the face, neck, and chest," injured the most seriously.[37]

Immediately guns flashed in the hands of whites. Realizing that "the situation had gotten out of hand," Sheriff Underwood telephoned Governor James McCord, asking for the "assistance of all highway patrolmen he could get." Still, although the shooting of police officers usually ranked alongside alleged attacks on white women in fueling mob spirit in the South, the knowledge that blacks in the Bottom were armed and willing to fire clearly dampened the ardor of the crowd on the square for an invasion of East Eighth Street.[38] With this advantage, the sheriff and his deputies, along with the remaining uninjured policemen, and three locally based state troopers "managed to hold back the white people and prevent them from proceeding to Mink Slide and engaging in a battle with the Armed Forces." The state troopers included Noles; police chief Griffin's son, William A. "Billy" Griffin; and Billy Fleming's brother, Flo.[39]

Lynn Bomar—chief of the Highway Patrol, state commissioner of safety, and former all-American football star—was "just outside the City Limits of Spring Hill" when he got the call from the governor telling him to proceed to Columbia. Siren wailing, he raced toward the county seat. "I was running a Roadmaster Buick, flying a little low, it didn't take me long to get to Columbia," he recalled.[40]

Shortly after Bomar's arrival, a group of whites commandeered a Monsanto Chemical bus waiting on the square to take employees to work and forced the driver to take them to the local state guard armory. Soon a crowd of between 150 and 200 white Maury Countians had congregated there. They were joined by highway patrolmen Noles and Griffin, who told the caretaker "to furnish them arms and ammunition, stating that they had been instructed by Commissioner Bomar to deputize some of the crowd . . . to quell the disturbance that seemed imminent." The caretaker refused and immediately contacted local members of the Tennessee State Guard. (The National Guard had not yet been demobilized from service in World War II.)[41]

When the officers arrived, the state troopers again demanded guns, and they threatened to "call the Governor if necessary to have him instruct State

Guardsmen to turn over arms and ammunition to them." An "excited" Lynn Bomar told Lieutenant Myron Peck to do the same, stating that "they needed guns badly." The situation grew increasingly tense. "A restrained report" later described not only a commissioner of safety who was "quite excited" but also a "rough" crowd of "25 to 30 white men" who got inside the Armory, though not into "the strong room" where the guns and ammunition were kept. "By God—we will take them if you don't let us have them!" one member of the throng yelled. Hastily, Major William H. Cotham Jr. contacted Major General Jacob McGavock Dickinson Jr., the commander of the Guard and of its Second Infantry Brigade. When Dickinson sustained the major's decision to withhold guns from state troops, the patrolmen left. Gradually, the crowd began to disperse.

Threats to the Bottom by no means ceased, however. Following the Armory incident, a crowd of about fifteen men watched as James Beard, the owner of a small auto repair shop and the son of Columbia's former fire chief, and his companion Borgie Claude headed down an alley toward East Eighth Street. Armed and carrying a half gallon of gasoline, the duo planned to set fire to the black business district. As they entered the alley, Claude handed his shotgun to a nearby taxi driver, but he kept a revolver in his possession. Beard carried a shotgun. As the pair made their way down the alley, shots from atop one of the buildings in the area zinged toward them. Both were struck, and both quickly hightailed it back up the street. Beard had buckshot removed from the front of his legs at the fire station; Claude was taken by cab to King's Daughter's Hospital.[42]

STATE FORCES MOVE IN

Under orders from their chief, highway patrolmen sped toward Columbia. Before the night was over, between sixty and seventy-five would arrive. The first to show up were members of the Middle Tennessee Division, who were based in Nashville and surrounding towns. Later this contingent would be reinforced by the East Tennessee Division based in Knoxville, a unit Lynn Bomar himself had once commanded. It would be the Nashville troops, however, under the leadership of Bomar and 35-year-old sergeant and later division chief, J. J. Jackson, who would carry out a predawn raid on the Bottom.

As his men began to arrive, the patrol chief positioned them at the two intersections leading into the first block of East Eighth Street, that is, at East Eighth and South Main and at East Eighth and Woodland. He also dispatched Tennessee Valley Authority (TVA) guards W. E. "Smitty" Smith and E. G. Flannigan, along with Constables Homer Copeland and Harry Shaw, to the Jackson Highway. Reports had been received that "armed Negroes from the phosphate mines at nearby Mt. Pleasant were moving to help the encircled Negroes on Mink Slide."[43]

As soon as the four policemen were shot, most African Americans in the Bottom had fled the area. Others gradually melted away, leaving only a smattering of men there. Several found refuge at James Morton's funeral parlor until they were discovered and arrested in the early hours of the morning. Two, William A. "Rooster Bill" Pillow and "Papa" Lloyd Kennedy, spent the night in Saul Blair's barbershop, where the 21-year-old Kennedy had worked for three or four years shining shoes. About half a dozen men stayed throughout the night on the second floor of the Lodge Hall, while a comparable number sought safety at the home of a relative, Daisy Lee, on Woodland Street, just around the corner from East Eighth.

About the time the armory episode occurred, Major General Dickinson was ordered to Maury County by the assistant adjutant general under the direction of the governor. After consulting with Major Carlton, he mobilized the Second and Tenth Regiments, and later the Seventh, bringing his entire Second Brigade into action. He also supplemented this force with a detachment from the Third Brigade. In all, "139 officers . . . and 648 enlisted men saw some service at Columbia," though only about 200 were present on the morning of the 26th, when the highway patrol commenced its invasion of the Bottom.[44]

When Dickinson reached the county seat, he learned that "the buildings along the south side of East 8th St . . . were occupied by an unknown number of negroes who kept up continual sniping upon all who appeared." He later reported that "the number of negroes in Mink Slide engaged in or threatening violence was variously estimated at from 75 to 150." Through his "own reconnaissance," the brigadier general also observed "many armed white persons in the surrounding area," and in conjunction with his "reconnaissance detachment," he concluded that "they equalled or exceeded the supposed number of negroes in Mink Slide."[45]

Because it would take the rest of the night for Dickinson's brigade to reach effective strength, he determined in consultation "with Safety Commissioner Bomar, Sheriff Underwood and City Officials" that "nothing further [was] to be done until about daylight." In his own hand, he scribbled in the meticulously typed Brigade journal: "Agreement—joint action 7 am."[46]

As Bomar and his troopers stood at the intersections of East Eighth Street, they were heckled by whites for not going immediately into the area. Although the chief and his men withstood this taunting, they did not prove so restrained as the evening wore on. Initially they were surprised when John Kincaid, a Nashville resident who had been asked by a United Press manager "to stick with Lynn Bomar most of the time," appeared at the intersection of Eighth and Woodland and informed them that James Morton was inside a nearby house and that he was going in to interview him.[47] Although the troopers had heard the phone ringing all evening as newspapermen attempted to reach Morton, no lights had come on in the house and they had assumed no one was there. When Kincaid showed up, a patrolman escorted him inside and left.

Shortly afterwards the patrol chief appeared at the door, asking who lived there. When he learned the identity of the occupants, he "walked in," proclaiming as he did so: "Morton, you are the bastard leading these bastards." As the undertaker protested, "No, sir, Mr. Bomar, I am sure you are wrong," the burly safety commissioner, with "one of those great big lights flashing," strode passed him into the room where the men were hiding, yelling as he did so, "Hey bring me some help in here, the house is full of negroes."[48]

At that point, according to James Morton, "about seven or eight patrolmen rushed in with machine guns." "The first son-of-a-bitch that bats his eye let him have it!" Bomar shouted. Someone struck William Dawson over the head, apparently with a blackjack. The troopers then "'ransacked' the place, searching for guns, ammunition, etc." They confiscated jewelry that belonged to James Morton and his wife. When they discovered "a pearl handle pistol" in a trunk, Bomar exercised his prerogative as chief, stating "'I will take that one.'" John Thompson of the Associated Press described Mary Morton as "extremely wrought up, almost hysterical, obviously nearly scared to death." Another, older woman, who was either Mary's mother or her friend Marcia Mayes was "weeping, and sobbing, and from her conversation," the reporter continued, "I gathered . . . that the negroes were all terrified."[49]

About a dozen men, including Morton, were removed from the house. As they were "loaded" into a truck, Saul Blair and George Nicholson were seized at the intersection of East Eighth and Woodland as they returned from Nashville. They too were placed under arrest. As this occurred, "a crowd of white people gathered around." All were armed, but no one attempted any action when the state guardsmen who were present "told them to stand back."[50]

Just after 6:00 on the morning of February 26, the Highway Patrol moved into the Bottom. Although the Tennessee State Guard "had presupposed almost the identical problem that took place in Columbia" and had had "simple basic drills, and various forms of advanced training," the force made a singular contribution to the patrol venture. As part of Field Order No. 1, guardsmen were to relieve troopers at the intersections leading into the first block of East Eighth Street. In turn, the guardsmen were to be supported by other Guard units, who would present such a show of force that neither blacks in the Bottom nor armed whites on the outside would want to cause trouble as the highway patrol attempted to remove those still on East Eighth. To this end, Colonel Victor H. Wilson, commander of the Second Regiment and Dickinson's second in command in Columbia, assumed guard duty with five of his men at the intersection of East Eighth and South Main Streets. He then ordered the gas company of the Second Regiment to move from the armory to this location.[51]

Before the company could arrive, however, Wilson had to confront a crowd of fifty to seventy-five armed whites. Walter Hurt, staff correspondent with the *Tennessean*, described the scene: "Shotguns, rifles and small arms bristled among them. They had been fed with rumors there would be a showdown at dawn following a night of sporadic firing. Several of their relatives and friends had been wounded in the shootings. Nerves were at the snapping point. The men were grim-lipped and gripped their weapons tensely."[52]

When the crowd heard "gunfire and wild yells" issuing from the Bottom, its members initially "hesitated," but, encouraged by "several hot-heads . . . obviously drinking," they "blindly started to move forward." At that point, Colonel Wilson, "weighing no more than 140 or 150" stepped up and told them to "Take those guns home." "We'll take care of any situation that needs them," he continued. "Again they hesitated. Again the fanatical would-be leaders urged them on." This time Wilson "singled out the leaders and practically read them a 'one-man riot act.'" Repeatedly "he kept pushing them back and [he] detailed one of his men to escort a man home and leave his gun." "Gradually the armed weapon carriers, some so tense there were tears in their eyes, broke up and faded from the scene."[53]

From the intersection of South Main and East Eighth Streets, J. J. Jackson and a contingent of the Middle Tennessee division of the Highway Patrol had advanced down the sidewalk toward Bomar and a force that was entering the first block of East Eighth from Woodland. Others, including Trooper Ray Austin and Sergeants Joe Sanford and Fred Waldrop, moved up the middle of the street. The forces met near Saul Blair's barbershop. Jackson peered through the door. "Look out, one is in there," he yelled. "He is going to shoot!" Trooper Dave White called back as he saw the man raise a weapon. At least one shotgun blast emanated from the facility. Austin,

State guardsman turns back mob members at the corner of South Main and East Eighth Streets. (Courtesy of United States Attorney's Office, Middle District of Tennessee)

Sanford, and Waldrop were all struck with buckshot, though none was injured seriously enough to consult a physician or even to leave duty. Armed with machine guns, several patrolmen immediately emptied 125 rounds of ammunition into the establishment. Miraculously, neither "Rooster Bill" Pillow, who crouched in a corner "just as low as he could get, with his hands buried in his face," nor "Papa" Lloyd Kennedy, who stood behind a partition in a shower stall "against the wall in a corner, just as straight as he could," were hit.[54]

The patrolmen maintained that they removed from the shop a double-barreled shotgun with two empty shells nearby and a single-barreled shotgun with a spent shell in the chamber, though they could produce none of these items in court. According to Pillow and Kennedy, once they were

Hollis Reynolds (left) shortly after being shot and seized by highway patrolmen during the invasion of the Bottom on February 26. (Courtesy of United States Attorney's Office, Middle District of Tennessee)

taken from the facility by the sheriff, who had accompanied state troopers into the Bottom, the patrolmen "took over in a big way, beating, kicking, stomping, cursing, abusing." Allegedly, they asserted: "You black sons of so and so, you had your alls way last night, but we are going to have ours this morning."[55]

From the barbershop, the troopers proceeded to other East Eighth Street establishments, "shooting off locks and kicking in the doors." Hollis Reynolds, who rented a room in the back of a restaurant, was dressing to go to work when patrolmen burst into the building and shot him in the arm. The most brutal attack occurred, however, at the Lodge Hall. There, Jackson and the officers accompanying him kicked down an entry set of double doors and made their way up the stairs. At the top, "some of the boys" went through a door "to the right," while the division chief and the others shot off the locks and kicked in another set of double doors as they proceeded into a large room with "a big stage" that was used by the Odd Fellows; the International Union of Mine, Mill, and Smelter Workers Local 546; and a host of others for meetings and celebrations. "They were cursing and said they ought to kill everyone of us negroes," Leonard Evans recalled. Jackson said only that "several negroes came out from behind this stage . . . with their hands up saying, 'Please don't shoot.' "[56]

J. C. "Charlie" Smith was seized by one trooper and struck by two others as he emerged from his hiding place behind a piano on the stage. They then "beat up some more boys." None was more savagely manhandled than John Blackwell. According to Jackson, a door to a "little room" off the main one opened and Blackwell "came out with a gun, shotgun in his hand." As the later division chief described his next action: "I didn't ask any questions, I hit him across the head and knocked him to the floor."[57]

Beyond taking "the shotgun away from him," the trooper offered no further details of Blackwell's arrest, but other witnesses described a fierce attack. Initially, when Blackwell had emerged from the small room with his hands in the air, patrolmen had "knocked him down with their fist[s]." "It was about two on him when they had him down hitting him in the head with a gun and he never did get up," Charlie Smith continued, so "They pulled him on down, caught hold of his breeches leg and pulled him down the steps." "His face was bumping the steps. . . ." Once on the street, "some highway patrolmen kicked him in the mouth," but another said " 'Don't kick that man no more, you done killed him.' "[58] At that point, Blackwell "groaned and moved his hand or leg, and the officer said, 'No he is not dead, but he ought to be.' " He then turned over the hapless Blackwell "with his foot," proclaiming, " 'God damn you, I ought to blow your God damned black brains out. I hope you die."[59]

As the men were removed from the Lodge Hall to the street, the maltreatment continued, amid cries by troopers of "reach to the sky!"[60] "You negroes are not as bad as you were last night," one shouted as he struck Army veteran Elmer Dooley "in the eye with a blackjack or a club." John Porter too described further abuse: "[a patrolman] come up . . . cursing and said, 'You damn negroes think you are bad' and hit me across the head with a rifle a couple of times." Likewise, Leonard Evans was thrown down the steps and struck with "either a tommy gun or rifle" and then "kicked and stomped" as he lay on the sidewalk. "I stood there in the middle of the street for a good long time, and the officers did mistreat them," prize-winning photojournalist Edward "Ed" Clark later told a federal grand jury. "One was

John Blackwell lies in the street after being beaten and dragged down the steps of the Lodge Hall during the Highway Patrol invasion of the Bottom on the morning of February 26. Two patrolmen are assessing his condition; Policeman Frank T. Collins and Constable Homer Copeland are in the background. (Courtesy of United States Attorney's Office, Middle District of Tennessee)

hit over the head with a Tommy gun, broke the stock off of it. I saw two or three hit with blackjacks, flashlights, kicked," he asserted.[61]

As the men from the Lodge Hall were joined by others seized in the East Eighth Street vicinity and then marched to jail, the abuse persisted. Running in front snapping pictures, Clark "saw them get hit and heard licks I didn't see." As the prisoners made their way up Woodland, "some white ladies, and some boys on the street" shouted, " 'Hit that negro, hit them, make them reach.' " As the patrolmen obliged these requests, the spectators yelled, "Hit them again!"[62] The prisoners were also struck by state troopers as they were placed in the Maury County jail.

As the raid by patrolmen proceeded, General Dickinson, infuriated at

Black Columbians are marched to jail from the Bottom after being rounded up by the Highway Patrol on the morning of February 26. The second person from the left is William Gordon, who two days later died at the hands of patrolmen while incarcerated in the county jail. (Courtesy of United States Attorney's Office, Middle District of Tennessee)

their early entry into the Bottom, raced down South Main "on the double . . . as mad as a wet hen . . . his neck . . . turkey cock red." When he arrived at Saul Blair's barbershop at 6:40 in the morning, it was already "pretty badly wrecked." As Blair described it:

> two plate glasses were broken all to pieces, and the door made out of little glasses, all the panes, six or seven panes was out. . . . the chairs was all cut up and shot up, all the mirrors broke up. . . . The cash register was

smashed so bad . . . National Cash Register Company . . . said they couldn't fix it. . . . They broke open my wardrobe where I kept my towels and linen and things . . . they shot holes through the shower bath and they taken my kodak, three pair of electric clippers, all my razors, and . . . two silver dollars.

"Just ramshackled, tore up," he summarized, "looked like rats made a bed out of it."[63]

Julius Blair described similar conditions at his soda fount: "I had a big clock knocked off the wall . . . the glasses, my showcases were all broken up, and the shelves where I had my glass, medicine, and things was broken out . . . the ice cream what they didn't eat up they put rat poison in it."[64]

As the raid ensued, Mary Morton saw a "group of State Patrolmen advance in a body across the street in the direction of her husband's funeral home. . . ." Though "her view was obstructed and she could not see them enter the place . . . soon she heard glass breaking." Ed Clark too "could see the blows come against the Venetian blinds and break the glass." When four officers emerged a short time later, "They were laughing and joking." Inside the place was in shambles: a sofa, chairs, drapes, and Venetian blinds were cut; lights were broken; files and mortgage notes were "torn to pieces"; embalming fluid had been poured "all through" a navy blue casket and the letters "KKK" scrawled with chalk or white powder across the top; and a lady's dress and a man's suit had been placed in other coffins and embalming fluid poured over them.[65]

In the end, not a single black-owned business in the first block of East Eighth Street was left unscathed. All were damaged through avid searches and wanton destruction, including the offices of a physician and the local agent for the Atlanta Life Insurance Company. An investigator for the two-year-old Southern Regional Council (SRC) concluded: "Any estimate of property damage would not be too high." Though a couple of state guardsmen later admitted seeing others in their ranks pilfer cigarettes, cigars, and candy, there was little doubt that members of the Tennessee Highway Patrol had perpetrated this swath of devastation.[66]

Following their foray—which troopers themselves labeled a raid—Lynn Bomar, accompanied by a few guardsmen and reporters, rode "in a command car . . . through the adjoining Negro residential sector speaking over a public address system." "There is not going to be any more trouble," he told residents, "Everything is all right. . . . We're down here to give you the same protection as we do the people on the other side of town." The patrol chief, his stiff neck swathed in a billowing yellow scarf, also urged his listeners to

Saul Blair's barbershop shortly after the Highway Patrol swept through the Bottom on the morning of February 26. A highway patrolman continues a search of the premises, while a state guardsman looks through the window from East Eighth Street. (Courtesy of United States Attorney's Office, Middle District of Tennessee)

"smile." Sixty-six patrolmen, plus Bomar, and fifty-nine state guardsmen, including Dickinson, then fanned out through black neighborhoods, seizing weapons and making arrests. In all, over 100 African Americans, overwhelmingly male, were placed in the Maury County jail.[67]

After her husband's arrest, Mary Morton was making a telephone call when "some Patrolmen came back into the house . . . cursed me and told me to stay off of the phone; and if I didn't, he would snatch the 'so and so' telephone . . . and throw it out in the street." That phone call was to a friend in Nashville; Morton asked him to alert the National Association for the Advancement of Colored People (NAACP) "about the impending danger to the Black community in Columbia." When Z. Alexander Looby, a West

Indian lawyer in Tennessee's capital and a member of the NAACP's national legal committee, received "news of conditions in Columbia," he tried to reach James Morton by telephone. Initially he was told "the circuits were all busy"; when he called back a few minutes later, he was informed, "they were not accepting any calls for Columbia except official calls."[68]

Help was on the way, however, from the national office in New York as well as from local attorneys, including Looby. At 9:35 A.M., shortly after the patrol raid ended, a radio station telephoned NAACP headquarters and reported: "Rioting Negroes who fought police all night were being subdued after twelve hours (12) of bloody fighting. . . . It is Tennessee's worst racial trouble." Immediately the national office wired assistant field secretary Donald Jones, who was in Chattanooga conducting a membership drive, and it conferred with Looby in Nashville, site of the NAACP's "largest and most active branch" in Tennessee. Jones in turn asked Maurice Weaver "to go to Columbia and make for the Association a fair and impartial investigation of the facts." A white lawyer, Weaver "was in [a] better position to get these facts for reasons that are obvious," Looby wryly observed.[69]

From Chattanooga, Weaver, "the CIO attorney" and a participant in the first meeting of the Southern Conference for Human Welfare (SCHW) in 1938, proceeded first to Nashville and then to Columbia. Reaching the county seat quite late on the 26th, the day of the patrol raid, he visited the sheriff's office early the next morning. Without hesitation, Underwood gave "a long and detailed story" of events the preceding Monday. Though he said that this account was "off the record," he readily retold "his version" before a court recorder that Weaver had brought from Chattanooga when Weaver met later in the day with the sheriff, James Morton, and Saul Blair.

Morton and Blair, who remained incarcerated, were brought from their cell at the behest of Underwood. Indeed, Weaver later emphasized, "There was no restraint as far as my being able to see them, and talk to them, to be able to get any facts I wanted from them." Neither did the sheriff try at that time to minimize the threat of mob violence that he had observed two days earlier. Feeling quite comfortable with the way the situation was being handled, Weaver returned to Chattanooga around midday.[70]

Following his departure, however, certain developments suggested that Highway Patrol officers were continuing to supersede local ones, including the sheriff. They also indicated that Underwood was willing to modify his version of events. Three times Julius Blair, who had escorted Weaver around town, was picked up by officers: first by Highway Patrolman Noles, who released him when Blair phoned the sheriff; second, by a "city policeman," who said he was ordered to take the action; and third, by "another bunch of highway patrolmen," one of whom asked, "Where is them goddam white lawyers you had?" When the senior Blair stated, "I think I have a right to know what you are arresting me for," the state trooper responded, "'Oh, never mind' and went up and shoved me in jail." Blair remained in custody until his release on bond late Friday night.[71]

That afternoon no one was released from jail as Weaver had anticipated and in the evening the local district attorney (then termed district attorney general) Paul F. Bumpus, and Ernest B. "Jack" Smith from the state attorney general's office began formal inquiries. Following the questioning of black funeral director V. K. Ryan, whose establishment was located two blocks from the Bottom, Underwood gave a statement in which he drastically altered the position he had taken with Weaver that morning. "Some threats" came from "a few irresponsible whites," he admitted, but he added, "We paid little attention to those threats." Even in the wake of the police shootings, when virtually everyone questioned agreed that guns flashed in the hands of whites and a crowd surged toward the Bottom, Underwood decided that the group "had become very quiet and reasonable."[72]

The next morning the investigation continued, as suspects were brought from their cells and questioned in the sheriff's dining room. (Underwood and his family lived at the jail.) As the interrogation proceeded under the auspices of Bumpus, Smith, and now Underwood, others, including Highway Patrol Chief Bomar, various state troopers, and an assortment of local officers, wandered in and out of the room.

Especially the first witness, James "Digger" Johnson, the son of restaurant owner Meade Johnson, seemed to corroborate an emerging official view that, rather than acting to protect James Stephenson, Morton and the Blairs had instigated trouble with whites, including the police. Before he could appear in court as the state's "star witness," however, Johnson was gunned down, victim of an aggressive attack by state troopers. Indeed, by 3:00 on the day he was queried, the 29-year-old poolroom operator lay dying in a pool of blood in the nearby jail office.[73]

Charged with carrying a concealed weapon, Johnson had been told following a lengthy interrogation by the "Board of Inquiry" that his father would be removed from jail and could "make your bond."[74] "Mr. Jim, don't do that. If you bring my father out of there now," Johnson told the sheriff, "the other negroes will think that I have told something, and they'll have it in for me."[75] Heeding his wishes, Underwood placed Johnson in the jail office until others had been questioned. Following their interrogations, both William Gordon and Napoleon Stewart were also placed in the office to await the bail that the sheriff felt certain their white employers would post.

Johnson and Gordon sat near one another, along the east wall of the office; Stewart sat farther away, toward the northeast corner. About three or four feet from Stewart were stacked all of the guns collected in Tuesday morning's raid and house searches. When several state troopers and a female reporter with the *Nashville Banner* left the room, only three individuals besides the prisoners remained: John Morgan, a photographer with the *Banner* who sat with his back to the others making notes on some pictures he had taken; 70-year-old Deputy T. R. Darnell, who was making a phone call; and the sheriff's newly deputized son-in-law, E. G. "Ed" Pennington, who lay sprawled across a bed gazing out the window.

Suddenly, Gordon grabbed a gun from the stack and pointed it in Darnell's direction! Observing his action from the corridor, Highway Patrolman Billy Griffin opened fire. As Griffin began shooting, other patrolmen near him joined in. In vain, Gordon attempted to crawl under the bed to safety. Whether or not Johnson tried to assist his companion is unclear. Some claimed he grabbed a gun; others were not sure. Regardless, he too quickly fell.[76]

Backing into the corner, Stewart threw his hands in the air. As the shooting died down, Flo Fleming struck Stewart in the left eye. J. J. Jackson then "knocked him to the floor." Lynn Bomar, who had joined his officers in the melee, testified, "I pulled out my pistol and put my foot on his neck and told him to lay there and not give us any more trouble."[77] Stewart was subsequently sent back to his cell. Johnson and Gordon both died en route to a Nashville hospital.

Following the fracas in the sheriff's office, forty-two prisoners, including the Blairs and Morton, were rushed to the Davidson County jail in Nashville in an armored trailer truck hastily procured from the state prison. That evening the Lebanon unit of the State Guard, which had left Columbia the preceding morning, was alerted that it might need to return to the county seat. At that point, "several score men and youths, including 45 former GI's in the Cumberland University Law School[,] . . . among them combat veterans, made a mass appeal to Capt. Same [sic] S. Bone, of the Lebanon Guard unit, for immediate induction and service."[78] The men were not accepted, however, and no additional units were needed, despite authorities' fears.

Meanwhile, Maurice Weaver had filed a petition for writ of habeas corpus in behalf of thirty prisoners who were still in custody, and on Friday, March 1, the day following the jail transfer, when all were returned from

Nashville, officials began releasing many on bond. They included Julius Blair and his two sons, Saul and Charlie, as well as James Morton and Calvin Lockridge. That night, "a volley of shots" was fired into the home of Julius and Saul Blair. Fortunately, neither was injured, though they found three bullets in the house the next morning, which the senior Blair later gave to Attorney Looby.[79]

On Monday, a week following the Stephenson-Fleming fight, county judge Washington C. Whitthorne set a hearing before circuit court judge Joe M. Ingram for Wednesday on the petition for a writ of habeas corpus. Weaver and Looby withdrew it, however, when District Attorney General Bumpus gave them the names and amounts of the bonds of thirteen African Americans still incarcerated. That afternoon, eight days after they were seized, the thirteen were released.

Bonds were set at $5,000 for those charged with attempted murder or conspiracy to commit murder and $250 for those accused of carrying a concealed weapon. Local black leaders, with James Morton and Julius Blair as principals, signed these documents. Morton's own $5,000 bond was signed by Finn Wray, a black barber and property owner in nearby Mt. Pleasant, and by John W. Frierson, a white Maury County businessman and the operator of a flour mill in Mt. Pleasant. Among those signing Julius Blair's $5,000 bond, as well as those of other black Maury Countians, was white Columbia attorney R. S. Hopkins Sr., a man to whom Weaver paid "high tribute" for braving "the wrath" of those who wanted to keep African Americans in jail.[80]

On Sunday evening the 800 state guardsmen, who had been in Columbia almost a week, withdrew; 65 highway patrolmen, including Chief Bomar, stayed. At midday, Mayor Denham broadcast over a Nashville radio station a very upbeat message about his community. In it, he paid tribute to well-known native sons James K. Polk and former U.S. senator Edward Ward Carmack as well as Edward "Pop" Geers, the "grand-old man of harness racing." He also spoke of Columbia's location "in the very heart of the Blue Grass Section of Tennessee" and of its fame as "the largest mule street market in the world." He closed with words of praise for state forces: "The State Guard, under the command of Brigadier General J. M. Dickinson and the Highway Patrol under the direction of chief Lynn Bomar, deserve the appreciation of all peaceloving people of both races."[81] Clearly, the mayor's remarks reflected the dominant white perspective. Most black Maury Countians probably did not hear them anyway, for they were attending the funerals of Johnson and Gordon. The mayor's speech was sandwiched between the two ceremonies.

In the wake of the jail killings, concern about developments in Columbia and about the possible outbreak of racial violence on a much wider scale intensified among liberal and leftist organizations throughout the nation. On Saturday, March 2nd, two days after the jail catastrophe, Mrs. M. E. Tilly conducted interviews in Nashville and Columbia on behalf of the executive committee of the Jurisdiction Woman's Society of Christian Service and the SRC. On the same day, Walter White, executive director of the NAACP, went with Looby and William J. Faulkner, dean of the chapel at Fisk University, to meet with Governor James Nance McCord.

In a separate meeting, also on that Saturday, the governor conversed with Ira Latimer, executive secretary of the Chicago Civil Liberties Union; New Yorker Samuel Neuberger, a lawyer for the National Federation for Constitutional Liberties and a member of the National Lawyers Guild; and Joseph Moore, a lecturer in pastoral theology and human relations at Seabury-Western Theological Seminary in Evanston, Illinois. The following day, the trio conferred with local and state officials in Columbia and then returned to Nashville where they participated in meetings spearheaded by White and the NAACP. On Tuesday, Neuberger met as part of a National Lawyers Guild committee, headed by William H. Hastie, with U.S. Attorney General Tom Clark in Washington.

Meanwhile the SCHW, which was at that time headquartered in Nashville, rushed into print 100,000 copies of a pamphlet entitled "The Truth About Columbia Tennessee Cases."[82] The SCHW, in conjunction with the National Federation for Constitutional Liberties and the International Union of Mine, Mill, and Smelter Workers, also orchestrated the National Emergency Conference to Stop Lynch Terror in Columbia, which convened on March 13 at the YWCA in Washington. Out of this effort came a short-lived United Committee Against Police Terror in Columbia, Tennessee.

Although the American Communist Party sent a representative to the March 13 meeting, it carried on its own separate publicity campaign, sending *Daily Worker* reporter Harry Raymond to cover events in Columbia from the day following the patrol raid through the fall trials. Robert Minor, then secretary of the legislative committee of the Communist Party and publicist of the Scottsboro case in the 1930s, was the featured speaker at the creation of a short-lived Maury County Voters League in April, and he published in the fall a ninety-five-page pamphlet entitled "Lynching and Frame-Up in Tennessee."

At the moderate end of the liberal spectrum, the SRC operated at a much quieter level. In addition to Tilly and W. B. Twitty, Guy Johnson, the organization's executive director, traveled to Columbia to conduct an investigation and authored "What Happened at Columbia," a report that appeared in the SRC's journal *New South* in May. Johnson also shared his findings with Turner Smith, head of the Civil Rights Section of the Justice Department.[83]

Of the plethora of labor and civil rights organizations interested in the Columbia case, the NAACP, above all, made it "a cause célèbre."[84] Skipping the March 13 affair in Washington, the Association convened its own gathering in New York the next day. Many of those who had been in Washington attended. They included representatives from the National Federation for Constitutional Liberties, the Congress of Industrial Organizations Political Action Committee (CIO-PAC), and the SCHW, but no one from the Communist Party. Eventually all, excluding the Communists, would follow the NAACP's lead. As early as March 2, the Association had procured the right to defend almost all of the African Americans who were charged in the Columbia case. At that time, only James Stephenson and Calvin Lockridge remained outside the fold, and both were on board within a month.

Through a variety of tactics, the organization strove to indict police for their excesses, to raise money for legal counsel, and to sound the alarm throughout the country that the Columbia episode could represent the commencement of a much-feared postwar revival of racial violence. Along the way, it also energized its own ranks. To coordinate its campaign, the NAACP hired Oliver "Ollie" Harrington, a former *Pittsburgh Courier* reporter. It appealed to local branches for support, organizing a speaking tour that included several of the defendants and holding mass rallies.[85] Additionally, it sought publicity through newspapers and radio and fashioned an ad hoc committee of prominent individuals and organizations.[86]

Headed by Eleanor Roosevelt and Channing Tobias, the National Committee for Justice in Columbia, Tennessee (NCJC), employed the services of a New York consulting firm that distributed 50,000 copies of the NAACP's pamphlet "Terror in Tennessee," along with an appeal signed by the chairpersons. Concomitantly, the "Committee of 100," a group of prominent Americans who had solicited funds in behalf of the NAACP's Legal Defense and Education Fund since 1943, mailed a letter signed by noted author Carl Van Doren asking for $50,000 for the Columbia campaign.

Like most of the organizations interested in the Columbia affair, the NAACP appealed to higher authorities in Washington for action. Letters and petitions poured into the White House, and so many organizations and individuals demanded to see the president that he began referring all to Attorney General Clark. Many of the complainants likened the behavior of Columbian authorities to fascism and made references to the recent, victorious war against Hitler and racism and in behalf of democracy.

These efforts yielded results. Although U.S. Attorney Horace Frierson, a native of Columbia, reported to Washington the day after the patrol raid that no violation of federal civil rights statutes had occurred in his hometown, the attorney general sent his special assistant, James E. Ruffin, also a Columbia native, to the scene. He also dispatched more FBI agents. When Frierson again found no civil rights violations following a week-long investigation by the Bureau, Clark summoned him to the national capital. On the day of his visit, the attorney general released a directive ordering a grand jury investigation.

Infuriated at this turn of events, federal judge Elmer Davies convened a jury, but he served notice from the outset that organizations that had publicized events in Columbia were on trial as much as the police. "Now, gentlemen of the jury," he declared in his opening charge to them, "I suggest that you subpoena before you the officials of the Southern Conference for Human Welfare and question them as to the facts contained in this pamphlet ["The Truth about Columbia"] and, if they are true, you should act accordingly and return indictments against the persons responsible for those acts." He continued: "If they are not true, then the circulators of this pamphlet should be exposed for deliberately agitating matters of this kind to cause difficulties between races which are trying to live together in peace and harmony."[87] To present the case to the jury, Davies assigned local assistant district attorneys A. Otis Denning and Z. Thomas "Day" Osborn Jr. to work with Justice Department lawyers John M. Kelley Jr., Arthur B. Caldwell, and Eleanor Bontecou, a move that caused considerable frustration among the Washington counsel as well as among its liberal associates (see Chapter 6).

From April 8 through April 18, jurors heard testimony from a number of witnesses. Except for James and Gladys Stephenson, no African Americans were called to the stand until the afternoon of April 15. Instead, jurors heard the official version of events first, as they listened to W. E. Hopton, the senior resident FBI agent in Nashville, and, following the testimony of those involved in the fight on the square, to Police Chief J. Walter Griffin, Magistrate C. Hayes Denton, Sheriff Underwood, Columbia mayor Eldridge Denham, Highway Patrol Chief Bomar, Assistant State Attorney General Smith, and State Guard Commander Dickinson. They heard also from white buckshot victims James Beard and Borgie Claude.

Finally, on the afternoon of the 15th, a week into the hearing, James Morton testified, along with a couple of journalists and one of the alleged leaders of the white mob, Roy L. Scribner. Morton was followed the next day by Saul and Julius Blair, Calvin Lockridge, George Nicholson, and three additional reporters. On the 17th, Horace Gordon and James Thomas "Popeye" Bellanfante testified, along with more journalists. At his own request, Maurice Weaver offered testimony on the afternoon of the 17th and the morning of the 18th. Napoleon Stewart also appeared on the 18th, and he was followed by State Attorney General Roy H. Beeler and District Attorney General Bumpus. A trio of inconsequential witnesses completed the testimony on the 18th, and attorneys Denning, Osborn, and Caldwell offered a few concluding remarks. Kelley said nothing. Eleanor Bontecou was not present; she had departed on the 15th for Germany to participate in the Nuremberg trials.

Although a report was expected from the jury the next week, on Monday, April 29th, Judge Davies requested further inquiry by the FBI. Specifically, he asked agents to investigate the destruction of property on East Eighth Street and to examine the publishers and circulators of accounts of "the Columbia disturbance." The jury then adjourned for almost a month. On May 27 and 28, FBI agent Hopton gave additional testimony. He was followed by Ira Latimer of the Chicago Civil Liberties Union and several members of the State Guard. At last, in a day-long session on the 29th, twenty-two black Columbians who had received abuse at the hands of state troopers got to tell their stories. This testimony was succeeded by an intense two-day grilling of James Dombrowski of the SCHW and Oliver Harrington of the NAACP.

On June 14, Hopton made a final appearance before grand jurors, and on the same day, they released their report. In their 4,200-word document, jurors determined that "fact and fancy were freely intermingled" in the wake of the Fleming-Stephenson fight "especially among the less stable elements of both races." They could, however, find no evidence that rope had been purchased at any Columbia businesses, and they decided that the "small groups of white individuals [who] gathered from time to time on the Public Square and in the streets nearby" were composed largely of "teenaged youths" who were "unarmed" and "responsive to orders." Likewise, "the majority" of the "20 to 30 white persons [who] . . . went to the county jail and demanded to know the whereabouts of the Stephensons" were "teenage boys . . . who appeared to be unarmed."

Although jurors acknowledged that "several negro witnesses, activated by the rumor of a possible lynching, armed themselves and assembled in the 'Mink Slide' area for the purpose of protecting James Stephenson from mob violence," they also noted that "several other negro witnesses" had "no genuine apprehension of impending trouble" and, they argued, this included Stephenson himself. They found "no evidence whatsoever" to substantiate the notion that the police "were accompanied by a crowd of armed white men" when they entered "the 'Mink Slide' area." While jurors did admit that "as word of the assault on the officers spread armed white people began to assemble on the Public Square and on South Main Street near the entrance to 'Mink Slide,'" they did this not to raise the possibility that whites were in fact armed all along, but to demonstrate the necessity of calling in state forces. In short, though grand jurors offered no explicit explanation as to why the police were shot, they clearly laid the onus of the fray at the door of black Maury Countians.

"After the arrest of the negroes found in 'Mink Slide' on Tuesday," jurors admitted, "various business establishments, the fixtures therein, and certain personal property . . . particularly the properties of James Morton, Sol Blair, and Julius Blair, were found to be in a wrecked and damaged condition." Though they desired "to remain in session and to continue our efforts to fasten responsibility for such property destruction," they found it "wholly impossible to determine the identity of such person or persons or to elicit facts upon which to predicate an indictment in this respect."

Not only did jurors fail "to ascertain the identity of the person or persons committing these acts of vandalism," they went on to exonerate all law officers involved in the Columbia episode, including members of the Highway Patrol, and in the same breath to lament their own inability to indict the purveyors of "nationwide misrepresentation." Though "during the course of the arrests certain negroes were struck by the arresting officers," the jury determined, "the force shown to have been used was not unreasonable." Similarly "the killing of the negroes Johnson and Gordon" constituted "justifiable homicide." All in all, jurors concluded,

> the Governor's prompt action in getting the State Patrol and the State Guard to Columbia is to be commended, as is the action of the state forces in sealing off the "Mink Slide" area, and in preventing any clash between white and negro citizens. The prompt arrival and deployment of state forces, in our opinion, prevented a bloody race war which threatened to arise out of the heat of excitement following the wounding of a number of officers of the law, who, it is evident, were acting solely in an effort to preserve the peace and to fulfill their sworn duties.[88]

It was clear that Judge Davies's opening charge to the jury had established the jury's priorities, and the publicists of "false-hoods and half-truths" incurred its wrath. "We have explored the possibility of returning present-ments against those sending such pamphlets through the mails," jurors noted near the end of their report, "but to our regret, we are advised that the mailing of such pamphlets does not constitute a violation of any Federal statute." They continued, clothing all liberal and leftist associations in Communist garb:

> In disseminating such propaganda the avowed Communist press of the country has been especially active, having carried a series of inflam-matory articles on the racial disturbances at Columbia. This technique is characteristic and dangerous, and manifestly is designed to foster racial hatred and to array class against class.
>
> In concluding our report we wish to sound a warning that the good citizens of both races be on their guard against insidious and false propa-ganda. In the opinion of this grand jury nothing is so likely to erode and ultimately destroy peaceful and friendly relations between the races.

STATE TRIALS

As the grand jury investigation unfolded, criminal actions against blacks and a few whites proceeded apace. On March 20, the grand jury of the Maury County Circuit Court began considering indictments related to the Columbia affair. Orchestrated by District Attorney General Bumpus, the hearing included testimony by Underwood, Griffin, and other city and county officials, as well as Bomar. Two days after it commenced, the jury handed down indictments against thirty-one African Americans and four whites.

Twenty-eight of the black Maury Countians faced serious charges. Twenty-six were indicted as either accessories to attempted murder in the first degree or attempters of murder in the first degree, stemming from the shooting of policeman Will Wilsford. Four of these men—Saul Blair, James Morton, Meade Johnson, and James Thomas "Popeye" Bellanfante—were indicted on both counts; Julius Blair was indicted as an accessory only. When the prosecution learned late in the trial held that autumn that one could not be convicted on both counts, it charged James Morton and Julius Blair as accessories and Saul Blair and the other men as attempters. If found guilty on either count, the men would receive from three to twenty-one years in prison.

In addition to these twenty-six, two others—William "Rooster Bill" Pil-low and "Papa" Lloyd Kennedy—were charged with assault to commit murder in the first degree for the wounding of state trooper Ray Austin outside Blair's barbershop during the patrol raid. As it turned out, the twenty-eight men charged with the most serious offenses were the only individuals ever tried on charges stemming from the February fray. No effort was made to indict the Stephensons on charges of attempted murder, nor were any indictments filed against several African Americans initially held on weapons charges. The four white men indicted by the local grand jury were never brought to trial.

A week after the indictments, Judge Joe Ingram announced that the jury box from which grand and petit juries were drawn was empty, that the jury commissioners must fill it with at least 750 names, and that the circuit court would adjourn until May 27. The following day Maurice Weaver filed pleas of abatement for three African Americans accused in the shooting of Wilsford, attempting to quash their indictments on the grounds that no black Maury Countians had served on the grand jury that brought the charges. Although Judge Ingram ruled that neither these pleas, nor additional ones that were filed, could be heard individually, he did stipulate that pleas on behalf of the men facing the most serious charges in the shooting of Wilsford would be heard first. The defense and the prosecution also agreed that this phase of the proceedings would occur without a jury.

For more than two weeks, one African American after another took the stand, stating that he was an adult, male householder but that he had never served on a jury nor heard of any black person who had. Of the 217 men who testified, only College Hill High School principal J. Thomas Caruthers had been summoned for jury duty. This, he explained, had occurred a year or two earlier, and he thought it was a mistake, so he had asked Sheriff Underwood to excuse him.[89] Left unsaid was the probability that Caruthers thought his summons was in error because no African American had served on a jury in Maury County since the turn of the century. Eighty-year-old county judge Washington Whitthorne was the only official who could remember such an event.[90]

On June 11, defense attorneys Looby, Weaver, and Thurgood Marshall, head of the legal arm of the NAACP, ceased calling witnesses to the stand when they reached an agreement with the prosecution that "'there are numerous other Negroes in the county' who could testify that they are qualified for jury duty, but had never been summoned nor served on a jury."[91] Following this agreement, defense lawyers called James Morton to the stand. Morton testified that Tommy Baxter, one of the twenty-six men indicted on the Wilsford charges, was dead. Baxter had caught cold while in the Maury County jail. Presumably he died from pneumonia.[92]

As the plea of abatement hearing, now involving twenty-five men, continued, Attorney General Bumpus, aided by Assistant District Attorney William A. Harwell of Lawrenceburg, and Columbia attorney Hugh Todd Shelton Sr., began putting on the stand whites who testified that they had never been summoned for jury service. Marshall and Looby tried to blunt this testimony by getting all to admit under cross-examination that although they had seen whites on juries, they had never seen a black person on "any jury in any courts within the county."[93]

Not surprisingly, their efforts were to no avail, as Judge Ingram denied all pleas of abatement. Reasoning very much as Bumpus argued, the judge ruled that the only question at issue in the hearing was "whether Negroes were excluded from the grand jury in February, 1946." Since the names of ten African Americans were included in the jury box, though not one was summoned for service, the motion to quash the indictments was rejected.[94]

Ingram also denied separate trials for each of the defendants, and he set the following Monday, June 24th, as the day for the change of venue hearing requested by the defense counsel. On that day, however, Bumpus asked to delay the hearing to prepare for the affidavits that defense lawyers had submitted. The latter agreed and subsequently attended the national NAACP convention in Cincinnati, a trip that the *Columbia Daily Herald* chose to highlight in its coverage of the venue hearing delay.

On Monday, July 1, the defense affidavits were read in court. They included statements by Saul Blair, courthouse janitor Will McConico, and Maurice Weaver and Z. Alexander Looby, as well as Jesse Owen, a white worker who was formerly employed at the fertilizer plant in nearby Godwin, Tennessee.[95] The defense also placed *Daily Herald* reporter Paul Page on the witness stand. Page verified that his newspaper, which had consistently identified the defense counsel as associated with the NAACP, had carried an editorial that merged "the NAACP, SCHW, CIO-PAC, and Communist press."[96]

In a surprise move, the prosecution attorneys offered no rebuttal to the defense's claim that conditions in Maury County would inhibit a fair trial for the defendants. Instead they submitted nine affidavits, three from blacks and six from whites, saying that the defendants *could* get a fair trial in *Lawrence* County, the home of Assistant District Attorney Harwell and another of the four counties in Bumpus's district. Knowing that two of the prosecution lawyers had close personal ties to Lawrence, that the county had a minuscule black population, that it abutted Alabama, and that its county seat of Lawrenceburg was less than half the size of Columbia, defense lawyers were horrified. As Looby exclaimed to the court: "It is a matter that would be worse than jumping from the frying pan into the fire."[97] Davidson County was the first choice of the defense, and Williamson, the home of Franklin, a distant second.

From the defense's point of view, the prosecution was selecting the location of the trial, a prerogative it did not have. Prosecution lawyers in turn argued that the defense had said that their clients could not get a fair trial in Maury or in any of the adjoining counties, with the exception of Lawrence County. "Technically," prosecutor Shelton contended, "the State admits the charges as to all the counties in their motion for change of venue with the exception of Lawrence and we have met that with rebuttal testimony."[98] The next morning the two sides met privately with Judge Ingram for three hours. At the outset of the afternoon session, the defense attempted, without success, to withdraw its change of venue motion entirely.

Ironically, many members of the Lawrenceburg establishment were as chagrined as the defense counsel that the trial was being moved to their community. Worried that negative publicity might result from such an event, Mayor R. O. Downy, "backed by the town's leading figures," began circulating petitions against it. In all, about 400 business and professional men signed these documents, which concluded by stating: "It is not our dirty linen. . . . We resent being called upon to launder it." Downy also declared that if Bumpus insisted on going ahead with the trial in Lawrenceburg, townspeople there would defeat him in the next election. On July 12, Downey led an eleven-man delegation to Columbia to meet with prosecution attorneys to try to effect a change. The local American Legion and Lawrenceburg's board of commissioners also passed resolutions urging the court to vacate its decision. As Bumpus himself summed the situation: "The attorney general is about as popular in Lawrence County since this matter came up, as a polecat in a perfume factory."[99]

As the anti-trial forces gathered momentum in Lawrenceburg, Weaver raced around the county and adjoining ones gathering affidavits for another change of venue motion, which the defense counsel would enter when the trial began in early August. Even Eleanor Roosevelt condemned the choice of Lawrenceburg, writing in her syndicated column on July 9, "I was discouraged on receiving word the other day that the trial of the Columbia, Tenn., Negroes was to be moved to a place where the tension and anti-Negro feeling is, if anything, stronger than it was in Columbia."[100]

Ill during the last three days of the initial venue hearing, Thurgood Marshall returned to New York as soon as it concluded. In mid-July, Ingram granted a continuance in the Kennedy-Pillow case until the November term of court, but he refused to postpone the Lawrenceburg trial, an event that Marshall would miss entirely because of a pulmonary infection and viral pneumonia.

Despite efforts by Looby, Weaver, and Leon Ransom of Howard University to enter pleas of abatement for the defendants in Lawrenceburg on the same grounds as they had in Columbia, Ingram ruled much the same—that is, that only methods of selecting the current panel were germane to the motion and that evidence existed that the names of some Negroes had been placed in the jury box for this term of court. In addition, the judge denied the second change of venue motion, and on August 10, jury selection commenced.

For five full weeks, the process inched along. In the painstaking search for "twelve good men and true," well over 700 veniremen were questioned. Fortunately for the defense, the anger that prevailed in Lawrenceburg about hosting the trial made opting out of jury service acceptable, even respectable, and many Lawrence County residents chose this course of action. A few avoided service by saying that they were so infuriated that the trial had been moved to their community that they could not give the state a fair hearing. Others offered medical excuses, some of which were undoubtedly ruses. (When Ingram asked one potential juror, "Can you hear me?" the venireman responded, "No.")[101] The vast majority were excused, however, because they admitted that, for one reason or another, they could not give an African American a fair trial.

In questioning potential jurors about their racial views, defense attorneys were relentless. After two weeks of their persistent grilling, the judge became so incensed at the slow pace of the proceedings that he stipulated that all questions related to feelings of racial prejudice should be submitted to him well in advance in writing and that he would conduct inquiries on this matter from the bench. Ever resourceful, Looby and Weaver then began asking questions about veniremen's views of the Ku Klux Klan. Weaver, in particular, was so insistent upon this line of questioning that Ingram threatened him two days in a row with contempt citations.

The intense interrogations by defense lawyers, coupled with the veniremen's willingness to share their prejudices and thereby opt out of jury service, meant that NAACP attorneys were able to ration carefully their 200 peremptory challenges. Despite the examination of well over 700 men, they did not exhaust their legal objections until they reached the alternate, thirteenth juror. At this point, Ingram allowed them fifty more challenges, half of which they used in making their final selection.

In the end, the meticulously selected jury consisted of six farmers, two carpenters, a country storekeeper, a sawmill operator, a school janitor and former member of the United Mine Workers, and an employee in a local blacksmith shop. The thirteenth and alternate juror was a truck driver. All were white—the prosecution had used a peremptory challenge to exclude the single black veniremen whose name was drawn from the jury pool—and all were male, a prerequisite for jury duty required by Tennessee law at the time. The oldest, a retired farmer, was 73; the youngest, the blacksmith worker, was 29. On the surface, they seemed an ordinary lot, but they would render a most extraordinary decision.

For a week, from September 19 through 26, the State placed its witnesses on the stand. They included Will Wilsford himself and the policemen who had accompanied him into the Bottom, as well as the sheriff and the policemen who had ridden into the vicinity early in the evening on the 25th and had seen African Americans there armed. The policemen especially named Julius and Saul Blair, James Morton, and Meade Johnson as men they had recognized. In cross-examination, however, the defense extracted from the law officers numerous references to dangerous whites on the square.[102] In addition, Underwood, Wilsford, and Griffin demonstrated their respect for the Blairs and Morton, referring to them as men of "peace and quietude." The sheriff described the Lockridge brothers in similar terms.[103]

A handful of black Maury Countians testified that the other defendants were armed and on the street ten to fifteen minutes before the police were shot. None, however, could say that they had actually seen the shooting, because all claimed to be elsewhere at the time it occurred. Under cross-examination, they testified to considerable mistreatment at the hands of law enforcement officers, especially the highway patrolmen, and Sheriff Underwood admitted that one of the defendants "did cry for a few minutes" while making his statement to interrogators.[104] Two of these witnesses also described seeing an armed white mob on the square as they headed for the Bottom that evening.

Three high school students acknowledged that James "Popeye" Bellanfante, their school bus driver, had said something as they departed from the bus on the afternoon of the 25th about a fight that day on the town square, the possibility of a mob that night, and the need for "some of your people" to come to town.[105] The defense in cross-examination emphasized the fear induced in these teenagers by officials through their interrogation procedures and by Bellanfante's expressed concern about a mob.

Other witnesses offered testimony that the men who were shot, including Wilsford, were recognizable as police by those bunched together on East Eighth Street. These witnesses included Roy Staggs, a white photographer who had taken a picture at Bumpus's behest that ostensibly showed the conditions as they existed that night. A photography buff himself, Weaver raised questions about Staggs's motives and methods as he grilled him intensely. Some of the officers also indicated on cross-examination that whites were indeed following them as they entered the Bottom.[106]

The most contentious—and embarrassing—witness for the prosecution was Lynn Bomar. Though on the stand to testify about such matters as the men and guns he found in James Morton's house, the patrol chief proved so dismissive of constitutional guarantees and so explosive as Weaver questioned him that he was not called to testify in the Kennedy-Pillow trial in November, even though it involved the shooting of one of his own men. The safety commissioner also caused quite a stir in the courtroom when he aggressively labeled noted writer and journalist Vincent Sheean " 'a lying Communistic yellow —— ' " before "several hundred spectators."[107]

The only evidence connecting anyone specifically with the shooting of Wilsford came from African Americans Mamie Fisher and Alexander Bullock. Initially Fisher stated that as she left the Ritz Club, which was located "about . . . six or seven blocks" from East Eighth Street, late on the 25th with "Bob" Gentry, John McKivens, and the driver of the car [Alexander Bullock], whom she did not know, Gentry, who was sitting beside her in the back seat, remarked: "We shot one of the policemen, but don't know which one did it." Bullock also testified that "Gentry said 'We were all shooting down there, and we think we shot an officer, but don't know who shot him.' "[108]

Fisher stated that Bullock and McKivens had shotguns and Gentry a pistol, while Bullock agreed that McKivens was armed with a shotgun. Fisher, however, retracted her statement about Gentry's remark and held fast to her retraction even when threatened by Prosecutor Shelton with contempt charges. She also noted that she was warned of a three-month jail sentence if she did not testify against Gentry. Although Bullock never retracted his statement, he talked during cross-examination about a beating that he received at the hands of officers on Tuesday morning when he went to the jail to learn the whereabouts of his car, which he had abandoned the night before on the Mt. Pleasant Highway.[109]

Though no ballistic evidence tied any of the defendants to the shooting of Wilsford, nor were there signs of premeditation, usually associated with charges of murder or attempted murder in the first degree, Shelton and Bumpus argued that neither was necessary. As they reasoned, "Concealing one's self for the purpose of killing another unawares is lying in wait," and, they argued, "The law allows no inquiry into the question as to whether or not deliberation and premeditation were present in fact, but they are conclusively presumed from the fact that 'lying in wait' appears."[110]

The prosecutors went on to argue that for conviction of "aiding and abetting," it was not essential that the defendants be "right at that spot where these guns were fired," that in fact "they could be a block away or several blocks away" or even "home asleep in bed." As for the other defendants who were accused of attempting murder in the first degree, Shelton insisted: "The rule is, if divers persons come with the intent to do mischief, as to kill, rob or beat, and one doeth it, all are principals in the felony." In summary, the prosecution made the following claims: Coming armed to East Eighth Street and taking it over was an unlawful act, and in the process of breaking the law in this fashion, someone shot Will Wilsford; *all* then who participated in the street takeover were guilty whether or not they actually pulled a trigger.[111]

To Weaver, Looby, and Ransom, the issue was plainly one of self-defense. Those on trial were armed, not to commit a felony, but to prevent one. Although, thanks to rulings by Ingram, the defense found it very difficult to get information about previous lynchings in Maury County into the court record, via cross-examinations they did obtain tidbits of testimony that pointed toward the presence of armed whites on the square on the 25th. They also prompted references to earlier mob murders—and details of the concern among African Americans about the possibility of another one—from the testimony of Julius Blair. Saul echoed his father's fears, as did James Stephenson's grandmother Hannah Peppers. An ailing Meade Johnson both underscored the feelings of friendship for Wilsford felt by the Bottom's leaders and served as a reminder to the jury of the death of his son at the hands of officials.

Several witnesses described the senior Blair's attendance at the school meeting on the evening of the 25th, and a few offered alibis for various defendants at the time of the shooting.[112] After four days of testimony, defense lawyers rested their case. Ingram allowed each side six hours total of summation, and on the afternoon of October 2, closing arguments began.

Prosecutor "Bud" Harwell led off with a dispassionate review of the evidence placing various defendants at the scene of the crime and noting conflicting testimony where it existed. Defender Ransom followed with a discussion of previous lynchings, of the fears they induced, and of the consternation generated by the Stephenson-Fleming fight. He pointed also to the lack of proof that any of the defendants were at the scene at the time of the shooting and to the absence of ballistic evidence. He concluded with an explanation of why those who provided alibis for the defendants should be believed and why black prosecution witnesses should not.

The next morning, Shelton provided the prosecution's legal rationale and, in a tone far more derisive and sarcastic than that of Harwell, reviewed the evidence against the defendants and their defenders. He closed with a not so subtle appeal to white solidarity: "You couldn't in my opinion, acquit these Defendants and go home and look the members of your family in the face."[113]

Weaver countered with a much more vivid description of the white mob than that furnished by Ransom, and he tore into the state's witnesses—into photographer Staggs, whom he had questioned so carefully; into the police whom, he said, the state had appear in uniform "to so impress this Jury with the dignity of law that you would ignore the facts"; into "Chief Bomar, the football player"; and into the circumstances under which black prosecution witnesses had been arrested and questioned but never indicted. He closed with impassioned references to the recent war—to "the forces of tyranny and oppression" and to "Negroes and whites . . . [fighting] side by side on land, on sea, and in the air."[114]

Absent from the trial for the preceding three days because of a severe problem with varicose veins, Looby sat during his closing remarks with his right leg propped up on a cushion. Like Weaver, he opened with a word of thanks to the citizens of Lawrence County for the "courtesy" and "almost impartial attitude" they had shown the defense attorneys and their clients. The real cause of the "unfortunate occurrence which happened at Columbia" he blamed on "the ignorance and inefficiency" of public officials, which amounted to "criminal negligence." He could not find in the State's case "one scintilla of evidence" that James Morton or Julius Blair "incited anybody to assault this policeman or anybody else." As for the other defendants, he derided Attorney Shelton's legal argument that all were guilty because someone shot a policeman while all were in the act of committing a felony as having no more to do with this case than "the price of beans in Boston."[115]

The Nashville attorney then proceeded to analyze the problems with the prosecution witnesses and the developments on the 25th that led him to charge law enforcement officers with negligence. From a legal standpoint, he argued that the defendants had "reasonable ground" to believe that their lives were endangered, that "every one of these people had lived through a lynching," and that they were there "to prevent the very thing that was happening." As to the state's claim that blacks were the aggressors, he noted that "all of the power and authority of Columbia is in the hands of the white people," and that "Negroes are in such small minority" that they "are too afraid of attack and in fact it is surprising that you can even get them together for defense."[116]

In conclusion, Looby joined the arguments that opponents of segregation long made as they looked back to the war against fascism and that they would eventually formulate as the Cold War intensified:

> We have spent millions, yea Billions of dollars to preserve democracy on earth; and why was democracy threatened? If I remember correctly, it was because of the existence of a so-called master race. . . . we sacrificed thousands of our young men in the flower of youth. . . . We did all of that that democracy shall not perish but take root and grow and cover the earth. . . . but how can we go to the United Nations and demand and insist upon democracy in other countries when we don't practice it ourselves? That is the question before us.[117]

Throughout, the defense attorney cast his appeal to jurors in religious terms. "There is no such thing as white man's country or black man's country or any man's country," he told them, and he continued: " 'Naked came I into the world, and naked shall I return; the Lord giveth and the Lord taketh away; blessed be the name of the Lord.' "[118]

For a few minutes the jury recessed, and then at 4:20 in the afternoon, Paul Bumpus took the floor. In a wooden attempt at humor, he remarked that he had enjoyed Dr. Looby's "sermon" and "felt very much like I was at church." In another, similar effort, he commented on the large number of "doctors over on the other side" and on his difficulty in keeping them straight. He then proceeded to refer to Weaver as "Dr." throughout, although Looby was the only one with legitimate claim to the title.

For the most part that afternoon, Bumpus spent his time arguing that a white mob did not exist on the 25th and that blacks, as the aggressors, had "lured" the police into the area. "Bear in mind that a mob can consist of colored people just as much as it can consist of white people," he repeated. The prosecuting attorney also personalized his appeal to jurors, recalling teachers that he had had when he attended public school in Lawrence County and suggesting that if any member of the panel believed him capable of persecuting anyone, he would resign. Only briefly did he hint at the blast that would come the next morning: "These people who take a delight in casting slanders and aspersions upon peace-loving communities for the sole purpose of breeding racial hatred and hostility, to further their purposes, in syndicated articles or otherwise, they are nothing but rats and dirty rats at that."[119]

Having fired the opening salvos that afternoon, the district attorney returned the next day to apply to the circumstances of the case the legal theory that Shelton had expounded, to explicate the reasons that Julius

Blair and James Morton should be convicted as accessories to murder and that black prosecution witnesses who placed defendants at the scene should be believed, and to explore the issue of whether or not the policemen who entered the Bottom could be recognized as officers. Along the way, he offered extravagant praise for Lynn Bomar, and he expressed a keen sense of victimization at the hands of the defense counsel.

Next, Bumpus trumpeted law and order, the absence of racial prejudice in the South and in his own thinking, and the anguished but glorious past of his state and region. Above all, he attacked those who "Like the filthy, loathsome birds of prey they are . . . swooped upon Tennessee's tragedy, and by means of the grossest misrepresentations of fact and most grotesque distortions of truth . . . poured out upon the American public a flood of sewage that would nauseate even a skunk." He continued:

If these lousy pinks and pimps and punks can't find some work more in line with attending to their own business—something closer home so they won't have to commute so far—the Federal Government had better take a hand before it is utterly too late. They are nothing but traitors and anarchists, who would crucify America on a cross of hate and bigotry,— in some instances for the dirty money they can grasp with their polluted claws, and in other cases to further a well-organized and far-advanced scheme to destroy every remaining vestige of democratic government in America.

At this point, Looby attempted to intervene. "I think our Supreme Court has ruled any objection to the argument ought to be made at the time," he explained, but Judge Ingram overruled him before he could even state his objection, and the attorney general, "his face livid with rage and emotion," persevered:

May it please the Court and you Gentlemen of the Jury, there are some persons in the United States, male and female, who need to learn to stay at home, and to quit gallivanting over the country spraying discord and racial hatred like a pole-cat.

If the canine kingdom would forgive me for the comparison, I should say they are too much like dogs in sticking their infernal, snooping, sniffing noses in everybody else's business. . . .

To these long-nosed men and short-chinned women—who have at-tained as near to perfect depravity as the infirmities of human nature will permit—the South replies: "Take thy beaks from out our heart and take thy forms from off our door. . . ."

Call them what you will—Reds, Yellows, Communists, or anything else; they are traitors and anarchists in reality; and by any other name they smell as vile. . . .

These subversive vermin and rodents are now crawling upon our body politic, and gnawing at its very vitals; and if our nation is long to survive, this government must have at once not only a bath, but also a fumigation.[120]

Bumpus then waxed euphoric about "a modest, simple cottage . . . too sacredly for words . . . [where he] first saw the blessed light of day." A cottage where "not for all the wealth of the world . . . no, not for the pomp and power and prestige of a throned and sceptred king, would [he] exchange the heritage of that birth, in that unpretentious home in Tennessee." He persisted: "No brighter birthright can spread its mantle of honor upon human existence than that given by kinship to the dauntless spirit of this valourous, intrepid people; a people who have ever answered the bugle-call of duty, so gloriously that Tennessee's immortal name and her deathless fame and her proud and valiant title[,] 'Volunteer State', are all enshrined together in the hearts of men forever."[121] With a flourish, he wound up his argument:

And so, Gentlemen of the Jury, in the name of such a people and of the noble citizenship of this State, in the name of the history and traditions of our people, in the name of a chivalrous manhood and a pure and precious womanhood, in the name of common decency, in the name of that law whose sworn ministers you are, in the name the peace and security of countless generations yet unborn, in the name of the gallant dust of all our great, heroic dead,—I plead for justice at the hands of this jury, for the sovereign State of Tennessee, justice that will be remembered forever in her borders.[122]

Following a ten-minute recess, Ingram read for two hours what newspaper accounts called his "carefully-prepared" charge to the jury. He reminded jurors that "the racial identity of the defendants must have no bearing on their consideration of the case," and he enumerated "the different degrees of the offenses contained in the charges under which the defendants were indicted." Those indicted for attempted murder in the first degree might be found guilty, for example, of that charge or of attempted murder in the second degree, assault with intent to commit voluntary manslaughter, or of the misdemeanor charges of simple assault or assault and battery.[123]

Both the State and the defense had submitted theories of the case, and

Ingram maintained that he had made only "minor changes" to both sets. Looby disagreed, however, so during an hour-and-a-half-long lunch break, the NAACP lawyers prepared eight requests that they wished included. Completely satisfied with the judge's instructions, the prosecution team wrote none. After the midday break, Ingram accepted Request 4, and he further instructed jurors that "the mere presence at the scene of the commission of any offense . . . is not sufficient to raise any presumption as to the probable guilt or connection of the person present . . . until other facts and circumstances arise to connect the person . . . with the acts done." Having lived in confinement for over a month, the jury retired once more to be alone at 3:07 in the afternoon.[124]

Pittsburgh Courier reporter Robert M. Ratcliffe described the next scene: "At 4:45 P.M. . . . a juror came out of the dirty, junky jury room, almost unnoticed . . . He borrowed a fountain pen . . . As he returned and closed the squeaky door behind him, a quiet excitement began to hang over the dingy courtroom . . . The news began to spread, and spectators sought front seats." Many of those present were family members of the men on trial. The NAACP attorneys sent for the defendants, most of whom were "in the courthouse yard, talking about everything but the outcome of the trial." Ratcliffe continued: "The bell in the town clock tolled five times . . . The courtroom was too quiet . . . All eyes were on that closed door of the jury room . . . At 5:02 P.M., a deputy whispered something to the judge . . . He left his sideline seat where he had been chatting with State's attorneys and walked to the bench . . . a seven-year-old white boy, who was rocking back and forth in one of the juror's chairs, was ordered to leave the jury box . . . The jurors strolled in and took their seats."[125]

The twenty-five defendants, "many of whom to all outward appearances, showed little interest during the long days of the hearing, leaned forward eagerly." The foreman of the jury handed the verdicts to Ingram. "Every eye was focused on the Judge. Terrific tension filled the courtroom." Ingram read silently. "He fingered his nose and then re-read the verdicts . . . He stared at the jury, and then returned his eyes to the signed papers on his desk." He seemed "to be trying to take it in." Then he addressed the jurors:

> Give me your attention, you twelve men. I notice dated October 4th 1946 written on the indictment, "We the Jury find the Defendants Julius Blair and James Morton not guilty as charged in the first count of the indictment."
>
> Gentlemen of the Jury, that is your verdict in this case as to the first count, so say all you men?

(The Jurors nodded in the affirmative.)

The second count, I notice written on the indictment, "We the Jury find the Defendants, Robert Gentry and John McKivens guilty of assault with intent to commit murder in the first degree as charged in the second count of the indictment and fix the punishment at not more than twenty-one years in the penitentiary of the State. . . ." Are these the only two verdicts returned by the Jury? Do you mean by these two verdicts you find the other Defendants . . . not guilty as charged in the second count?

(The jury nodded in the affirmative.)[126]

Twenty-three of the twenty-five men had been freed! "Maurice Weaver slapped Julius Blair's knee with a clap that could be heard all over the courtroom." "This makes a man proud to be an American," he shouted as he nearly "jumped from his seat." Looby "almost forgot" his ailing leg, while the senior Blair "nodded his white head in accord." The "wives of the defendants sent up a deep sigh." Bud Harwell rushed forward to congratulate the NAACP lawyers. Shaking their hands, he told them "they had put up a wonderful defense and he was happy over the outcome." Bumpus and Shelton "sat for several minutes as if stunned by the verdict then stood slowly and turned away from the court." With the judge's permission, Weaver thanked the jurors, and he and the other members of the defense team, along with the defendants, grasped the hands of the "twelve shy and somewhat embarrassed men" as they filed out of the courtroom.[127]

Attorney Ransom immediately appealed the convictions of McKivens and Gentry, and Ingram set October 18 as the day for arguments for a new trial. On October 26, the judge granted the defense's motion, and at the end of January 1947 the State decided not to go forward with further proceedings. Free on the $5,000 bond that was posted for them before the Lawrenceburg trial, neither man served a day in prison beyond their initial stay in the Maury County jail.

The only other persons brought to trial from the Columbia affair, William "Rooster Bill" Pillow and "Papa" Lloyd Kennedy, appeared in court in November 1946. Already that summer, pleas of abatement in the case had been denied and with the upcoming trial in Lawrenceburg staring them in the face, defense lawyers had chosen not to ask for a change of venue. Once a new group of veniremen was selected in November, however, Weaver and Looby, joined by a now healthy Thurgood Marshall, requested a change from Maury to Davidson County, and they tried to quash the jury panel on the grounds that blacks had been systematically excluded from petit juries in Maury County for over fifty years. Ingram ruled against the change of venue and, as earlier, maintained that the only real consideration was the present jury panel and that because four African Americans had been called for possible service—three of whom he had personally added—no evidence of discrimination existed.

The judge also moved the jury selection process along rapidly. On November 12, a panel of seventy-five had been chosen, but it was exhausted by the next day, so another panel of seventy-five was selected. Because only thirty-five appeared, Ingram ordered "instant subpoenas" in midafternoon, and court resumed that evening at 8:30. By 11:05, jurors had been named. Among those summoned by Ingram were "by-standers" and "outstanding business men and leaders of Columbia." The latter were selected from the Rotary Club, Kiwanis Club, Lion's Club, and the Junior Chamber of Commerce, all exclusively white organizations. Probably for this reason, Ingram handpicked three African Americans to serve as veniremen, but all were either excused or excluded by the State through its peremptory challenges. Among those chosen for jury service were the superintendent of the Armour Fertilizer Works and the manager of the Monsanto Chemical Company.[128]

For two and a half days, the jury heard testimony and summations, and on the third day, it found Pillow innocent and Kennedy guilty of attempted murder in the second degree. Evidence against both men was mixed, and even Harwell admitted in his closing remarks that it was unclear to him whether "one, two, or three shots" were fired from the barbershop. (The defense contended none were.)[129]

The outcome of the trial was probably determined more than anything else by the presence of two white businessmen who testified in Pillow's behalf and by Kennedy's defiant attitude on the witness stand. The assistant attorney general of Tennessee himself argued before the state supreme court that the jury may have concluded that "Pillow was not guilty because of . . . a good reputation proven for him" and that because of Kennedy's demeanor, the jury might have surmised "that this attitude existed at an earlier time, to-wit, upon the morning of this assault and that such attitude of defiance caused him to fire upon the Patrolmen when they were seeking to arrest him."[130]

In December, a motion for a retrial for Kennedy was denied by Judge Ingram, and the young man was sentenced to prison for no more than five years. Kennedy remained free on bond, however, while his case was appealed to the state and federal supreme courts.[131] In May 1947, the Tennessee Supreme Court upheld his conviction, and on March 18, 1948, the U.S. Supreme Court refused to hear the case. Still, the convicted man was pardoned by the governor and served only four months of his term.[132]

A final, bizarre episode ended the sojourn of Marshall, Looby, and Weaver in Columbia. Shortly after the verdict was rendered in the Kennedy-Pillow trial, the trio went to Julius Blair's drugstore, where they purchased soft drinks and snacks, and then, accompanied by Harry Raymond of the *Daily Worker*, headed for Nashville in Looby's car. Three times just outside the county seat, they were stopped by a car carrying several men who shined flashlights in their faces. Although these men wore civilian clothes, Marshall thought they might be deputy sheriffs or constables. Each time Looby's car was stopped, a state highway patrol car hovered nearby. In the first instance, the men searched the car for whiskey; the second time, they examined Marshall's driver's license; and the third time, they told him to get in their car, that he was under arrest for drunk driving. Marshall's companions, they suggested, should go on to Nashville.

Initially the car bearing Marshall headed toward the Duck River, but Looby, Weaver, and Raymond followed it, and the vehicle turned toward town. There Marshall was taken before a magistrate. Weaver informed the justice that this was a "frame-up" and suggested he smell Marshall's breath. Upon doing so, the official declared "This man isn't drunk, he hasn't even had a drink." With this statement, all the men who had brought Marshall into the office faded away, except for the one who had issued the original warrant, and he agreed with the justice! The defense lawyers and Raymond then headed back to the Bottom where they procured another automobile and proceeded safely to Nashville. The next day, some of Looby's friends in Columbia returned his car.[133]

Like this strange ending, the Columbia story, though filled with drama, leaves many questions unresolved. First, *who participated in the African American effort to protect Stephenson and why were they there?* After all, this community had experienced two lynchings within less than twenty years, and acts of mob violence are usually regarded as potent intimidators of black populations. Even Looby had commented that it was "surprising" that black Maury Countians would congregate "even . . . for defense."

Second, *why did the white mob form, and even more significantly, why did it fail?* Not only had white vigilantes terrorized blacks in recent decades in this community, but they had been pervasive during Reconstruction, when Maury County constituted one of the leading Klan counties in Tennessee. What happened in 1946? Was it a simply a matter of armed African Americans making a stand, or were other factors involved?

Third, *why did law enforcement officers play such divergent roles in this affair?* Virtually all were white, male, Tennessee natives. Yet the State Guard

apparently tried to maintain law and order, while state troopers enthusiastically subverted it. Similarly, Sheriff Underwood initially appeared more
favorably disposed toward the Stephensons than the local police. Yet, he
began rapidly backtracking on the issue of the severity of the white mob
within two days after it had formed.

Finally, *why did the federal grand jury and the Lawrenceburg jury reach
such different conclusions?* Their members too resembled the State Guard
and Highway Patrol in gender, race, and native origins. Yet the verdict
reached in the federal case represented a staunch victory for conservatives,
while the one in the Lawrenceburg trial was an enormous coup for liberals.
Why did such disparate outcomes occur?

The remainder of this book attempts to answer these questions. Chapters
2 and 3 deal with the black effort to prevent the lynching of James Stephenson and the trends and circumstances, past and present, that gave rise to it;
Chapter 4 confronts the issue of the mob and the role played by whites in its
formation and failure; and Chapters 5 through 7 explore the relations of
African Americans with the police and the courts in the mid-forties. Together, these chapters demonstrate a shift in emphasis during World War II
from unequal protection of African Americans by the law to unequal enforcement of the law.

RACIAL VIOLENCE

THE
BOTTOM AND
ITS BROKERS

The selection of the Bottom as a place to make a stand in behalf of James Stephenson was *not* happenstance. Most simply, the first block of East Eighth Street was a confined physical space long controlled by African Americans. Frequented by a multitude of low-wage workers and owned by a handful of middle-class entrepreneurs, the establishments of the Bottom reflected the larger social structure of the community. At once, they offered mute testimony to the vitality of black institutions and to the limitations imposed on them by white society.

On February 25th, the owners of East Eighth Street businesses and their customers came together in defense of Stephenson. Their actions resulted from a confluence of long-term historical processes and from more recent developments, namely local lynchings and a world war. This chapter focuses on the proprietor side of the equation. It deals with the acculturation process that entrepreneurs experienced as they shifted from white to black clienteles and with the strategic roles that they played both within their own communities and between the black and white worlds. The chapter points especially toward a militant defensiveness that certain members of the black middle class could assume during times of crises, and it explores the memories and events that triggered such a response in 1946. Above all, it reveals a criminal justice system aimed at controlling rather than protecting black citizens, and it highlights the men who stepped into the breach. Almost inadvertently, local proprietors took actions that enhanced black pride and effected wider changes.

Throughout the United States—from the growing cities of the Northeast and Midwest to the coalfields of southern West Virginia, from the Mississippi Delta to the San Francisco Bay—black businesses expanded rapidly in the late nineteenth and early twentieth centuries, as owners everywhere shifted from white to black customers. By the 1920s, only one black proprietor in four serviced whites, and the black business district or "Negro Main Street" had emerged as "a fixed institution."[1]

In large measure, the shift in clienteles and the construction of black business districts resulted from an intensification of white racism and a hardening of racial boundaries. Large-scale structural factors and shifts in black attitudes were important as well.[2] The Great Migration northward also afforded black proprietors the opportunity to continue familiar service establishments in a markedly different environment, while the community building and institution building initiated by African Americans in southern towns and cities during the Civil War decade provided fertile soil for the flowering of black businesses in the latter part of the century.

Black communities and their public expressions—"Negro Main Streets"—thus resulted from a dual process of African American initiative operating in a wider context of racial inequality. The Bottom in World War II Columbia represented the culmination of these forces.

ROOTS

The genesis of the black community in Maury County lay in a tiny number of pre–Civil War, free black households, situated in Columbia, and in changes stirring in the countryside, as the Union army entered the region in the early months of 1862 and slavery began to crumble.[3] The end of slavery laid a basis for the expansion of black businesses in Columbia in two ways: (1) by creating a rural populace in need of services and (2) by promoting both migration to the town itself and the construction of an institutional and organizational framework that would sustain a vibrant business district well into the twentieth century.

In some ways, African Americans in the Maury County countryside, like those in the other twelve "heartland" counties of Middle Tennessee, were better positioned to achieve a degree of economic independence and to build institutional support networks than their brethren in the cotton belt.[4] For a variety of reasons, general farming offered better opportunities to newly freed persons to acquire land than did the cotton culture, which produced the lowest levels of black landownership in the South.[5] Additionally, those who depended upon grain and livestock for their livelihood "experienced fewer anxieties over basic sustenance." As historian Lester

Lamon points out, "Their work was not seasonal, more of their food was home-grown, and they depended less upon distant markets and unscrupulous merchants."[6]

Although the landholdings of most African Americans remained small and their circumstances, like those of all small farmers, grew more precarious as the twentieth century progressed, the ownership of property offered definite advantages over working as a sharecropper or as a farm laborer for cash wages. For one, property ownership permitted blacks "to offer their labor to the market under circumstances of their own choosing." Too, because landowners made the decisions regarding agricultural production, black farmers could consciously choose general farming and thereby avoid the "vicissitudes" of a staple, nonfood crop like cotton. Finally, in an agricultural society, the acquisition of land not only provided a measure of economic autonomy and independence, but also it was regarded as a social advancement, resulting in greater self-esteem for the individual farmer and his family.[7]

The discovery of rich veins of phosphate in southwestern Maury County in the early 1890s offered alternative sources of employment to rural Maury Countians and contributed to the development of the small town of Mt. Pleasant.[8] By 1942, the region was the nation's largest producer of phosphate. Mines, fertilizer plants, and two chemical companies devoted to the production of elemental phosphorus, an ingredient used in the construction of bombs, altered but did not supplant the county's agricultural orientation during the World War II years.

For newly freed blacks who found few opportunities in the countryside, Columbia offered the possibility of a new start. More blacks than whites moved to town during the 1860s, and in 1870, for the only time in the county seat's history, African Americans comprised over half the population (52 percent).[9] Indeed, during the 1860s, the movement of blacks to Middle Tennessee towns was so large, and that of whites so limited, that it contributed to historian Stephen Ash's conclusion that "the Civil War in Middle Tennessee—more precisely, black initiative unleashed by the war—had liberated black society and pointed it toward the future, only to immure white society and point it toward the past."[10]

But life in the county seat was not easy. Frequently segregated in "shanty-towns" such as Macedonia on the outskirts of the city limits, many black town dwellers found it difficult to procure the basic necessities of life. Nimrod Porter observed in the winter of 1866, "'a verry great scuffle with the blacks to get houses & places to live[.] [T]hey are in a pitiful condition

& many of them almost starving & naked.'"[11] Similar reports to the Freedmen's Bureau from teachers working in the South indicated that "poverty remained an all-pervasive characteristic of black life and loomed above all others" during Reconstruction.[12]

Despite changes that included relatively high rates of black landownership, the opening of the phosphate mines, and migration to town, most African Americans in Maury County, including Columbia, remained mired in low-wage, dead-end jobs throughout the first half of the twentieth century. In turn, the scarce resources of most of the county's workers and the growing disinclination of whites to patronize black businesses limited drastically the opportunities for black proprietors and professionals, and in turn, the size of the middle class. The occupational structure thus resembled a steeply sloped triangle, with a vast number of people clustered at the base and a tiny fraction perched unsteadily at the apex.[13]

Yet while black Maury Countians were vastly underemployed and low paid, they were *not* unemployed and unpaid. Jobs were arduous, often insecure, and low-paying, but in the labor-intensive economy that prevailed in most parts of the South at least until the early 1950s, they *were* available.[14] Although private and public funds for institution building were scarce, they could be scraped together. Paid employment thus served not only as a source of individual self-esteem but also as a critical building block in the construction of an all-black infrastructure.

The creation of this infrastructure began as early as the Civil War years and continued unabated at the time of the 1946 altercation. At the conclusion of the Civil War, African Americans in the county were determined to arrange their own households whether or not they farmed as owners, tenants, or day laborers. Remarks by the *Columbia Herald* in 1870 revealed the attempts, prevalent throughout the South, by Maury County women and children to withdraw from field labor: "It has been the experience of the whole South and especially Maury County, that one of the greatest differences between slave and free labor, is in the matter of hoeing cotton. The negro woman and children did most of the hoeing in slave times, but the freedman keeps his wife at home doing nothing, and sends his children to school, or lets them do nothing and steal."[15]

Black churches apparently served as hiring halls for whites seeking black laborers in the years immediately following the Civil War, and they functioned as sites for political meetings.[16] The growth of these houses of God marked the emergence of rural black "spiritual and social communities," even as many of their members continued to live in isolated dwellings on their employers' land.[17]

"Cotton pickings," in which African Americans assisted one another in harvesting the crop in the late 1860s, also testified to agrarian bonds of mutuality and support, while the "June meeting," a daylong religious and social gathering of blacks from throughout the county, persisted and expanded. Additionally, "black barbecues, hoedowns, and camp meetings soon became familiar features of the Middle Tennessee countryside, exuberant symbols of rural black communalism." "The Colored People's Benevolent Society," organized at the hamlet of Campbell's Station, affirmed the same spirit.[18]

Intense Ku Klux Klan activity in Maury County in 1868 testified not only to white hostility but also to determined efforts by African Americans to participate in the political process. It was a sign of the times—and of times to come—that a John Lockridge served as a delegate from Maury County to the Freedmen's Convention in Nashville in 1865, while in the midst of the Klan outrages, "one Bellefonte" was whipped with "'a strap and buckle.'"[19] African Americans continued to be active in Maury County politics throughout the late nineteenth century, and a number were voting in the 1940s, but their service as officeholders—and as jurors—were clearly distant memories by the World War II decade.

During the Civil War era, parents also struggled to obtain adequate clothing for their children so that they might attend school, and they sometimes exchanged firewood for school fees.[20] The first black school in Maury County was housed in Columbia in the Mt. Lebanon Missionary Baptist Church, located one block from the Bottom at the corner of East Eighth and Glade Streets. Established by preacher "Cap" Jordan in 1864, shortly after the town fell to Union forces, the school persisted through the war years, "despite threats and brutal physical abuse at the hands of Confederates, Yankees, and local whites alike."[21]

The hostility of whites toward schools was bound inextricably with their belief that black and northern white teachers, the Freedmen's Bureau, and Republican organizations known as Loyal Leagues were fostering anger by freedpersons toward their former masters and encouraging "uppityness" and political activity.[22] "Cap" Jordan became so discouraged that he was reputedly leaving for Florida in 1869 and trying to "take all negro population" with him.[23] In 1873, the county provided some teachers for black public schools, although they drastically cut funding in 1874 in the face of a proposed Civil Rights Bill that would have mandated integrated facilities.[24]

By the 1920s, College Hill School, located two blocks from East Eighth on East Tenth Street, served town and county students alike from first grade through high school. Although it was crowded and inadequately funded, to young Herbert Johnson, a World War II Army sergeant who grew up just around the corner from the school, College Hill was nevertheless "imposing," and his first teacher "amazing."[25]

By completing high school, Johnson, the nephew of a teacher who remained fifty years in the profession and the son of a former teacher who frequently recited poetry to him, was more fortunate than most. In 1950, 84 percent of the adult black population in Maury County, and 79 percent in Columbia, had no schooling beyond the eighth grade. Median school years completed stood at 5.9 years for the county and 6.4 for the town.[26]

Despite continued resentment—and at best indifference—on the part of whites toward black education, African Americans persisted in their long-standing efforts to improve opportunities for their children. Nothing demonstrated this more clearly than the fund-raising campaign for a new school that was underway in February 1946.

Along with the schools, churches, benevolent societies, and fraternal organizations were also part of the emerging social scene in 1860s Columbia just as they were in the countryside. Founded in 1843, Mt. Lebanon Missionary Baptist represented one of the oldest black churches in Tennessee. Within a few years after emancipation, black Columbia boasted five churches, including Mt. Lebanon, and was home to the Young Men's Aid Lyceum Society, a relief organization, and to an Odd Fellows Lodge and a Masonic chapter (Myrtle Lodge No. 6).[27] By the mid-1940s, sixteen black churches were located within the town, and the Colored Ministerial Alliance had formed, with Mt. Tabor Presbyterian minister Joseph P. Blade as its head.

Both Masons and Odd Fellows, who held their meetings in the Lodge Hall on East Eighth Street, remained an integral part of Columbia's social fabric, and an Elks Club (Harland Flippin Lodge No. 1155) was organized in July 1945.[28] More directly a product of war were the Hill Gordon American Legion Post, which was founded in the wake of World War I, and the Global War Veterans, which originated following World War II. A small social group, composed mainly of young veterans and known as the Royal Duke Club, also emerged briefly following the Second World War.[29]

Women joined sister organizations of the men's associations, including the Women's Division of the Elks, the Masonic Order of the Eastern Star, and the American Legion Women's Auxiliary. They also participated in the Columbia Art & Social Club, "Stitch and Chatter," and the Green Garden Club. Teachers and businesswomen were usually members of the Columbia Negro Women's Business and Professional Club.[30]

Columbia's black population in the mid-forties clustered in five distinct areas of the town: East Hill (also known as East End) and College Hill were adjacent to one another, south of Main Street; Macedonia and West End, which included a small district known as Fairview Heights, lay north of Main Street; and a few families lived along the southern end of Main in an area that would expand dramatically in the years after the war and become known as Southside. Each vicinity had churches and grocery stores, as well as homes.

Class differences were discernible. West End—or "Happy Hollow," as whites euphemistically dubbed it—was home to a larger working-class population than was South Main or College Hill, the latter so named allegedly because of the large number of college graduates who lived there. Macedonia and East Hill were socially more mixed. Almost one-third of the householders in Columbia owned their own homes in the early 1940s, and men predominated among household heads by more than two to one.[31]

THE BOTTOM

The community and institution building that persisted in Maury County in the midst of a wider context of racial disparity found its most visible expression in the Bottom. There, the twin themes of initiative and inequality could be seen in the compression of respectable and "less respectable" establishments in a single block; in the tiny cadre of successful black proprietors and their far more numerous working-class clientele; and in the combined spirit of comraderie, machismo, and contentiousness that flourished luxuriantly in the district.

As on other "Negro Main Streets," churches, meeting facilities, service establishments, and places of entertainment bunched together in the first block of East Eighth, only a couple of streets from the courthouse square, the heart of the white business district. Frequently, black business vicinities were divided, with one side home to "high-class businesses" and the other side "just the opposite."[32]

In Columbia, such a class demarcation line also existed, but it was not hard and fast. The north side of East Eighth Street was occupied by an ice plant, the First Baptist Church, and Morton's funeral home. The south side was anchored on the west end by the Lodge Hall and the offices of a physician, a lawyer, and an insurance agent and at the east end by the Holy Comforter Episcopal Church and a kindergarten, but it was the plethora of restaurants, pool rooms, and barbershops crammed between the Lodge Hall and the Episcopal Church that defined the block's character.

A view of the south side of the first block of East Eighth Street (the Bottom) from the northeast corner (at South Main) after highway patrolmen cleared it on the morning of February 26. The three-story building in the center of the photo is the Lodge Hall; note the ironic juxtaposition of the billboard advertisement for Castner-Knott, the store to which Gladys Stephenson had taken her radio for repair. (Courtesy of United States Attorney's Office, Middle District of Tennessee)

Three barbershops, including that of Saul Blair; the "soda fount" with a pool room in the back, operated by Julius Blair and his son Charlie; a beauty shop; five restaurants, including that of Meade and Sallie Johnson; and a separate pool room operated by Meade's son, James "Digger" Johnson, gave testimony to both the vitality of the dreams of black proprietors in Columbia and the reality of working conditions for most of the community's black citizenry. Some of those who operated businesses in the area, like the Mortons and Blairs, were genuinely and consistently successful for more than one generation, though their businesses tended to be small and undercapitalized in comparison to many white establishments.[33]

Most who wiled away their hours in the business and recreational sites of East Eighth Street were employed in the low-paying jobs so prevalent among black Maury Countians. Many of these people were male and single. Because they frequently held jobs that were inhibited by inclement weather, they often had time on their hands. In February 1946, a number were soldiers recently released from the military. Whether veterans or civilians, few of these men had attractive job prospects in sight.

The atmosphere in the Bottom was at once communal and contentious. As Julius Blair explained at his trial, "The colored population, the boys . . . come down to the pool room and to get sandwiches and to get everything and they congregate there when they have not got anything else to do."[34] In addition to Saturdays and Sundays, he continued, "most colored people have blue Monday," and on rainy days, they could be found "right in there in a bunch."[35] Some of the "boys" also worked in the Bottom and were there on a very regular basis.[36]

The predilection among the Bottom's frequent visitors to call one another by nicknames created an intimate distance among them. Many knew one another only on a first-name basis or as "Popeye," "Moot," "Toady," "Junior," "Mule," "Papa Lloyd," "Rooster Bill," or "Buster." With the exception of Meade Johnson's son, "Digger," and "Big Louise Wilkes," who ran a restaurant, nicknames were reserved for the customers, and not the owners, of East Eighth Street establishments. They thus served to delineate the clientele and employees, on the one hand, from the proprietors on the other, creating some distance between the two.

Nicknames also allowed the young men who frequented the area to maintain a sense of familiarity without the acquisition of intimate knowledge of one another. This familiarity encouraged a group response in behalf of Stephenson, while the distancing helped preserve anonymity in the wake of the police shootings. No one was eager to give law enforcement officers any details, but the men in the Bottom often honestly did not know the last names of others on the street that night or of those who sought refuge in various locations such as the Lodge Hall. Most tended to have personal knowledge only of the members of the specific group with which they hung out.

In the clustering process, friendship was often fortified by kinship. All five of the Edwards brothers were removed by the highway patrol on the morning of the 26th from the home of their aunt, Daisy Lee, at the corner of Eighth and Woodland Streets, at the Bottom's edge. Also taken from Lee's house were brothers Early and Lee Andrew Shyes and cousins Clarence Brown, Louis "Junior" Miles, and Paul Miles. Brown was also a cousin of

James Stephenson's father, and James "Popeye" Bellanfante was a cousin of Stephenson himself. Almost all of these men, as discussed further in Chapter 3, were World War II veterans.

As life quickened in the Bottom on weekends and "Blue Mondays" and men, and some women, poured in from around the county to eat, drink a little beer or bootleg liquor, possibly gamble for low stakes, and enjoy companionship, tempers often flared. Sometimes, shootings or stabbings were the unhappy result. Undertaker V. K. Ryan's son, Ronald, recalled that "on Saturday or Sunday morning you could go back to the morgue room cause there would be somebody dead." White landowners such as "old man Ritley" who reputedly told his black workers, "If you stay out of the cemetery, I'll keep you out of the pen," contributed to this devil-may-care atmosphere.[37] Additionally, in Columbia, as elsewhere, police indifference and "light patrolling" of black areas did little to curb violence.[38]

Many women avoided the recreational sites on East Eighth Street. Julius Blair's daughter-in-law recalled that she did not eat in the vicinity, although her husband Charlie lunched there every day. Similarly, Marcia Mayes, a friend of the Mortons who happened to be visiting them on the night of the 25th, mentioned at the trial that she always walked on the north side of the street, while restaurant worker Sadie Flippen maintained to the police that she did not "go in them places" on south East Eighth.[39]

Ronald Ryan and grocer Jim Martin's daughter Patricia Martin Bowman remembered that black youngsters were cautioned by their parents not to walk on the south side of the street. Ryan was taken to Guy Hamlet's barbershop near the corner of the block for haircuts and warned to remain until he was picked up, but Patricia surreptitiously scampered across the street for the free strawberry ice-cream cones that the Blairs knew she adored and invariably offered her. Standing six feet tall, Charlie Blair, lover of dogs, horses, and quail hunting, epitomized the vibrancy and danger that was East Eighth Street as he stood on the sidewalk, frying fish, a pistol strapped to his side.[40]

THE BROKERS

As proprietors both contributed to and imbibed East Eighth Street culture, they grew more physically assertive than their predecessors who had operated businesses on the town square a few years earlier. The younger generation was not poorer, less educated, or darker in skin color than those that preceded them, as some scholars have maintained; instead, the new group came of age after segregation lines hardened and the Bottom materialized as a cultural entity. Younger business leaders, who interacted daily with their working-class customers, thus developed more aggressive personas than older entrepreneurs who dealt largely with middle-class and elite clienteles. Their tough visages were much more often turned toward their customers, however, than toward whites, with whom they seldom came in contact. In addition, compared to the previous generation, they proved more willing to accept segregation and much less likely to interact with whites on something approaching an equal footing.

No one demonstrated more clearly the generational shifts that occurred as African American businessmen shifted from white, middle-class patrons to black, working-class customers than Julius Blair and his sons Saul and Charlie. The son of former slaves, the senior Blair was born in the early 1870s and spent his childhood in the countryside near Columbia. With a father who "had about sixteen in the family and couldn't make over $1.25 a day to save his life," Julius left home and began working in the streets of Columbia as a bootblack around the age of twelve or fifteen.[41]

He got his courage, Blair later told his daughter-in-law, one Thanksgiving, when his mother told him that there was no money for a turkey. Upon hearing this dismal news, he acquired some apples, sold them on the street in Columbia, and bought the traditional Thanksgiving bird, carrying it home with the proud announcement, "Mama, here's a turkey." If he could sell those apples, Blair reasoned, he could do something else.

After bootblacking in the streets, the young entrepreneur moved his operation into a black-owned barbershop, possibly that of Saul Wilkins, whose daughter Blair married. Sometime in the early 1890s, he acquired a shop of his own. Astutely, Blair also opened a shop in nearby Mt. Pleasant just as phosphate mining was beginning to boom there. As he recounted the story to his daughter-in-law Addie Blair Cooper, he had intended to rent a place in Mt. Pleasant but was able to purchase one on credit. After "those folks [in Mt. Pleasant] got settled in" and "spent their good money," Cooper chuckled, Blair took his savings and bought property on East Eighth Street.[42]

For over twenty-five years, Julius Blair operated a shop on the Columbia square, serving white, largely middle-class and elite customers. Like two other successful African American businessmen—John Merrick, barber and founder of the North Carolina Mutual Life Insurance Company, and Alonzo F. Herndon, barber and founder of the Atlanta Life Insurance Company—Blair's "indirect tutelage" from his businessmen-patrons no doubt reinforced his own business acumen.[43] But the timing of the commencement of Blair's operation was also very important, for he started his shop when he had access to both the central business district and a white clientele. Significantly, he abandoned his shop on the square in Columbia, concentrating all of his business efforts in the Bottom, in 1918.

At his trial, Blair explained his relocation in his customary blunt terminology, "I thought I had worked long enough and quit."[44] But his decision very likely had a discriminatory dimension, for black barbers increasingly lost out to whites after 1900, as they were "shunted aside into Jim Crow locals, denied leadership in mixed unions, and threatened with state licensing requirements." Although licensing bills proposed by white barbers failed in the Tennessee legislature in 1903 and 1905, "the economic squeeze continued and the traditional black barbering monopoly collapsed rapidly."[45]

Much more than their father, Saul and Charlie Blair were products of the Bottom. Except for a brief foray in the taxi business in the late forties and early fifties, Charlie spent his life managing the poolroom and drugstore with his father. By 1946, Saul had operated the barbershop on East Eighth Street for almost thirty years. With the exception of four months in the military in 1918, he had spent virtually all of his adult life in the East Eighth Street vicinity. At the trial, he commented tersely that after signing the bonds for the Stephensons he had gone "back down in the Bottom where I belonged," but he also seemed to accept the situation in ways that his father did not. Julius, for example, refused to attend the motion picture show in Columbia because he would not enter via the door reserved for blacks; both his sons as well as James and Mary Morton—all of whom were in the same age cohort—demonstrated no such qualms.[46]

In retrospect, Julius was described as "firm," but Saul "and his bunch" were recalled as "fiery." Although Raymond Lockridge remembered Saul as more "fiery" than Charlie, Ronald Ryan depicted the younger Blair brother as "really rough."[47] Julius was also closer to whites like Sheriff Underwood than were his sons, and he retained on a regular basis a white lawyer, R. S. Hopkins, one of the local establishment's few Republicans. Both relationships dated from Blair's days as a barber on the town square.

The fieryness and roughness of the younger Blairs may have been in part a matter of personal proclivities, but these were likely reinforced by internal frustration born of living throughout their lives in a rigidly segregated, discriminatory white world over which they had little control. Undoubtedly, their demeanor was also attributable to their incubation in the tough East Eighth Street world, a place where many of those with whom they interacted on a daily basis shared their sense of frustration and bellicosity.

In contrast to his sons, Julius Blair, who obviously felt quite angry about segregation but who had matured in a less circumscribed age, seemed to feel freer to express his frustration and was thus less inclined toward physical aggression. Indeed, he went well beyond his offspring in his willingness not only to work with whites but also to say whatever he chose around them. At the same time, Blair's relocation to the Bottom was not without impact. Although he differed from his sons in personal style, he resembled them in his fierce protectiveness of the Bottom's patrons, and because he knew key white officials like the sheriff better than they did, he assumed the lead, along with undertaker James Morton, in brokering in his customers' behalf when they ran afoul of the law.

Morton served as another example of the way operating a business in the Bottom could produce militant defensiveness as well as divergence within the black middle class. A quintessential member of the bourgeoisie, who ate "dinner" rather than "supper" and who was deeply chagrined the night of his arrest that he had to wear his bedroom slippers to jail, Morton nevertheless carried a double-barreled shotgun at his side when he walked out in the street to talk with police on the night of February 25th, and he warned officers not to permit whites to come into the area. According to defendant William "Moot" Bills, Morton also "seemed to be giving instructions" to the dozen or so armed men who were gathered in front of his funeral home, and he eventually invited the men inside where they remained until their discovery by the highway patrol.[48]

In contrast to Morton, none of the other three undertakers in Columbia, including his Uncle Lorraine Morton who operated a funeral parlor on South Main Street, participated in Stephenson's defense. V. K. Ryan, whose funeral home was located two blocks from the Bottom, informed FBI agents that he had "no first hand knowledge" of the events of the 25th and 26th, because he had "made it a point to remain on the outside of that area."[49]

Similarly, neither Samuel E. Jones, principal of College Hill High School, nor Reverend Joseph P. Blade, minister of Mt. Tabor Presbyterian Church and president of the Colored Ministerial Alliance, even knew about the fight between Stephenson and Fleming until Morton appeared, "a bit disturbed," at the school fund-raising meeting on the evening of the 25th with the announcement that a crowd was gathering uptown.[50] Furthermore, Jones stated at the trial that he was only "fairly familiar" with East Eighth Street between South Main and Woodland (that is, the Bottom), and Patricia Martin Bowman recently recalled that teachers always shopped in Nashville rather than Columbia before local stores were integrated.[51]

In retrospect, a number of black Columbians surmised correctly that

Morton was forced to adopt a militant stance because of the location of his business in the Bottom. The funeral director did not, however, act against his will or better judgment. Instead, while unquestionably middle class, Morton had been toughened by his day-to-day association with the men who frequented East Eighth Street. He had also developed considerable allegiance to the area's patrons, as he chatted with them while sitting on his front porch, guided their choices in elections, and—along with the Blairs—bailed them out of jail.

In sum, Morton's behavior on the night of February 25th stemmed from his immediate and sustained contact with workers who frequented the Bottom. Businessmen who did not have such contact, even other funeral directors, did not follow suit. Neither did ministers and teachers, who had little exposure to the rough side of working-class culture.

A Missionary Baptist minister who carried "an Army paratrooper's semi-automatic machine gun and several clips of ammunition," Calvin Lockridge seemed a contradiction to this generalization, but Lockridge, who labored daily as a carpenter, was not nearly as removed from the underside of working-class life as a full-time minister like Reverend Blade. A "peppery" individual, whose wife was a cousin of the young man most recently and brutally lynched in the community, and himself a cousin of the woman engaged to Charlie Blair, Lockridge also had personal reasons for acting as he did. Lockridge, then, was the exception and not the rule in the degree of militancy shown by ministers in the Columbia affair.

Eventually the gap between the operators of establishments on East Eighth Street, especially the south side, and "respectable" elements within the black community might have widened. A thorough fissure within the middle class did not exist, however, in 1946. The small size of black Columbia, the relative wealth of men like the Blairs, the middle-class lifestyles that entrepreneurs maintained, the leadership positions that they held in community organizations, the firm but moderating influence of an earlier generation symbolized by Julius Blair, and, above all, the strictures placed on all African Americans by a Jim Crow society and the quotidian harassment that this system spawned—all these factors mitigated against the separation of south East Eighth Street business owners from the rest of the bourgeoisie. Nothing better demonstrated the continued middle-class status of Saul and Charlie Blair, despite their "fieryness" and their close association with young men of the streets and countryside, than the printed invitation delivered to Columbia homes three months after the trial in which Julius and Saul were deemed not guilty by the Lawrenceburg jury. It read:

Just We Three,—S. W.- C.E. and Me
Feel indebted to Columbia S-O-C-I-E-T-Y
So we'd like to repay
In the usual way
All of Columbia's society at a ball
Given by
J. W. Blair and Sons
Friday night, Feburary [*sic*] 14 from 10 'til?
at the
Odd Fellows Hall
Music by
Chick Chabis
Hours 10 Until ?
Formal[52]

The continuing ties of East Eighth Street's proprietors with other members of the middle class were important, because they enabled business owners to make working-class concerns middle-class causes. During the lengthy criminal trial in the fall of 1946, money and other forms of assistance from area churches poured in to African American defendants who could not work. Some of this support would no doubt have been forthcoming anyway, but without question, the charges levied against men like Morton and the Blairs insured middle-class attention and help.

Because of their middle-class status and their leadership positions within their community, black businessmen experienced both advantages and disadvantages in their relations with whites. To African Americans whom they knew, like the Blairs or Morton, white Columbians offered property when they decided to sell it. Even ammunition found its way into the hands of farmers and laborers via men like the Blairs, for the local hardware stores sold them boxes of shotgun shells, and they in turn resold to other blacks, three or four shells at a time. A $5 box of shells could earn the owner as much as $15 or $20.[53]

Yet at the same time that whites offered business opportunities to African American leaders, they held them responsible for the behavior of other blacks. For this reason, officials indicted them for inciting others to commit murder in the first degree following the February fray.

In fact, because of their relative wealth and power, black entrepreneurs did discipline as well as assist their customers, although their ability to control them, especially in late February 1946, was not as great as whites liked to believe. Black agricultural agent George A. Newbern recalled that when he moved to Columbia in 1944 it was difficult to buy property. "All the rest of them, the Johnsons . . . the Blairs and Mortons and all of them, they were the ones who had the money and had all the rest of the illiterates, black, around them, and that's just the way they lived. . . . if you didn't get in with them, you couldn't get anything."[54]

Similarly James "Digger" Johnson stated to investigators on February 28, just hours before he was killed, that "Blair and James Morton, they got other people, you know, to do like they wanted them to do, all colored to do like they did." Johnson's charge that Charlie Blair had struck him with a fire poker a few years earlier serves as an explicit example of the enforcement of physical discipline by the Bottom's leaders, as well as of Charlie's "roughness." Along with their wealth, this physical exercise of power also undoubtedly helps explain some of Johnson's anger toward them. Again, later in his testimony, the young poolroom operator exploded in reference to Saul Blair and James Morton: "We do what the big men say and them two owns the world."[55]

But the money and influence of Columbia business leaders could be used to help as well as command. Hannah Peppers's appeal to Julius Blair on the morning of the 25th to make bond for her daughter and grandson was not an isolated occurrence. Morton and the Blairs had bailed so many people out of jail in the past that some officials had attempted to convict them for signing bonds without a license. The attempt failed when a local judge refused to try the case. In the wake of the massive arrests on February 26, they signed bonds for so many of the defendants that the prosecution tried to use their actions as further proof of a conspiracy on their part to incite others to shoot policeman Will Wilsford. As Julius Blair explained on the witness stand in regard to himself and James Morton: "We got tired of fee grabbers taking a Negro up there without any help or backing, and fine him what they wanted to; and if he didn't have the money, put him on the County Road, and that was our purpose. We didn't get a cent out of it and didn't look for anything out of it. We got tired of the fee grabbers catching a man and doing that because he didn't have no help. We went to his rescue."[56] They didn't sign bonds for "no thieves, bootleggers, and whiskey drinkers," Blair made clear, "It is just when we think they are mistreated." "Do you have sympathy for people that steal or criminals?" the defense asked. "Not a bit," Blair responded, though he hedged, "when they are in good health."[57]

Above all, black entrepreneurs were multifaceted. In dealing with their customers, they were at once empathetic and tough. In conjunction with other members of the middle class, they served as community boosters. In relations with whites, they were usually circumspect. None relished a show-down with the establishment. Yet because of their acculturation in a tough environment, they were not encrusted in a middle-class shell of respectability. Instead, they were comfortable with physical assertiveness in ways that other members of the black middle class—like preachers and teachers—were not. Additionally, over the years, black proprietors with a large number of working class customers had assumed the role of protector, as well as disciplinarian, within their domain. Thus when the circumstances appeared to warrant it, they could respond with considerable alacrity and militancy.

The threat of white violence in 1946 proved such a catalyst in Maury County. Since the 1920s, black leaders had witnessed a racially motivated murder in the courthouse itself and two lynchings. Too often, law enforcement officials were interlaced with the perpetrators, while the criminal justice system proved ineffectual in finding and punishing offenders. At best, mob members appeared to bear a legal imprimatur; at worst, they seemed to flaunt all judicial institutions and constitutional protections.

Owners and customers alike shared a collective memory of nightmares. The actions of both in 1946 would be informed by them, but anguished recollections would prove especially important in galvanizing middle-class entrepreneurs who had assumed a guardianship role within their community. Never before had they turned their tough visage toward white officials. This time, however, the historical path that they had trod, coupled with the war's effects and, most important, with the searing memories of rope and untimely deaths, compelled them to bare it. When William Fleming's older brother John was asked recently if he thought African Americans had previous lynchings on their mind in 1946, he responded, "I doubt it; I doubt it very seriously."[58] He was wrong.

SHARED NIGHTMARES

In a Columbia courtroom in 1924, an ominous drama unfolded. Robert Wilson, an African American who probably hailed from West Tennessee, was arrested in May for the rape of a young white woman. Evidence against Wilson was apparently quite flimsy, for in his June trial an all-white jury sentenced him to only two years in prison, and Judge Thomas B. Lytle promptly set aside the seemingly mild sentence. Immediately following the judge's pronouncement, shots rang out in the courtroom. The alleged victim's brother, Davis J. "Dacie" Twomey, had killed Wilson. So many white Maury Countians rushed to sign Twomey's bond that additional sheets of paper had to be added to the bail form.[59] One year later, an all-white jury declared Twomey not guilty.[60]

Although the criminal justice system had in the end freed Wilson, it could not, or did not, protect him. His murder in the courtroom was a stark reminder of that fact, and the behavior of whites, both in rushing forward to sign Twomey's bond and in readily freeing him, served notice that in Maury County, as in neighboring Alabama, "The 'honor' of one white woman was more important than the life's blood of a black man."[61] White behavior also made clear that when it came to protecting one of their own, white Maury Countians stood united.

African Americans in Columbia did not forget the Wilson-Twomey affair, although many whites seemed to do so. In May 1946, after an FBI investigation that had occurred off and on for two and one-half months, an agent heard about the Wilson case for the first time. Joe Braden, the black owner of a taxi business, prefaced his comments to the white interviewer with the qualifier that "the white and colored people in Columbia had enjoyed generally good relations," but he continued, "The white people do these things to keep the colored people cowed." When asked specifically to what he was referring, Braden described the Wilson episode. Though some of his "facts" were not quite accurate, his understanding of the import of the affair was right on target. As he explained it, "the colored boy died instantly but no action was taken to prosecute the white boy."[62]

Three years following Wilson's murder, another racial atrocity occurred at the courthouse, this time in the form of an overt mob killing. On the morning of Friday, November 11, 1927, a young white woman, who lived about ten miles outside of Columbia on Hicks Lane, claimed she was accosted as she made her way to catch the school bus. According to her story, she successfully fought off her attacker; then she ran to the home of her uncle, Marvin Pickard. Sheriff Luther C. Wiley was summoned.

A man claimed to have seen 18-year-old Henry Choate coming from the direction of Hicks Lane shortly after the alleged crime. Choate, who was working as a road construction laborer in Coffee County, was off for Armistice Day, and he had come for a visit with his grandfather, Henry Clay Harlan. Harlan, a black farmer who resided on land that he owned and on which he had been born a slave in 1861, was approached that morning by a group of white men. As he walked across the field with them, exchanging ideas about how they might apprehend the alleged attacker of the young woman, he learned to his horror that they had come for his grandson. Choate was taken to the home of Pickard. Although the young woman could not identify the young man as her attacker, the sheriff allegedly had difficulty getting him safely away from Pickard's home and lodged in the Maury County jail.

About 8:00 that evening, a mob of fifty to seventy-five men approached the jail. When the sheriff's wife refused them entry, one member of the crowd rushed to a nearby power station, grabbed a sledgehammer, and began to batter down the jail door. Once the men gained entrance to the jail, they rushed to the second floor, where the cells were located. Obtaining the keys from a deputy, they seized young Choate, dragging him down the stairs, outside, and to the West Seventh Street entrance of the courthouse.[63]

Whether the young man was killed prior to his arrival at the courthouse or after he got there is disputed. The accounts of events after Choate's death do not differ, however. A rope was slung over the railing of the second floor balcony of the courthouse, and the teenager's body was hung from it. The conservative *Nashville Banner* reported the day after Choate's murder that he had confessed to his crime as he stood before the courthouse entrance; Henry Clay Harlan maintained to journalist Carl Rowan in 1951 that "a few days later they found for sure that another lad was the guilty party."[64]

Law officers were not as deeply implicated in the killing of Choate as they would be in the death of Cordie Cheek six years later. Nevertheless, the forty-member executive committee of the Tennessee Interracial Commission, a body that represented over 600 members statewide, resolved that: "All available information indicates that the sheriff of Maury county failed to meet his obligation as an officer. Other sheriffs in Tennessee and in other states have prevented lynchings under more difficult circumstances. That this lynching should have taken place on Armistice Day and in the very citadel of justice, and that no effort was made to defend the prisoner or to spirit him away to a safer place, adds to the seriousness of the offense."[65]

A deepened awareness that the criminal justice system could fail dramatically in the protection it afforded African Americans was certainly one lesson that blacks in Maury County drew from the Choate lynching. They no doubt perceived that the possession of deep roots in the community and the ownership of property, both attributes of Harlan, offered no protection either.

The aspect that they associated most closely in their minds with the horror of that evening, however, was the *rope* used to hang Choate's body from the courthouse balcony. Today—as in 1946—African Americans recall that the rope dangled menacingly "for months and months . . . as a symbol of what would happen to anybody else."[66] In contrast, Communist Robert Minor attributed in his booklet the hanging of a rope for many months to a lynching that occurred in a courthouse located 162 miles from Columbia.

Some reports noted that Choate's body was cut down only a few minutes after it was hung and thereby implied that the rope may not have remained either. But the transposition of factual information, if that is indeed what happened, serves only to underscore the special association made in the minds of black Maury Countians between rope, the courthouse, and racially inspired murder.[67]

On the afternoon of February 25, 1946, as whites began to cluster in front of the Fair Store across the street from the courthouse, a rumor, pregnant with dire implications, flew around the county: a rope, intended for the Stephensons, had been purchased at a local hardware store! The federal grand jury meeting in the spring of that year tried diligently to confirm this report, but in doing so, the jurors overlooked the particular meaning that rope held for black Maury Countians. Whether the purchase of rope generated anxiety about Stephenson's safety or whether concern for his safety sparked rumors about a rope purchase, that specific rumor indicated that Choate's killing formed an integral part of the mosaic of fears that informed black actions that day. A mob murder that took place six years after Choate's would become an even more important part of that mosaic.

THE LYNCHING OF CORDIE CHEEK

The black Cheek family and the white Moore family had long resided near one another in the small farming community of Glendale, about six miles southeast of Columbia. At the time of his son's death, Fate Cheek, Cordie's father, had labored for nine years as a section hand for the L&N Railroad. The victim's mother, Tenny Cheek, had worked for many years as a cook, maid, midwife, and nurse for the Moore family.[68]

In 1929, Mrs. Moore died, and three years later, in the winter of 1932, her husband, Lauris Moore, committed suicide. An elder daughter and her husband continued to live in the house, along with her brother, 19-year-old Henry Carl Moore; an 11-year-old sister, referred to as "Lady Ann"; and two younger brothers. Tenny Cheek, who "had treated the Moore children as her own," "did what she could for the family" after the mother's death and "still helped out" after the father's suicide. She also arranged for Cordie to do chores for the Moores.[69]

Formerly Henry Carl and Cordie, who was only two years younger than Moore, had been playmates. Now, under the new arrangements, "social friction evidencly [sic] of a status nature" developed between the two.[70] Additionally, Henry Carl owed wages to both Cordie and his mother. When Cordie asked for his, a fight ensued, and Henry Carl was "worsted."[71]

On the afternoon of November 16, 1933, Cordie was chopping wood at the Moore household. As he brought a load into the house, he brushed past "Lady Ann" and accidentally tore her dress. Shortly afterwards, Cheek discussed his next day's work with Henry Carl's older sister and departed for home.

About an hour after Cheek's departure, Henry Carl allegedly persuaded his younger sister, in exchange for a dollar, to say that the young man had tried to rape her. He then proceeded to a local store-filling station owned and operated by Dawes Hancock and his son Robert "Bob" Hancock. Phone calls were made to the nearby farming community of Culleoka and to Columbia. Soon a crowd, which included the Moore children's uncle, C. Hayes Denton, began to gather. About 6:00, a black employee at the store raced to the Cheek home to alert Cordie that a crowd was coming to punish him because he had "gotten too 'biggity.'" When an incredulous Tenny and her daughter Ann Pillow went to the store, they found "people in a hubbug," and Henry Carl cursed and slapped the older woman.[72]

When his mother returned home, Cordie fled, running up a ravine and along a railroad track. It took him most of the night to travel the fourteen miles to the home of his sister and brother-in-law, Bob and Ann Pillow, who lived on the farm of white landowner Joel Cheatham. Meanwhile a mob that included, among others, Henry Carl Moore and Dawes and Bob Hancock, made their way to Cordie's home. They also went to the home of Bob Pillow's brother as well as several others. Two of the men whose homes they visited recognized Maury County deputy Pillow Dew in the crowd that appeared at their doors.[73] About 10:00 that evening, Dew telephoned Joel Cheatham to ask permission to search his plantation for a "prisoner" that had escaped. Cheatham thought he was referring to a convict.

Thirty minutes later Dawes Hancock knocked at Cheatham's door. So inebriated he had to lean against the doorframe, Hancock maintained to Cheatham that Cheek had raped Lady Ann Moore and that a crowd was down in the road looking for him. Sheriff [Claude] Godwin and others were up on the highway, he said. Cheatham gave Hancock permission to search his tenant houses and their barns. They made "considerable commotion among the tenants," so finally, "feeling that they had been prowling around long enough," Cheatham told the crowd to leave.

The next morning Bob Pillow, "greatly agitated," approached Cheatham's home. He explained that his brother-in-law was hiding in the cornfield near Pillow's house. At that point, Cheatham directed his tenant to hide Cordie in a "sinkhole" in the woods, and he proceeded to Glendale.[74]

After buying gas from Bob Hancock and observing a crowd inside the store that C. Hayes Denton seemed to be directing, Cheatham headed for Columbia. There he spoke with a Deputy Witherspoon, and the two men made their way back to Cheatham's plantation, where they procured Cheek; then, they headed to Lawrenceburg. When they arrived, they found the jail quarantined because of small pox, so they proceeded on to Pulaski, where Cordie was placed in jail.[75]

Upon his arrival home, Cheatham discussed the case with his son-in-law, Evans Hardison. Both were concerned about Cheek's safety. When Hardison returned to his home in Nashville, he phoned Governor Hill McAllister's wife, and shortly thereafter the governor sent a heavily armed car to retrieve the prisoner. Cheek was brought to the state capital and lodged in the Davidson County jail. He stayed there for almost a month.

On Wednesday, December 13, Maury County sheriff Claude Godwin telephoned Davidson County sheriff I. A. Bauman to say that the local grand jury had not indicted Cheek and that he should be set free. Bauman replied that he needed written confirmation before he could release the young man. Friday's mail brought the necessary document. A deputy gave Cheek directions and carfare to his uncle's home, which was located on the edge of the Fisk University campus, two doors from the home of the dean of women.

Cordie arrived at the Jackson Street address around 3:00 or 4:00 in the afternoon. His aunt, Leona Cheek, and his 26-year-old first cousin, Rush Cheek, were there. They invited Cordie into the kitchen and began to prepare something for him to eat. Their visitor explained that he wanted to rid himself of the "jail smell," so they placed water on the stove in preparation for a bath. Cordie was immensely relieved to be out of jail, and he was excited. His father was supposed to bring him some money so he could go to Indianapolis.

Suddenly the Cheeks heard a car door slam in front of the house. "A heavy set man," "about five feet, eight inches in height," "apparently above forty years of age," appeared at the door. Six or seven other white men stood in the yard; some of them were armed. The man asked if this were the home of "Cheek." When Rush Cheek identified himself, the stranger replied, "You are not the one." Just then Cordie stepped to the door. When he gave his name, the man said, " 'Consider yourself under arrest.' " He then turned to those in the yard, saying, " 'Here he is boys, come on and get him.' " The men surged forward and it seemed to Leona Cheek as if "more than two [took] hold of him." "Cheek made no reply but walked on with them," his aunt later recalled.

Two Ford automobiles, one bearing Cordie, then careened through the heart of the Fisk campus. Henry Carl Moore stood on the running board of the second one, a pistol in his hand. Two women students, who were eating in a restaurant across the street from the Cheek residence, jotted down the license numbers of the two cars. One belonged to C. Hayes Denton; the other to Bob Hancock.

Very frightened—and probably quite unaccustomed to turning readily to law officers—the Cheeks made no effort to seek help.[76] About 7:00 or 7:30 that evening, Leona Cheek's husband, Jackson Cheek, telephoned Blair's Drug Store on East Eighth Street in Columbia. Charlie Blair told them that an automobile had just arrived in town. Cordie Cheek's dead body lay crumpled in the rumble seat.[77]

A laborer and a domestic worker—honest, upright, and hard-working but far from affluent—Fate and Tenny Cheek were people with whom most African Americans in Depression-ridden Maury County could easily identify, and they were very visible within the community. Uncomfortable in their home after their son's death, the Cheek couple moved to Columbia, though they still tended a garden near the Moores' at their old homesite. Their anguish was obvious. Seven months following her son's murder, Tenny Cheek murmured disconsolately, while Fate Cheek always spoke of his child "in a rather broken way."[78] Much more than the elderly Henry Clay Harlan and his wife, who rarely made visits to Columbia from their remote farm, the Cheeks were living symbols of powerful forces gone awry, forces that could not be allowed to rampage unchecked in the future.[79]

Even those who did not know the Cheeks personally knew a great deal about the nature of their son's alleged "crime" and his abduction. Certainly details of his murder circulated, for not only had numerous whites witnessed it but also James L. Garrett, a teenager from "a very interesting Negro family, thrifty, intelligent, and in good financial circumstances," had been forced to view it as well.[80]

The account of Cheek's slaughter was quite gruesome even by previous county standards. Well in advance of the murder, "many people in Columbia and environs" knew that it was going to occur.[81] For half an hour the lynchers waited at the lynch site, while phone calls were made, letting people know the time had arrived. Shortly thereafter, cars began to appear "from every direction." The crowd included "women, children, and men—everybody."[82]

Garrett saw a "tall thin-like person and two shorter thin-like ones" standing beside Cheek. The tall one and one of the shorter ones had pistols. They "had hold" of the young man. His hands were bound behind his back with "a strong rope," and a rope was tied around his neck. "It was a big rope," the young witness added, and it was "up on a limb of the tree and a step ladder about four feet high [was] under the limb of the tree." Cordie "was standing there trembling." Was he crying or did he struggle or fight? Garrett was asked. "No sir," the teen responded, "he was just trembling."[83]

As people began to gather, "Some of them said; 'Kill the nigger.'" Once the crowd had assembled, "they opened Cordie's trousers and castrated him by severing the testicle sack from his both."[84] Next, they blindfolded him and forced him up the ladder. Garrett continued: "Then the heavy-set man took a pole and pushed against Cordie's hips like and pushed him off the step ladder and hung him. Then the tall fellow shot at him and the short fellow shot at him. Then they passed the pistols around and lots of people shot at him. . . . They formed a circle and went around and looked at him. Then they began to get in their cars and go away."[85]

In the Choate lynching, the sheriff had been chastised for not being present when the mob arrived and thus for not doing all that he might have to save his prisoner. In the Cheek killing, the charges—and the knowledge—of the involvement of Maury County officials and law officers went much deeper. At every phase of the episode—from the initial search, through the abduction and killing, to the protection of the lynchers— officials were involved. Indeed the presence of so many in the events of 1933–34, the "procedures" that they followed, and even the language that they used as they seized Cheek, makes one wonder if mob members managed to convince themselves that they had legal sanction for their actions.

Deputy Pillow Dew, it will be remembered, called Joel Cheatham for permission to search his tenants' homes on the night of November 16, and reference was made to Sheriff Godwin's being with other men on the road as the search was conducted. Constable Austin Harlan was in the crowd that abducted Cheek from Fisk, and he returned to the Cheek residence in Nashville late one evening in June 1934 with three men, two of whom he identified as "city detectives." For two days, Cordie's cousin Rush Cheek was held in the Columbia jail and queried as to whether or not he would recognize any of the men who had spirited Cordie away. When he told them he could make no such identification, "they seemed pleased by their manner." Cheek was subsequently freed when a relative paid "costs."[86]

Additionally, though his role was murkier than that of Harlan, Ann Moore's uncle, Magistrate C. Hayes Denton, continued to surface throughout the Cheek episode. Although Joel Cheatham recalled that Denton was directing affairs on the morning of November 17 when Cheatham arrived at Hancock's store, the magistrate assured Tenny Cheek that he would protect her son. He also appeared solicitous of Fate Cheek, informing him that he had "kept the mob off of you" and that he had always been Fate's "friend."

Denton had added, however, that Cheek had "better keep quiet and be careful."[87]

As the drama unfolded, Denton's role remained elusive. The "Squire" maintained that he did not move his car from a parking space in Columbia all day on December 15, 1933, and no one claimed to have seen him at the residence of Jackson Cheek. But his vehicle was unquestionably one of the two used in Cordie's abduction. Too, because telephone "party lines" were prevalent in the rural South in the 1930s, it was common knowledge that phone calls were placed from Denton's home informing people that the lynching was about to take place, and at least two white women maintained that it was Denton's voice that they heard. Thus Denton's warning to Julius Blair in February 1946, that he should leave the Stephensons in jail for their protection, could have reflected legitimate concerns based on Denton's past failure to deter a mob, or it might have emanated from regrets over his participation in a mob murder. It is possible, too, that Denton's warning was designed to keep the Stephensons in jail where they would be readily available to a mob. Whatever Denton's intent, Julius Blair clearly knew about his alleged involvement in the Cheek case and mistrusted him. Blair's response that there would be no more "social lynchings" in Maury County made that fact very clear.

If Denton's role in Cheek's murder was obscure, Earl Allen's was not.[88] A member of a county road crew in 1933, Allen had been elevated to chief mechanic of county road operations by the summer of 1934. He also served as county coroner in 1933, a post he continued to hold in 1946. Allen was a friend of Deputy Ed Pugh of Nashville, and Pugh apparently called Allen to inform him of the timing of Cheek's release and of his whereabouts.[89] Indeed, Fate Cheek saw Allen getting into Bob Hancock's car on the afternoon of his son's abduction, and Allen informed Cheek that they were going to Nashville. Cordie's father, of course, had no idea of their mission at the time. Additionally, witnesses maintained that Allen knocked on the door of the Jackson Cheek home and informed Cordie that he was "under arrest," stopped James Garrett's truck on the road, and used a pole to push Cheek off the ladder to his death.[90]

Why the former chief mechanic and coroner played such a prominent role in this sordid affair is unclear. He may have been related to Ann's older sister's husband and felt that the family's honor necessitated his participation.[91] Henry Carl Moore was also a member of a road crew in 1933, and he and Allen may have worked together. Information unearthed by Arthur Raper, research director for the Commission on Interracial Cooperation (CIC) and one of the nation's foremost authorities on lynching in the 1930s, suggested that Ann *was* molested on November 16, possibly by her own brother-in-law![92] Allen thus may have been sucked into a scheme initiated by Henry Carl that stemmed from his own relative's offensive behavior.

The enigma only intensifies when one considers the conflicting descriptions of the shadowy Lady Ann. To her aunt, Ann was "such an untruthful and incorrigible child that no one could put dependence in what she said." In contrast, in reference to "an undersized [*sic*], undernourished child of between seven and ten years of age," Cordie Cheek told Joel Cheatham, "She looks just like that poor little thing out at Glendale that they are trying to kill me about."[93]

Just what occurred in the Moore household on the day Henry Carl inflamed hostilities toward Cordie Cheek will probably never be known, but it is clear that virtually no one in the black community—and probably a sizable group in the white community—believed that Cordie Cheek had attempted to assault the 11-year-old child. In the first place, Cheek had not been indicted by a Maury County grand jury because no one testified against him, including Ann Moore. Ostensibly, the family believed the trauma would be too much for her, but others speculated that there was concern the child would alter her story.

Additionally, Cheatham maintained to Scarritt College professor Albert E. Barnett and to Dr. Thomas E. Jones, president of Fisk University, that Cheek "was so evidently innocent that nobody could honestly doubt him." According to Fate Cheek, the older sister of Henry Carl and Ann told his wife and others in the community that "she didn't believe a word of the accusation against Cordie."[94] Finally, Sheriff Godwin's deputies—whom Cheatham labeled "the worst men in the county" with the exception of Witherspoon—stated that they did not know whether Cheek had assaulted Ann Moore and that "nobody seemed really to be clear as to just what had happened."[95]

Nevertheless Maury County officials, along with a number of leading citizens in the community, closed ranks to block indictments against the alleged lynchers, and neither state nor federal forces overcame their resistance. Not only did Sheriff Godwin label C. Hayes Denton as "'one of our best citizens'" to journalists in Nashville at the first of three grand jury hearings, but a statement made by the sheriff that "as long as Negroes rape white girls in Maury County they will be killed and there is nothing anybody can do about it" appeared to be a "deliberate misrepresentation." No one had accused Cheek of rape; the charge prior to the sheriff's comment was "attempted assault." "Did he not use the word 'rape' in an attempt to create and maintain a public opinion which would condone the crime of kidnapping and lynching, and help shield from punishment those guilty of them?" Raper queried in his report.[96]

Too, officials in Davidson County appeared adamant about bringing Cheek's lynchers to justice until the sheriff and the state attorney general traveled to Columbia, where they met only with Maury County officials, relatives of the Moore family, and Ann Moore herself. After that trip, Jones, Raper, and S. L. Smith of the Julius Rosenwald Fund found "sentiment reversed." "The boy was supposed to be guilty and deputies and others did not think anything should be done about it," Jones observed.[97]

In addition to the jailing of Rush Cheek by Austin Harlan and his cohorts in June 1934, other pressures were brought by Maury County officials, as well as some white citizens, to halt indictments. Lawyers converged on Chester K. Hart, a Nashville judge, to try to persuade him that he was wrong in informing a Davidson County grand jury that they could indict Cheek's abductors for both kidnapping and murder. Maury County authorities and businessmen informed officials in Nashville not only that Cheek was guilty, but also that prosecution of the case would provoke "riots" in the community. Leading citizens and bankers from Columbia promised that they would raise any amount of money necessary to bail anyone indicted out of jail.

Meanwhile Maury County relatives of members of a Citizens' Committee, created in Nashville to bring the lynchers to justice, urged them to cease their efforts.[98] Finally the supervisor of road work in Maury County spent most of the day prior to Joel Cheatham's scheduled appearance before the third and final grand jury trying to convince Cheatham not to testify, and on the day of the hearing several Maury County men appeared in the hall leading to the Grand Jury room, apparently to discourage would-be witnesses.[99] In short, powerful forces in Maury County, intimately interlaced with local officialdom, were arrayed against those trying to bring Cheek's killers to justice.

Confronted with this pressure and interlocked politically with various individuals in Maury County, state officials meandered along, sometimes blundering and always dragging their feet.[100] When the Citizens' Committee in Nashville raised $1,000 for a special prosecutor, the governor refused to appoint one, although he nominated with alacrity a special investigator for a burgeoning bank scandal that "took all of the time of the attorney general" just after Cheek was killed. The district attorney in Nashville, who would have prosecuted the case if a grand jury had brought indictments, reputedly condoned the lynching in a speech at a banquet in East Nashville, while the state attorney general, who was finally persuaded to visit the Fisk campus to take depositions from eyewitnesses to Cheek's abduction, greatly incensed one of the witnesses by asking if she were a prostitute![101] Eventually the Interracial Commission determined to hire its own attorney to assemble the case for the final grand jury. The Citizens' Committee, discouraged "with the promises and dodges of the attorney general," wrote him a "sharp letter" and agreed to the Commission's plan.[102]

At the federal level, Tennessee senator Kenneth D. McKellar, who adamantly opposed federal antilynching legislation, refused to intervene locally or to encourage the government to take action. In part, discouragement over the Cheek affair prompted the Southern Methodist Woman's Missionary Council and its constituent conferences in Tennessee and Alabama to endorse federal antilynching legislation in 1934.[103] Similarly Professor Barnett's frustration over the Cheek case resulted in his testifying in behalf of federal action before the Senate Judiciary Committee in February of the same year. But no federal legislation or assistance were forthcoming. In the only federal action taken, President Roosevelt dismissed Bob Hancock as Glendale postmaster.

For Maury County blacks, the message was crystal clear: any defense afforded African Americans against would-be lynchers in the future must derive from within their own community. Above all, East Eighth Street proprietors, who had assumed the role of protector as well as disciplinarian, heard the charge. Julius Blair made this very explicit when he was asked at his trial what he meant by "social lynching," the term that he had used in his warning to Magistrate Denton. Without hesitation, Blair replied:

A When they hung Cordie Cheek, they cut up the rope and had a social gathering after that. That is what I meant. They cut up the rope and hung it around and had a social gathering.
Q Did you mean to keep a social lynching from occurring in Maury County? I will ask you in what way you proposed to keep down a social lynching?
A By getting the boy out of the way.
Q Getting the boy out of the way?
A Out of town.[104]

Charlie Blair also insisted to FBI agents that the occurrence of "three lynchings or murders" in Maury County in the past twenty-five years rendered it "entirely normal" that armed black people would congregate in the Bottom on February 25th.[105] To the dozen or so men gathered in front of his funeral parlor, James Morton stated quite plainly that "They 'should not fire on the law,' but that they were to prevent any white mob from coming in there."[106]

Thus, though the proprietors of East Eighth Street had long witnessed what they regarded as unlawful arrests of black workers, it was above all the failure of authorities to *protect* black citizens that drove them to action. In this way, the Columbia episode points not only toward changes that black businessmen experienced during the first half of the twentieth century, but also toward the most important, though nowadays less noticed, aspect of law enforcement that undermined the trust of African Americans.[107]

Although the Cheek case in 1933–34 and the Stephenson-Fleming fight in 1946 seemed very different—one involving an alleged assault on a white female and the other a fight between two men—it is clear in retrospect that they shared many similarities. Whether Fleming fell or was pushed through the plate glass window at the Castner-Knott Department Store, it obviously appeared that Stephenson had "worsted" him, just as Cheek had worsted Moore. Additionally, Fleming hailed from a large family with deep roots in Culleoka, the small rural community located near Glendale to which phone calls had been made as the initial crowd gathered at Hancock's store in mid-November 1933. Fleming's father John had served as a deputy under Sheriff Claude Godwin, while an African American who had reputedly killed John Fleming's brother, Eugene, also a deputy, had died under mysterious circumstances. All of these facts were no doubt well known in black Columbia.

Black Maury Countians also felt that whites were responding to the Fleming-Stephenson fray all out of proportion to the seriousness of it. As Robert Frierson viewed the situation, the incident at Castner-Knott's was "a 'clean case' involving no reprehensible conduct" on the part of Stephenson, while James Morton termed it "a trifling incident."[108] In comparison, the accusation against Cheek had been more severe. Frierson himself described rape as well as murder as "serious," but it was widely believed that Cheek had done nothing to warrant this charge and his death. C. H. Denton's insistence that the Blairs and Mortons leave the Stephensons in jail for their own safety obviously aroused suspicions further, while the continued presence of Magistrate Denton, Coroner Earl Allen, and Constable Austin Harlan among Maury County officials did nothing to allay fears.

But if there were striking similarities between the Cheek and Stephenson situations, there were new, explosive factors in the Stephenson-Fleming altercation. Among black Maury Countians, Gladys Stephenson's public display of anger at the radio repairmen and her aggressiveness in assisting her son when he was attacked by Fleming were not subjects of discussion, but they symbolize much about the war and its implications for workers at the lower end of the economic spectrum. The presence of tenants, farm laborers, and chemical workers among Stephenson's defenders signaled similar alterations. Equally important, though unnoticed by the *Columbia Daily Herald* in reporting the story, was James Stephenson's status as a veteran. Like Stephenson, a multitude of young black men had had their lives transformed by military service, and most had returned to the small towns and rural communities in the South from which they had departed.

On the white side, too, the war experiences were important. Not only was Billy Fleming a veteran, but so were his six brothers. Moreover, the Fleming family had made the supreme sacrifice when Fred, Flo's twin, was killed in action at the Battle of Guadalcanal. One of the leaders of the mob that appeared at the jail demanding the Stephensons was a veteran; a soldier asked specifically for them. If Stephenson had committed defenders, Fleming possessed ardent avengers. In short, it was no coincidence that white intrusion into the black community in Maury County materialized, and black resistance crystallized, in the wake of a wrenching world war.

Relatively powerless before the white establishment in the early 1930s, African Americans turned to God and to supernatural forces to punish Cheek's murderers. James Garrett's mother had heard "that the Lord was taking a hand in it, and that one of the men had committed suicide, another had been killed [in an automobile accident], and another had had his house burned."[109] Dawes and Bob Hancock had allegedly fled the county after they had encountered a seven-passenger black car filled with "big, black Negroes" who had stopped them near the spot where Cheek was lynched and had a talk with them. In another account, the Hancocks were killed in a car crash on the Culleoka road near the tall cedar tree where Cordie was hung.[110] Only the Hancocks' departure from the community was a confirmed fact. In 1946, the circumstances were altered; protection for James Stephenson was left neither in the hands of God nor fate. Not only the owners of East Eighth Street establishments but also their patrons saw to that, and it is to the latter that we now turn.

WAR, ESTEEM,
EFFICACY, AND
ENTITLEMENT

Without question, World War II affected middle-class leaders such as Morton and the Blairs. As the organizers of war bond and Red Cross drives in Maury County, James and Mary Morton felt their commitment to a "Double-V" strengthened as the war progressed. Saul Blair also both imbibed and circulated word of the "Double-V" effort as he distributed the *Chicago Defender*, a black newspaper that minced no words in the campaign's behalf. Additionally, the flush of wartime prosperity and the quickened pace that it brought to the business community undoubtedly reinforced the prestige and position of established leaders like the Blairs and thereby encouraged their assumption of responsibility in repelling a potential lynching.

Yet despite the important role played by local businessmen in leading a defense effort, decisive, combative action welled up from below. "White officials believe Mr. Morton and Mr. Blair and his son had something to do with it [the congregation of blacks and shooting of police]," investigator W. B. Twitty reported to the Southern Regional Council. "I believe they could have made it worse," he continued, "but doubt seriously if they could have stopped it."[1] Instead, he concluded: "It was a spontaneous reaction." The FBI reached the same conclusion in an investigation that it completed in May 1946.

The gathering of so many men in the Bottom and the action that they took in Stephenson's behalf stemmed, not from blind loyalty to East Eighth Street's leaders, but from changes resulting from the war. Already from family, friends, and community, black Maury Countians had developed a strong sense of personal esteem. As the national rhetoric intoned freedom and democracy, as black citizens themselves or their relatives and friends donned military uniforms, and as the workplace widened, they experienced an enhanced sense of entitlement and personal efficacy.[2]

Especially the greater sense of personal efficacy for those who remained at home derived from an economy that, for once in the twentieth century, needed *all* of its workers. The country's voracious appetite for civilian and military personnel reached those on the lowest rungs of the economic ladder, as sharecroppers, day laborers, and domestic workers all found greater room to maneuver. Those who participated in unions created even more latitude for themselves.

This section focuses on African Americans' expanding sense of entitlement and personal efficacy at home, while the following one details similar processes at work among black members of the armed forces. Together they shed light on the emergence of a black populace "not disposed to be 'pushed around.'"[3]

THE HOME FRONT

WAR AND THE UNORGANIZED WORKER

One of the major results of the war in the South was the departure of many people from small towns and rural areas. As historian Pete Daniel recounts, "Like [singer-performer] Muddy Waters, a lot of southerners got the 'Walking Blues.'"[4] This trend was especially pronounced among African Americans who were hit hard by the Great Depression.[5]

Like their counterparts throughout the South, the largest number of black men in Maury County on the eve of the war were farm laborers or tenant farmers, while the overwhelming majority of black women worked in domestic service. Because these jobs were arduous, arbitrary, and low paying, it was especially men and women from these walks of life who walked away.[6]

As the number of tenants and farm laborers decreased across the South, those who remained found their bargaining position temporarily enhanced.[7] This did not mean that the balance of power in the workplace had shifted drastically in the rural South. Police continued to arrest reluctant workers on charges of loitering, vagrancy, and disturbing the peace, while informal, extralegal controls on farm laborers remained. In Lowndes County, Georgia, for example, the U.S. Employment Service representative refused to certify farm workers for defense jobs unless they had permission from their employers or, in the case of independent renters, from the white county extension agent.[8] Employers who got blacks deferred from the military for farm work also threatened to have them declassified if their performance was unacceptable.

But the pressure was not unidirectional. Exempt workers, often more than willing to be declassified and depart, exhibited newfound freedom in a variety of ways, such as reporting late for work or slacking off as they tired. White employers throughout the South complained that only the poorest quality of workers remained on the farms, and they noted that "particularly Negroes" (and in the Southwest, Mexicans) were becoming "too independent" and having "to be humored." Too, they described "concessions" that were "not in harmony with traditional race relations." These included making more improvements in tenant houses than usual, furnishing ice water and even cows to cotton pickers, as well as competing among themselves for the use of local labor.[9] Employers also worried that blacks might be called by draft boards for examination, knowing that few were likely to return regardless of whether or not they were inducted. Glen L. Shadow of Ruston, Louisiana, summed up the laments of many large landowners as he remarked that "labor once on your place are very independent, and the majority will not take an interest in their work as they are so independent they do not mind being fired."[10]

The tighter labor market and the war's democratic thrust had a decided impact on the perception farm workers had of themselves and their situation. In addition to blacks' demanding higher wages and alterations in work habits, many blacks and whites in the Clarksdale, Mississippi, vicinity reported that "the Negroes were becoming more aware of their second-rate citizenship status." A Farm Security Administration official remarked that "even the poorer Negroes are becoming convinced that they are mistreated here," while the white county school superintendent noted that blacks were beginning to use titles like Mr. and Mrs. when speaking of one another in front of white people.[11]

Small farmers who remained on the land also found their situation improving. Because the war sharply increased the demand for agricultural products, and thereby improved the environment for the acquisition of land, and because tenants left the countryside much faster than owners, the rate of ownership among black Maury County farmers rose from 46 percent in 1935 to 63 percent in 1945.[12] In the long run, a decided shift during the war years away from "the Jeffersonian ideal" and toward "corporate values" among federal policymakers would have drastic implications for the future of American agriculture, but at the time school bus driver James Bellanfante issued his clarion call throughout the countryside in behalf of James Stephenson, signs of struggle mingled with those of success.[13]

As the opportunity structure widened, farm owners, like tenants and laborers, determined that more general improvements should follow. Riley Miller, a black landowner and World War I veteran from Lowndes County, Georgia, who was "rather well accustomed to the local race situation," indicated to interviewers in 1944 that he wanted to vote and be treated with more consideration.[14] In a spontaneous demonstration of a similar feeling, African Americans in Coahoma County, Mississippi, "literally booed" local newspaper editor and former lieutenant governor J. D. Sneider when he proclaimed in a speech at the annual black agricultural fair that Negroes would never vote in Mississippi. Following the speech, a number of residents canceled their subscriptions to Sneider's paper, although he continued to carry a page devoted to news of special interest to blacks and published an editorial trying to explain his position. African Americans could tolerate a white man who said that "in order to get along where you are now do thus & so," researchers surmised, but not one who proclaimed "'Never vote in Mississippi.'"[15]

Just as the war had profound implications for African American farmers, most of whom were men, it also drastically altered conditions for domestic workers, the vast majority of whom were women. Essential family members and important citizens in their communities, domestic workers had long played a vital role in black society. When the war provided opportunities to escape the drudgery of household employment, many departed.[16]

Concomitantly, the bargaining position of those who remained was strengthened just as it was for farm workers. Furthermore, as mothers and wives of soldiers, many household workers grew increasingly incensed at indignities inflicted on their children, their spouses, and sometimes, themselves.[17] Accustomed to hard work, less inhibited by cultural trappings than business and professional women, and intimately acquainted with the foibles of white people, domestic workers grew more likely during the war to display in public some of the tenacity that had long marked their relationships with their family, friends, and neighbors.[18]

Gladys Stephenson's outspoken behavior in the radio repair shop, and her aggressive defense of her son, reflected the combination of toughness, fortitude, anguish, pride, frustration, and consternation that the war had heightened among the South's household workers, especially mothers of men in uniform. Her conduct also suggested the improved options and the enhanced sense of personal efficacy and entitlement that the conflict produced.

The 37-year-old Stephenson, in her work as a maid, had until that cold February day maintained a demeanor that ensured harmony with her white

Gladys Stephenson, with NAACP attorney Maurice Weaver (left) and Saul Blair (right), shortly after the Columbia episode. At the time the photo was taken, both Stephenson and Blair were charged with attempted murder. (Courtesy of NAACP)

employers.[19] Yet that deportment was only one aspect of her personality. A hard-working, independent woman who provided for herself and her four children, Stephenson ran a household in the West End of Columbia. Her role as stalwart breadwinner, along with her recognition of her son's recent service to his country, produced the initiative that sparked her loud comments in the store and her aggressiveness outside.

Undoubtedly, Stephenson was proud of her eldest son and protective of him. Because James preferred the Navy, his mother had written a letter in his behalf, gaining him entry although he was only 17 at the time.[20] Without question, her goal in attacking Fleming was to aid her son. Excitedly she had approached the police when they arrested James, urging them "not to hurt her boy," and she demanded that Police Chief Griffin "investigate" before he did anything.[21]

As black Columbians reconstruct the story, James Stephenson was going to the aid of his mother when he fought Fleming. In fact, his wariness of the radio repairman was probably fueled by a remark by Fleming that Gladys overheard as they exited the store. Certainly, following this comment,

James consciously placed his mother in front of him so that he was between her and Fleming. But to view the extension of protection as a one-way affair is to miss an important part of the story. Gladys Stephenson was infuriated on February 25, 1946. The rhetoric of the war demanded better treatment for African Americans than she was receiving. Even more significant, given the military record of James Stephenson and others like him, he did not deserve a punch by William Fleming, and he certainly did not deserve to be manhandled by both Fleming and an accomplice from across the street who came to Fleming's rescue!

As Gladys Stephenson lunged at Fleming with a piece of glass, she allegedly screamed at him, " 'You yellow yap!' "[22] The term "yellow" could simply have indicated that Fleming was a coward in her view, and the "yap" may have been a substitute for profanity. Indeed, one witness suggested that she yelled "You yellow s-o-b."[23] But the "yellow," especially when coupled with "yap," could have had a different meaning. Having lived for five years in a society rabid with hatred for the Japanese, Stephenson's remark could have represented the most awful nomenclature she could think of. If so, the expression is freighted with symbolic meaning—about the war and personal enhancement—for some of the most lowly on the nation's economic chain.

WAR AND THE ORGANIZED WORKER

While farmers, agricultural laborers, and domestic workers continued to fight individual battles, miners and factory workers seized opportunities during the war for collective expression. Just as the New Deal had altered the agrarian landscape, it had also strengthened the bargaining position of the nation's industrial workers through the National Industrial Recovery Act in 1933 and, more permanently, through the National Labor Relations Act (Wagner Act) in 1935. But it was World War II, with its mammoth appetite for workers, that gave labor the chance to take full advantage of the tools that government had provided. Especially in the South, the war proved a boost for industrial unionism and its spearhead, the Congress of Industrial Organizations (CIO).[24]

In Maury County, phosphate workers had struggled as early as 1919 to affiliate with the International Union of Mine, Mill, and Smelter Workers (Mine Mill), an outgrowth of the Western Federation of Miners, an organization that had helped establish the Industrial Workers of the World in 1905. In 1937, Mine Mill, under the auspices of the CIO, renewed its activities in the Mt. Pleasant vicinity and in Wales, in neighboring Giles County, near Pulaski.

After a protracted struggle with the International Mineral and Chemical

Corporation (IMCC), a subsidiary of the International Agricultural Corporation, Mine Mill finally got a contract with IMCC in December 1940.[25] Local 547 represented workers at the Mt. Pleasant facility, Local 486 those at the Wales' operation. Other Mine Mill locals were established in Mt. Pleasant at the Federal Chemical Company (Local 545), Virginia-Carolina Chemical Company (Local 278), and the Hoover-Mason Phosphate Company (Local 583).[26] All these companies, as well as the Tennessee Valley Authority and Armour Fertilizer in Columbia, mined phosphate rock for fertilizer production and prepared it for market. IMCC's Wales plant, Virginia-Carolina, and Armour also operated fertilizer divisions.

Not surprising, demand for these products shot up during the war. In addition to companies involved in producing phosphate for fertilizer, Victor Chemical and Monsanto Chemical were producing elemental phosphorus for use in the construction of bombs, and the increased wartime activity of these companies was reflected in the awards they received from the Army and Navy for their outstanding performance in the production of war materials.[27] As U.S. defense efforts continued to expand in the spring of 1941, Mine Mill representatives began meeting with workers at the Armour plant in Columbia. There, a prolonged struggle, comparable to that experienced by Mine Mill with IMCC, finally culminated in Local 546 in the summer of 1943.

A radical, "left-led" union that was committed to interracialism, Mine Mill followed a formula established by the United Mine Workers. Whites in each local served as presidents and financial secretaries, blacks as vice presidents and recording secretaries. In keeping with this policy, African American James Wade served as vice president of Local 546 in the mid-forties. Although Wade lived in the 500 block of East Eighth Street, whether or not he or any other members of Mine Mill participated in the coalition to defend James Stephenson is unclear. (It may be significant, however, that Wade, who was an officer in 1944 and 1945 was not serving in that capacity in the summer of 1946.) Without a doubt, some workers from the unorganized Monsanto plant were there, including Jesse "Peter" Harris.[28]

Yet regardless of whether Mine Mill members were on East Eighth Street the evening of February 25th, the presence of the union in Maury County contributed, at least indirectly, to the coalition that emerged there and to the events that followed it. Ultimately successful in protracted struggles with very powerful companies that were closely allied with local officials in both Mt. Pleasant and Columbia, phosphate workers set an important example of achievement in defying authority. Certainly their triumph was visible in the Bottom, for Local 546 met in the Lodge Hall and its

Monsanto worker Jesse "Peter" Harris is searched by a highway patrolman following his arrest on February 26. (Courtesy of United States Attorney's Office, Middle District of Tennessee)

banner routinely hung there—until it was taken as a souvenir by a state guardsman.

On a more tangible note, the union improved wages and benefits in nonunionized plants like Monsanto, as well as in unionized ones, while war demands increased the need for workers and gave contract negotiators the opportunity to improve wages and benefits further. Some of this wartime bounty no doubt found its way into the coffers of black businessmen in the Bottom, as well as in Mt. Pleasant, strengthening their personal finances, their leadership position, and their willingness to defend members of their community. More significantly, the improved economic environment, like union participation itself, further augmented the sense of efficacy among black workers as well as white.

In the spring of 1951, Local 546 prepared for Armour employees a fact sheet informing them of the gains the union had made since its inception in 1943.[29] Number twelve on the list read: "Last but certainly not least— Recognized for the first time as a man, (a Human), rather than a piece of equipment."[30] For a few short years during World War II, many African Americans would have agreed with this statement, and they began insisting that others recognize it as well.

THE WAR ZONE

As the war strengthened those who remained at home, it also had a dramatic impact on those who left to join the military. In turn, veterans comprised one of the most significant components of the East Eighth Street coalition. James "Digger" Johnson estimated in his testimony to local and state officials that nineteen (about 20 percent) of those held in jail as suspects had served *overseas*. At least nine of the twenty-five defendants in the Lawrenceburg trial had been in the armed forces. In addition, Robert Edwards, who was taken from a house on the edge of the Bottom but was not charged, was in the Army, while two of the veteran arrestees, Early Shyes and Leonard Evans, were forced to testify for the prosecution.

A "yellowish colored negro" standing beside the car window of policeman Bernard Stofel on that fateful evening stated emphatically that "he had fought for freedom overseas and he was going to fight for it here." Also, the terms "Halt" and "Fire," used by African Americans as the police approached, had a certain military ring to them. Finally, although most of the weapons confiscated by the police were rifles and shotguns, along with a smattering of pistols, defendant Clarence Brown carried a carbine rifle that he had brought from the Army. Not surprisingly, SRC investigator W. B. Twitty determined that black Maury Countians, "lead [sic] principally by veterans and their spirit," determined to take action against a potential lynching.[31]

Prior to June 1943, when the need for manpower intensified, the Army did not accept men into service who were illiterate. With the exception of Robert Edwards, who did not turn 18 until 1944 and was thus too young to enter service before 1943, the twelve veteran defenders of Stephenson who were identified in this study joined the military before the literacy requirement was abolished. Yet, though able to read and, like most African American soldiers, members of noncombat units, these servicemen undoubtedly encountered a lexicon and a set of responsibilities that were at once mentally challenging and broadening. Directions, for instance, might be framed in terms such as "'discipline, sentinel, compensation, maintain, observation, barrage, [and] counter-clockwise.' "[32] Topics to master in just over six months included:

> storage and issue (warehousing, space utilization, prerequisites for issue); vehicle loading; daily telegrams and the computation of supplies on the basis of information furnished therein; railhead arrangement; use of road nets and sidings; receiving, sorting, and checking supplies; accounting for supplies; inspection of subsistence stores; salvage operations; selection of sites for railheads, including plans for defense, camouflage, and protection from air attacks; practical operation of railheads; map reading; security (including reconnaissance, defense against guerrilla, chemical, air, and paratroop attacks, concealment, dispersal, and camouflage); decontamination apparatus and its use; demolitions; safety measures; night operations.[33]

As Ulysses Lee, a member of the Office of the Chief of Military History from 1946 to 1952 and "the military history specialist on Negroes in the Army," summed it: "The range of subjects to be covered in twenty-six weeks was greater than many of the men assigned had encountered in all of the preceding years of their lives."[34] Certainly not everyone perfected all of the assignments, but it is not surprising that 19-year-old James Stephenson informed radio repairman LaVal LaPointe that he had "done some radio work in the Navy" and thought he could repair the one belonging to his family.[35]

African Americans serving in World War II interacted with men in their units who had backgrounds considerably different from those they would have encountered had they served in World War I. In the First World War, one in five black enlisted men came from the North; only 3 percent of those from the South and 14 percent of those from the North had attended high school. In contrast, in World War II, one in three African American enlisted men came from the North, and they hailed primarily from large metropolitan centers such as New York, Chicago, Philadelphia, Detroit, and Pittsburgh. Even more significant, 33 percent of the black southerners and 63 percent of the black northerners had attended high school, while 24 percent of the black northerners were either high school or college graduates. Among all blacks in the Quartermaster and Engineering Corps, the branches where African Americans most often served, better educated men appeared in the same proportion as they did in combat units such as the infantry, field artillery, and coast artillery.[36]

The horizons of African Americans from rural areas like Maury County and small towns such as Columbia were widened not only by the men they encountered in the armed forces but also, for most, through service outside the United States. Smaller black units within the engineering and quartermaster branches were especially in demand, and they were among the first to go overseas. Later, as the U.S. intensified its global buildup after mid-1944 and black soldiers who had been inducted in 1942 and 1943 were made available, their numbers abroad increased. By the close of the war, a higher percentage of black troops than white troops was serving abroad. Overall, about 77 percent of the black enlisted men in the Army served overseas at some time during their military careers.[37]

While abroad, black troops performed numerous important duties, and sometimes found themselves in the midst of heavy fighting, as the line between service and combat blurred. The experiences of Mt. Pleasant resident John W. Orr, who served with the 477th Amphibious Truck Company, illustrate this point.

An electric motorman who operated a trolley at IMCC in Mt. Pleasant before the war, Orr was initially assigned the job of truck driver in the Army Air Force. After entering service at Camp Forrest, located about sixty-five miles from Columbia in Tullahoma, Tennessee, in August 1942 and completing basic training at Fort Benning, Georgia, Orr spent five weeks in Washington state at Paine Air Force Base. By May 1943, he was bound for Pearl Harbor. While in Hawaii, Orr not only had the pleasure of visiting with his brother Eugene, a boatswain's mate 2nd class, but also he was switched from driving a land-based vehicle to operating an amphibious truck known as a Duck.

As a Duck driver, Orr worked with the Marines, the Field Artillery, and the Airborne—"all of them, wherever they needed us," he explained. His job involved ferrying men and ammunition to shore from an LST (Landing Ship, Tank). He and his assistant driver could carry twenty-six men or two one-and-a-half-ton nets of ammunition. The bottom of the LST opened, and the Ducks backed out. Keeping the motor running was essential; otherwise, the Duck would sink.

Orr participated with the 2nd and 4th Marine Divisions in the invasions of Saipan and Tinian, and with the 1st and 6th Marines in the invasion of Okinawa. He was also involved in the recapture of the Philippines. Three times his unit attempted to land at Saipan. At one point, the shelling and bombing grew so intense that an order was given to disperse, and Orr had to head his vehicle out to sea. A tenacious struggle, the battle for Saipan engulfed Japanese women and children. "The Americans were losing a lot of men so the general or admiral or somebody, gave orders to kill everything that was big enough to die," Orr remembered. "And they did, too," he added. "While I was there, I saw women with babies in their arms lying dead across machine guns."[38]

As they prepared for the invasion of Tinian, the captain warned them: "Well, we're going into Tinian. It's going to be as bad as Saipan. One thing about it, try to be careful and do the best you can. Sometime you will be on your own, so use your best judgement God Almighty gave you. It's going to be hot and plenty Damn Hot." Orr found the description accurate as he hauled ammunition to the beach and carried dead bodies back to the shoreline. The Duck held six corpses; some days, he brought out as many as 42. "They stacked the bodies up on the beach just like stacking up wood," he recalled.[39]

Rather than eating K rations, Orr and his assistant driver were usually given a plate of food on the ship from which they were hauling ammunition. Periodically, they would eat while the ship was being loaded, or one would eat while the other one drove the Duck. Once Orr went without sleep for seven days and seven nights consecutively. "If they run out of ammunition, we had to go," he explained. Sometimes they slept in their clothes "in a slit trench." On one occasion, sniper fire blew a hole in one of the tires on Orr's Duck. He used an emergency measure to keep air flowing into the tire to keep the truck moving. He had a spare on the back, but a week passed before he was in a position to get it changed. Had he stopped sooner, he might have been killed by snipers.

Another time the Duck driver and his assistant were caught out by themselves during an air raid. Orr had to make a quick decision, so "What I did was ease on up to a battle ship," he recalled. He was invited on board, but because he was not supposed to leave the Duck unless it was sinking, he chose to stay with it. He was thrown a line from the ship, however, and remained tied to it throughout the night—and the air raid. The next morning, land was nowhere in sight, but acting on orders from the battleship to "set your compass on 180 degrees North," Orr and his assistant successfully made it back to "Yellow Beach 2."[40]

Prior to the invasion of Okinawa, it seemed as if they stayed on board the LST "several weeks . . . with the battle ships firing, shelling the island to get it softened up so we could go in." Within an hour after arriving in the Philippines, Orr's unit was strafed by a low-flying Japanese plane. "When the siren went off, he was over us and all that fire was jumping out and bouncing off that Duck. . . . Them bullets looked about the size of a golf ball," he recollected. Quickly, Orr dug a foxhole in the loose sand and burrowed inside. Although he did not know it at the time, the shells he was carrying on his truck had not been fused, though the fuses, as well as the shells, were part of the cargo. Two cans of gasoline, however, perched on the back of the truck. From his vantage point in the hastily constructed foxhole, Orr could "see them red tracers" as American forces shot down the attacker. "I thought he was going to hit the cans and shells and the whole thing would blow up," Orr vividly reminisced.[41]

Like many veterans, John Orr is partially deaf, probably a result of encountering massive shell fire. Although a member of a noncombat unit, Orr, who was stationed overseas for more than two and a half years, received the Good Conduct Medal, the World War II Victory Medal, the Asiatic-Pacific Theater Service Medal with two bronze battle stars, the Philippine Liberation Medal with one bronze battle star, and the Meritorious Unit Award. The latter was given to the 477th Amphibious Truck Company for hauling the most ammunition to Saipan, Tinian, Okinawa, and the Philippines.[42]

As in the Pacific, black units all over the globe built roads and airfields, repaired bridges and highways, unloaded ships, scrubbed hospital floors, hauled garbage, and manned trucks and amphibious vehicles. One-third of the 10,000 construction troops who built a highway through the frigid wilds of Canada and Alaska were black engineers, as were 60 percent of the 15,000 involved in the principal construction effort in Asia, a road from Ledo in Assam through northeastern Burma to China. The only barrage balloon unit of its type, which unleashed balloons to provide protection of soldiers from low-flying aircraft during the cross-channel invasion at Normandy, was African American. Black amphibious truck, quartermaster service, and ammunition companies swung into action during the invasion with tasks that they would continue until the war's conclusion. Three-quarters of the truck companies in Europe were manned by black drivers, mechanics, and administrative clerks. Black truckers sped fuel, ammunition, and other supplies from the French coast to the armies advancing upon the Germans via the "Red Ball Express" route, as they did along the Motor Transport System in Iran and the Stilwell Road in Burma. As Army historian Lee explains: "These were all normal functions for units of their types. But the variety in the employment of Negro troops so far outstripped anything seen in World War I or contemplated at the beginning of World War II that this fact alone is of prime significance in any account of the use of Negro troops in World War II."[43]

Milton Murray, an Army PFC who recalls vividly today the armed defense of Stephenson, served with the 3581st Quartermaster Truck Company. As a construction foreman who served in Europe, Africa, and the Middle East, he participated especially in campaigns in Italy—Rome-Arno, the northern Apennines, and Po Valley.[44] Like Murray, Stephenson defenders Clifford Edwards, Leonard Evans, Early Shyes, and Milton Johnson were also in the European, African, and Middle Eastern theaters. Shyes, a PFC longshoreman with a port battalion in the Transportation Corps was in three campaigns. Edwards, serving with a fire fighting platoon in the Engineering Corps; Evans, as a PFC and squad leader with the 365th Engineers; and Johnson, as a cook in a quartermaster gasoline supply company, were all in campaigns in Normandy, northern France, the Ardennes, the Rhineland, and central Europe. Similarly, Louis "Junior" Miles served with the Signal Corps in France, Luxembourg, and Germany. Clarence Brown, assigned to the Asia-Pacific theater, was engaged in campaigns from New Guinea to the Luzon Sea in the Philippines.

To Herbert Johnson, Army sergeant and brother-in-law of Early Shyes, who was in the Bottom on the day of the 25th, though not that evening when the shooting occurred, landing in Oran in North Africa inspired religious thoughts: "from the way the people dressed . . . you'd read about the robes and all that were in use in Jesus' time . . . who knows what our Lord and Savior might not have passed this way." He remembered the Muslims, who were attached to his outfit, as a particularly devout people. "I still think if we as Christians were as religious as they are," he commented, "our world would be a different world." Equally exciting was the sight of former history lessons coming to life as he gazed at the leaning tower of Pisa and at the ruins of the ancient city of Pompeii. While they were there, Mt. Vesuvius erupted:

> And we woke up that evening . . . you could hear the roar, just ROAR! and the earth shaking. Then next we would see the lava just coming down the sides, and oh, it was a frightening thing. . . . We went to sleep and that morning when we woke up, it was as dark as I've ever seen any sunrise. Cloudy, clouds all around and the birds, the gulls—we were right on the ocean front and they were just flying in circles, they couldn't find any place to land. . . . I said, "Lord, is this going to be the end of the world or is this what is going to happen?"[45]

As tasks, responsibilities, and opportunities to meet new people and see new places multiplied, the self-esteem of black soldiers was enhanced, and pride in their units abounded.[46] These feelings, coupled with continued segregation and discrimination, served to heighten militancy and a sense of racial solidarity. The very act of partitioning black soldiers into separate units gave every hardship a racial tinge. Indeed, one former member of the training command at the Tuskegee Air Base in Alabama attributed unit pride in part to segregation. "Any group that is handled in a special way begins to think of itself in a special way," he commented, and he continued, "Consequently, the individual's loyalty is, first to the group, and second, to the parent organization."[47]

Still, it was not simply the separateness that black troops underwent that made them cognizant of discrimination, but the relentlessly unequal and unfair treatment that segregation imposed. Rigorously separated from their entry into military service, African Americans were usually consigned to "the fringe" of the main arena on military bases. They endured living quarters and other facilities that were almost always inferior to those of whites. At Camp Claiborne in Alexandria, Louisiana, where Milton Murray was stationed for awhile, the area assigned to blacks "seemed to have no geographical relationship to the rest of the camp." Additionally, black soldiers there performed guard duty "with pick and axe handles."[48] Until 1944, black and white soldiers remained staunchly segregated by Army policy in post exchanges, theaters, and service clubs, as well as on buses operating on the base. Even a widely touted policy shift in July 1944, which presumably eliminated separation by race in all facilities, brought little meaningful change. By that time, bases had constructed separate "Negro sections" with their own recreational facilities.[49]

In addition, most black enlisted men (55 percent in 1943) trained in either the Fourth or the Eighth Service Commands. Another 10 percent were in the Third Service Command. As part of eight Army administrative units, these three commands encompassed all of the states of the old Confederacy.[50] Hence, the large majority of African Americans were stationed in states with sizable black populations, states where Jim Crow laws were rigidly enforced and where most white civilians were very resentful and fearful of black troops.

Bases through which Maury County blacks passed proved no exception to these generalizations. A part of the Fourth Service Command, Tennessee's Camp Forrest in Tullahoma served as a reception center for African Americans from the county entering the Army. In 1943, the post was headed by a Commander who was described by a black soldier stationed there as "an individual who makes no bones about his feelings toward Negroes and Negro officers." "As far as he is concerned," the young man continued, "they just aren't."[51]

From Tullahoma, African American Army entrants from Maury County proceeded to Fort Benning, Georgia. There they received clothes and other necessities prior to their assignment to camps for basic training. Unfortunately, though not unexpectedly, Fort Benning offered little, if any, respite from Camp Forrest. Even before the U.S. officially entered the war, the base earned, via an alleged lynching, the dubious distinction as the site of the "first major symbolic event in the long chain of racial violence" that marked the war era.[52]

Although the Recreation Hall at Fort Benning served as the induction center for black troops in the Fourth Service Command, no black officers were assigned to it. Furthermore, an investigation at the war's conclusion discovered that before shipment to other units, African American soldiers at Fort Benning were held in a stockade, "allegedly to keep them from going AWOL," though no white soldiers were accorded such treatment. Additionally, black soldiers had to get off the bus as it entered the gate of the camp to have their passes checked, another procedure from which whites were immune. Finally, despite the policy alteration in 1944, Fort Benning remained rigidly segregated at the end of 1945. No recreational facilities, such as swimming pools and service clubs, could be used by white and black soldiers together, and separate bus stations were maintained.[53] In an obvious understatement, one GI concluded, "The racial policies at the fort were certainly not going to build morale or patriotism in young Negro draftees."[54]

Meanwhile, service in areas where segregation and discrimination were less stringent than in places like Camp Forrest and Fort Benning offered many black soldiers a glimpse of alternatives. John Orr recalled:

> The best and most enjoyable time I had was what little time I was in Everett, Washington. We would get passes to Seattle. The people were so nice to us. When you walked out the gate we hardly ever had to catch a bus. There was a big sign there, "Give a Man in Uniform a Ride." They'd stop and make room for us. If there was too many of us, they'd say there would be another car along to pick us up, and there was. I caught the bus only about one time the five weeks I was there. That was about the nicest place. Of course, Hawaii was a nice place.[55]

Service abroad could be especially frustrating for black troops, because often they initially encountered native populations who received them positively, and then, the situation altered. One document, which described the racial climate in Italy, is particularly revealing:

> The attitude of the people toward the colored troops was very friendly at first. Negroes were a subject of curiosity and often of affection and the Italians tended to be shocked at the discriminatory attitude of white soldiers. The situation changed. Causes of the changes are: (a) an insis-

tent propaganda by Italians who dwell in the United States that Negroes must be considered inferior and white people must not freely associate with them; (b) a tendency on the part of the American troops to blame the colored troops for all the misdeeds and pecadillos occurring in the liberated areas; (c) the growing hostility or rather a decreasing love for the American troops which focuses itself particularly on the Negro soldiers. Rumors and propaganda point out that the Americans sent to Italy soldiers whom they considered racially inferior. In other words, they submitted Italians to a treatment to which they would not submit white Americans. (d) [T]he behavior of white troops toward colored operates in Italy pretty much as it operated in Britain with the same results.[56]

Herbert Johnson, who spent considerable time in Italy, recalled a common story spread by white soldiers that "the black American was a monkey and he had a tail and his tail would come out at night." "That followed us all the way through every country you were ever in," he recollected. Revealingly, Johnson relied on his deep religious convictions to deal with this potentially destructive anecdote. "You didn't let it get you down," he quickly added, "you would just know that God was still God of all people."[57]

Not surprisingly, the segregation and discrimination that plagued African American troops throughout their war experience, dogged them as they prepared for the journey home, and in the victory celebrations that followed. From the Philippines, where Clarence Brown and John Orr served, came the report that two men who had left their unit one morning, with all good wishes for a successful departure home, had returned in the evening. The reason for their return? "This replacement depot does not accept colored troops."[58] In the gigantic parade staged in Washington welcoming Admiral Chester Nimitz and his forces home, "There were heroes from Saipan, Iwo Jima, Guadalcanal, Coral Sea, the Philippines, Okinawa and other Pacific islands." John Orr and Clarence Brown were not among them. Neither were seamen Paul Miles, William Dawson, Eugene Bailey Orr, or James Stephenson. Only the presence of a Coast Guard training school unit prevented "a complete lily-white-turn-out to welcome home the hero of the Pacific."[59]

As black soldiers progressed through a war whose aims enunciated freedom and democracy, a war in which they encountered alternative possibilities in social relations which were often spoiled by white soldiers, and one in which they saw their own contributions as quite valuable and the treatment they received as highly discriminatory, many experienced a transformation. It was not that they were unfamiliar with segregation and discrimination in civilian society, though many nonsoutherners had never confronted Jim

Crow as formally as they did while based in southern camps, but black troops felt a special moral claim to fairness and justice. Furthermore, relegated to racially defined military units, they inhabited a world that encouraged their *insistence* on equity and fair play, while the comraderie that they experienced as a cadre of young men with shared responsibilities and grievances often prompted *collective*, and sometimes *militant*, responses.[60] All of these factors, including their negative encounters with civilian and military police (described in Chapter 5), combined to shape the response of the black community in Columbia.[61]

Additionally, black veterans carried home the same psychological baggage as all vets, and they encountered similar problems and challenges as they readjusted to civilian society.[62] This produced among them, as among whites, a tendency to associate with one another after their return.[63] In Maury County, this occurred on a formal basis in the Gordon American Legion Post and the newly formed Elks Club.[64] Some in black Columbia founded their own organization, the Global War Veterans.[65] On a less public note, about twenty young men, most of them vets, affiliated with the Royal Duke Club.[66]

As before the war, black Maury Countians also wiled away time together in the establishments along East Eighth Street. Veteran Clarence Brown had been in the College Hill section on the 25th. He had dinner at a cafe in East Columbia and then proceeded to the Bottom. He was wearing his Army cap (and carrying his carbine rifle) at the time. Veteran Luther Edwards had also been in the College Hill neighborhood during the day, as well as "a few places in town where they had restaurants and like that and hang around." His veteran brother Clifford Edwards arrived on the block between 6:00 and 7:00 in the evening. After visiting a few cafes "just as usual," he had dinner at the same East Eighth Street cafe as his brother and veteran, Robert Edwards.[67]

Seven veterans, including Brown and the Edwards brothers, were removed by the Highway Patrol from a single house at the corner of East Eighth and Woodland. For a few hours on February 25th, the military unit was reconstituted. Weapons were borne. There was a comrade to protect. White civilians and the police were behaving in a threatening manner. Former military men from Maury County knew what to do, and they acted accordingly.

Scholars increasingly point to "mass militancy" among African Americans as an integral part of World War II. Historian Lee Finkle claimed further that "if we seek the roots of the 'black revolution' of the 1960s in the World

Arrestees just after they were seized from Daisy Lee's house during the patrol raid on the morning of February 26. The three men in full view in the front row are (right to left) veterans Clifford Edwards, Clarence Brown, and Luther Edwards; Daisy Lee is standing next to Luther. Note that Brown is wearing his Army cap, jacket, and boots. (Courtesy of United States Attorney's Office, Middle District of Tennessee)

War II era, a study must be made of the black masses, not their leaders."[68] The Maury County experience provides insights into the specific process at work. Relegated to a partial Jim Crow world from freedom's dawn in the 1860s and rigidly segregated from the turn of the century forward, African Americans built organizations and institutions from which they drew psychological sustenance. White abuse hurt and angered, but it did *not* destroy self-confidence and personal esteem. These, black Americans derived from one another—from friends, from relatives, from coworkers, and from co-worshipers. If anything, mistreatment by whites fortified a sense of community and, sometimes, of self.

Lasting far longer than World War I, World War II provided a framework in which some of the hopes and dreams seemed realizable. The national rhetoric intoned freedom and democracy. The workplace widened. Industrial unions and military units provided forums for collective expression. All of these factors intertwined in February 1946 to spark insistence on fair treatment by Gladys Stephenson, by her son, and by his protectors. Personal and racial esteem, personal efficacy, and a sense of entitlement coalesced, and the war's meaning for African Americans was concentrated in a single, visible moment in actions taken on the streets of Columbia, Tennessee.

THE MAKING
AND UNMAKING OF
MOBOCRACY

Unfortunately for African Americans, the improved job opportunities that accompanied World War II disappeared quickly, and the GI Bill did not offer black veterans the same advantages that it presented whites. Nevertheless, black southerners, through the growing sense of entitlement and personal efficacy that they experienced during the war, were in a better position to repel mob actions immediately following the war than they were before it.

Unquestionably, the fierce defense of Stephenson by black Maury Countians deterred the would-be lunch mob on the town square. As noted in Chapter 1, the crowd milled for hours, coalescing only briefly when about fifty men approached the jail. Sheriff Underwood commented to federal grand jurors that those on the square "were not so dog-goned hot to go down there [to the Bottom]," and he added knowingly, "They probably would have got shot."[1] In short, as demonstrated by the defense of Stephenson, as well as by a ninefold increase in NAACP membership during the war, black Americans were strengthened both materially and psychologically just at the time when extralegal violence by whites appeared most propitious.

Other factors, however, had already dampened mob actions in the region. Lynchings had declined in part as a result of the Great Migration of African Americans out of the South, which began during World War I. In addition, organizations like the Commission on Interracial Cooperation and its affiliate, the Association of Southern Women for the Prevention of Lynching, had further emboldened local authorities to act, so that by the 1930s, sheriffs in particular took steps to prevent mob murders.[2] The lengthy, though unfulfilled, drive for federal antilynching legislation by the NAACP, underway since 1909, had helped achieve the same goal.[3] During World

War II, the greater involvement of the Justice Department in lynching cases, stemming from Cleo Wright's murder in Missouri in 1942, was also important in curbing mob killings.[4]

The accelerated movement of African Americans out of the rural South and into urban areas during and following World War II not only further dampened mob actions in the plantation belt but also created conditions in the cities that discouraged extralegal violence. This occurred because as African Americans migrated in large numbers to urban centers, they were limited by whites to specific geographic locales. From Birmingham to Chicago during the postwar years, the most explosive issue (literally) stemmed from efforts by whites to keep blacks out of their neighborhoods.[5] Yet because African Americans were forced to crowd together in urban areas, they were better positioned to resist white intrusion, whether in the form of lynchers, race rioters, or Ku Kluxers. Whites might hound individual blacks out of their vicinities or struggle with them for public space after they arrived, but they did *not* penetrate large urban enclaves of black residents.[6]

Another exodus from the rural South that has received far less attention than the departure of blacks but which was very important in the decline of mob violence, was the migration of white small farmers out of the region. Their departure, which was greatly facilitated by World War II, was important because they had long sustained a culture capable of spawning mob actions in times of crisis. Additionally, as part of a unified white citizenry, yeomen had the support and protection of the local establishment when they perpetrated mob murders.

The commitment to racial violence as a means of achieving power and social control and the establishment of white solidarity occurred during the Civil War and Reconstruction, but social cohesion in the countryside had even earlier origins. The first two sections of this chapter explore how the enduring link between white leaders and white followers was forged and describe the conditions that prevailed in the small-farmer South from the antebellum years through the 1930s. Both contributed to mob actions. The third and fourth sections investigate the reasons for the propensity among some whites for racial violence immediately following World War II and the unraveling of one side of the white coalition, a development that dramatically diminished that propensity.

THE ROOTS OF WHITE SOLIDARITY

Mob actions were no strangers to Maury County. As early as the 1860s, a culture encompassing mob murder materialized. Both a mass, public lynching and extensive terrorist campaigns perpetrated by the Ku Klux Klan appeared in this decade.

The Klan in particular became an intrinsic element of Lost Cause ideology, a "civil religion" that bound white southerners, regardless of class, gender, or rural or urban ties.[7] At the same time, the lynching left in the public memory a storehouse of symbols and rituals that could be drawn on at a later date. The 1860s thus bequeathed to white Maury Countians a legacy that (a) isolated African Americans and any sympathizers they might have, (b) ensconced within the criminal justice system the dominant white perspective, (c) legitimized extralegal racial attacks and established models of form and ritual that those attacks would follow, and, above all, (d) bound white authorities so tightly to the white citizenry that the dissolution of mob actions would have to come ultimately from the side of the perpetrators.

THE RITUAL OF LYNCHING

White residents in the early twentieth century dated the community's first lynching as 1862, "about the time the cherries were ripe." This macabre affair inaugurated a particular strand of extralegal violence within the community. In doing so, it combined old and new aspects in a way that revealed how continuity melded with change as attempts to dominate slaves became efforts to control free blacks.

Gilbert Dowell was a striking man. Remembered variously as 30, or 35 to 40, years of age, he was "about 6 ft. 2 inches high, well formed, copper colored, very muscular." Another account depicted him as "large, stout, and fine looking, bright, 'likely', and smart." Though enslaved, he was probably accustomed to having considerable latitude in handling his own affairs. One observer commented offhandedly long after the lynching that his owners, the Dowells, "had never controlled their slaves," and on the morning that Dowell was seized, he was plowing at a farm that did not belong to his owners. Gilbert Dowell was married to Martha, a slave who had grown up about three miles from Dowell's Branch on the farm of James H. Gregory. They had two children. Sometime in the summer of 1862, "after crops were laid by," Gregory took Martha and the children to Louisiana where he sold them. As one Maury Countian summed it succinctly, "Gilbert was left behind."[8]

In retaliation, Gilbert Dowell allegedly turned to incendiarism, burning Gregory's barn. Following the fire, suspicion fell immediately on Dowell, and a couple of men headed for "Lem Prewetts" near Culleoka, the vicinity where Cordie Cheek was later lynched, to obtain Prewitt's "negro trailing dogs." According to Dave Gregory, however, he and D. T. Chappel did not wait for the return of the dogs but went immediately to the farm where Dowell was plowing and "arrested" him. Throughout the night, Dowell was kept a prisoner in a barn or corn crib.[9]

To this point, the narrative contains many elements typical of the antebellum South: slaveholders, especially smaller ones, using their slaves in a variety of arrangements, such as renting them to other farmers, to earn extra cash; the resultant latitude that allowed some slaves to develop considerable autonomy; the marriage, at least in the eyes of those in bondage, of slaves with one another; a nagging shortage of cash that prompted owners to sell slaves southward and thereby tear families asunder; the rage and despair that enveloped separated family members; an apparent act of desperation; the assessment of guilt by the aggrieved parties; and the resort to "negro trailing dogs" to find the alleged culprit.

But at this juncture in the story, events in Maury County begin to depart from the traditional antebellum scenario. Punishment was not meted out to Gilbert Dowell privately by his owner, nor by the aggrieved party acting alone. Instead, the morning following Dowell's "arrest," a "great crowd assembled" at the site of the burned barn. One estimate placed the number as high as 1,000 people. Whole families were represented: "all the Murphys: Bill, Henry, old man Murphy; all the Wests; all the Sellers; all the Porters (Dock, Ed)." At least three ministers were there. "A great many ladies" were present. Significantly, the assemblage included two constables, and one, Coleman Goad, played a key role in Dowell's murder. Some people were undoubtedly present simply to witness the excitement; a few tried in vain to halt the proceedings; others were bent on exacting the ultimate price, Dowell's life, for his alleged crime.[10]

As John S. R. Gregory recollected the scene, "A court was formed with —— as Judge. Witnesses were examined, but no attorneys. All parties present were heavily armed, mostly with double barrel shot guns." Dave Gregory remembered that "there was not much of a trial." According to another spectator, the "trial" was "all sober, quiet, and in order." John S. R. Gregory, along with schoolteacher John. D. McGill, Reverend W. O. Roberts, and Mrs. Ben Dowell, Gilbert's owner, all pled "that the law be allowed to take its course." Not only were they "hooted at, but threats of personal violence" were made against the three men. Dowell, who was described as "very calm, not excited," had allegedly confessed that morning to "Davy" Chappell and "an old colored preacher" that he had burned the barn and a corn crib, and he reportedly did so again publicly before the assembled crowd. Green Irvine stood on a cart with Dowell and took a vote. "All 'aye' crossed a line and hollered yes." Reverend Irvine then reputedly had a talk with the doomed man about preparation for death. Already a wide scaffold, with "a sort of trap platform," had been constructed. Constable Coleman Goad tied a knot around Dowell's neck and hung him immediately. Shortly after a doctor pronounced him dead, his body was carried to a nearby barn where it remained all night. The next day, "he was buried not far from the burned barn."[11]

Clearly the episode of folk justice that occurred in Maury County in 1862 was transitional. The reasons for Dowell's demise were born of slavery, and the tensions and anomalies that the institution generated. Some of the mechanics of control, such as "negro trailing dogs," also derived from the past, but the means to Dowell's end represented phenomena much more characteristic of the New South than of the Old: a manhunt and the seizure of a black culprit; the forcing of a "confession," although in this case without mutilation; a large crowd acting as judge, jury, and executioner; and the unwavering conviction among most whites in the aftermath of the fray that the victim was guilty and deserved the punishment rendered.[12]

Yet despite the early appearance of a mass lynching in Maury County and a persistent public ideology that denigrated African Americans, the lynching epidemic that accelerated in many parts of the South in the 1890s did not materialize there, nor was there any consistent trend of mass, public murders. Instead, they were sporadic, occurring in 1862, possibly 1877,[13] 1927, and 1933.

The lynchings that scarred parts of the South from the late nineteenth century well into the twentieth did not occur in Maury County because the community had neither the socioeconomic features nor the labor relations to produce it. Mob violence was most persistent in the single-crop plantation regions of the South, where a small number of white landowners presided over a vast cadre of black sharecroppers.[14] In Maury County, there were large plantations, especially southwest of Columbia along the Mt. Pleasant turnpike, where the Polk family held large tracts, and in the Zion Church vicinity, where wealthy Scotch-Irish Presbyterians from South Carolina had located.[15] Slaves there grew cotton and tobacco, but above all, farmers and planters alike specialized in livestock, both before and after the war.[16] They also grew wheat, corn, rye, potatoes, and rice. In short, Maury County had a diversified agronomy before the war as well as after, and the same set of circumstances that created a favorable climate for the acquisition of land by African Americans after the Civil War mitigated against chronic violence and dampened potential mob actions.

When lynchings did occur, they originated in the sections of the county where small farmers predominated and at times when those areas were under duress. The lynching of Gilbert Dowell occurred in a vicinity where small farmers like James Gregory (Martha and her children were his only slaves) were probably reduced to desperate circumstances early in the Civil War. Similarly, the mob that killed Henry Choate in downtown Columbia in 1927, at a time when the fortunes of southern agrarians were rapidly deteriorating, apparently originated in the vicinity just across the Duck River from Dowell's lynch site. Finally, the murder of Cordie Cheek happened in the middle of the Great Depression in the eastern half of the county in the Culleoka-Glendale vicinity, where yeomen also prevailed.

THE ROLE OF THE KLAN

If mass lynchings derived from small-farmer regions of Maury County, Ku Klux Klan activities in the late 1860s saturated the entire community. This occurred because the conservative impulse of small farmers coalesced with the goals of the county's antebellum elite to produce a terrorist orgy.

Founded in Columbia in June 1867, a year after its birth in Pulaski in neighboring Giles County, the local Klan chapter made its first public appearance in Maury during an African American Christmas celebration in downtown Columbia in December 1867. Soon its membership had reached "several hundred." Additionally Columbia was the birthplace of the Order of Pale Faces, an association that had spread throughout much of Tennessee by 1869. Less secretive than the Klan about their organization and membership, the Pale Faces claimed to be a charitable group, but their membership probably overlapped with that of the Klan, and they may have had associational ties with some Klan chapters as well.[17]

By late January 1868, the Maury County Klan had accelerated its night-riding, terrorist activities. They included beatings "administered on the bare back with 'hickories,' sticks or small branches torn off a nearby tree." Sometimes their victims were left permanently scarred or crippled. "Typical raids were accompanied by a great deal of profanity and obscenity as well as indiscriminate physical abuse," with the treatment worsening when the victim tried to resist. Frequently, a group of Klan members carried out several raids per night. Murders were also part of the Klan's stock in trade.[18]

Virtually always the targets of Klan violence were Republicans, and very frequently they were African Americans. Revealingly, Klan atrocities subsided only after Conservatives regained political control at the local and state levels in August 1869. Still, Klan goals were not always narrowly political. Sometimes, as in the case of freedman Henry Fitzpatrick, who was seized from his Maury County home and first hung and then shot, there appeared little or no motive.[19] In the broadest sense, non-Conservatives were attacked for reasons that fell under the general rubric of social control. "Klansmen must . . . have enjoyed their work to engage in so much of it," one scholar has mused, "but they also regarded themselves as purveyors of a rough justice."[20]

This perception derived, at least in part, from guerrillas, who materialized in locales where Yankee soldiers appeared early. Indeed, it is difficult to find a more striking anticipation of rank-and-file Ku Kluxers—and lynch mob participants—than the wartime resisters described by historian Stephen Ash:

> The guerrillas of Middle Tennessee were not, however, merely footloose partisans waging ruthless war on the Yankee invaders. They were men (and boys) of the rural communities, known to their families and neighbors, harbored and supported by them, and committed to safeguarding their world. Federal authorities misinterpreted guerrillaism in the region as evidence of anarchy, an irony because it was in fact just the contrary. An extension of rural society, the guerrillas of the occupied heartland became the surrogate instruments of communal integrity and discipline when the customary instruments faltered or disappeared under the stress of war; and they enforced with loaded guns the deeply conservative values of the communities they embodied.
>
> Tapping (and simultaneously helping to sustain) the nervous system of rural society—the traditional network of neighborly contacts and communication, the communal sharing of news, rumor, and opinion—the guerrillas, acting now in place of the generally defunct churches, courts, and less formal bodies, identified deviants and transgressors who jeopardized the purity, the unity, or the very existence of the community. Then, with threats and violence, they endeavored to bring the wayward back into the fold, or failing that, to expel them, so that the community might retain its virtue and cohesion.[21]

Targets of wartime resisters were "those who took the oath [loyalty to the Union], sold goods to the Yankees, in any way cooperated with the invaders, or opposed guerrillaism." They also "endeavored to safeguard slavery and white supremacy as vigilantly as they did white unity." Equally important for Klan construction, guerrillas were "faithful subjects" who "loyally championed the local aristocracy." In turn, the local elite "patronized the guerrillas in their role as watchdogs of the social order."[22]

At no time did local aristocrats need watchdogs more than when slavery ended and Radical Reconstruction commenced. Prior to the war, Maury was one of the most prosperous of middle Tennessee's heartland counties, but it was ravaged by both Union and Confederate armies. At the end of the conflict, "the politics, society, and economy of Maury County were in chaos."[23]

Many local Democrats, who had long held office and who had grown accustomed to exercising power within the community, found themselves disbarred from politics because of their service to the Confederacy. Those who were able to participate grew quite frustrated in the wake of the gubernatorial election in August 1867 when African American men, who had just been enfranchised, voted overwhelmingly for the Republican party. Indeed more than twice as many voters participated in this election as in any previous ones in the county, and 91 percent favored Republican candidate William G. Brownlow.[24]

Local Democrats were incensed not only by the results of the election but also by the participation of former slaves in the process. According to the Democratic *Columbia Herald*, African Americans received their instructions and ballots that morning, and then they proceeded to the polling station "en masse." "If not difficult," it was "very disagreeable" for a white man to vote, the paper continued, "unless he happened to love *L'odour d'Afrique.*" The summer of 1867 was thus "a turning point in race relations in Maury County": "After two years of Radical control, now sustained by the freedmen's votes and continued Rebel disfranchisement, coupled with Northern instigation and support of freedmen's rights through schools and the [Freedmen's] Bureau, white Conservatives began to organize to recapture control."[25] For many, that organization assumed the form of hoods and robes.

Unquestionably, former Confederate soldiers joined the Klan, as they endeavored to keep intact hierarchies at home that they could not secure on the battlefield. The Grand Titan of the Ku Klux Klan for the district containing Maury and Marshall Counties was Joseph Fussell of Columbia, initially a private and later commander of Company E, First Tennessee Cavalry.[26] Along with their commanders, it was also "a natural step for the rank-and-file Confederate soldiers to become rank-and-file Klansmen." Historian Charles Reagan Wilson concluded that "in the Reconstruction years, before the Confederate [veterans'] organizations had emerged, the prominence of Confederates in the Klan kept alive the holy memory."[27]

The marriage of whites in the Klan across class lines, coupled with the return of Conservatives to power, had grave implications for African Americans generally and for their relationship with the criminal justice system. The *Columbia Herald* in 1870 expressed the opinion that "the negro is working better and is more content now than at any time since his liberation from slavery," but the newspaper also gave evidence of the way many were dealing with the worsening situation when it reported in January 1870 that "Negroes at Santa Fe [in western Maury County] nearly all leaving old homes—unsettled and restless."[28] Likewise, it was no accident that black preacher and school-founder "Cap" Jordan was reputedly going to Florida in 1869 and that he was trying to "take all negro population" with him.[29] By the mid-seventies, the *Herald* was lamenting "a shortage of manual labor," as Maury County blacks established a course of resistance through departure that many would pursue throughout the twentieth century.[30]

The election of men like former Klan leader Fussell, who served as attorney general of the Ninth Judicial Circuit for sixteen years beginning in 1870, did not bode well for black political or civil interests. Although African Americans won offices as constable and as magistrate in the mid-1870s, such victories were becoming increasingly rare. Indeed, the *Columbia Herald* described the black magistrate's trying of a case as " 'a novel but disgusting sight.' " Meanwhile, though it was illegal, Maury County sheriffs by the mid-seventies were excluding blacks from jury duty even when another African American was on trial.[31]

Finally, the participation of the elite and the rank and file in the Klan bound leaders and followers in a way that gave both groups license to operate beyond legal boundaries in their relations with blacks well into the twentieth century. This occurred as the Klan was construed as the South's savior and enfolded as a central tenet into Lost Cause ideology.

The participation of former Confederate soldiers in the Ku Klux Klan helped tie it to an increasingly romanticized antebellum and wartime past, as did its leadership by members of the prewar and postwar Conservative elite. By the early twentieth century, a glowing depiction of the organization had reached full flower. As Mrs. Grace Meredith Newbill of Giles County, home of Pulaski, the birthplace of the KKK, described it in 1912:

the Ku Klux Klan . . . has proven the greatest organization the world has even [*sic*] known, protecting our noble women, our innocent children, and our defenseless old men from dangers far worse than death. It has truly been said that the Ku Klux Klan was the salvation of our beloved Southland during the dark days of the reconstruction period. . . .

Klans were organized in every district of the County; they were always composed of the best and most honorable men in the community . . . when the originators learned that the grotesque costumes, great secrecy and weird mystery of the Klan wrought with superstitious terror upon the minds of the ignorant and vicious Negroes and undesirable whites, they turned this Klan into a more useful channel. . . .

The missions of the Ku Klux Klan was doing good, protecting the weak and oppressed. And in the terrible reconstruction days when William G. Brownlow had control of Tennessee, and outrages innumerable were committed under the sanction of military despotism then it was, women and children blessed the sound of the Ku Klux Klan whistle around their homes, knowing they could sleep soundly while this noble band was standing guard over the homes of their stricken South.

Newbill had in her possession at the time of her talk "in perfect state of preservation" various documents related to Klan organization and dissolution. Given to her as a "young wife" by her husband, she "cherished them sacredly, guarded them faithfully when it was still perilous to keep them, and will leave them to my children as a priceless legacy when I die."[32]

Thus in the hands of Lost Cause devotees, the Klan was not merely excused for its violent activities; it was lauded for them, as white lawlessness was recast as protection for the defenseless. This romanticized version of the Klan and its inclusion in Lost Cause ideology was extremely important, for this dogma was shared widely by white southerners, regardless of their class, gender, or Klan experience. Equally significant, the organizations designed to celebrate the Lost Cause were created and sustained largely by members of the ruling class.

Hence, Conservative leaders sanctioned racial violence by both condoning it and participating in it during Reconstruction. Then they and their descendants enshrined it in the South's "civil religion." This patrimony endowed all whites with the authority to control blacks, and it resulted in license for those who resorted to violence to do so. Such an arrangement might appear a logical outgrowth of an antebellum system in which whites governed and blacks were enslaved, but it was not inevitable. New possibilities flickered briefly during Radical Reconstruction and again in the Populist movement of the 1890s, but extralegal violence helped squelch the alternatives both times, and a united white citizenry resulted. Sheriffs, encouraged by concerned citizens and associations, began to step forward by the 1930s to prevent lynchings, but almost never did local authorities seriously attempt to find and punish the culprits once the deed was done. Neither did juries convict in the rare instances when alleged culprits were brought to trial. Their historical legacy simply did not allow it.

SOCIAL COHESION IN THE COUNTRYSIDE

While small-farmer enclaves like those in the Glendale-Culleoka vicinity in eastern Maury County shared Lost Cause ideology, they had their own special forms of association and neighborliness. These forms, which had deep roots, gave continuity and meaning to their lives. They also defined their enemies—and their victims—as well as their friends.

For the vast majority of the residents in eastern Maury County, whether in the nineteenth century or the twentieth, life involved struggle and hard work. Although an occasional large slaveholder could be found there before the Civil War, the basic economic and social unit in the antebellum period was the self-sufficient family farm, and "modest-sized" farms continue to characterize the area to this day.[33]

"Situated . . . on the impoverished land where the limestone ledge that makes Maury County so fertile thrusts upward and leaves the soil thin and unproductive," this region saw "the prospects for ambitious farming . . . inhibited . . . by the realities of geography." The production of corn, always the area's principal crop and used for feed for cattle, mules, and hogs rather than for cash, was very taxing, especially in the pre-tractor era. As a local study reports, "pulling the disk harrow was a mule killing job." In some cases, the hillside land was so steep that farmers used single mules to plow because "the possibility of controlling a team of mules or horses along such uneven terrain would have taken a measure of adroitness for which neither beasts nor men were equipped." Preadolescent and adolescent males alike were expected to contribute to field work, "and when the occasion demanded, girls and women lent a hand as well."[34]

In addition to the daily struggle of working the farm, the pre-World War I generation confronted "exorbitant" railroad rates and the vagaries of the weather and the marketplace. They also battled a variety of worms and insects, and in 1915, hog cholera hit. World War I proved a boon to the region, as demand for foodstuffs accelerated and the need for horses and mules skyrocketed in a way that would happen in no subsequent war. The appearance of the boll weevil cut short a temporary cotton surge in the 1920s, however, and the "startling turn of economic events after 1929" meant for many "a total financial loss."[35]

In the early days of settlement, "a young core family," accompanied by relatives and often neighboring families, migrated into the area from Virginia or North Carolina. Through the years these families continued to dwell near one another, as their offspring intermarried and settled on adjacent land. Near a road and a deep creek or river, one or more of the families might establish a mill for grinding corn, and then a store, a church, and later, perhaps, a school would be added. Eventually, railroad stops also encouraged the growth of businesses, although no settlement would grow larger than the village of Culleoka, and "the average hamlet could be travelled on foot within five minutes." Even when their economic activities extended beyond the farm, "family members often cooperated, going into business together or investing in a common enterprise." Ultimately, "closely bound . . . by blood, property, and mutual interest," family networks formed small, though similar, enclaves or neighborhoods throughout eastern Maury County.[36]

Churches, overwhelmingly Protestant in denomination and fundamentalist in character, were important in knitting families and neighborhoods together. One resident of the eastern Maury community of Rock Springs estimated that among local residents "no more than five per cent transfer from one church background to another." As camp meetings of the nineteenth century gave way to revivals in the twentieth, Protestant fundamentalist culture generally and churches specifically served as "sources of spiritual continuity," although many, too small and poor to maintain full-time ministers, used itinerant preachers. "Man's capacity for 'wickedness'" and sins of the flesh were routine topics for sermons, and intimidation was often the means for encouraging personal reformation and salvation. "A little old fire-eatin' preacher" was remembered because whenever he received a negative response to his invitation to members of the congregation to come forward to the altar, he closed the service with the admonition: "All right, you're dismissed—just go on to Hell!"[37]

The churches served, of course, as much more than spiritual referents. "Religion and romance mixed in ways both the church leaders and the congregation appreciated," and this helped explain not only the creation of interlocking networks of families but also the lack of need for adults to switch churches. In addition to entertainment, including opportunities for courtship, the houses of worship provided assistance in times of crisis. Barker Hardison remembered that Rock Springs Baptist Church members quickly provided food and clothing whenever a house burned in the community, that food was taken to the wake when someone died and that "the men in the community always dug the grave in the cemetery." The twentieth century "brought neither religious nor secular ideas that challenged spiritual values" in eastern Maury County; only "an atrophying of membership," as young people left the community in increasingly large numbers, undermined "the quantity and vitality of church activities" and the "sense of mutual belonging" that they had sustained.[38]

Before and after the Civil War, "work parties"—which included "corn-shuckings, sugar camps, house-raisings, log rollings, cotton-picking bees, and quilting bees"—not only had the practical import of getting difficult tasks accomplished but also "generated a sense of community and solidarity" within rural neighborhoods. This sense was reinforced as families gathered together to celebrate Christmas, birthdays, and weddings and as women in particular routinely visited with one another. Along with veterans' associations, the temperance movement gained momentum in the 1870s, and temperance societies, like Sunday Schools, held picnics, dinners, and excursions. Other popular, organized forms of activity dating from the nineteenth century included fraternal orders, Grange chapters, debating societies, and spelling contests.[39]

"Quiltings and shucking bees" continued in the twentieth century, while the arrival in 1916 of the Agricultural Extension Service inaugurated a series of organized community activities, which included boys' corn clubs, 4-H Clubs, canning and poultry clubs for women and girls, as well as Home Demonstration Clubs. Increased emphasis on livestock diversification in the 1920s yielded the first cooperative lamb market in 1923, a dairy herd association, a Men's Baby Beef Club, and a boys and girls Jersey calf club. "Hamlet reports," regular features in the *Columbia Herald* and the *Maury Democrat* that chronicled local happenings, also molded a sense of identity, while country music provided a shared cultural experience throughout the region.[40]

Sports held a particular fascination for eastern Maury County men, and in addition to hunting and fishing, nothing captured their imagination as much as baseball. Here money was not initially so important, as "the school boys of Culleoka" proved in 1875 when they scored a very satisfying victory over the "uniformed team of men" from Columbia. Not only did they win but they did so before fifty Columbians who had ridden a special train the twelve miles from town for the occasion! By 1929, however, despite an energetic fund-raising drive that added a gymnasium to Culleoka High School, "the village possessed neither the resources nor the school population essential to sustain the caliber of sports competition identified with nearby Columbia."[41]

Like the gymnasium and the ball team at Culleoka High, schools mirrored both the pride and the poverty of eastern Maury County. They also demonstrated the lingering effects of an antebellum slaveholding society in which some people could afford to send their children to very good private academies while most made do with an exceedingly spartan public system.[42] Undoubtedly the nineteenth century's main legacy to the twentieth century in eastern Maury County, as in the rest of the rural South, was one of primitive, one-room schoolhouses, attended sporadically by students for only a few months each year and conducted by teachers with inadequate schooling themselves.

An infusion of money and enthusiasm from southern and northern educational reformers, under the auspices of the Southern Education Board, and the enactment of laws favorable to public education by the Tennessee legislature in the first decade and a half of the twentieth century brought about much needed improvements in eastern Maury County. Local residents "were not merely passive recipients," however. "Communities like Rock Springs, Leftwich, Culleoka and Fountain Heights" engaged in numerous ice cream suppers, fiddling contests, plays, rallies, and barbecues in behalf of local schools, and as they did so, they built not only educational institutions but also local pride and solidarity. By the 1920s, the village of Culleoka had changed from "a setting in which more privileged young people attended school" to "an environment where sons and daughters of struggling farmers could learn to read and write," and they learned more as well. "Pride in the community" was one quality routinely instilled. A teacher at a two-room grade school incorporated this attitude "as one vital feature within 'civics' lessons" whenever she taught Tennessee and American history.[43]

Yet despite the efforts of reformers from outside and inside local communities, the improvement in schools in eastern Maury County was uneven at best, with "those which had more people and a solid educational base from which to build" benefiting the most. Some communities, like "Lickskillet"—so called because residents there were reputedly so poor that they had to "lick the skillet"—possessed a very small resource base from which to work. In the 1920s, even Culleoka High, located in the area's largest hamlet, still housed both the high school and an elementary school, and clear differences separated the sports programs at Culleoka and Columbia. Only two other communities in eastern Maury boasted high schools at all in the twenties, while a newly consolidated school serving Rock Springs and Bear Creek consisted of two rooms, divided so that instruction for grades one through four took place in one and for grades five through eight in the other. The Depression, then, "forced whites to alter fundamentally their expectations of the public schools . . . [and] the succeeding decade represented an era of sharply reduced accomplishments and hopes."[44]

Not surprisingly, the strong localism that characterized communities in eastern Maury County rendered them suspicious of and hostile toward outsiders, although in this inclination they were more similar to than different from their neighbors in the county seat. Still, eastern Maury farmers carried their suspicions to an extreme to which town dwellers did not go.[45]

On racial matters, eastern Maury Countians also shared similarities and manifested differences with Columbia and with the more affluent farmers and livestock breeders in southwestern Maury County. Historian John W. Cell referred to segregation as a "city slicker," and in an important sense he was right. Residential segregation did prevail, even in small towns like Columbia, and it was largely from the South's towns and cities that segregation laws emanated.[46] In contrast, in the southern countryside the dwellings of blacks and whites were interspersed, whether in large-planter domains or small-farmer regions.

Still, living near one another did *not* insure an integrated lifestyle or mindset. From the whites' point of view, African Americans were not kin, at least not recognized kin, and in rural neighborhoods, kin networks were the basis for cohesion and continuity. This did not mean there was an absence of conflict among whites. The preponderance of guns and alcohol, the self-righteous resort to violence born of isolation and religiosity, and the prevalence of hair-trigger tempers wired to individual and family honor: all combined to ensure a contentious culture very similar to that in the Bottom. But white contentiousness was expressed within a framework of solidarity, a framework from which blacks, by virtue of their race, were excluded.[47]

Although rural black Americans had their own forms of association, they did not participate in white birthdays, weddings, or Christmas celebrations, other than as servants in homes that could afford them; and except for an occasional camp meeting or corn shucking, they were excluded from all formal and informally organized white activities. They were not at church, at school, in the local veterans association, in the Masonic lodge, or even in the government-sponsored agricultural extension clubs. So rigidly were they excluded from white consciousness that one white woman repeatedly confused a sociologist trying to reach rural homes in the 1930s by omitting the houses of blacks from those to be counted in her directions. Another appeared quite puzzled when asked about a school that was supposedly located about a mile and a half from her home. After stating "positively" that no such school existed and then hearing a description of it by her visitor, she laughed and responded, " 'Oh, that's a nigger school—I knew there wasn't any school on that road.' "[48] Though rural black southerners lived among whites, Ralph Ellison's sense that he was "invisible" and Pauli Murray's discovery that she was passed by white schoolchildren each morning "as if I weren't there" were just as applicable in the southern countryside as on the sidewalks of America's towns and cities.[49]

Especially those who were most engaged in community endeavors—and involvement usually correlated positively with income—were the most isolated from any sense of equality with African Americans. Even in eastern Maury County, where farmers as a whole were poorer than in the southwestern district, there were wealth distinctions, and the relatively affluent served as government officials and civic leaders. They were also more likely, too, to have black tenants and household help, and they in turn felt confident that they knew and understood African Americans. In fact, it was among lower-class whites, in rural as well as urban areas, that "neighborly relations" between blacks and whites sometimes developed. In contrast, lower-middle-class whites almost never achieved harmonious relations with blacks, even when they lived near them. Instead, they were "generally antagonistic." Upper-class and upper-middle-class whites occasionally offered protection to blacks, and more often, a veneer of politeness, but such forms of behavior engendered little equity between the two groups.[50]

Thus the same forces that melded rural white neighborhoods together rendered blacks outsiders and, under certain conditions, made them targets of extraordinary white malevolence and ferocity. As historian Barbara Fields so aptly reminded us:

> There may be charm in quilting bees and logrollings, in the various traditions of mutuality and reciprocity, and (for some) in country music. But there is also a somber side to that culture, not unrelated to the first: for example, the personal violence and the do-it-yourself justice of the necktie party. Those inclined to romanticize, sentimentalize, or take vicarious comfort in the flowering of cultural forms among the oppressed which challenge their subordination . . . would do well to remember that these autonomous cultural forms need not be gentle, humane, or liberating.[51]

The important point is that solidarity and exclusion flowed from the same cultural wellspring, and both were essential to mob actions. Solidarity yielded mobilization, and in the wake of a lynching, silence. Exclusion defined the targets.

What prompted a rural neighborhood to gear up for a lynching? The timing, causes, and conduct of mob murders in small-farmer areas differed from those in the South's plantation regions, and the differences themselves provide not only insights into black-white relations in areas like eastern Maury County but also additional clues about the reasons for the killings.

In the Black Belt, where mob violence was most pervasive and enduring, alleged murder most often prompted lynchings. The affairs were usually orderly, "blatantly public," and often involved "the open complicity of local officials." In contrast, lynchings outside the plantation South were sporadic affairs, stimulated by rapid social and economic change. Even more revealing, the causes of mob murders in the Upper Piedmont of Georgia were alleged sexual assaults or, second most often, "overstepping the boundaries of acceptable conduct," for example, "by arguing with an employer." These killings were usually conducted in "the form of mass lynchings, replete with elaborate ritualism."[52]

The lynchings of Dowell, Choate, and Cheek in Maury County conform to the sporadic nature of mob killings outside the plantation South and to periods of dramatic change—change for the worse in the case of Maury County farmers. The murders of Choate and Cheek were spawned by alleged attempted sexual assaults and involved crowds and considerable ritual. The circumstances of Cheek's murder in particular correlated with the findings of Arthur Raper's 1930 study of lynchings during the Great Depression: most lynchings happened in "open country" or exceedingly small towns in counties that were "economically below average" and usually had no "economic need for Negroes." While these characterizations do not fit Maury County as a whole, they most assuredly apply to the eastern section. Raper continued: "As would be expected from their poor economic rating, the educational facilities in many of these counties were far below the state average. Baptists and Methodists account for over three-fourths of all church members in nearly three-fourths of the counties, and two-thirds of them regularly poll Democratic majorities."[53] The reasons most often given for the lynchings in Raper's study were alleged rapes or alleged attempted rapes.

Clearly, the characteristics of lynchings inside and outside the Black Belt South reflect different terms on which race relations were conducted. The openness and impunity with which lynchings occurred in the plantation regions demonstrated the extraordinary influence of planters and the relative powerlessness of black tenants, while the sustained mob actions pointed toward the integral role of violence in day-to-day relationships. Routinely threatened and brutalized, defiant African Americans were forced to resort to desperate measures, and hence the charges of murder against those killed in mob actions.

In contrast, the sporadic nature and timing of mob violence outside the plantation South suggested a fluidity in race relations that could reach dangerous levels in periods of flux. White small farmers, who lived in areas where blacks made up a much smaller proportion of the population and were more apt to be landowners, encountered blacks in nonhierarchical situations more frequently than did whites in the plantation South. Equally significant, because rural African Americans in these areas had relatively greater autonomy and space—and their own well-established associational networks—they themselves were more apt to behave in ways that challenged the status quo as whites perceived it. In the midst of such circumstances, particularly in times of disarray, charges of sexual assaults were credible to whites, regardless of their validity, while allegations of "overstepping the boundaries of acceptable behavior" defined quite accurately the situation as whites-in-crisis perceived it.

Especially black teenagers in the process of becoming adults tested society's boundaries, while white youths avidly defended them. Thus over two-thirds of the victims lynched in 1930 were under twenty-five, while "the majority of persons known to have taken an active part in the lynchings were unattached and irresponsible youths."[54] Readily one thinks of the contestation between 19-year-old Henry Carl Moore and 17-year-old Cordie Cheek and the disastrous consequences that flowed from it. Similarly, Flo Fleming recalled threatening James "Popeye" Bellanfante with a gun when both were youths.[55] Undoubtedly, such encounters occurred routinely in the small-farmer South. If the area were experiencing severe economic and social dislocation, whether from war or a savage depression, and the participation of white adults could be elicited, serious consequences could result. This kind of competition, however, reveals less about a permanent state of dominance and subordinance than about a constant tug-of-war being waged as blacks, through their behavior, tested society's limits, and whites, in pursuit of racial hegemony, strove to enforce their version of those limits.

Not every white rural family participated if a lynching occurred in its vicinity, but kin and neighborly ties exerted a powerful pressure. An alleged attack against the member of one family quickly engulfed others. Even if one managed to remain beyond the fray, the combined forces of cohesion and exclusion that characterized rural neighborhoods rendered highly unlikely any attempts to halt the gathering storm or to bring its perpetrators to justice.

On the last matter—as was readily demonstrated in the wake of Cordie Cheek's murder—rural neighborhoods usually had the full cooperation of the local establishment. Forged in the violence of the Civil War and the Ku Klux Klan, seared with the religion of the Lost Cause, and awash in white supremacy and parochialism, the union of perpetrators and authorities stood impenetrable, even in the face of mob murder, and even as some in urban areas raised their voices in opposition to it.

WAR AND THE REAPPEARANCE OF MOBOCRACY

The persistence of white solidarity was demonstrated in Columbia in 1946 in the tendencies of law officers to focus their attention almost exclusively on African Americans and to merge periodically with white civilians as they tried to maintain order (see Chapter 5). It was also confirmed in the site the crowd chose for assembly. Just as black Maury Countians marshaled their forces in *their* physical space, the Bottom, whites poured into the area of town they considered *their* territory: the public square.

This area represented not only the heart of the white business district but, more importantly, the seat of power in the county. First and foremost, the courthouse sat in the middle of it. City Hall was located one block north on North Main Street, while the office of Magistrate C. Hayes Denton was just across the street. The jail and fire station were close by, within the "white vicinity" as well. In short, the mob claimed as its space the area that included the major public buildings within the county, including all of those associated with the criminal justice system.

The crowd that milled around on Columbia's town square did so against a backdrop of national disquietude and sectional alarm on the part of whites regarding racial affairs. Convinced of black inferiority and of the fairness of their segregated system, most were irate at the greater sense of personal efficacy and entitlement displayed by African Americans during the war. Even "the most sympathetic observers as well as . . . those habitually critical of the Negro," referred to their "'chip on the shoulder'" attitude, while "correspondence panels" following the Detroit riot of 1943 described "rude, aggressive, or disorderly behavior" as "the Negro's contribution to inter-racial friction."[56]

As home to 77 percent of the African American population and to legal segregation in 1940, the white South was especially sensitive to racial challenges. During the war, rumors involving the hoarding of ice picks, knives, and other weapons by blacks flew around, and in a twist that had not been heard since the Civil War, southern whites worried over conspiracies and race wars initiated by black Americans against all whites.[57]

Because white southerners linked the prospect of racial change in the public sphere with threats by black men toward white women in the private sphere, those who were most distressed by the alterations that the war portended focused their fear and fury on African American males. Letters like the following one from a couple in Prescott, Arkansas, poured in to President Roosevelt and other Washington officials: "Due to the fact that so many negro's are turned down [for military service], it leaves more negro's in purportion then [sic] white men. And they are becoming more arrogant every day. It is almost unsafe for a white woman to be on the streets on Saturdays or at night."[58]

Southerners, even more than northerners, saw the induction of more

African American men into the Army as a solution to their difficulties. Both groups wanted them in combat, rather than behind the lines, despite the problem, as many whites saw it, of having soldiers return home emboldened by their military service and more experienced in the use of sophisticated weaponry.[59] Once black men were in the armed forces, however, the woes of white southerners were not ameliorated, for the vast majority of black troops, an estimated 80 percent, were trained and stationed in the South.[60]

If black civilians were worrisome, black soldiers appeared even more so. African American troops aroused intense concern as they traveled through the southern countryside, lived on nearby bases, and participated in normal military routines. In line with their fears about black civilians, whites agonized over advances made by African American soldiers toward white women, and even more than with the civilian sector, they grimaced over the apparent dissolution of racial boundaries.

F. S. Craig, an attorney in Mansfield, Louisiana, was infuriated when a "negro troup [sic] train" drew near his teenaged daughter and her friend and "negro soldiers all up and down stuck their heads out of the windows, cat called and whistled at them." Similarly, a salesman for a St. Louis chemical company fumed at the sight of "a buck negroe lying in his berth stripped down to army shorts reading a magazine" when he boarded a train near Jacksonville, Florida, while Lizzie Rains of Marthaville, Louisiana, sparked a full-blown military investigation of the all-black 93rd Division as it conducted maneuvers near her home. The charges she made, military investigators concluded, were "inspired by the fear of what *might* happen to unprotected women in a rural community."[61]

Along with white civilians, a number of white soldiers also had their negative stereotypes of African Americans reinforced while serving in the military.[62] As Columbia policeman and Army veteran Bernard Stofel recently explained, "I don't believe they had but one or two combat outfits . . . in the whole war. All the rest of the blacks was in supplies and driving trucks, behind the lines."[63] Not surprisingly, the preponderance of black troops in these positions was frequently offered by whites as evidence that African Americans managed "to avoid combat and stay in safe jobs," although the decision to put them in noncombat positions was made by high-ranking whites.[64] In turn, the placement of black troops in rear-echelon and service units buttressed the frequently held view among whites that African Americans were "lazy" and "slackers in work."[65] It no doubt also reinforced their perception that the appropriate role for blacks was serving whites.

Additionally, though no survey ever focused specifically on the racial attitudes of white soldiers serving in the Pacific region—the area where Billy

Fleming was stationed—it appears that the strongly racist attitudes held by white Americans toward the Japanese may have contributed to more negative images of African Americans by whites.[66] E. T. Hall Jr., a white officer who led black troops for two and a half years during the war and who analyzed race relations afterwards in a scholarly article, noted that from the outset of their arrival in the Pacific theater, he and his men "heard stories of conflict between white and colored troops," and he described the situation there as worse than in Europe.[67]

Nothing, however, made white soldiers more indignant than contact between black servicemen and white women. According to Hall, "the competition [between black and white troops] for women" was greater in the Philippines than in the western theater, but black involvement with English and European women proved especially infuriating to white soldiers. In England, outbreaks of violence over black men associating with local women were so numerous that restrictions were sometimes placed on leave policies so that black and white soldiers did not visit the same town at the same time.[68]

Amidst this context of hypersensitivity and unease, the fight between Fleming and Stephenson assumed major proportions in the minds of many white Maury Countians. In turn, certain groups stepped forward to assume the mantle as defenders of the Fleming family and of the wider white community.

In the wake of events on February 25th and 26th, local and state authorities tried to downplay the seriousness of the mob by dismissing its members as "irresponsibles" and "late teen-age white boys." These labels obscured more than they revealed, however. Sheriff Underwood *had* arrested two white men at the jail who were drunk and disorderly, and he later described them as "characters about town." Yet the two were a farmer who had brought a cow into Columbia for sale before he headed for a local pool room and an auto mechanic who was a married veteran.

Similarly, the presence of young people in the crowd should not detract from the peril that they posed. Henry Carl Moore's wild ride across the Fisk campus in 1933, as he stood on the running board of a car waving a pistol, illustrated the palpability of youthful danger, while Arthur Raper's 1930 study confirmed it. Carl Hugh Kelly, a 19-year-old who demanded the Stephensons when the mob appeared at the jail, was in the Army at the time, serving as a mortar crewman. Furthermore, a recent analysis of the Detroit riot of 1943 indicates that, although most of the younger rioters of both races in that fray committed only misdemeanors, almost 65 percent were under the age of 23 and the median age stood at 20.[69] Nothing in lynching statistics for the 1930s or for riots of the 1940s or the 1960s suggests an intrinsic link between youth and harmlessness.

The crowd that milled around on Columbia's town square on February 25th included phosphate employees from the nearby Godwin plant as well as blue-collar service workers. Unquestionably, neighbors and acquaintances of the Fleming family in the Culleoka vicinity sparked the conflagration.[70] White veterans, who were scattered throughout the various constituencies, comprised the crowd's most volatile element.

In part, the success of the CIO union Mine Mill, discussed in Chapter 3, encouraged phosphate workers at the Godwin fertilizer plant to join the crowd. In competing with Mine Mill, Godwin's local, the AFL (American Federation of Labor) Operating Engineers, had stirred racial antipathies by guaranteeing primacy to white workers, while the specter of a strong interracial union at Mt. Pleasant obviously heightened tempers.

Blue-collar service workers who milled about on the town square included auto mechanics, filling station attendants, and cab drivers. They represented a phalanx of men who knew one another, and their motivations were probably similar.[71] Although anthropologists who studied Natchez, Mississippi, in the late 1930s described white filling station attendants speaking courteously and even tipping their hats to affluent black customers, they also noted that whites who served African Americans seldom achieved "superordinate relations to many Negroes." Even more important—and undoubtedly more galling—as service workers, they were at least occasionally in a "subordinate position" to blacks. Therefore these scholars concluded that people in these situations "achieve superordination through direct force."[72]

In addition, the participation in the crowd of men like cab driver Ichabod Cox probably resulted from the informer-enforcer role that white taxi drivers frequently played in southern communities and which James Morton specifically acknowledged when he told Columbia policemen on the 25th to keep all "white taxis" out of the Bottom. Finally many of the whites who milled around on the town square were imbibing alcohol, and those from the service sector were very much a part of this culture.[73]

Culleoka residents were catalysts for the mob's formation, because of their understanding of time-honored traditions of support, loyalty, and reciprocity, counterposed against their perception of African Americans as "the other." The successful, unpunished killing of Cordie Cheek no doubt strengthened their conviction that their actions in 1946 were both safe [for them] and appropriate. Also, the relatively poor economic circumstances of many eastern Maury Countians apparently made them jealous of the wealth that some black Columbians had accumulated, and their resentment probably increased during the war as the prosperity of black businessmen accelerated.[74]

Veterans were prominent in the Columbia conflict, not only because their military service heightened their animosity toward black men but also because of their respect for the Flemings' service records. A former soldier who rose to the rank of lieutenant during the Spanish-American War and a captain in the National Guard for twenty-seven years, John Fleming Sr. had watched all seven of his sons march off to battle during World War II. All had served overseas, and two in particular had been highly decorated— Billy, while serving as a heavy machine gunner in the Pacific theater, and Luther, as a captain in the Signal Corps in the European, African, and Middle Eastern theaters. Flo received a discharge in the summer of 1944 because of a wound he received at Gela in the Sicilian campaign, while his twin brother Fred paid with his life when his ship, the USS *Little*, was sunk by the Japanese early in the war near Guadalcanal in the Solomon Islands. Sheriff Underwood underscored the close ties between the Flemings and other white servicemen when he noted that "veterans in uniform had been taken off of busses and voted a number of times around the county by Flo Flemming [sic] and his political associates" in an obviously fraudulent attempt to capture the recent primary, in which Fleming had narrowly defeated the incumbent sheriff.[75]

Underwood also commented that while it was true that "Mr. Blair and Mr. Morton had made too many bonds for rough and tough negroes . . . equally business men and politicians in the white community had made too many bonds for rough and tough whites, most of them veterans." Initially, the sheriff had ordered his deputies "to go easy on these veterans and let them have a great deal of range," but when he discovered that this approach "was a serious mistake," he issued orders "to tighten up and bring anybody who was drunk or who had committed any disorder[ly] conduct . . . before the Court." In retrospect, he believed that his initial leniency had led "to the disrespect for law and order on both sides that prepared the way for this affair."[76]

WAR AND THE UNRAVELING OF MOBOCRACY

Despite the Flemings' veteran status and the strong support among many veterans for them, the most notable fact about the family was the generational split that characterized their response to Billy's fight with James Stephenson. While John Fleming Sr. was on the square in the afternoon, drunk and encouraging a lynching, his sons were noticeably absent. Apart

White civilians on the road the night of February 25. Driver Sidney Dorris Minor served in the Navy from June of 1944 till January 1946; one of the unidentified riders in the back is in Navy uniform, the other wears an Army jacket. (Courtesy of United States Attorney's Office, Middle District of Tennessee)

from John Jr., none of the others appeared, with the exception of John's younger brother Flo, and he was there not as a member of the mob but as a highway patrolman. Even more significantly, John Jr., in marked contrast to his father, attempted to *discourage* a lynching. Not only did he appear on the square both before and after the police were shot, but he also rode around in a car that evening with three young men from Columbia "to keep them from killing somebody."[77]

Without question, the absence of members of the aggrieved family, and the resultant leaderless condition of the crowd on the square, contributed to its inability to take decisive action, expressed in its milling quality. In conjunction with Sheriff Underwood's release of James Stephenson to black leaders and the subsequent protection offered him by armed African Americans in the Bottom, the lack of leadership on the part of the Flemings prevented the seizure of the young Navy vet and the success of another lynching effort in Maury County.

What accounted for the departure of the Fleming sons from the traditional ways of their father? In large part, it derived from economic and geographic mobility that they experienced as a result of World War II. After the war, the South was much better positioned to sustain economic opportunities than it had been before. Coupled with New Deal minimum wage standards, the alterations that the war initiated sent local and state authorities scurrying for outside investments. Combined with the capital that poured into the region via defense-related construction and manufacturing, the internal market that they generated, and the emergence of the Cold War, the changed orientation of southern leadership set the South firmly on the road toward a high-wage economy.[78] The GI Bill in turn equipped many southerners, especially whites, with the education and skills needed to take advantage of this situation.[79]

To posit a relationship following the war between expanded job and educational opportunities for white veterans and a decline in extralegal violence is *not* to suggest a direct, facile association between wealth and education on the one hand and racial tolerance on the other. Nor do rising income and educational levels necessarily insulate one from concerns about interracial contact. Indeed, objections by white Americans to personal involvement with black Americans tend to increase as the number of African Americans rises in a given setting, regardless of the ed   el of the whites. Moreover, the higher the socioeconomic stat   e more apt they are to think that blacks are inferior in intelligence.[80]

Class and its implications for white actions are discussed further in Chapters 5 and 7; the significant point here is that after experiencing extraordinary financial loss and vulnerability during the Depression of the 1930s and serving away from home and family during a lengthy war (75 percent of white soldiers served overseas), former servicemen returned obsessed with economic security and personal advancement.[81]

This did not mean that their racial attitudes had changed. Neither "revolutionaries" nor "reformers," the vast majority of soldiers in World War II saw military service as a "detour" on the road of civilian life and not as a great social crusade.[82] Although some grew more tolerant toward African Americans as a result of their wartime experiences (see Chapter 7), the number in this category remained small.[83]

Most, however, had neither time nor interest in monitoring black behavior after the war ended. Either because of growing educational or job opportunities at home or because expanding horizons that accompanied military service encouraged migration, southern whites were on the move. Like blacks from the plantation region, they poured out of the rural South by the millions, with the most extensive departures occurring in the 1940s and 1950s.[84]

To look at a decrease in extralegal violence and its relationship to economic and geographic mobility from a slightly different perspective, Bettelheim and Janowitz noted a positive correlation between downward mobility and intense racism. Further, they found that "dubious feelings or outright doubt that [the white veteran] would be able to achieve his occupational ambitions were *significantly* associated with the degree of a man's anti-Negro attitudes." Likewise, a 1944 survey concluded that "widespread unemployment among [white veterans] would serve to re-vitalize a whole series of resentments," and, it continued, "in such an atmosphere, . . . anti-Negro attitudes could be expected to flourish."[85] A 1945 survey expressed the situation in similar, though less explicit terms: "Hostility toward civilians was not generalized. What increases in hostile attitudes were expressed appeared only when questions focused attention on those groups which had a vital relevance to the soldiers' dominant desires to get back into civilian life on reasonably favorable terms." Or, as analysts of this study explained further: "The anxiety of the soldier about his future economic security and opportunities was a central one and any group which appeared to threaten this future would very likely become a target of hostile attitudes."[86]

Nothing made this point more explicitly than the riot in the summer of 1946 in Athens, Alabama. There, as former white servicemen spearheaded the altercation, they invaded "shops and stores that employed Negroes" and demanded "that the Negroes' jobs be given to white veterans."[87] The combined awareness of the danger of an economic downturn and of the positive repercussions of financial prosperity led Samuel Stoffer and his associates to conclude four years after the war ended that the tensions in the immediate postwar years might have been greater had it not been for two conditions: relatively full employment and the GI bill.[88]

No one demonstrates better the changes that the war encouraged in the white rural South than the Fleming family. Residents of eastern Maury County for at least three generations, the Flemings became landowners during the boom years of World War I when John Sr.'s father managed to buy 450 acres of property, a "large farm for Culleoka at that time," John Jr. noted—though he felt compelled to add, "not as big as down toward Mt. Pleasant" (in southwestern Maury County). The farm, which was eventually left to John Fleming Sr., had tenants, all of whom were black, but family members themselves worked strenuously. John Jr. milked eight or nine cows twice a day, and he commented in retrospect that the family could not have handled any more than the 450 acres that it possessed. Life on the farm was "hard enough," he recollected, and he swore that he would never milk another cow in his life![89]

Like many in the small-farmer South as late as the 1930s, John Fleming Sr. and his wife, Minnie Hancock Fleming, had a large family: ten children, eight of whom survived to adulthood. Although John Sr. eventually acquired the farm, he also served as a deputy under Sheriff Claude Godwin, and he earned some money as a twenty-seven-year member of the National Guard. By the time Flo was growing up, the family had left the farm and resettled in Culleoka. John Jr. completed school there and then went to Cumberland Law School. While there, he earned a little cash, like his father and two of his brothers, as a member of the National Guard. In 1935, he moved to Columbia and established a law practice. He had his "law-abiding" instincts strengthened further when he served part of the time he was in the Army as a member of the Provost Court in Hawaii.[90] Louise, the only daughter in the family, became a schoolteacher.

Clearly some of the Flemings experienced social mobility prior to the war, but economic alternatives remained sparse in their vicinity. At some point, probably during the war, Louise and her husband, Webb Bowman, moved to Richland, Washington, while all of her brothers, in part because of their economic circumstances, entered the military prior to the Japanese attack on Pearl Harbor.[91]

All seven men served overseas; none returned on a permanent basis to Culleoka. Like the vast majority of other white servicemen who planned to migrate after the war, three of the Flemings moved to the Pacific Coast, joining their older sister and brother-in-law in Richland.[92] There they found opportunities provided by a growing Cold War. John Jr. worked as a plant protection inspector for the Atomic Energy Commission (AEC), while Billy and Emmit were employed by firms that had contracts with the AEC— Billy as a security officer, Emmit in shipping and receiving.[93]

Billy, who had initially gotten a job as an assistant in the appliance repair shop at the Castner-Knott Department Store in downtown Columbia, was advised by John Jr. to leave the area after his fight with James Stephenson. Neither he nor Emmit ever returned to live in Maury County. Billy died in Richland in 1983, Emmit succumbed there in 1987. John Jr. eventually came back to Columbia but only after working twenty-six years with the AEC and living in, in addition to Richland, San Francisco, Chicago, and

Pittsburgh. Upon his return to the county seat in 1972, John opened a law practice and then served for a decade as a municipal judge.

The eldest Fleming son, Luther, who left the Army as a captain, ensconced himself firmly in the South's expanding middle class after the war, working first in a bank in Birmingham, then at the Maury National Bank and the Commerce Union in Columbia, and finally for nineteen years as head bookkeeper at the *Daily Herald*. He also remained outside Culleoka, and he honed his white-collar skills by serving during the Korean conflict as an aircraft warning officer in California and as an aircraft warning instructor in Florida.

Jack William ("J. W.")—as his brother Flo recalled, "a roamer" who, like his father, imbibed frequently, and "didn't care if the world turned over," though he was "good as gold"—worked in a variety of jobs, including an exterminating business owned by Flo. Eventually, he made his way to Chicago where he joined the Police Department. He died there at the age of 54, just a couple of months before the disastrous encounter between the Chicago police and antiwar demonstrators at the 1968 Democratic National Convention.

Flo Fleming made a career in law enforcement and investigative endeavors. A state trooper in 1946, he was elected sheriff of Maury County for the three terms allowed by the Tennessee Constitution. He then held several other law enforcement positions, including director of security at the Tennessee State Prison, criminal investigator for the state Attorney General's Office, and chief law enforcement officer for the Department of Motor Vehicles. He also worked briefly as a security officer for the Manhattan Project in Oak Ridge, Tennessee. In 1964, Flo sought a congressional seat. Running on a segregationist, anti–civil rights platform, he was defeated in the district as a whole, though he won in Maury County. Finally, for a number of years, he ran a private investigator business and even in retirement continues to conduct occasional investigations for attorneys and insurance companies. "Can't get it out of the blood," he explained.[94]

For eastern Maury County, the changes represented by the Flemings in the postwar years meant "the accelerated abandonment of sites and activities commonly identified with community life." Now vacant schools at Park Station and Rock Springs testify "to a dwindling school age population" after the war, while a deserted brick Masonic hall in Culleoka exemplifies further the outmigration that sapped community vitality.[95] But as the associational life of rural southern neighborhoods disintegrated, so too did the less gentile expressions of the collective spirit. No lynchings have been attempted in Maury County since 1946. The nation as a whole witnessed in 1952, 1953, and 1954 its first lynching-free years since record-keeping began in the 1880s, and Tuskegee University, long the careful recorder of these gruesome affairs, ceased its monitoring activities.

This is not to suggest that racially inspired murders disappeared from the southern landscape, but as one of the most assiduous scholars of the lynching phenomenon has reported: "as the number of lynchings declined sharply during the 1940s, the tradition of mob murders by mass mobs, with their attendant public rituals, virtually came to an end."[96] On occasion—for example, in the ethnic neighborhoods of working-class Catholics in Chicago—community solidarity was reestablished, and extralegal, violent efforts at race control resulted, without the attendant rituals but with social cohesion reminiscent of the rural South.[97] The agrarian southern folkways that had produced "assaults on jails . . . public rituals of torture and mutilation of mob victims, and . . . carnivalike gatherings to witness the victim's corpse" were, however, history.[98]

Moreover, most former soldiers, reunited with their families and engaged wholeheartedly in getting ahead, rejected appeals in 1946 and 1949 to revitalize the Ku Klux Klan, while the limited organization that did emerge was much more a city phenomenon than a country one.[99] The Klan would revive in response to the civil rights movement, and it would prove especially deadly in many of the towns and cities in the Deep South as it bombed schools, synagogues, and churches. This time, however, the Hooded Order garnered little of the appreciation and the subsequent glorification that it captured in the wake of the Civil War when kith and kin from rural neighborhoods united with the local elite to swell its ranks.

To the growing white southern middle class, separated from Ku Kluxers by income and residential area, donning hoods and robes was no longer respectable. Those from this social stratum who did attempt organizational means to thwart a burgeoning civil rights movement did so briefly in the mid-1950s in the "white-collar Klan" known as Citizens Councils. By the mid-1960s, white southerners themselves, in pursuit of law and order, began turning against Klansmen and holding them accountable for their deeds.[100]

Thus, as a result of forces accelerated by World War II, a white consensus regarding the use of extralegal violence for racial control, forged in the 1860s, fell apart. Important in making this happen were the increased concern among local and state authorities about the image of their communities, the greater attention of the federal government to the problem, and the campaigns of organizations dedicated to the eradication of mob vio-

RACIAL JUSTICE

THE
POLITICS OF
POLICING

Ironically, while the migration of African Americans to the nation's cities discouraged attacks by white civilians, it increased the possibility of negative encounters between police officers and black residents. This occurred because after World War II, police in the urban South were more likely to abuse blacks than were those in small towns and the countryside.[1] Police abuse was also rising in certain urban locales in the postwar era.[2]

While both developments were undoubtedly related to the growing number of African Americans in cities, the very anonymity of urban blacks often led police to typecast all with whom they came in contact as "bad niggers" and to confront them aggressively. When officers were exceptionally abusive, African Americans frequently responded in kind, so that killings by police and killings of police tended to be high in the same locales.[3] Although the specific personnel of the police force, especially the chief, helped explain the different death rates from one city to another, police behavior ultimately rested on a more fundamental bedrock—namely, politics and the distribution of power.

Nothing demonstrated better the differences that political arrangements could make in the safety and security of African Americans than the contrasting treatment blacks received at the hands of the Columbia police and the Maury County sheriff. Although Justice attorney Eleanor Bontecou described both Police Chief Griffin and Sheriff Underwood as "two very gentle spirits," subtle but important differences distinguished the two.[4]

While the Columbia police did not behave as viciously as some law officers, they, like their counterparts in towns and cities across the South, answered to white officials, and indirectly to an overwhelmingly white electorate, that expected perpetuation of the status quo. Relations between black Columbians and the local police had changed since the late nineteenth century, but the changes were more ones of style than substance. Meanwhile, a very different political matrix—one that looked backward to the First Reconstruction and forward to the Second—had developed between Underwood and black voters.

This section sorts out and explains these distinctions; the following one compares the Highway Patrol and the State Guard. Together they demonstrate how political machinations both protected and offended black rights. They also challenge the truisms that state law officers are inherently more impartial than their counterparts at the grassroots level and that the intermingling of law enforcement and politics is innately bad.

THE LOCAL SCENE

As upholders of a legal and social order that had sustained first slavery and then segregation, the vast majority of southern law officers were not held in high esteem by most African Americans.[5] Some improvement had occurred in the rare locales that had hired black policemen, but as a Georgia resident summed the prevailing sentiment: "We have no Negro police and most of the white policemen are nasty."[6]

Although the Columbia police in 1946 did not engage in the savagery that some did, their behavior was at best mixed. W. E. "Clyde" Frazier, the radio operator at the Columbia police station, struck Gladys Stephenson several times as she attempted to protect her son on the morning of the 25th, and local fire chief J. P. White may have hit her as well.[7] Constable T. I. "Harry" Shaw of Spring Hill and TVA guard W. E. "Smitty" Smith also pummeled Alexander Bullock with their fists and blackjacks when he arrived at City Hall the morning of the 26th in search of his car.

In addition to the physical abuse accorded Stephenson and Bullock, Police Chief Griffin clearly discriminated against the Stephensons in the matter of arrests. As James Stephenson explained, when the police appeared, "the other two [white] guys [who had been in the fight] walked upon the sidewalk."[8] No one questioned them, and obviously Griffin never thought of taking them into custody.

The chief did not consider arresting any of the whites involved in the Stephenson-Fleming fight, nor did he question the propriety of white civilians and officers abusing black Maury Countians, because the social function of the police in the South, as in much of the nation, was to *control* African Americans, not protect them.[9] In this mission, all whites were presumably united. For these reasons, the law officers involved in the Columbia fray focused on the men gathered in the Bottom, not on the armed whites roaming around the town square. Even Sheriff Underwood made no effort to disarm white Maury Countians, and like the town police, he paid a visit to the Bottom, though his actions in behalf of the Stephensons went well beyond any taken by the local police.

Initially it appeared that the criminal justice system in Maury County operated at cross purposes. As noted in Chapter 2, Julius Blair and James Morton frequently went to the rescue of men who were seized by "fee grabbers" and either fined or "put . . . on the County Road."[10] At the same time, Blair and Morton, along with several other black citizens, wrote an open letter to the newspaper asking the circuit court judge "to give the colored people more severe penalties, than they had been given in the past."[11] This apparent paradox emanated from a criminal justice apparatus that snared poor, working class blacks while treating black-on-black crime very lightly, especially if the accused African American had the sanction of an influential white person.[12]

In short, the police operated as the frontline guardians of an arbitrary criminal justice system and a social order that controlled black Americans in their relations with whites but that offered blacks little protection from whites or from one another.[13] These conditions especially ensued in Columbia in the case of working-class blacks, and they prompted African American leaders like the Blairs both to assist and to discipline their customers. Julius Blair described the dual nature of law officers who ensnared without safeguarding as he explained at his trial in regard to the Columbia police: "I don't know of anything they could have against me, only one thing, they think I takes up too much time protecting those unfortunates. They don't do as much as they could by them having some protection."[14]

If the relationship of the Columbia police and African American workers turned openly on the issue of control, the officers' orientation toward black leaders appeared more protective and cordial, at least on the surface. When the State Guard departed, Police Chief Griffin took it upon himself to notify personally all the business owners on East Eighth Street so that they could go into the area and take care of their possessions, and he gave testimony at the Lawrenceburg trial that was very favorable to Julius and Saul Blair and to James Morton, saying that he had known them for many years and that they were men of "peace and quietude." When pressed by defense attorney Maurice Weaver, policeman Will Wilsford agreed with this positive assessment, although he noted that Saul Blair had been arrested for allowing or operating a "dice game or something [in his barbershop]."[15]

In turn, Julius Blair commented that his relations with Wilsford had always been "nice" and that he "only had sympathy" and was "sorry that he got shot." Likewise, Meade Johnson, the father of the slain Digger Johnson and owner of a restaurant and pool room on East Eighth Street, regarded Wilsford as "a friend of mine," adding "He always treated me all right."[16]

The mutual respect that the leading proprietors of East Eighth Street and Columbia police officers Griffin and Wilsford accorded each other stemmed from many years of acquaintance on a basis that did not involve dominance by the whites and subordinance by the blacks. The 66-year-old Wilsford had known the 76-year-old Julius Blair forty or fifty years, while the 70-year-old Griffin had been acquainted with the senior Blair "thirty-five years or longer." In both instances, the associations stretched back to the days of Blair's barbershop on the town square. Griffin, who said he had known Blair's 55-year-old son Saul "about as long as I have Julius," was acquainted with him through his father. He had also known the 36-year-old James Morton twenty-five or thirty years, since he was a boy working with his mother in the family funeral operation. Morton's mother, who operated the business after her husband's death, had been a friend and contemporary of Julius Blair.[17]

The cordiality of these men with one another masked two important points, however. First, despite the favorable impressions of Morton and the Blairs held by the elderly Griffin and Wilsford, the white police officers actually had little conception of organizations and institutions within the black community, of the ways in which these had evolved through time, or of the roles that leaders played within them. Second, as segregation crystallized and then ossified, some of the younger law officers grew openly derisive toward blacks, while middle-class leaders like Julius Blair became increasingly contemptuous of younger policemen.

The police and the more affluent blacks in Columbia were divided, as they were throughout the South, by class as well as race. Like virtually all southern policemen, the Columbia police worked long hours for low pay. Bernard Stofel recalled that when he joined the force in 1946, he worked twelve hours a day, seven days a week. The standard pattern was two weeks of night shifts, followed by two weeks of day shifts, with no time off in between. An annual two-week vacation constituted the sole days off during the year. The pay of $150 per month represented a step up for white unskilled workers, but the job of policeman was not one to which middle-class white southerners aspired.[18]

Prior to joining the police force, Stofel worked occasionally in the livestock business, probably with his father James Wesley Stofel, who ran a

The four police officers who were fired upon as they attempted to enter the Bottom the night of February 25 (left to right): Columbia Police Chief J. Walter Griffin, and officers Bernard O. Stofel, Will Wilsford, and Sam Richardson. The 66-year-old Wilsford was the most seriously injured of the four. (Courtesy of Bernard O. Stofel)

livestock market with another Columbian. Stofel had also hauled tobacco from the farm of Judge Armstrong, "the place where the Gordons was raised." William Gordon had in fact helped him load tobacco "off and on before I started policing." Similarly, Will Wilsford had been in charge of keeping the Columbia streets in good repair before he became a police-man, while Sam Richardson had apparently disposed of junk or scrap items for private citizens.[19]

Because policing represented an advance for white unskilled laborers, few left the job once they acquired it, and their average age tended to be high. Griffin at 70 and Wilsford at 66 illustrated this phenomenon.

Not surprisingly, southern policemen tended to have "little general edu-cation or special police schooling."[20] Stofel did not receive any profes-sional training until he attended the FBI Academy in Washington for three months in 1951, although in his view his military service in World War II stood him in good stead, since he "had all kind of training on the firing range with pistols and rifles."[21] Still, despite their limited credentials, the

Columbia police did not misinterpret the events which unfolded on the 25th. On the contrary, they proved much less likely than officials at the district and state level to leap to exaggerated conclusions about a planned insurrection by blacks. As Stofel recently explained: "I've thought about it lots, and I just don't believe that those people come in down there and armed theirself . . . to whip all the whites. That's just out of the question. I think they thought it was going to be another lynching. That's my honest opinion, because you know you couldn't take no 200 people, or 250 say, with shotguns and rifles and think they could whip Columbia. They're too smart for that."[22]

However, the low socioeconomic position of the police did mean that in addition to overcoming an enormous racial divide in working with African Americans generally, they had to surmount a class difference in relating to black leaders. Failures on both counts surfaced when Will Wilsford was questioned at the Lawrenceburg trial about Morton's contributions to the community during the war. When Attorney Weaver asked "You know he is an active leader in Red Cross drives?" the elderly policeman, who had lived within a block of the Bottom for almost thirty years, could only respond: "I know he is an active leader in the undertaking business." Weaver then pressed the matter, inquiring if the officer knew of Morton's involvement in bond sales during the war. To this query, the hapless policeman replied, "No, sir, I don't know how many bonds he has got."[23]

Thus, despite their insistence that they knew African American leaders, even elderly police officers Griffin and Wilsford were unaware of the ways in which long-term changes within the black community had toughened and emboldened the proprietors of East Eighth Street. They also had little understanding of the sense of personal efficacy and entitlement that black businessmen, as well as their customers, had gained during the war. To the aged Griffin and Wilsford, these changes were not simply unknown, they were unfathomable, and it was for this reason that they led the foray into the Bottom, "antigoggling" into a darkened East Eighth Street, guns in their pockets, calling as they advanced, "Boys, we just want to come down to talk to you."[24]

As segregation solidified after the turn of the century, the same negative processes that restricted the Blair brothers to the Bottom, and that made R. S. Hopkins Jr. angry and ashamed of his father's continued friendship with Julius Blair, affected local officers and their relations with the leading proprietors of East Eighth Street. Not surprisingly, older policemen, as well as younger ones, lost touch with a younger generation of black business-men. On the witness stand in Lawrenceburg, the elderly Will Wilsford admitted, that while he knew Meade Johnson, "several of those others that have grown up, I don't know them."[25] A decline in civilities was also made manifest in police terminology before the Lawrenceburg court. While the oldest member of the force used the archaic "darkeys" throughout his testimony, the youngest officer resorted consistently to the more pejorative "niggers."

In turn, men like the senior Blair grew increasingly contemptuous of younger policemen with whom they were not well acquainted and who were less affluent than themselves. This situation was exacerbated in many communities during the war as new officers were rapidly added to police ranks, either as replacements for those who entered the military or because the exigencies of war demanded an expansion of the force. In Columbia, four men were added to the police force between 1942 and 1946: Sam Richardson in 1942, T. I. Collins in 1944, and George Reeves and Bernard Stofel early in 1946. All were new to the force, with the exception of Stofel, who had been a policeman briefly in 1943 before he entered the Army. While these men could have been replacements, they may have represented a wartime expansion, possibly hastened by the nearby location of Camp Forrest. Regardless, they were officers with whom longtime black leaders like Julius Blair were not well acquainted.

Blair, the indomitable patriarch, made his feelings about two of the younger policemen quite evident at his trial. He maintained erroneously that Stofel, whom he had known "just since this thing come up," was added to the force after he had his picture taken "peeping around a wall with a gun in his hand down there on the corner, of Eighth Street." This reference to a photograph that was taken the night of the 25th and that made those in it look exceptionally silly, indicated quite clearly Blair's estimation of the 26-year-old officer. Additionally, when asked if he knew Sam Richardson, Blair derisively dismissed him with the comment, "Quite a while. He drove a dump cart around for a number of years."[26]

Obviously, the financial and social distance that separated successful black entrepreneurs and the local police, coupled with police harassment of poor African Americans and the leniency with which the criminal justice system dealt with black-on-black offenders, fostered a sense of contempt among many members of the black bourgeoisie toward white policemen. This sentiment grew increasingly palpable as black proprietors like Julius Blair were forced to withdraw from competition with whites and to situate themselves in an all-black world. It not only explains the orientation of older residents like Blair toward younger, newly appointed officers, but also it undoubtedly contributes to the findings of recent polls that higher-status blacks hold more contrary attitudes toward the police than do higher-status whites.[27] Similarly, it yields insights into the ready emergence of cross-class coalitions in the African American community in the face of police abuse.[28]

Still, whether civility or disparagement characterized relations between the police and East Eighth Street entrepreneurs, the basic orientation of law officers toward black leaders had not changed. When four of Columbia's policemen rode into the Bottom and encountered armed business owners instructing *them* to keep white people out, they were incensed. There were ways that black people, including leaders, were supposed to conduct themselves around whites, and that deportment extended even to speech. Sam Richardson was angered because Julius Blair and James Morton "Didn't talk right." How did they talk? "Like they were mad," he fumed, and that was "the biggest thing" in the way they showed "disrespect." Stofel put the issue more forthrightly, as he explained that the problem with the Blairs and Morton lay in the way they were "talking, expressing themselves." "Can you describe that a little more carefully for us?" Attorney Ransom asked. "They were using a loud tone and the way a 'nigger[']' wouldn't be talking to a white man," the officer exploded.[29]

Following the Lawrenceburg trial, the size of the Columbia police force increased rapidly, and police monitoring of the Bottom and maltreatment of owners and customers alike accelerated. Nothing demonstrated more clearly the control function of the police than their behavior when they sensed, as a result of the "not guilty" verdict at the trial, that they were losing control and that changes in relations between blacks and whites were imminent.

As the trial of William Pillow and Lloyd Kennedy drew near, the defense sought a change of venue, averring that "the police of the City of Columbia have, particularly for the past several weeks, oppressively policed the Mink Slide section." Saul Blair confirmed that "the City Police" had been "arresting and abusing Negro citizens for little or no reason at all," though as usual, it was his father who articulated the situation with force and barely suppressed rage. "The police would come down, five or six at a time and arrest a man, either beat him up or curse him, and say, 'We, are going to kill all you dam [sic] Negroes,'" he fumed at the venue hearing, and he continued:

> I sat out there in my place Saturday Night in front and seen the policemen, people walking as good as I ever walked in my life, one fellow came out with four bottles of beer and they arrested him and put him in jail. They arrested five or six people down there that it wasn't necessary and

they had no protection, didn't have any business being arrested. They were walking as straight as anybody else, and they didn't have any business arresting a man unless he was boisterous or down or something. I saw that part, I know that. They don't have to do anything but walk along and they think he has been drunk before and think he is drunk all the time and arrest him and carry him to jail.

"Have you seen that, Julius, yourself?" District Attorney Paul Bumpus asked in response to Blair's reference to the police beating black prisoners. "No, sir," the Bottom's patriarch replied, though he added instructively, "I have seen the knots they brought back." Ultimately the situation grew so deplorable that Blair asked the mayor for a conference with the police chief and the city manager. "I thought it best if we could get it checked," he explained, "better for both races."[30]

In comparison to the town police, Sheriff Underwood was on much better terms with black workers. He not only knew East Eighth Street proprietors well but also had a good working relationship with them. Time and again, Underwood's more positive interaction with members of the working class surfaced. He had known Gladys Stephenson's father "well" and "thought the world of him." He also knew her mother and he "had a sympathy for her, because of that fact."[31] No one asked James Stephenson if he were hurt after his fight with Fleming or what happened—until he arrived at the county jail and Underwood inquired. Even more important, the sheriff accepted without hesitation the Stephensons' version of events on the square that morning.

Although Underwood had discovered no panacea in his relations with less affluent African Americans at the time of the Columbia confrontation, his interaction with other black workers was similar to that which he displayed with the Stephensons.[32] Likewise, the sheriff demonstrated a close working relationship with black leaders, especially Julius Blair. Though Saul Blair labeled it "a rare thing" for the sheriff or police officers to drive into the Bottom and "call me and ask questions and tell what to do," Underwood noted on the witness stand in Lawrenceburg that he "advised with him [Julius Blair] very often." Indeed, he went to East Eighth Street in the middle of the afternoon on the 25th when the elder Blair called him to confer about the Stephensons, and he confirmed in that meeting with the Blairs and James Morton that a crowd was gathering uptown. At 5:00, he released the Stephensons to the Blairs and Morton for safekeeping, and he subsequently confronted with a machine gun a white mob that appeared at the jail, actions that contrasted sharply with those of previous law officers in Maury County.[33]

Black leaders in turn seemed to like Underwood and to feel that he could be trusted. On the evening of the 25th when the sheriff and his chief deputy drove into the Bottom, Calvin Lockridge gave the county's chief law officer protection from the man who was threatening to shoot him on the spot. Morton suggested that newspaper reporter J. A. Kincaid bring the sheriff with him to the Bottom when Kincaid expressed reluctance to interview the funeral director at his home following the shooting of the police, and it was Underwood that Julius Blair called the first time he was arrested.

Underwood's intimate knowledge of the leading proprietors of East Eighth Street and his concern for them manifested themselves in a number of ways. James Morton he termed "very public spirited," and in contrast to police officer Will Wilsford, who knew nothing about Morton's community activities, Underwood indicated that whenever there was a drive for the Community Chest, Red Cross, or Victory Bonds, "almost invariably [Morton] helped."[34] The sheriff regretted that he had not been present when the Highway Patrol entered Morton's residence, and he reassured the undertaker while he was in jail that his family was safe. On the morning following the Patrol raid, Mary Morton appeared at the jail and procured from Underwood written permits to operate the family's funeral parlor.[35] That evening, when Julius Blair was placed in jail, Underwood moved the Blairs and Morton at their request to a better, less crowded location within the facility. He chose the women's cells, which were at that time unoccupied, and he brought them mattresses.

At the Lawrenceburg trial, Underwood vouched for Calvin and Raymond Lockridge, declaring "I have never known them to be in any trouble before in their lives," and he went out of his way to give a realistic assessment of the Blairs and Morton at the federal grand jury hearing, when Attorney Denning tried to smear them as "the trouble makers of the race." The sheriff's response to this derogatory label was revealing not only because he contradicted it, but also because his testimony demonstrated that Underwood knew and could evaluate these businessmen as individuals, warts and all:

Julius Blair has always had the respect of a great many white people. He goes a great many bonds, he and Saul and James Morton, far more than they should be permited [sic] to. . . . Julius Blair is a man, that if he agrees to pay you a thousand dollars or a hundred dollars, he will pay it. He has been considered honest and honorable. He doesn't in any way fool with whiskey. I don't think he ever drank any. He has gambled, been a big gambler, but I think he has now quit that, although his son, Saul, has picked it up and is carrying along as big as he can. Morton, I don't think is a drinker. I have never known him to be drunk, although the officers brought out a quantity of whiskey and wine from his home on that early morning search. I never knew him to be drunk, I never knew him to drink much, and he also will pay his debts. That is the type of negroes [*sic*] they are.

When asked by Denning if the Blairs and Morton owned property, Underwood continued his efforts to underscore the positive qualities of the trio by contrasting them with stereotypical images held by many whites of blacks as he replied: "Yes, sir. Get me now, these are not negroes who would bludgeon you in the dark and take your money. They are not negroes that would take an undue advantage of you to rob you. I don't mean that they would do that at all. I think they are honest. I think what they have got, they got it either by gambling or careful trading, or in most ways that would be considered legal."[36]

The nature of Underwood's relationship with the proprietors of East Eighth Street, as well as with their customers, was most succinctly revealed in the terminology he used to describe the area. Whatever the origins of the term "Mink Slide," used as a designation for the first block of East Eighth, in the 1940s, as now, African Americans who frequented the vicinity viewed the name as a derogatory, white appellation.[37] James Morton made that very clear to the FBI as he explained "I realize that the negro business district is referred to as Mink Slide but I prefer to call it 8th street." Similarly, when Julius Blair was asked by Attorney Bumpus if he operated a place of business "in this area referred to as Mink Slide," the elder Blair responded, "Down on Eighth Street, yes."[38] Other black Maury Countians used the term almost generic to many black communities, "the Bottom." In contrast, whites invariably opted for Mink Slide with one exception: to Sheriff Underwood, it was "the 'Bottom' or 8th Street." "You refer to that as Mink Slide too?" Attorney Denning asked the sheriff at the grand jury hearing. "Yes, sir," Underwood responded, but in fact as long as he was sheriff, he never did.[39]

The more positive relationship between Underwood and local leaders derived in part from their backgrounds and patterns of interaction over time. Although the 59-year-old sheriff had lived in Columbia "practically all the time" from 1900 forward, he had spent his early years on a farm about five miles outside the county seat. When he was 17, his father died, and the young man inherited 250 acres of land, which he expanded during his own

Sheriff James J. Underwood Sr. (far left) after the Highway Patrol raid and the roundup of suspects and weapons from African American homes in Columbia on February 26. Highway Patrolman E. B. Noles is to the right of Underwood; Constable Homer Copeland is at far right. (Courtesy of United States Attorney's Office, Middle District of Tennessee)

lifetime to over 550 acres. A cattle raiser, Underwood operated a butcher shop in Columbia for several years and also had a postal route for about a decade.

While the sheriff's farm was only slightly larger than that of John Fleming Sr., it was not located in the hardscrabble zone of eastern Maury County. Neither was it northwest of town in the vicinity where the lynchings of Gilbert Dowell and Henry Choate originated, nor among the vast landholdings southwest of Columbia on the Mt. Pleasant Highway. Instead, it was situated in a somewhat more modest but nevertheless verdant vicinity northeast of town, between Columbia and Spring Hill. Underwood thus escaped the areas of the county with lynching traditions, but at the same time, he was not part of an elite that was suffused with an insurmountable paternalism. In class terms, then, he was positioned to achieve reciprocity with black leaders, given the appropriate circumstances.

Prior to his election as sheriff in 1942, Underwood served as deputy sheriff from 1936–40 under the man who later became his chief deputy, J. Claude Goad. Since it was Goad who warned Saul Blair that he should get James Stephenson out of town (see Chapter 1), it appeared that Underwood and the deputy shared similar perspectives on black leaders and the desirability of including them in efforts to defuse potential lynching threats. Thus Underwood, who was 49 when he became a deputy sheriff and 55 at the time he was elected sheriff, came to law enforcement relatively late in life, and he had no experience with the Claude Godwin regime. Instead, he gained his exposure to policing under a man whose views probably reinforced his own.[40]

Underwood's negative views of lynching were shaped early and remained with him throughout his life. As a boy, he heard from his father about how he and a group of others had saved the life of a white man who was about to be lynched in Arkansas. Underwood never forgot that account. As an adult, he picked up his two sons from a movie theater in downtown Columbia one day, told them that what they were about to see was not going to be pleasant, nor did he want it to happen, but that it would teach them a lesson. He then took them to a lynching at the courthouse, probably that of Henry Choate in 1927. Calvin Lockridge also maintained that Underwood had "carried me up some secret steps in the court house and showed me where he had carried a boy once to keep the mob from him." Clearly, his father's role in thwarting a mob was on Underwood's mind as whites milled around the Columbia square on the 25th, because he relayed the story to the Blairs and Morton when he paid his first visit to the Bottom to discuss with them getting the Stephensons out of jail.[41]

The sheriff's association with those who played leadership roles on the 25th also began early in his life, and they stemmed from both his country and his town experiences. One black man, who was possibly the father of Calvin and Raymond Lockridge, made enough money farming on Underwood's land to buy the adjacent farm.[42] Occasionally, Underwood signed notes for his neighbor and loaned him money. In turn, the sheriff asserted to the grand jury that the farmer's son "has been carrying the keys to everything I have got out there for 14 years." At the Lawrenceburg trial, Underwood noted that he had known both Calvin and Raymond Lockridge "all their lives," and though they were considerably younger than the sheriff, as

Raymond remembered the situation, he and his brother and the sheriff "grew up together."[43]

Twenty-three years older than James Morton, Underwood had also known the funeral director "ever since he was a boy," while his relationship with Julius Blair was equally long, and in some ways more reciprocal than the one he had with the younger Morton and the Lockridges. At the outset of their affiliation, Blair was the authority figure: he cut Underwood's hair when the sheriff was a youngster. Later, after he left the square, the former barber and his older son Saul were steady customers at Underwood's meat market.[44] Thus, the geographic location of Underwood's birthplace and subsequent home within Maury County, his socioeconomic position, the reinforcement that he received as a deputy sheriff, the antilynching traditions within his own family, and his patterns of interaction with black Maury Countians, especially Julius Blair, were important in predisposing him toward working with African Americans when he became a law officer. Still, his overall orientation might have remained largely paternalistic, despite his more egalitarian association with the senior Blair, had it not been for an additional factor: politics.

Although blacks in rural Maury County, as in most of the agrarian South, remained largely disfranchised, many in Columbia were voting in the 1940s. Exactly when an organized black vote emerged is unclear. Some middle-class blacks in the county seat may never have lost the franchise, since the suffrage restrictions enacted in 1889–90 focused primarily on rural African Americans in Western and Middle Tennessee and hit especially hard at those who were illiterate, mobile, and poor.[45]

Other black Columbians may have resumed participation at the ballot box in the 1920s, a decade when significant black political activism occurred in Chattanooga and Memphis. Raymond Lockridge recalled recently that black Columbians were voting in the twenties, while "a growing tendency in the state Democratic party to acquiesce in reenfranchisement" occurred in North Carolina during the same period.[46] Historian Lester Lamon concluded on the basis of his analysis of Tennessee politics during the 1920s that "racial solidarity" could be maintained at the polls "in spite of caste restrictions and white hostility" "when strong leadership emerged."[47]

In Columbia, Julius, Saul, and Charlie Blair, along with James Morton, were providing that leadership in the 1940s, and African Americans there usually voted as a bloc. In close elections, they potentially held the balance of power. While this condition may have contributed indirectly to the relatively benign attitude of the town police prior to the Lawrenceburg trial, it was critical to Underwood, who looked to black Columbians for the margin that he needed for victory.[48] Primary contests like the one the sheriff had just lost to Flo Fleming by a mere twelve votes demonstrated the extraordinary closeness of some elections and the importance of every ballot.

Although black votes had not provided the margin that Underwood needed in the recent campaign, they had unquestionably gone to him. Mayor Eldridge Denham doubted that Fleming "received ten votes from the negro element in Maury County." Several factors explained the lack of enthusiasm for Fleming. First, the Fleming family hailed from Culleoka in eastern Maury County, the home of " 'tough' country stock" and scene of Cordie Cheek's lynching. Not surprisingly, "most of the negroes in Columbia did not have too good a feeling toward the white element of the Culleoka Section," the mayor explained to the FBI.[49]

The Flemings were also tied closely to former sheriff Claude Godwin, the sheriff at the time of the Cheek murder. John Fleming Sr., Flo's father, had served as a deputy under Godwin, and Flo recalls with considerable pride to this day the gold badge that Godwin gave him when he was elected sheriff. As a law officer, the senior Fleming had the reputation "of being tough on negroes," and according to black Columbian Albert Wright, he "was regarded by the colored population of Columbia as a poor one." Fleming's brother, Eugene, had also been a deputy. "Gene" had been killed while an officer by an African American allegedly involved in the illegal liquor trade. Gene's murderer was later found dead "in a house in the hills." John Fleming Sr. insisted that he had frozen to death; rumor had it that he had two bullet holes in his body.[50]

In contrast to Fleming, Underwood "was well liked by the negro element in the Columbia area." Black pastors worked to solidify the vote for him, and their ranks included carpenter-minister Calvin Lockridge. "When he was elected sheriff [in his earlier, successful bid for office]," Lockridge told grand jurors, "I had a part in it."[51] Similarly, Underwood himself acknowledged that Julius Blair had supported him "in every campaign I have ever been in."[52] On the afternoon of the 25th, during Underwood's initial visit to the Bottom, he and the Blairs were "talking politics." According to Police Chief Griffin, "the negroes had been boasting that they could throw a good block of votes for a good strong independent candidate." Whether or not such "boasting" had occurred, the Blairs were discussing with Underwood on that fateful afternoon the possibility of having the sheriff or perhaps his son run on an independent ticket against Flo Fleming in the general election in August.[53]

Not everyone approved of the working political relationship that Underwood had with the Bottom's brokers. In the wake of the police shootings, a deputy sheriff and a magistrate decided that Underwood had caused the entire problem. As they viewed the situation, the sheriff "couldn't go in Mink Slide and make an arrest, because he would go down there and buddy with them."[54] *Tennessean* reporter Beasley Thompson theorized on the basis of his own investigation that Underwood was "trying to make political capital" out of the situation, and his views were echoed recently by Flo Fleming partisans. Fleming himself believes that the sheriff and some of his allies stirred up blacks in the Bottom in an attempt to beat him in the summer election. Columbia policeman Bernard Stofel concurs in this assessment, although he thinks African Americans themselves were "in earnest if they'd been told what I was told they was told"—that is, that a white mob was going to lynch the Stephensons. Like Stofel, Fleming's older brother John refers obliquely to "some political things in there too" when he describes black actions on the night of the 25th.[55]

No evidence exists that the situation festered in the Bottom because Underwood's relations with black Columbians prevented him from doing his job, nor is there any sign that he warned black leaders of a white mob for political reasons. The alacrity with which these notions materialized and the tenacity with which they have been held, however, underscore both the centrality of politics in southern communities and the refusal of whites to believe that black Americans can seize the initiative. Instead, most attribute black action to white manipulators, either in the form of local politicians like Underwood or outside agitators who are allegedly linked in a conspiracy, a theory that found fertile soil in Maury County. Additionally, the firm, tenacious conviction regarding Underwood's alleged partisan motives indicated that any white politician who attempted to work with African Americans, even a long-time resident like Underwood, was subject to ready suspicion by other whites, including close coworkers.

The most important point, however, lies less in what Underwood's rivals believed happened than in what actually occurred: In the interest of getting elected, a white law officer worked with African American leaders, and his association with them led him to surrender to them for safekeeping a black man who was in danger of being lynched. By no means was Underwood the first sheriff to offer protection to a would-be lynch victim. As noted at the outset of Chapter 4, southern sheriffs increasingly stepped forward in the 1930s as Jesse Daniel Ames and the Association of Southern Women for the Prevention of Lynching targeted them in their vigorous campaign. Columbia was distinctive not because Sheriff Underwood helped prevent a lynching, but because of the *source* of the pressure on him and the *manner* in which he carried out his duties. *Blacks, not whites, were central in his calculations.* This condition existed because of the direction politics had taken in the community.

Unfortunately for African Americans in Columbia, they constituted such a small minority of voters that their political influence remained minimal unless whites divided sharply. Moreover, in a tight race one of the white candidates had to be sympathetic to their concerns and willing to work with them, a condition that did not always prevail. To make matters even bleaker, voting did not translate into better jobs and economic circumstances for most black workers, and the location of black Columbians within the larger context of state and region severely limited the protection that they were afforded during crises like the one that occurred in 1946.

Nevertheless, politics, like union membership, mattered. Holding the balance of power brought a measure of personal safety to black Columbians that their disfranchised brethren in other parts of the South, including the Maury County countryside, did not have. Once he was in office, even Flo Fleming attempted to work with Julius and Saul Blair, at least on routine policing matters, as he labored "day and night" to solve a couple of robberies at their business establishments.[56]

As reform-minded individuals and organizations were noting with increasing frequency in the 1940s, voting and personal security were inextricably linked. "There is a direct correlation between Negroes voting in appreciable numbers and in improved treatment by police and in the courts," an Atlanta survey proclaimed. Similarly, Will Maslow of the American Jewish Congress declared before President Truman's Committee on Civil Rights, "Nothing is as basic to the Negro's security in the United States as the right to vote." As part of his advocacy of "self-help" rather than "federal dependency" for African Americans, Howard Law School dean Charles Houston also stated unequivocally to the President's Committee that if he "had to make a choice," he would "prefer enforcement of suffrage over the mere matter of protection against mob violence." The war was important in this equation, because it propelled black Americans from the rural South into towns and cities where voter registration was more feasible, and because it resulted in the expansion of organizations concerned with this issue.[57]

Without question, Underwood's support of black Maury Countians was tenuous at best. A white man steeped in the ideology of the Lost Cause, the sheriff himself was susceptible to pressure from other middle-class whites (see Chapter 6). Too, as a local official, he found his authority quickly usurped by Chief Bomar and the Highway Patrol. Ultimately, as he was buffeted by conservative forces, the sheriff was perceived by both blacks and their liberal white allies as "weak" and "hemmed in." Nevertheless, Underwood's political affiliation with African Americans in Maury County demonstrated the *potential* of such an alliance, as well as the inveterate association between politics and policing.

LAW, ORDER, AND DISORDER: STATE FORCES

Confronted with a spate of mob murders and a race riot in the World War I era, black Tennesseans held numerous public meetings in support of a "State Police" or "Constabulary" bill introduced into the legislature in 1919. The newly formed Nashville branch of the NAACP worked especially hard for the bill's passage, delivering a petition to the state assembly "in the name of righteousness, justice and fair play . . . and in the name of the soldiers who bled and died to make the world a better place to live."[58]

In view of the high hopes that black Tennesseans held for a state police force, it was ironic that Sheriff Underwood proved most helpful to black Maury Countians in 1946, while the Highway Patrol inflicted the most damage. It was particularly in relation to the State Guard, however, that differences *between* state forces were the most striking.

The different approaches of the State Guard and the Highway Patrol stemmed from the origins and reputations of the law enforcement units themselves, and hence from the men that they attracted. They also derived from the dissimilar orientations of their leaders, but, above all, the latitude given state troopers resulted from the politicized nature of the force and the state officials who guided it.

THE STATE GUARD

The emergency of war produced the State Guard. Under an act passed in January 1941, Governor Prentice Cooper created "a volunteer defense unit" to be activated whenever any portion of the National Guard was called into federal service. Composed initially of the First, Second, and Third Regiments, stationed respectively in West, Middle, and East Tennessee, the State Guard was restructured in 1942 into three brigades. The largest of these units, the Second Brigade, was headquartered at Nashville and commanded by Jacob McGavock Dickinson Jr. Dickinson also served as brigadier general of the entire Guard. The Second Brigade, which he personally commanded, consisted of three regiments: the Second, headquartered at Nashville; the Seventh, at Cookeville; and the Tenth, at Pulaski. Colonel Victor H. Wilson headed the Second Regiment. The entire Second Brigade, supplemented by a detachment from the Third Brigade, served in Columbia.[59]

Although anyone between the ages of 16 (with parental permission) and 65 could volunteer for service in the Guard, the absence of adult males during the war meant that many of the enlistees were teenagers. Their youth in turn strengthened the role of their commanders in shaping their conduct. "We could not afford to leave them without officers," Dickinson commented to grand jurors.[60]

The commanders, like the enlisted men, were civilians who participated in the force on a voluntary basis. Most lived in Nashville or other towns in Middle Tennessee, and they worked in professional or white-collar positions.[61] In contrast to National Guardsmen, few received any financial remuneration while on active duty or maneuvers, and they regarded themselves first and foremost as private citizens and not as soldiers or law enforcers. As Walter W. Hogan, an employee of the Methodist Publishing Company in Nashville, explained: "On Thursday nights I am a company commander in the State Guard but on Sunday nights I am just an ordinary citizen of Tennessee."[62]

The part-time nature of Guard participation did not mean that Guardsmen were ill prepared to meet the kind of emergency they encountered in Columbia, at least not the men who served in Dickinson's Second Brigade. The great-nephew of a lieutenant colonel in the Confederate Army and the son of President William Howard Taft's secretary of war, Dickinson possessed a strong yen for the military. Upon graduating from Yale Law School, he had planned to pursue a military career, until his eyes were damaged by gas while he was serving with his National Guard unit in the First World War. Unable to follow his dream, he nevertheless retained a keen interest in military affairs all his life.[63]

At the behest of the governor, Dickinson organized the initial units of the Second Regiment of the Tennessee State Guard in the summer of 1941, and he enthusiastically directed the organization of the Seventh and Tenth Regiments, which joined with his original Second, to form the Second Brigade. As brigadier general, he toured the eastern United States in the summer of 1945 on behalf of the adjutant general to study training methods and programs applicable to the State Guard. A man who "had a horror of anything getting out of hand," the Guard commander also had a lifelong interest in riot control, which may have stemmed from his living in Chicago at the time of the race riot there in 1919.[64]

In staff meetings and in drills with officers, Dickinson had "presupposed almost the identical problem that took place in Columbia" the year before it occurred. Under Dickinson's Plan B, "Riot and Rebellion," Guardsmen were "to isolate the troublemakers" and arrest those "*of either side and*

Three young members of the State Guard in Columbia on the night of February 25. (Courtesy of United States Attorney's Office, Middle District of Tennessee)

State Guard Commander Jacob McGavock Dickinson Jr. (facing camera) gives instructions at the command headquarters that he established at the Columbia City Hall on the night of February 25. (Courtesy of United States Attorney's Office, Middle District of Tennessee)

prevent any race riots." "The whole theory," Dickinson explained to grand jurors, "is based on a show of force." Because his men were part-time soldiers who could not be expected to develop "a high degree of personal efficiency," they were to demonstrate so much strength that the disorderly would back down, and there would be no need for "active force." If active force were needed, Guardsmen would use chemicals, followed by bayonets, and as a last resort, fire power. Chemicals in their arsenal included smoke, tear gas, and "sickening gas," none of which were lethal.[65]

As educated, middle-class citizens who were equipped with a clear plan of action that demanded evenhanded treatment of all "trouble-makers" and that included the use of firepower only as a last resort, the officers of Dickinson's Second Brigade were inclined away from independent initiatives and personal rowdiness and toward collective, impartial measures, regardless of their individual racial attitudes. From the detailed journal, the field orders, and the active duty reports that the brigadier general required from the time the Guard entered Columbia until it departed almost a week later, it was obvious that Dickinson ran the Second Brigade like a well-oiled machine. Some improper conduct occurred, but the performance of the Guard generally stood in marked contrast to that of many state troopers.[66]

THE HIGHWAY PATROL

Although the Highway Patrol prevented armed whites from entering the Bottom on the evening of the 25th, and they killed no one during the course of their morning raid on the 26th, a number engaged in actions that were less than impartial and restrained: raking East Eighth Street establishments with machine-gun fire, wrecking them through avid searches and acts of wanton destruction, stealing, cursing and striking suspects as they took them into custody or placed them in jail. They also blasted Johnson and Gordon to their deaths and beat Napoleon Stewart when Gordon attempted to grab a gun in the sheriff's office. Their history and their leadership inclined state troopers toward a physically tough posture that knew few boundaries where African Americans were concerned.

Formed in 1929 along modified military lines—with captains, lieutenants, sergeants, and troopers—the Highway Patrol in the mid-1940s consisted of what a chronicler of fifty years of Patrol history referred to as " 'gung ho' " individuals who "didn't want to miss anything."[67] Its symbol was a motorcycle, and the ability to ride or to learn quickly constituted a prerequisite for service in the early years, because all patrolmen below the level of district chief roared around on Harley Davidsons.

In part, the rough-and-ready attitude of many patrolmen stemmed from the legacy of a short-lived state police force. In 1919, the Tennessee legislature had authorized the Constabulary Bill, creating a force of 600, but it was never funded. Instead, a State Police Act established a fifteen-person unit in 1926. Superseded by the Highway Patrol three years later, the State Police were described by the Nashville *Tennessean* as " 'obnoxious, bullying and disgraceful to the state.' " Although patrolmen were reminded upon the completion of their training that they should "go not as Lords, but as servants of the people," several of the earlier state policemen made their way into the Patrol ranks, and the state police chief, Johnny Burgess, became the Patrol's first inspector, the officer second in command to the head of the Highway Patrol.[68]

Although Tennessee authorities did not empower highway patrolmen as

Highway Patrol officers search men from the Lodge Hall shortly after seizing them on the morning of February 26. The man on the far right is Joe Daniel Calloway; Horace Gordon, brother of William Gordon, is the third person from the right. Note the soldier-policeman appearance of the highway patrolmen. (Courtesy of United States Attorney's Office, Middle District of Tennessee)

state policemen, they seemed to envision for them a role like that of the New York state police: "brave Anglo-Saxon soldier-policemen."[69] Clad in white shirts and forest green jackets, caps, and trousers, troopers also wore sets of leather puttees, and they were well armed. Those who entered the Bottom in 1946 carried semiautomatic weapons that could fire twenty-five shells per round, and some, like Nashville division chief J. J. Jackson, bore fully automatic Riesen machine guns.[70] The Tennessee Highway Patrol, like its counterparts in other states, barred both African Americans and women from service for decades.[71]

The Highway Patrol "look" also embraced large, athletically oriented men, and they in particular rose to leadership positions. Greg O'Rear of

Lawrenceburg, a baseball pitcher and star basketball player on a local factory team, was initially solicited for Patrol duty by Prentice Cooper because O'Rear, at six feet, eight inches tall and weighing 245 pounds, stood "head and shoulders above the crowd outside the courthouse" where Cooper was campaigning for governor in 1938.[72]

From the outset, patrolmen were made to feel special. Chosen from a pool of 3,250 applicants, the initial 55 five were addressed by the governor following a brief training course at a banquet held at a Nashville hotel. Organized into four divisions based geographically across the state, the force remained small into the late 1940s.[73] A sense of comraderie established at the beginning of the troopers' experience endured.[74] This orientation encouraged them to remain silent regarding the actions of their comrades in the Bottom even when they knew infractions had occurred.[75]

Initially empowered to enforce traffic regulations and collect state taxes and revenues, the Tennessee Highway Patrol saw its authority increase significantly in 1939 under Governor Prentice Cooper. A series of laws, the most important of which was the Local Option Liquor Act, resulted in patrolmen serving as general law enforcement officers, especially in rural areas. The enforcement of "the whiskey law" oriented troopers toward "raiding" of illegal liquor stills and "gambling . . . and bootlegging joints." This orientation did not change to "sav[ing] lives on the highway" until the early 1950s, and even then the Patrol maintained a vice or "raiding" unit, and it continued to enter communities during racial crises and labor disputes.[76]

Along with its raiding mission, extremely difficult, hazardous working conditions promoted physical toughness among troopers. Greg O'Rear rode his 80 Harley Davidson over "mostly rock dirt roads" even "if the temperature was down to zero." Frequently when O'Rear was chasing an automobile, the driver of the car, who had a definite advantage over a motorcycle rider, attempted to force him off the highway. Working alone, troopers immediately locked their motorcycles "on the spot" whenever they arrested a drunk driver. They then drove the inebriated person to jail in his own car and hitchhiked back. Given these circumstances, it is not surprising that "early day troopers" were "rough and tumble" men.[77]

World War II added a host of new duties to the Patrol's agenda. They included dealing with a sudden influx of servicemen and assisting with troop movements in Middle Tennessee when the U.S. Second Army began extensive operations there, guarding bridges and other vital installations until civilians could be hired, escorting boats and submarines through the state, enforcing gasoline rationing regulations as well as laws related to prostitution and venereal disease, and quelling racial disturbances.[78] When patrolmen arrived in Columbia, then, they had an enhanced sense of their own importance and authority. Notably troopers from Middle Tennessee's Second Brigade, which provided significant services to the U.S. Army, carried out the raid on the Bottom.

Unfortunately, encounters between state troopers and African American soldiers participating in the Second Army's maneuvers in Tennessee and Arkansas in the summer of 1941 did not bode well for black Maury Countians. Neither did meetings during the following two years between black soldiers and the state police in Louisiana. At both the Middle Tennessee town of Murfreesboro and in the vicinity of Gurdon, Arkansas, black servicemen from the 94th Engineer Battalion met severe treatment at the hands of highway patrolmen. Sergeant Lester Duane Simons recalled that "the Tennessee State Police really worked some of our guys over unmercifully." Specifically, he remembered an incident in which he stood helpless as troopers assaulted his friend and fellow soldier David Hughbanks. "Yes, I stood by and watched," he later explained; "two fists are no match for billy clubs, 45s, and rifles; ask any man who has been there."[79]

In Prescott, Arkansas, state policemen followed trucks of African American servicemen into town and threatened them as they disembarked. This followed an evening in which the 94th Engineers—then on maneuvers in Arkansas, unable to find any recreational opportunities in the town of Gurdon, and harassed by white military police—had marched uproariously down the main street as they departed the community "in a crude and noisy formation liberally spiced with profanity and uncomplimentary remarks about the South." In an even more severe reprisal for the boisterous exit of the 94th from Gurdon, state troopers struck sentries near the battalion's bivouac area the same night as the Prescott affair. Two days later, accompanied by a deputized force of white civilians, the troopers dispersed the demoralized 94th and drove them from the road as the soldiers attempted to march to a new bivouac area farther from Gurdon.[80]

In remarks that presaged the Columbia raid five years later—and that demonstrated quite clearly that Tennessee state troopers were not unique among southern state law officers in their treatment of African Americans— a soldier from the 94th wrote to his sister in the midst of the Arkansas crisis:

We are scared almost to death. Yesterday we went on a 10 mile hike alongside of the highway off the concrete. All of a sudden six truck loads of mobsters came sizzling down the highway in the other direction. *They jumped out with guns and sub-machine guns and [revolvers] drawn, cursing, slapping and saying unheard of things.* Sis it was awful. They took us off the highway into the woods. Daring anyone to say a word, they hit two of our white officers who try to say something back. But the bad part of it all, the military police were among them and against us. The State police passed out ammunition to the civilians. We are now about five miles down in the woods hoping that they don't come down here. No one has pitched a single tent today, nor yesterday, we are afraid to, half of our company has left for Michigan already, hoboing. Few have train fare, others went deeper into the woods. . . . Our officers are nearly all as afraid as we are. They call them "Yankee Nigger lovers," us black "Yankees."

We have guards, guarding a place and the State police deliberately came off the highway, took his gun (rifle) which was empty and beat Yankee Doodle on his head. These people are crazy, stone crazy. Or I am.[81]

In Alexandria, Louisiana, state troopers reinforced the city and military police early in 1942 as they rampaged through a black business district following the arrest of a black soldier and the subsequent stabbing death of a white military policeman. Ten African Americans were killed, and scores were forced to flee the vicinity, with some, as in Arkansas, taking refuge in nearby woods. A year later, a Louisiana state trooper shot and killed a black military policeman who was unarmed and on duty. Although the attorney general described this incident as "a case of apparent murder," the head of the state police refused to take any action, declaring flatly in a telephone conversation with a General Donovan, " 'It was just a nigger killing and we don't intend to do anything about it.' "[82]

Like Flo Fleming, a number of Tennessee troopers had been in service, and their military experience may also have informed their demeanor during the early-morning invasion of East Eighth Street. Forty-two patrolmen were in the armed forces by mid-1943, and the description of black veteran Luther Edwards suggested parallels between the war experience and the East Eighth Street incursion. As Edwards gazed out the window of Daisy Lee's house, he saw "firing all in the back, firing the same as . . . if they was in the army." Similarly, the *Columbia Herald* declared: "To the war veterans, the scene was reminiscent of American troops going through a captured town in Europe."[83]

Finally, the atmosphere created in Columbia by white civilians encouraged severe treatment of black Maury Countians by the Highway Patrol. When troopers arrived on the scene on the evening of the 25th and set up roadblocks at the intersections leading into East Eighth Street, they were heckled by a crowd of about thirty white men for not entering the area immediately. As a patrolman shoved one black man along toward the jail the next morning, the crowd through which they passed was so volatile that *Tennessean* photographer John Malone testified he "thought they were going to have a sure enough mob violence." Even white women and boys egged on troopers as they marched suspects to jail, urging that they strike them more often. In short, a law enforcement agency with a tough legacy, whose members had grown accustomed during the war to greater authority at home and excessive physical force abroad, was placed in a highly combustible situation in which fellow whites urged more, not less, maltreatment of blacks.[84]

The Patrol's leadership would be important in determining its response under these conditions; at the same time, the law enforcement unit would not have faced quite the same set of circumstances had it not been for its immediate supervisors and the higher officials who underwrote their authority. A game plan existed for patrolmen to invade the Bottom and for the subsequent treatment of its inhabitants. Less consciously formulated than Dickinson's Plan B, it was no less historically patterned. Its specific features lay in the crime-stopping methods and personal characteristics of Patrol chief Robert Lynn Bomar Sr.; its direction derived from those who placed him at the helm.

The Local Option Liquor Act of 1939 provided Bomar with an opportunity to make a name for himself in state law enforcement, and from 1942 until 1949, he both reflected and shaped the Tennessee Highway Patrol as its chief. A native of the small town of Bell Buckle in Middle Tennessee's Bedford County, Bomar was formed above all by his experiences as a star athlete. A prep school standout, he played football first at Fitzgerald and Clarke at Tullahoma and then at Castle Heights Military Academy in Lebanon, Tennessee. In 1921, he entered Vanderbilt University at the same time that his coach at Fitzgerald and Clarke, the famed Wallace Wade, became an assistant coach there.

Standing six feet tall, weighing 200 pounds, and "lightning fast," the "Big Blond Bear" played forward on the basketball team and catcher on the baseball nine, but it was at football that he excelled, leading Vanderbilt to two Southern Conference championships and tying for another during the four years he was at the school. Named an all-American on the teams of Grantland Rice and Walter Camp, Bomar "plucked passes out of the ozone that seemed impossible to get, and then raced through the enemy like they were tied." Often he started games at fullback, shifted to halfback or end, and finished at tackle. In backing up the line, "he hurled back all comers with the same savage vigor." His favorite refrain to his opponents? "I-hope-you-don't-like-it." For two years following his highly successful days at Vanderbilt, Bomar played professional football with the New York Giants, but his career ended abruptly in 1926 when he dislocated a knee in a game against Brooklyn. For the rest of his life, Bomar sought the thrill of those Saturday afternoons when he led the charge and pulsated to the roar of the crowd.

After his football career ended, the former star worked for seven years as assistant manager at the Colonial Hotel in Springfield, Tennessee, the home of his new bride. He also attempted to capitalize on his fame by selling life insurance, but "there was no excitement," his son Robert Bomar Jr. recently explained, "in essence no Saturday afternoon cheers."[85] The work of a deputy U.S. marshal seemed to hold promise, and Bomar tried that position from 1934 until he became a division chief with the Highway Patrol in Knoxville in 1939. A year later, he was appointed director of public safety, overseeing the police and fire departments, for the City of Knoxville. When antiadministration forces won office and eliminated the public safety position, Bomar again served for a few months as Highway Patrol division chief. Then late in 1942, he was promoted to chief on a trial basis by Governor Prentice Cooper when the current occupant was ordered to active duty in the U.S. Army Air Corps. In 1945, just months before the Columbia episode, Bomar reached the pinnacle of his success and authority as a law officer when he was made both state commissioner of public safety, a newly established cabinet-level office, and Patrol chief, a dual post that was eliminated in 1949.

As Highway Patrol division chief and then as head of public safety in Knoxville, Bomar honed the style and methods that characterized the Patrol's foray into the Bottom. As division chief, he launched "a series of sweeping seizures within a hundred-mile radius" of Knoxville, personally participating in the confiscation of illegal liquor stores one night near Johnson City and showing up the next day at a gambling house near Chattanooga to cart away people and equipment.[86]

Knoxville, the entertainment center for "a swollen Tennessee Valley payroll" but one of the few large cities in Tennessee in which hard liquor remained illegal, offered Bomar almost limitless opportunities to continue his "active war on outlawry." Desirous of eliminating police graft and with little concern for constitutional niceties, he took out search warrants himself, called together officers from a number of units, and immediately led them on raids. With "gusto for personal participation in vice crusading," the public safety director's "bulky but nimble figure" headed "blue-coat flying squads" that raided "back-street so-called 'hotels' and nuisance beer parlors." Every other day during his first year in office, Bomar averaged at least one, and sometimes as many as twenty-five, such forays. While some, possibly most, of the raids were carried out without any evidence that a law had been broken, Bomar explained with customary bluntness that they were necessary because "more than 85 per cent of crime is planned at the lower type of these hangouts. . . . They are the primary breeding places of crime."[87]

In light of these activities, it is not surprising that the patrol chief arrived, siren wailing, in Columbia only a short time after receiving the governor's call about problems there. The Bottom, as Bomar himself depicted it, with "so many beer joints and barber shops, that is about all there is," no doubt resembled the countless arenas the safety commissioner had previously invaded. Certainly it was not unusual that he participated in the raid on the 26th "right up to my neck," nor that he proceeded into East Eighth Street ahead of the time on which he and Dickinson had earlier agreed. "Committee & consultation dealing with problems did not occur to him," his son explained. In short, as Walter S. Hurt Jr., a member of the *Tennessean* editorial staff, characterized the foray into the Bottom, it was "BOMAR's show," and its precursors lay in other shows he had conducted throughout eastern Tennessee.[88]

Though mixed in his attitudes toward individual blacks, Bomar's orientation toward African Americans as a group became crystal clear as he related . to *whites*. Like the Columbia police and Arkansas troopers who passed out guns to white civilians, the Patrol chief treated whites throughout the entire affair as if he and they were on the same side, with the same common enemy: black Maury Countians.[89] This orientation, coupled with his placement of physical toughness at the heart of law enforcement, his rambunctious style, and the license he permitted his forces, rendered officers free to indulge their individual racial proclivities. Some struck no one; others went on a rampage.

Whether troopers abused black Maury Countians because they were black or because patrolmen saw toughness as an integral part of their job was difficult to discern. Yet whether the primary motive or one of a cluster of factors, racism undoubtedly contributed to the Patrol's excesses. It appeared in the exclamations that troopers hurled at African Americans as they arrested them.[90] It surfaced even more clearly in the contempt and ridicule patrolmen heaped on East Eighth Street's middle class leaders: in the profanity hurled at James and Mary Morton as officers burst into their home, in the cursing and shoving of Julius Blair during his arrest, and in the desire of a trooper to see that "goddam undertaker" as Morton boarded the truck for Nashville. It appeared too in the malicious frivolity with which East Eighth

Highway patrolmen and armed white civilians on South Main Street peering around the corner into the Bottom on the night of February 25. The patrolman in the center of the photograph facing the camera is Flo Fleming. Note the free intermingling of highway patrolmen and armed white civilians. (Courtesy of United States Attorney's Office, Middle District of Tennessee)

Street businesses were destroyed: in the consumption of ice-cream by troopers at Blair's drugstore and the lacing of the remainder with rat poison; in the placement of the outfits of a man and a woman in coffins at Morton's funeral home and the inscription of the letters "KKK" on one of the caskets. Particularly striking was the hilarity with which the funeral parlor was wrecked. Reporters, in fact, rushed to the scene because troopers were "having a big time over there," and the officers emerged from the building "laughing and joking."[91]

Less affluent whites, like working-class blacks, often experienced the heavy hand of law officers, but few middle-class whites encountered it. For patrolmen to destroy a white business district and to treat members of the

Morton's Funeral Parlor in the aftermath of the patrol raid on February 26. (Courtesy of United States Attorney's Office, Middle District of Tennessee)

white middle class as they treated East Eighth Street's proprietors would have been inconceivable. Jim Crow's fusion in the same block of establishments that served the entire African American community—like the funeral parlor, churches, and Lodge Hall—and those that catered to a working-class clientele, such as the pool rooms and cafes, no doubt masked to some extent for troopers the middle-class status of the Bottom's entrepreneurs. But there is simply no getting around the fact that their rude conduct toward members of the black bourgeoisie, and the conscious devastation and theft of their property, signified among patrolmen the denigration of *all* black Maury Countians. As Flo Fleming acknowledged: "Yeah, yeah, it was, quite a bit of damage done in this funeral parlor . . . and in a number of places, a quite a bit of damage done . . . because of relations, because they were black people, that's it."[92]

As Justice Department attorney Eleanor Bontecou recalled, Bomar and

Dickinson "wanted to carry out totally different policies" in Columbia.[93] No one summarized the pair's differences and their import better than Methodist Publishing Company employee and State Guard captain Walter W. Hogan. In a letter to Dickinson drafted during the grand jury hearing, Hogan agonized over the havoc wreaked in the Bottom by state troopers, and he lamented the unequal justice they meted out to blacks and whites. "On that Tuesday morning when all the shooting was over the Mink Slide area was pretty well wrecked," he began, and he continued:

> I would not criticize the Highway Patrol for any plate glass they shot out or anything else they did to get those negroes out of there, and I think they are to be commended for not killing anyone in the process of getting them out. But I feel very strongly on the matter of deliberately wrecking places after the shooting was over. I have no idea what the Federal Grand Jury will do but I have an idea they will do nothing about the Highway Patrol—yet I know they stole cigarettes by the carton out of those stores and I know at least one brick was thrown through an undamaged window because those things I saw.

Hogan wrote Dickinson that at a recent practice session, he had been startled to learn from George Pellettieri, chief of records at the Nashville post office garage and a State Guard major, that shortly after arriving in Columbia, Pellettieri had seen a white man with a rifle shooting at a fleeing Negro. Himself unarmed, Pellettieri recruited another, armed guardsman from a nearby restaurant, and together they pursued and caught the white civilian. Then they handed him over to the Highway Patrol, "and there the story ends," Hogan lamented. He continued: "When negroes fire at white men it is very rightly called assault with intent—yet when a white man fires at a negro with State Guards and State Highway Patrolmen standing around he is not indicted for anything. Frankly that is not the sort of justice I like to think we are trying to uphold and I know it is not the sort of justice you have taught us to uphold."

In his conclusion, Hogan drew very sharply the lines between the commander of the State Guard and the chief of the Highway Patrol, and he showed quite plainly and succinctly the significance of those demarcations:

> Criticism alone is poor stuff. As a remedy for the situation that seems to exist could you not clear up with Chief Bomar some of the more elementary points of justice and fair treatment? I have an idea Lynn Bomar is trying hard on his job and he deserves every encouragement but he lacks so sadly many of the things you have in abundance. Can't you show him

that two wrongs do not make a right and that justice goes right down the middle of the road, and ask him to get it across to his men. Our men followed you and didn't do those things, his men followed him and stole and looted. It[']s as clear as day and while I know you must be sick of the whole thing, won't you try to help him see the differences?[94]

Although Lynn Bomar held considerable power as both safety commissioner and Highway Patrol chief and exercised enormous influence in shaping the Patrol's behavior in Columbia, he did not act in isolation. A highly politicized official who operated under the purview of the governor, the chief of the Highway Patrol, along with his troopers, reflected the sentiments and inclinations of those in power at the state level of government.

Southern highway patrol and state police systems alike were distinguished by the dominant role played by the governor in their direction, and the Tennessee Highway Patrol was very much a part of this pattern. As early as 1932, just three years after the Patrol's inception, so many troopers fell "prey to the temptation to play politics" that almost 40 percent "found their jobs 'gone with the wind'" when a new Democratic faction, dominated by political boss Edward Crump of Memphis, assumed power. Not surprising, when Greg O'Rear joined the force seven years later, "it was strictly a political job," and the only stipulation aside from patronage that E. B. Noles could recite recently was that "They wouldn't employ radicals!"[95]

The extension of civil service status to Patrol members in 1941 made little difference for two reasons. First, with a plethora of Patrol candidates who met the minimum requirements, the governor could easily play politics with the selection process. Flo Fleming recalled that when he wanted to join the patrol following his service in World War II—and three years after the passage of the Civil Service Act—he and his father visited the governor's office. "Governor, I want my boy to have a job on the Highway Patrol," John Fleming Sr. said. "Well, I think we can take care of that," the governor responded, and "so he did," Fleming added. Similarly, E. B. Noles's family, who were friends with their state senator, took E. B. to Nashville, where all visited the governor's office, and the young man was added to the force that very day.[96]

Even more important in diluting the impact of civil service requirements on the orientation of the Highway Patrol, the 1941 act exempted from coverage the safety commissioner as well as his secretary, the Highway Patrol chief, and the four division chiefs. Thus the act did not extend to men at the levels of Lynn Bomar or J. J. Jackson. Long-time secretary in the

Department of Safety, Martha Remslinger O'Rear remembered there being a patronage committee when she went to work in the Safety Department in 1947. She explained, "Back then you had to have some political advantage . . . to be appointed."[97]

As had occurred when he was Knoxville's public safety director, Lynn Bomar lost his job in 1948 when the Crump faction was ousted by an antiorganization coalition that included Gordon Browning as governor. Similarly, E. B. Noles, who was so close to Browning's opponent, two-time governor James McCord, that McCord included the trooper in his will, left the force that same year. Both Greg O'Rear and J. J. Jackson managed to hang on through the Browning years, though Jackson in particular suffered a temporary setback.[98] O'Rear and Jackson then experienced long-term security once the pre-Browning faction reassumed office under Frank Clement four years later, and Clement and Buford Ellington, both members of the same faction, traded the governorship back and forth for almost twenty years.[99] Both Patrol officers understood, however, that partisan activities remained a requirement for keeping their jobs.

Thus as the governor went, so went state troopers, and the governor of Tennessee had little reason to include black concerns in his political calculations in the mid-1940s. Stemming from the late-nineteenth-century passage of suffrage restrictions, many rural blacks were systematically disfranchised, while many nonaffluent whites became too discouraged to continue participation in the political process. Thus, by the 1920s, Tennessee gubernatorial elections, like those in other southern states, were marked by very low voter turnouts and by the prevalence of the propertied at the polls.[100] Rarely did more than a quarter of the potential electorate participate in either the Democratic primary or the general election. Typical of the times, the election of 1946 saw only 22 percent of the state's potential voters choose the governor.[101]

Although, as in Columbia, African Americans sometimes held the balance of power in local races, they did not constitute a cohesive, statewide voting bloc. Most blacks in Shelby County, like the vast majority of whites, voted for candidates backed by political boss Ed Crump. Outside the Memphis area, the majority of blacks probably supported the antiorganization faction, but their ranks were rife with dissension.[102]

There was no statewide association concerned with political action among black Tennesseans. Ironically, the lack of initiative by whites in thwarting the black vote in Tennessee cities may have contributed to this disunity, since obtaining the vote did not constitute a common, unifying concern. Organized labor was also divided, with the CIO leaning more toward the antiorganization faction than the AFL, and the entire urban vote was diminished by a rural-dominated legislature that refused to give growing cities their due.[103]

These characteristics of electoral politics narrowed drastically the range of interests among state officials. None were beholden to African Americans, and most had to weigh the loss of rural votes against potential support from organized industrial workers. The governor of Tennessee in 1946, Jim Nance McCord, reflected these conditions.[104]

A "'self-made man' from a poor family of eleven children," McCord began clerking in a hardware store in 1894 at the age of 15 in Shelbyville, the county seat of Bedford. (Bedford County was also the birthplace of Lynn Bomar.) Two years later, McCord moved to Lewisburg in neighboring Marshall County, just a few miles east of the Maury County line and the Culleoka community. Like Maury, Marshall had been a hotbed of Ku Klux Klan activity during Reconstruction.

In Lewisburg, McCord and an older brother opened a bookstore, which Jim operated while his brother practiced medicine. A few years later McCord hit the road as an itinerant soap and flour salesman. Traveling "here and there over the state" for a decade, he "became known as a fellow with 'a good line' . . . that included a ready smile, a quick wit, and a good story or two." In 1910, he bought an interest in his father-in-law's newspaper, the *Marshall County Gazette*, and settled down in Lewisburg. Eventually he would acquire the entire newspaper and serve as president of the Tennessee Press Association, but with "a flair for salesmanship" and "a voice suited to oratory," McCord's first love was auctioneering, and he completed a school for auctioneers in Chicago in 1920. Specializing in livestock, McCord was so fond of Jersey cattle that he kept a clay statue of a Jersey cow on his desk while he was governor. He also slipped away while campaigning for governor in 1944 to conduct an auction for the American Jersey Cattle Breeders Association in Ohio.

Billing himself as a "pure and wholesome plain country Democrat," McCord gained considerable political experience, but with the exception of a two-year stint in the House of Representatives just prior to his assumption of the governor's chair in 1944, it was entirely within the confines of his small rural district. In addition to serving for a quarter century as mayor of Lewisburg, he was also a member of the Marshall County Court. In this arena, according to veteran Nashville political reporter Ralph Perry, the eventual governor "judged the farmers' livestock as well as their babies at the county fairs, officiated at one-room school box suppers, preached the funerals of his neighbors and listened with the boys while the hound pack made music among the Middle Tennessee hills."[105] A fellow Tennessean described McCord "as a former auctioneer with 'a voice like a golden gong.'" "A wonderful speechmaker," he added, "He never says a damn thing that means anything, but it certainly sounds good."[106]

An intimate associate of Ed Crump, McCord broke with the political boss only once. In 1947, he supported a sales tax that was used to finance ambitious educational reforms. Like Crump, he remained adamantly opposed to the CIO, sending the Highway Patrol to break a strike by the Steelworkers Union in Nashville in 1948 and presiding over a legislature in 1947 that outlawed the closed shop, made labor unions liable as organizations for damages, and denied unemployment benefits to striking workers.[107]

As governor, McCord also followed the standard Crump–West Tennessee line on race, which historian Michael Honey has recounted in detail. Initially in need of African American votes, writes Honey, "Crump's paternalistic racism viewed blacks as children to be managed rather than as enemies to be exterminated," but by the end of the thirties, the situation had changed. Black votes were less necessary to the Crump organization, while black wards in Memphis were controlled almost completely by the Crump machine. Given these conditions, the machine became "less reticent" about keeping "the black community in its place." Indeed, conditions deteriorated to such an extent under Police Commissioner Joe Boyle that a number of black Memphians appealed directly to U.S. Attorney General Frank Murphy. In January 1941, a LeMoyne College professor and NAACP supporter wrote to the national association, "It seems as if Ed Crump, working through Joe Boyle, has gone stark raving mad."[108]

During the last two years of the war, according to Honey, "race relations reached their boiling point in Memphis." In 1943, "the Crump machine came down hard on every black leader it could find" to stop a meeting at which A. Philip Randolph, president of the Brotherhood of Sleeping Car Porters, was to speak. Increasingly concerned about racial liberalism that seemed to accelerate within the national Democratic Party as a result of the New Deal and the war, Crump worked with other southern leaders in 1944 to deny Henry Wallace renomination for vice president. Like Mississippi senator Theodore Bilbo, who in 1946 denounced the SCHW as "that 'un-American negro social equality, communistic, mongrel outfit,'" the Memphis boss "increasingly veered [in the postwar years] toward such vitriolic rhetoric as well." Late in 1947, he refused to allow the American Heritage Foundation's "Freedom Train" to visit Memphis, because "integrated viewings of the train's [historic] documents would cause whites and blacks to jostle each other and lead to race riots." In 1948, he abandoned Truman for

Strom Thurmond and the Dixiecrat Party in part because of his firm opposition to any liberalizing trend in race relations.[109]

Enshrouded in his own provincialism and strongly influenced by an aging, bitter patron, the 67-year-old McCord let his imagination run wild in the wake of the Columbia confrontation. When SRC activist Mrs. M. E. Tilly and fellow churchworker Mrs. E. C. Robinson visited McCord on March 8, he insisted that when he had spoken at a Rotary Club meeting at Mt. Pleasant the week before the episode, a man had whispered to him that "at a Negro funeral that week 65 Negroes marched in the funeral procession armed with army rifles." He then quickly followed this account with the assertion that "400 guns and 132 pistols" had been seized from Negro homes in Columbia. When asked why he thought Negroes were so fearful, he cited the executive secretary of the SCHW, "Domboski," and insisted on reading the SCHW pamphlet "The Truth about Columbia" in its entirety to Tilly and Robinson. "He was pretty hot before he got through," Tilly observed. To his visitors, the governor maintained that Clark Foreman, the head of the SCHW, was "being played upon by this *Communist*, Domboski." When asked what he thought church people could do, he responded with alacrity: "Preach the gospel and nothing else!"[110]

McCord had also recoiled in horror at a proposal that Mary McLeod Bethune speak to an interracial audience in Nashville on January 17, 1946, as part of an SCHW-sponsored tour. Fyke Farmer—a liberal Nashville attorney, chair of the March 3rd meeting to inaugurate defense preparations for black Maury Countians, and friend and admirer of James Dombrowski—visited the governor, along with Dombrowksi and two prominent Nashvillians. When the visitors requested permission to use the auditorium of a state-owned building, the governor "turned red . . . his veins, his face, he was so shocked!" "You know that's breaking the custom," he sputtered, and he was considerably dismayed when Farmer informed him that "he'd caught the point, that's what we were trying to do."[111]

Although McCord initially spoke out for a unified Democratic Party in 1948, he changed his position within hours of Crump's announcement of his opposition to Truman. Lashing out against the president's ten-point civil rights program, he attacked the Fair Employment Practices Committee in particular as "unconstitutional, unenforceable, and unnecessary." After meeting with the governor a few days after the Columbia fray, NAACP national secretary Walter White commented simply, "McCord is an ex-mule auctioneer and that just about characterizes his mentality."[112]

Not surprisingly, the governor surrounded himself with men whose outlooks paralleled his own. His executive secretary Bayard Tarpley—whom

Walter White described as "a bumptious, vicious anti-Negro person"—hesitated to let Attorney Z. Alexander Looby and Dr. William J. Faulkner, dean of the chapel at Fisk University, see his boss when they visited with White on March 2nd. Apparently, Tarpley could see clearly that Looby and Faulkner were African Americans, but he was uncertain whether the lighter-skinned White was "white or colored." Finally, Tarpley decided to admit White alone, saying that "these others could see the Governor some other time." Just then, McCord walked in, and Tarpley began claiming that "the Negroes were buying arms in every shop and hardware store in Nashville and all over the United States." He also denied that there was ever a white mob in Columbia, boasting instead that "we have positive evidence that . . . there has been outside influence stirring up trouble."[113]

Brigadier General Dickinson blasted state officials before the federal grand jury, asserting that "all our trouble in the State Guard was among the higher officers in the State Administration, which was pretty punk."[114] Five months later, Dickinson himself tendered his resignation as both brigadier general and commanding general of the Second Brigade.

No one demonstrated more clearly the racial provincialism in which the McCord administration was mired, however, than the governor's attorney general, Roy Beeler. Called upon to assess the constitutionality of the actions of law officers in Columbia, the 54-year-old Beeler asserted before grand jurors: "I am not making a speech here or rendering testimony against the negro," and then he volunteered, "I call them 'niggers.'" Throughout his testimony, Beeler depicted African Americans as lazy and criminally inclined. Even when describing their alleged equitable treatment before the law in Tennessee, he remarked "I have to keep after them all the time," as he launched into an account of how he had "to haul one out home to cut my lawn." Beeler then proceeded with an anecdote about how the first black juror in Knox County tried to impress his fellow white jurors by buying them whiskey, and he wound up with a flourish, indicting both blacks and their defenders:

> We are not after these negroes here, as long as they behave themselves, I had one the other night, according to the paper, kicked in a door, drug a woman around, I guess you saw it, General Denning, but the main thing they need to do, these negroes, is to let the white women in this country alone; not create a lot of disturbance and things of that sort. We are not much in a humor to have the rights infringed on by them. . . . Here, we have got too much outside interference. . . . As the result of the war time situation, everybody wants to run everybody else's business.[115]

Like his boss, the assistant attorney general from Beeler's office sent to investigate the Columbia affair, Ernest F. Smith, saw few distinctions among African Americans, and he made no attempt to get their side of the story when he visited Maury County. He reported that all in "the slide"—a term he obviously relished using in referring to the Bottom—were "armed and resentful" or "sullen and determined." After conferring with white officials on February 27th and making "a casual inspection of the street [East Eighth] *in company with Chief Bomar and Inspector Jackson*" on the 28th, Smith returned to Nashville to write his report. In it, he determined that "the record shows conclusively that Sol, Julius and Charles Blair and James Morton [whom he confused at one point with Morton's arch-rival V. K. Ryan] had so inflamed irresponsible negroes in Columbia that they would at the slightest provocation start a riot." The assistant attorney general based his conclusions on the testimony of James "Digger" Johnson, a man he initially thought was called "Nigger" Johnson and then decided was "Jigger."[116]

Investigators like Smith played a key role in shaping the state's cases against black Maury Countians (see Chapter 7). The important point here, however, is the tone that McCord and like-minded state officials set for the Highway Patrol and the nature of the leaders that they chose. Lynn Bomar developed the tactics that he used in Columbia over the course of several years. McCord, his immediate superior, knew what those tactics were and elected not only to retain Bomar as patrol chief but also to enhance his power by combining it with the newly created cabinet-level position of safety commissioner. If Lynn Bomar did not bear all of the responsibility for what happened in Columbia because of the individual behavior of the men who served under him, he was even less to blame than those above him, who retained him and inflated his influence, along with his ego.

GRAND (JURY) MANEUVERS AND THE POLITICS OF EXCLUSION

By the close of World War II, the extension of civil rights to African Americans had become for white liberals "an acid test" of their creed.[1] Conservatives meanwhile continued to defend the status quo, and some southern officials, like Theodore Bilbo and Ed Crump, grew increasingly shrill and vociferous as they detected enhanced personal efficacy among black Americans and the growing centrality of civil rights to their white allies. Those seeking improved treatment for African Americans in the 1930s and 1940s looked especially to the president, the Justice Department, and, whenever they could force the issue, the Supreme Court. Those endorsing the status quo had their supporters in the federal government as well, especially in Congress where longtime southern Democrats used their seniority to exercise influence far out of proportion to their numbers.

All of these elements came into play as liberals and conservatives clashed in the legal battles that emanated from the Columbia events of February 25 and 26. National and state forces did not appropriate a local conflict for their own purposes. Instead, the proponents of change on the one hand and the defenders of the status quo on the other had direct ties to opposing Maury County constituencies, and these ties shaped their perceptions of the Columbia episode and defined their respective positions. Columbia was less swept up into the vortex of state and national politics than part and parcel of them. Without competing forces external to the community, no sharply contested legal battles would have resulted from the Columbia encounter, but at the same time, without conflicting constituencies within Maury County, there would have been no confrontation. Local clashes like those in Columbia are by their very nature about power and politics. Not surprisingly, the legal proceedings that flow from them envelop political contenders at all levels of society.

The very fact that a federal grand jury met to consider indicting police officers for their excesses in Columbia reflected the growing power of liberals in the war and immediate postwar years; their resounding defeat signified the solid, institutional entrenchment of their opponents. This chapter explores this clash and the forces that shaped its outcome. For those seeking redress for black Maury Countians, difficulties arose from (1) the kind of campaign they were forced to conduct; (2) the constraints faced by Washington-based Justice attorneys, especially in their relations with the FBI; and (3) the conduct of state-based federal officials.

Running through all of these obstacles was the outsider status of liberals themselves. Whether southerners or northerners, those allied with black Maury Countians stood outside the mainstream consensus on race in the mid-1940s, and largely outside the political establishment that shaped the criminal justice system, especially when it dealt with civil rights and the disciplining of police officers. Liberals were in a position to pressure the president and the attorney general, but changes in the predisposition of these offices represented only recent, progressive buds on the highest branches of a large, sturdy oak of conservatism. The success of liberals in defending African Americans in the state trials in the autumn of 1946 resulted not from their destruction of the tree but from their reaching around it—to marginalized citizens who stood on the edge of the political apparatus, and whose lives and livelihoods were not intimately connected to it. This possibility was effectively blocked in the grand jury hearing by members of the establishment itself.

THE LIBERALS' DILEMMA

As described in Chapter 1, a host of representatives from private organizations arrived in Columbia in the wake of the February conflagration. Spearheaded by the SCHW, the Communist Party, and, most importantly, the NAACP, liberals and leftists alike engaged in vigorous publicity campaigns in behalf of black Maury Countians. The NAACP in particular proved very successful in its publicity and fund-raising endeavors. Telegrams and petitions from Association chapters poured into the White House, especially following the deaths of Johnson and Gordon, and at the conclusion of its legal battles, the organization disbursed a surplus of almost $9,000 (over $50,000 in 1990 terms).

The NAACP was able to organize an effective, multipronged campaign for a number of reasons. First, because Columbia returned it to an issue that had long been a prewar focus, racial violence, the Association was able to utilize established techniques and to draw on organizations, such as the American Civil Liberties Union, with which it had traditionally worked.[2] Too, with a ninefold increase in membership between 1940 and 1945, the NAACP itself emerged from the war in a much stronger position.

Equally significant, in the wake of the conflict the NAACP was able to draw on two invigorated constituencies. Inspired by "the politics of self-interest," labor leaders had embraced civil rights in the 1930s. They had also enjoyed tremendous success in organizing as a result of New Deal legislation and a wartime environment of worker scarcity. Chiefly the CIO had taken advantage of these opportunities, while in particular "the so-called Communist labor unions had good relations with the civil liberties organization."[3] Within a few short years, the CIO's momentum would slow, as right-wing unions within the organization expelled left-wing ones like Mine Mill. Although this development augured ill for the civil rights movement, in 1946 the NAACP had in the CIO an ally considerably strengthened by World War II and not yet weakened by the Cold War.

The Association also tapped into a wellspring of concern among middle-class white liberals whose numbers had grown as the nation confronted the fascist challenge abroad. Most notably Gunnar Myrdal's 1944 tour de force, *The American Dilemma*, helped legitimize the struggle for civil rights by "counterposing the American creed to Nazi ideology." According to historian Walter Jackson, "public censure of racial prejudice and discrimination increased notably after the war," as "clergy, journalists, and educators" all joined the ranks of liberal crusaders. An "upsurge of liberal activism at the local level" resulted in a dramatic rise in organizations "designed to reduce prejudice and improve the public's knowledge about minorities and their role in American life."[4]

Nowhere was the gap between American ideals and practices more noticeable than in the legally segregated South, and this region in particular served as a target of the growing concern. Not surprisingly, most of the liberal sentiment developed outside the South, although the southern-based SCHW experienced its best year ever in terms of membership and annual income in 1946.[5]

In the wake of World War II, many African Americans and white liberals alike worried that attacks on black Americans would mushroom as they had following World War I, and they feared that the riots of 1943 in particular were harbingers of the future. Columbia figured importantly in these concerns in three ways. First, it represented the initial interracial clash following the war. Second, it raised the specter of mob violence, even though the attempted lynching there was unsuccessful. Third and most important, it tapped into a growing awareness of police violence toward African Americans, which stemmed from wartime changes that both encouraged official abuse and publicized it.[6]

This is not to suggest that all eyes were riveted on Columbia and the difficulties faced by black Americans in the months following the war's conclusion. Walter White had to go to considerable lengths to ensure major press coverage of the Lawrenceburg trial, while journalist Vincent Sheean—once induced to travel to Lawrence County—wrote in one of his articles: "The nation as a whole, concentrated primarily upon wages and prices and, as a very bad second, on our foreign relations, has shown no sign of interest in a case which goes to the roots of our national structure."[7] Still, liberal forces, which had been gaining ground since the 1930s, reached a kind of crescendo immediately following the war, and this momentum was essential to those seeking redress for African Americans in Maury County.

Publicity was a critical component of the strategy of the NAACP and its affiliated associations, because they had leverage at the top of the political structure, and the effective use of that leverage depended on the mobilization of public opinion and the generation of a large public outcry. Thus, while liberal groups encouraged Governor McCord to take action in the wake of the Patrol raid, they directed most of their attention to the president and the attorney general.

President Truman's role in the positive response that liberals received should not be underestimated or regarded solely as the result of political calculations. As John T. Elliff concluded after a careful study of the CRS, "In civil rights, more than in most other areas of national policy, the attitudes of the man in office made a vital difference," and Truman was "'hipped' on the subject of individual rights." The president's orientation was important, however, "not because he intervened in specific decisions, but because [Attorney General Tom] Clark could count on his ultimate support."[8]

Clark's position on civil rights in turn was influenced especially by "the role of the Attorney General's Office itself." As Elliff explained: "It had to be responsive to political demands, and the pressure from the NAACP and other groups, as well as the volume of mail demanding action in notorious cases, was too great for the Attorney General to ignore."[9] Assistant Attorney General Lamar Caudle stated in regard to Columbia that Clark insisted on a grand jury "because of the 'leftwing groups' in this situation." Walter White also observed during his initial trip to Nashville that the attorney general was "anxious to prove to the public that as a Texan he is not too bad." The possibility existed that Clark would become Truman's running mate in 1948, and Columbia would "give him a chance to prove his worth."[10]

Like Clark, Caudle, who headed the Criminal Division, and Turner Smith, chief of the CRS in 1946, hailed from the South, and as native southerners, they were anxious to demonstrate to liberal reformers that they were just as sensitive to civil rights issues as their nonsouthern predecessors. One member of the CRS staff believed that they "'leaned over backwards' to avoid charges of sectional bias."[11]

In the midst of these pressures and commitments, the channeling of the postwar liberal surge by the NAACP and its allies produced results. Within hours of the Patrol raid on the Bottom, Smith telephoned the FBI to say that the attorney general had already received several phone calls regarding Columbia, and he himself was expecting a call from the White House. The CRS chief urged the commencement of an investigation. Scarcely a week later, David Niles, Truman's administrative assistant on minority affairs, sent Clark a batch of telegrams that the president had received "in conjunction with the disorders in Columbia, Tennessee." He stated explicitly: "While the President is receiving telegrams in this vein, I believe it is incumbent on us to satisfy ourselves and them that the Federal Government is doing all it can in order to protect civil rights." Meanwhile, Clark asked local United States Attorney (USA) Horace Frierson to make a preliminary check to see if any civil liberties had been violated. At the same time, he sent his special assistant James E. Ruffin to Nashville so that he might receive "full reports daily of any developments."[12]

Once Frierson announced that no infractions of civil rights had occurred, Clark called him to Washington and, on the day of his visit, released a carefully worded directive expressing his concern over the Columbia situation and ordering Frierson to assemble a grand jury "at the earliest possible time." In convening the grand jury, federal judge Elmer Davies read word for word indictments that had been composed in Washington within the CRS. Only in his decision to place liberal organizations on trial did he deviate seriously from his scripted text.[13]

The strategy employed by the NAACP and its cohorts had advantages and disadvantages. Clearly, without pressure at the top from black Americans and their liberal white allies, no federal grand jury would have convened in Nashville in the spring of 1946. Additionally, the intense publicity given the Columbia case served as an effective means of procuring money and members for future campaigns.

In their eagerness to initiate action at a time when they feared burgeoning racial attacks, however, liberals encouraged a hearing that did not have all of the attributes needed for success. Former CRS chief Victor Rotnem noted that a criminal case was best if "it doesn't get too old and have whiskers on it." The first lynching indictment in Mississippi, which happened during World War II, occurred when the grand jury convened and voted on the same day. "Had they gone home and met again the next day, there would have been no indictment," he added.[14] In contrast, the grand jury convened in Nashville well over a month following the Columbia events of late February and early March. Jurors then stayed in session over two weeks, adjourned, reconvened, and did not deliver a report until mid-June.

In one sense, the Justice case appeared solid. Less than a year earlier in the all-important *Screws v. United States* decision, the U.S. Supreme Court had for the first time in eighty years endorsed the constitutionality of Section 242 of Title 18 of the U.S. Criminal Code.[15] A remnant of the civil rights laws enacted by Congress during the Reconstruction era, Section 242 was one of only three statutes under which the CRS could prosecute.[16] It held that persons acting "under color of law" could not wilfully deprive other persons of rights guaranteed by U.S. laws or by the U.S. constitution. In comparison to the murkiness of many lynching cases, police officers were clearly embroiled in the Columbia episode and thereby met the "under color of law" criterion. They also appeared to have violated rights guaranteed by the Fourteenth Amendment, which declared that no state could "deprive any person of life liberty or property without due process of law; nor deny to any person within its jurisdiction the equal protection of the laws."

The Court had gone on, however, to clarify the scope of the rights secured by Section 242 and to define the word "wilful," a term that was inserted in 1909 when the Criminal Code was revised.[17] In doing so, it essentially decreed that in a police brutality case "a general evil purpose was not enough"; instead, "a specific intent to deprive a person of a Federal right made definite by [a Court] decision or other rule of law" must exist. Such a ruling was a problem, Turner Smith explained to the President's Committee on Civil Rights (PCCR), because "most acts of police brutality are actually occasioned by and result from either a sudden burst of passion on the part of the police officer or secondly, because of some personal revenge or feelings between the police officer and the victim." He continued: "We cannot seriously believe nor sincerely urge in most of these cases that the police officer in question was actually thinking about any Federal right or civil right the victim might have when he was hit with a billy. Most police officers have only a bare speaking acquaintance with the United States Constitution. *Therefore, it is only in cases which are particularly and peculiarly reprehensible in nature that we can successfully prosecute.*"[18]

The *Screws* case had "involved a severe and prolonged beating" in which "the victim's skull was broken and 'the brains were running out.'" In the subsequent *United States v. Crews* case, which the Justice Department prosecuted successfully during the fall of 1946, the town constable rode "the victim around during the night . . . for a long period of time, administering beatings with a cow whip and with the butt of his pistol, finally forcing him into the Suwannee [*sic*] River where he drowned." These cases were strong precisely because "the conduct of the officer and the very nature of the injuries inflicted" spoke "louder than legalistic arguments."[19]

In Columbia, only John Blackwell sustained serious injuries during his arrest, and state troopers testified that he had been struck when he leveled a gun at them. Similarly, everyone present at the jail, including Napoleon Stewart, maintained that Johnson and Gordon had been killed while they were attacking a deputy. One might have argued that the force used against them was excessive, but this point was quite subtle in contrast to the egregious cases in which the CRS had been successful. Likewise, though he had to be hospitalized, Blackwell's injuries paled in comparison to those administered to their victims by Sheriff Claude Screws in Georgia and by Town Marshal Thomas Crews in Florida. Hence, as far as the police brutality issue was concerned, Blackwell's treatment offered the best hope for indicting state troopers, but it did not really possess the characteristics that Smith described.

The matter that most clearly involved a Fourteenth Amendment guarantee was the "deliberate destruction of physical property." Lamar Caudle labeled it "the only possible civil rights violation."[20] Lawyers in the case initially missed the centrality of this issue, however, in part because they had to rely on the FBI for their information. Additionally, even if CRS attorneys had discerned it, agents might not have produced the evidence necessary for an indictment. Certainly they did not do so in their second round of inquiries.

Besides encouraging action in a case that had discernible weaknesses, the widespread publicity given the Columbia episode permitted Judge Davies to place liberal and leftist organizations on trial along with law officers. Even more important in aiding jurors in their decision, the tactics of loudly broadcasting missteps in Columbia, and of working through top officials in Washington, adversely affected the testimony of the two witnesses most likely to testify favorably on behalf of black Maury Countians: Sheriff Underwood and General Dickinson.

While Underwood downplayed before grand jurors the seriousness of the threat from whites milling around on the town square and the fears that he and black Maury Countians had on the 25th, Dickinson refused to criticize the behavior of Lynn Bomar and his state troopers. Underwood's and Dickinson's lack of forthrightness concerning the danger from whites in turn placed the onus of the fray on blacks.

As early as February 27, Underwood's remarks shifted markedly between the time of his morning talk with Maurice Weaver and his formal statement in the evening to state and local officials. By the time the hearing convened, he could not even remember having informed the FBI that when he turned the Stephensons over to their bondsmen, he had said, "Here they are; take care of them." After court on the 25th, the sheriff told grand jurors, he had heard that "the Fleming boy had been badly cut and that some of them, probably a half drunk or something of that kind had made a statement something ought to be done about it." "Can you give us a little more detail about that?" CRS attorney A. B. Caldwell asked. "Really," Underwood responded, "I don't know much detail about it because I just dismissed it from my mind." When it came to the term "lynching," Eleanor Bontecou recalled, "The poor old sheriff wouldn't use the word."[21]

The timing of Underwood's turnaround suggested that he was heavily influenced by members of the local district attorney's office and by state authorities. But the sheriff did not reverse himself solely under pressure from other leaders. Instead, as he discerned the overwhelming attention the Columbia episode was generating, his view of the situation grew more in line with their own. When asked by Caldwell what he did following the Patrol raid, Underwood replied, "most of the time dodging reporters." As the lawyer explained that he and the other Justice attorneys were just trying to get the facts, Underwood exploded: "My God, how I hope you get them because nobody else in the United States seem to have them." "[The] thing that really had my father upset was newspaper articles. . . . incorrect publicity bothered him terribly," James Underwood Jr. reflected recently.[22]

Underwood, like other Tennessee officials, recoiled in part at the fanfare given the Columbia episode, because he believed the publicists made false accusations, and he was not entirely wrong. Although the liberal version more closely matched actual circumstances than the conservative one, both liberals and leftists exaggerated and sensationalized their accounts in attempts to inflame—and mobilize—public opinion.[23]

Yet, regardless of its accuracy, southern leaders abhorred negative publicity and were inclined to unite in response to it for a number of reasons. First, as members of the middle class, they viewed appearances as extremely important. Social status for them was not "an inherent quality," as lineage was for the upper class; instead, it depended on their behavior as well as their income. Not only were they deeply chagrined when they were painted in pejorative terms by the mainstream press, but also strong pressure for conformity existed *within* the group.[24]

Additionally, as the proud nurturers of an heroic Lost Cause who chafed at the Yankee invasion and occupation that their forebears had endured—and who were well aware that race relations were less than harmonious above the Mason-Dixon line—members of the southern establishment bristled at finger pointing by northerners on racial matters. Maury County and the state of Tennessee had been sullied over a decade earlier when the Cordie Cheek lynching hit the front page of the *New York Times*. Officials were determined to present themselves to the nation in a more positive light this time, and this consideration overrode all else as they conducted their investigations and legal proceedings.[25]

Finally, many southern authorities—though Underwood was probably not one of them—resented interference by liberals and leftists in their affairs, because they believed it made African Americans difficult to control. Firmly convinced, as the Columbia *Daily Herald* expressed it, that "no serious race troubles have ever arisen before," they could find no other explanation for the increased assertiveness that they detected during the war as black Americans experienced a greater sense of personal efficacy.[26]

For the sheriff, community honor and personal honor began to merge as Columbia achieved notoriety. In response to questions posed by Assistant USA Denning, he repeatedly drew on personal examples to show that "the relation between the races [in Maury County] has been . . . better than any other classes on earth."[27] In short, Underwood was not simply weakened by his position as an isolated, lame-duck Sheriff. Instead, as a middle-aged, middle-class, white southerner, reared in the heyday of the glorification of the Lost Cause and confronted after World War II with the wrath of an invigorated, largely nonsouthern, liberal coalition, he was highly susceptible to the pressure of his colleagues.

Over three-quarters of a century after it was forged, white solidarity endured among southern officials. If anything, concern over appearances grew stronger in the wake of the New Deal and a war that put a premium on attracting outside capital to the South.[28] This occurred at a time when a chorus of voices rendered first mob actions and then police violence so unsavory that they could damage communities and states in the eyes of potential investors. While black southerners would orchestrate these concerns to their advantage in the 1960s, in Columbia in 1946, as after the Cheek lynching in 1933, worry over negative publicity served to unite white authorities rather than divide them.

If southern middle-class officials were obsessed with appearances, elite leaders like Dickinson had a somewhat different, though related, concern. This worry informed the State Guard commander's behavior before the grand jury as well as in Columbia. It, too, dated from the Civil War–Reconstruction era, but it had much more to do with the overt exercise of power than with the projection of respectability, an issue that bothered very little an independently wealthy, socially secure man like Jacob McGavock Dickinson Jr.

Of all the witnesses testifying at the grand jury hearing, none were in a better position to indict Lynn Bomar and his state troopers than Dickinson. First of all, the brigadier general made a very impressive witness.[29] Even more important, Dickinson knew a great deal about the Patrol's comportment in Columbia. In private communications to Adjutant General Hilton Butler, the Guard commander urged "that the Governor issue immediately, and in advance of further trouble, a definite directive . . . placing all troops and other armed forces under one single authority." In a separate set of confidential recommendations, he advocated the State Guard as that authority, at least until the National Guard was demobilized.[30]

Yet, although he knew and deplored what had happened in Columbia, Dickinson prevaricated when he appeared before the Grand Jury. On the one hand, he described precisely what was supposed to have occurred, reading his Field Order No. 1 verbatim, but he refused to blame Bomar in any way for the Patrol's early entry, saying only, "Unfortunately something broke, I don't know what it was, never have been able to find out." Similarly, he admitted that he had recommended to the governor that one authority be in charge in future disturbances, but he added "not because of any friction [between himself and Bomar], of course, we didn't have any."[31]

As a man whose wealth, education, and lineage made him impervious to the concerns of many other white southerners, why was Dickinson not more forthright before the grand jury? Clearly, he felt strongly about the issues of fairness and justice in law enforcement, and he knew that they had been violated in Columbia. His supplement to his confidential recommendations to the adjutant general made that very evident. Still, at best, his testimony was exceedingly evasive. Why?

In part, Dickinson was angered by aspersions cast against his young soldiers, and his number-one priority at the hearing was clearing their name.[32] However, he had more fundamental reasons for camouflaging his differences with Lynn Bomar, and ironically, they stemmed from the same impulse that led him to advocate clearer organizational lines, the avoidance of violence, and fairer treatment of African Americans in future domestic disturbances. This impulse was intimately connected to his own family legacy.

Although Dickinson's father moved the household to Chicago in 1899 when he became general solicitor for the Illinois Central Railroad, he never lost touch with his elite Confederate background, and he bequeathed to his third son a very strong sense of his southern heritage. Immediately following his father's death, the younger Dickinson returned to Nashville, where he devoted himself full-time to the breeding of Arabian horses. The youngest of three brothers, the Guard commander had a deep and abiding sense of his family and its place in the South. Like numerous Confederate officers before him, he was known as "General" following his State Guard service, a nomenclature that he liked and that remained with him the rest of his life.[33]

For Dickinson, social status stemmed from his patrimony; appearances in and of themselves were not especially important. His paramount objective on the witness stand then was not the projection of a positive image of Maury County or Tennessee. Instead, his understanding of history and his kinsmen's place in it informed his position. Reconstruction, an era when federal forces occupied his beloved southland and families like his own lost control, held a special horror for Dickinson, and it was this perception that motivated him to downplay his differences with Lynn Bomar and to stress privately the need for improved law enforcement. As he explained to the adjutant general: "In the event law and order cannot be maintained by local law enforcement agencies augmented by such state police as are immediately available, and in the further event that there is insufficient state military force to restore and maintain law and order, it may be considered inevitable that Federal troops will intervene."[34] Revealingly, Dickinson then reminded Butler, "Tennessee has already come through one reconstruction."[35] Thus the brigadier general's concerns centered around the maintenance of control by the southern elite, and for this reason he informed grand jurors: "Please understand this. There never was any friction or disagreement between the authorities down there. We tried to cooperate, and they were all very cooperative with us. There was no lack of authority which manifested itself there."[36]

Dickinson undoubtedly focused on the reentry of federal troops because of his military appointment and orientation, but his preoccupation with the growing power of Washington was a concern that he shared with other members of his social class. By the end of the nineteenth century, according to historian David Chappell, most had come to see "the threat of renewed federal intervention" as "a paper tiger," but their fears resurfaced during the New Deal and World War II.[37] Whether the concerns were, as historian Numan Bartley put it, "economic and ideological" or "more distinctively racial and sectional in nature," apprehensions mounted as the welfare state expanded and some high-placed Washington officials grew more favorably disposed toward civil rights.[38] The irony for a man like Dickinson was that his emphasis on order, fairness, and impartiality emanated from the same taproot as his concern about the retention of control. Above all, he wished to avoid a Second Reconstruction, and unfortunately for liberal reformers, this impulse remained paramount, even when law and order broke down.

Middle-class officials too were concerned about maintaining power, but for them the issue was always refracted through a prism of appearances and respectability. For this reason they worried about how they looked, even in private reports. Families like Dickinson's were accustomed to ruling—or to having in office public servants who were amenable to their goals. Reconstruction represented the single, searing instant of their having lost this prerogative, and they did not intend for it to happen again. As J. Edgar Hoover explained to the president's cabinet in 1956: "Race relations still are affected by the deep and bitter feelings which have been handed down from generation to generation in the deep South. Memories of the Civil War period are being revived. There is still talk among some cultured and educated Southerners of rule by the 'blacks,' 'carpetbaggers,' and 'scalawags.' "[39]

The strategy employed by liberal defenders of black Maury Countians thus alienated both middle-class and elite authorities, and this estrangement severely hampered the procurement of an indictment against state troopers for their deportment in Columbia. It was not so much that liberals made bad decisions, as that they had bad choices. They could do nothing, and thus forfeit any chance of a hearing, or they could generate such an outcry that national figures would be forced to act, and in the process, jeopardize their chances for a successful outcome. Either route presented a dilemma.

OUTSIDERS AND INSIDERS

In an important sense, CRS attorneys resembled the liberal organizations with whom they so frequently interacted. Marginalized within their own department and their own profession, estranged from their own investigative arm, and interlopers in the eyes of many USAs, they dwelled on the periphery of the criminal justice establishment. In marked contrast, the FBI, the agency that carried on their inquiries, was deeply immersed within it. Both conditions had major implications for the outcome of the hearing in Nashville.

THE CIVIL RIGHTS SECTION

Established by executive order rather than congressional statute, and thus devoid of its own fiscal appropriation, the CRS under Tom Clark continued to be funded haphazardly, and the staff remained small, despite a dramatic increase in the workload during the war years. As Eleanor Bontecou explained: "It was not a popular section. They looked upon us as 'do-gooders' and what-not, and it didn't, at that time, lead to anything outside the Department. A young attorney wouldn't make his reputation or be asked by a good law firm to come in."[40]

To make matters more difficult, the trio of lawyers who traveled to Nashville—John M. Kelley, Eleanor Bontecou, and A. B. Caldwell—were in a state of flux. Bontecou, who had the trust of civil rights leaders, was on her way to Nuremberg for the war crimes trials and would be in Nashville only a week. Caldwell, who sustained a lifelong interest in the CRS because "he got so interested in the problems as he saw them through this case," was only at the beginning of this turn in his career. Kelley, who was supposed to be the lead attorney in the case, obviously had little patience for the intricate maze of hurdles he had to face, and he returned to Washington before the grand jury report was written, an action that infuriated his boss, Lamar Caudle.[41]

Kelley, Bontecou, and Caldwell had far more serious problems, however, than a heavy workload, flux within their own ranks, and marginality within their organization and profession. They relied for almost all of their information on the FBI, an agency whose racial orientation diverged considerably from their own and one whose allegiance lay far more in the direction of the law officers it was supposed to be investigating than toward Justice attorneys for whom it was ostensibly working.

THE FBI

The FBI played an extremely influential role in the Nashville hearing in several ways. First, its initial report of March 10 provided Justice attorneys with almost all of their information throughout most of the proceedings. Even more important in the direction taken by the grand jury, the lead FBI agent in the case, W. E. Hopton, set the stage by testifying at length as the first witness. He then reappeared two more times as additional information was requested, and he closed the hearing as the final witness on June 14.

Hopton's written synopsis of the March 10 report gave jurors even more direction than his oral testimony, because the report itself consisted only of detailed summaries by agents of their interviews with various persons involved in the Columbia episode. Though arranged chronologically from "The Fleming-Stephenson Incident" through "Inspection of Property Damage—Mink Slide Area," the summaries offered little in the way of analysis or evaluation of witnesses. Lawyers plowing meticulously through the 197-page, typewritten, single-spaced document might piece together their own interpretation, but grand jurors, most of whom were farmers, had other chores to do in the evenings. Indeed, the proceedings adjourned every day in time for them "to get back to milk their cows."[42] Hopton's four-page, single-spaced summary thus provided a very handy interpretive framework, and it was not surprising that the Bureau in Washington received word in late April that "the grand jury will use the synopsis of the FBI report as its basis and guide for their findings."[43]

Hopton's testimony and his synopsis undoubtedly also impressed jurors because of the reputation of the FBI and the lead agent's own credentials. Thanks to a well-publicized war launched by the FBI director in the 1930s on notorious outlaws like John Dillinger and Bonnie and Clyde, "only illiterates could have missed reading about Hoover and the FBI, and even they would have had to have been deaf," political theorist Eugene Lewis concluded, "because the Bureau's radio publicity was so thorough and intense." World War II provided equally fine opportunities for the agency to grab headlines, although the targets shifted from bandits to spies and saboteurs. By the time the grand jury met, the director and his G-men were well established as national heroes.[44]

W. E. Hopton no doubt represented his organization well. A 40-year-old native of St. Louis, Missouri, who had graduated from Washington University Law School in the midst of the Depression, the senior resident agent in Nashville had turned to the Bureau on the recommendation of Wiley Routledge, the dean of his law school and later a Supreme Court justice. Impressed with the "other young men in the same boat that I was in," Hopton never returned to practice law as he had originally intended. "Mr. Hoover was very, very fortunate," he recalled recently. "He got the cream of the crop from the United States, all over." Involved in a number of renowned cases, including the capture of "Pretty Boy" Floyd, Hopton had served for two years as an administrative assistant in the Bureau's headquarters in Washington and, at his own request, was transferred to Nashville in 1943.[45] Well-educated, experienced in FBI matters, and quite at home in the state's capital, Hopton unquestionably made an impressive witness.

The mission of the FBI in Columbia, as Hopton described it to the grand jury, was twofold. It was to determine what caused the affair and whether anyone's civil rights had been violated. His testimony, which differed from his synopsis only in its fuller detail, actually directly addressed both issues only briefly in closing. Hopton spent most of his time chronicling events from the fight on the town square through the shootings at the jail.

Although his account appeared careful and straightforward to anyone unfamiliar with the details of the case, it derived almost exclusively from interviews with local officials and with Lynn Bomar. Even in his search for explanations of the property damage in the Bottom, Hopton relied solely on the Patrol chief. "We went down into Mink Slide to look at the business establishments of James Morton, Saul Blair, and Julius Blair, and we noticed there was considerable destruction in both Julius and Saul Blair's places," Hopton told jurors. He continued:

> Some of it was from gunfire, other destruction no doubt was not from gunfire. *We went back again and questioned Bomar* to determine, if possible, what had caused the destruction other than that which was caused by gunfire. *Commissioner Bomar stated* that he was positive that his highway patrolmen didn't do the damage. *He called attention* to the fact that in Saul Blair's Barber Shop, there are three barber chairs, that there were long cuts and holes made through the chairs. We had noticed that at the time we looked at it, and *Bomar was of the opinion* that those were done by bayonets. None of his men carried bayonets. . . . *he called attention* to the fact that a number of the State Guardsmen at the time this took place were individuals in their teen age. . . . *He expressed the opinion* that the damage that was done there, outside of the damage done by the gunfire, was done by some of these youngsters. . . . *Bomar stated very definitely* that some of the windows [at James Morton's] were broken on his orders, but *he stated he was positive* that none of his highway patrolmen had done any of the damage to these places outside of that which was done by gunfire. Any questions?[46]

Thus ended Hopton's analysis of the causes of damages in the Bottom; the views of no other person, including Dickinson, were cited.

Not surprisingly, given the sources of his information, Hopton painted a picture of blacks as bellicose, whites as nonthreatening, and law officers as acting entirely within legal bounds. Although he did not presume, as state officials were prone to, that African American actions on the 25th were Communist inspired, nor did he conclude that they resulted from a "pre-arrangement," he made no mention of earlier lynchings within the community. Instead, he dismissed mob concerns with the statement that "rumors circulating among the negroes to the effect that a white man had bought some rope at a local store for lynching purposes were unfounded." Only James Morton, Saul Blair, and Julius Blair had complained that their civil rights were violated, Hopton added, but rather than commenting on the legitimacy of their claims, he stated simply, "Investigation tends to indicate that these 3 negro leaders organized the negroes in this disturbance."[47]

Hopton's inquiry was complicated by a number of factors. Even State Guardsmen like W. W. Hogan who were chagrined at what had happened in Columbia refused to say anything to the FBI. Instead, as noted in the preceding chapter, Hogan encouraged his commanding officer to speak out. Certainly the solidarity among state troopers made it difficult to obtain information from them about one another. This task was made even more daunting because only a small cadre of men had intentionally damaged businesses in the Bottom, and they were all from the same division. Additionally, federal agents did not really focus on the destruction of property issue until late April, that is, after considerable time had lapsed. Patrolmen thus had time to synchronize their accounts and to grow less concerned about the need for cooperating with investigators.

Still, the FBI had cracked some very tough criminal cases, and the question of why the senior agent chose to interpret and present evidence as he did remains. Reasons derived in part from the racial views of J. Edgar Hoover and, in turn, of his agents. They also emanated from the way the director ran the Bureau and the role that he established for it within the larger framework of American law enforcement. Finally, Hopton's views flowed quite naturally from both personal and professional relationships that he developed within the context established by the FBI director.

Hoover's racial views, like his outlook on radicals and "pseudo liberals" (which he pronounced "swaydo liberals"), were very circumscribed and stereotypical. When asked by the PCCR if there were "a number of Negroes in the Department," he responded, "Oh yes, we have them as Agents and as experts in regard to subversive activities, and matters of that kind." In fact, there were only three: Hoover's chauffeur, James Crawford, to whom he gave agent status in 1946 in an attempt to placate the NAACP; his "office retainer," W. Samuel Noisette; and James E. Amos, a 68-year-old veteran of the Marcus Garvey case who was hired by Hoover's predecessor and whose duties as a regular agent largely ended with the Garvey affair.[48] The FBI chief demonstrated very clearly his limited understanding of African Americans when he explained to the PCCR why he would not want to send a black investigator into a lynching case like that which occurred in Monroe, Georgia, in the summer of 1946: "the local Negro I think would be more *disinclined* to talk to him because the particular type of Negro living in Monroe was a very ignorant type of Negro, and for that reason they were scared, they wouldn't talk hardly to anybody, and I don't think they would talk to a Negro agent."[49]

The terminology agents used in their reports and the way they conducted security clearances, a responsibility that they assumed during the war, demonstrated quite plainly that most shared Hoover's racial attitudes.[50] Without question, they shared his racial identity.

The racial composition and orientation of the force was especially important in a civil rights case such as that in Columbia, because the heart of an agent's job in a criminal investigation—like a Section 242 violation—was *interviewing*. As James Q. Wilson explained in his description of the duties of FBI agents:

> Whether developing an informant, speaking to a victim or witness, or canvassing the neighborhood of a crime, the essential task and critical skill of the detective [i.e., the agent] is his ability to conduct a productive interview. In this, the detective's craft is not unlike that of the newspaper reporter. . . . Detectives, like reporters, are expected always to identify themselves, to take full and accurate notes, to get all the essential details, and to have a flair for inducing worried or suspicious people to trust them or at least to tell them more than they intend. And they must have the judgment to distinguish the statements of persons who are self-aggrandizing, unreliable, or gossip-mongers from those of subjects who are candid, detached, and factual.[51]

Above all, Wilson summarized: "The work of detectives [agents] consists essentially of interviewing or manipulating apprehensive persons in intimate settings regarding complex or sensitive matters."[52]

Dressed in the "conservative, businesslike clothes" and conducting themselves in the "orderly, conventional manner" that Hoover demanded, nine white southerners set out early in March 1946 to interview the customers of East Eighth Street's establishments.[53] Many of these patrons had already had numerous encounters with the police with whom they saw the FBI allied and most had recently been arrested in conjunction with the shooting of the Columbia officers. It is difficult to fathom a more unlikely scenario for the development of an understanding on the part of interviewers of their interviewees. Indeed, there is little to suggest that Hopton and his men managed much insight into the views and concerns of East Eighth Street's middle-class proprietors.

Not surprisingly, the agents' queries did little to elicit honest responses, and these results took their toll. In a high-level review undertaken in Washington at Hoover's behest, veteran Bureau official Hugh H. Clegg wrote: "It is interesting to note that of the more than forty negroes [*sic*] interviewed by Agents all had some excuses or alibis concerning the night in question. They were either asleep and didn't know what was going on or just happened to drop in 'Mink Slide' and saw that something was wrong or had gone to go to some other town and was not there."[54] Although Clegg noted that "None of the negroes admitted participation in any shooting," this was *not* the issue the FBI was supposed to be investigating. Instead, the agency was supposed to be determining whether anyone's civil rights had been violated. Yet investigators used the respondents' prevarication on questions related to their whereabouts on the 25th to make determinations regarding civil rights infractions. In explaining why "there was no deprivation of civil rights," Clegg listed seven reasons. Among them, number 6 read: "The statements made by all of the law enforcement officers are substantially in accord whereas the statements made by the negroes arrested are, by and large, at considerable variance."[55] Thus the circumstances under which agents sought information from black Maury Countians were maximally conducive to producing erroneous or misleading statements. In turn, the FBI used the transparently evasive answers it received to conclude that the interviewees were untrustworthy and the violations they alleged, untrue.

Though the racial views of Hoover and the lily-white agency that they produced strongly influenced the FBI's evaluation of the case, other personal qualities of the director appeared more explicitly throughout the investigation and may also have affected Hopton's analysis. First, "the Boss" insisted on being informed very quickly about all proceedings.[56] Second, he demonstrated a now familiar obsession with the reputation of the Bureau. Hoover's insistence on speed may have encouraged Hopton to form opinions much faster than he should have, while his obsession with the Bureau's image, and his concomitant impatience with errors, may have discouraged Hopton from reconsidering earlier, hastily drawn conclusions.[57]

However, far more factors than prevarication by blacks and a desire for efficiency on the part of Hoover led Hopton to rely overwhelmingly on local authorities and the state Highway Patrol chief in reaching his conclu-

Like many other local policemen throughout the country, Columbia policeman Bernard O. Stofel strengthened his ties to the FBI—and the agency in turn to him—as he completed training at the FBI National Police Academy. Graduating from the Academy in 1951, he is seen here examining a file used for the identification of cars involved in hit-and-run cases. (Courtesy of Bernard O. Stofel)

sions. Unquestionably, the relationship that the director established with local and state law enforcement agencies and the ties that Hopton created personally influenced his choice of sources.

As Hoover sought to enhance the power and prestige of his organization, he confronted local and state law enforcement officers and politicians from "many shades of the political spectrum" who feared a national police force. To allay this concern, and perhaps because it fit so well with his own states' rights philosophy, Hoover sought "cooperative relationships." Through the establishment of the Identification Division (1924), the Uniform Crime Reports (1930), the FBI Laboratory (1932), the FBI Law Enforcement Bulletin (1932), and the FBI Academy (1935), Hoover was able "to bind state and local police forces to an ever-growing state of dependencies." Especially the FBI Academy—which Bernard Stofel eventually attended—served as "the West Point and the Harvard of law enforcement people for more than a generation."[58]

Yet, as the Bureau bound law officers to it, it pledged itself and its agents to those same policemen. Hopton, who joined the force one year prior to the founding of the Academy, became a qualified police instructor. As such, he held classes in the field for local policemen, teaching them "how to deal with law violators in such a way that was scientific rather than [using] brutality." In turn, the "local constabulary" carried out much of the investigative work for federal agents. Attorney General Tom Clark estimated that "90 percent of the direct cases were done by the local people." The resident agent who was stationed in Columbia at the time of the February crisis undoubtedly interacted with local law officers on a regular basis. Although Lynn Bomar told Clark that the FBI was "not too friendly, but friendly enough," both Sheriff Underwood and Police Chief Griffin indicated that they knew FBI agent James English "very well."[59]

Structurally the FBI was also bound very closely to the local USA's office. Whenever agents served in their investigative or detective capacity, it was usually to gather information for criminal cases that the USA or one of his assistants would prosecute. As Hopton expressed it, "out in the field . . . the United States Attorney . . . was the big dog." Hopton especially admired Tennessee's chief assistant USA, A. Otis Denning, a man whom he regarded as "brilliant" and "one of the finest lawyers in the state of Tennessee."[60]

Relations with the local federal judge were also very important, and as Agent-in-Charge D. S. Hostetter of Memphis pointed out, the FBI had "a good friend in Judge Davies." No one exemplified and cemented that friendship more than Hopton, who had originally requested the capital city as a base because he loved to hunt and fish, interests that he shared with the judge. Both had bird dogs, and they frequently hunted and fished together. Often Hopton visited Judge Davies's "fish camp."[61]

Even more indicative of the close ties between the federal judge and the FBI were the facts that Davies, as it turned out, had talked with Hopton about the case "from time to time" and that he was the "confidential source" who supplied "part of the information" that had been submitted to FBI headquarters! Additionally, the judge offered to "discuss with the Director personally everything which had taken place."[62]

As Eugene Lewis summed it, "The interinstitutional and intergovernmental linkages of the FBI in its maturity were a sight to behold."[63] Agent Hopton and Judge Davies represented one form of those linkages. The FBI's close relationship with local and state law officers illustrated another. CRS attorneys, like the liberal organizations with whom they worked so closely—and the clients those associations represented—were largely out of the loop. Since the New Deal, liberals had made gains at the top of the governmental structure, primarily within the executive branch, and they experienced a surge of grassroots support immediately following the war. For these reasons, Hoover and Tom Clark worried about their reactions, but liberal tentacles simply did not stretch very deeply into the criminal justice apparatus, especially when it came to disciplining the police.

Thus even the CRS's investigative arm had other ties and allegiances that were stronger than those to the attorneys for whom it ostensibly worked in civil rights cases. In the end, it was the FBI's cohorts in Tennessee—the federal judge and the lawyers from the USA's office—who did the most to shape the outcome of the grand jury hearing. It is to them—and to their location within the larger context of state and national politics—that one must turn to understand fully the decision reached in Nashville.

FEDERAL OFFICIALS AND THE POLITICS OF STATE

No one did more to influence the grand jury hearing than Judge Elmer D. Davies and the lawyers from the USA's office who worked closely with him. Spearheading the first round of proceedings was 56-year-old A. Otis Denning, the veteran attorney whom Hopton so greatly admired and who was one of Davies's "close personal friends." Assisting Denning and assuming a more prominent role after the grand jury reconvened following the FBI's second investigation was 26-year-old Z. Thomas "Tommy" (also called "Day") Osborn Jr.

Initially, Caldwell reported "friendly conferences" with members of the USA's office, but he described "a marked change" in their attitude "as soon as the grand jury met." Then it became obvious to the Washington lawyer that they did not intend to let the CRS "have much to say about the running of the grand jury or the presentation of the case." Even more worrisome, Caldwell doubted that the USA would present it with even "a pretense of fairness to both sides." "Unless more restraint is exercised," he warned, "intemperate language and discourteous conduct may pervert this investigation of the facts into a 'witch-hunt,' which will only result in even more criticism of the Department of Justice."[64]

Caldwell was not wrong in his assessment of the direction the Nashville attorneys wished to take the case. Although Hopton relied overwhelmingly on official sources for his conclusions, he at least searched for answers to questions such as why African Americans had gathered on East Eighth Street on the 25th and who had caused the damages in the Bottom. In contrast, Denning and Osborn clearly had an agenda they wished to pursue, and they did so relentlessly, asking leading questions and reworking responses to achieve their goals. In essence, they behaved like defense attorneys for the Highway Patrol and prosecuting attorneys when questioning black witnesses. As Eleanor Bontecou explained on her return to Washington in the midst of the hearing:

> It soon became apparent that a story had been agreed upon by all the State officials. . . . As the investigation proceeded it became evident that there was not only an effort to place the blame upon the State Guard [instead of the Highway Patrol], and to discredit the Southern Conference and especially Mr. Dombro[w]ski, but that the grand jury proceedings were also being used to discredit the three Negroes who were the leaders in the . . . area, representing them as disreputable and rather sinister characters who had long been stirring up discontent among the Negroes against the whites.[65]

In the eyes of the executive committee of the National Committee for Justice in Columbia, Tennessee (NCJC), Denning and Osborn behaved so outrageously that they deserved to be disciplined or removed from office.[66]

Why did federal officials in Tennessee choose this course of action? Racism undoubtedly played a part. Denning was the only person in the grand jury hearing to use consistently the outmoded term "darkies" in his references to blacks. Judge Davies, a native of Magnolia, Arkansas, had joined the Ku Klux Klan in Louisiana in 1919 just prior to entering law school and had once made a "sort of charade" of a black man who appeared in his courtroom without a coat and tie by forcing the man to wear ill-fitting apparel that he kept for such emergencies.[67]

Yet even NAACP Counsel Robert L. Carter determined in regard to Davies, "We cannot prove that his past membership in the Klan has any bearing on his attitude in our case."[68] The judge was also described as "a judicial tyrant" who was "very tough" on everyone, including the lawyers who practiced before him. Even more significant, upon assuming the bench he had taken action that resulted in the seating of the first African American ever on a federal grand jury in the Middle Tennessee District.[69] In short, racism does not always prevail among human characteristics even when it is present.

Further clues to the prism through which federal officials in Tennessee viewed the case lie in statements by Bontecou and Hoover's top assistant, Edward Tamm. As Bontecou explained it, the case "involved bitter political issues." She continued: "We discovered after we got there that the judge in the case was convinced that we'd been sent down by the Justice Department to block [Senator Kenneth D.] McKellar's election. . . . that ran through the whole case. Instead of collaborating with the local United States . . . [Attorney] we found ourselves feeling as if we were the prosecutors and he was the enemy." Similarly, Tamm reported when the Justice lawyers arrived in Nashville, they discovered "that the District Judge was distrustful of these Assistants and had instructed two Assistant United States Attorneys to direct the grand jury proceedings." He then elaborated: "Caudle indulged in some smoke-talk about the Judge's desire to protect the McKellar group supported by the Nashville Banner from the hostilities of the other Nashville newspaper, The Tennessean." Bontecou too mentioned "the two rival papers there."[70]

In response to the notion that CRS attorneys had been sent to Nashville to block the nomination of McKellar, Bontecou declared, "Well that was a brand new idea to everybody!" Caldwell also insisted that they tried to "convince all concerned that we are here only to be of assistance and are not possessed with a crusading zeal but desire only a full and impartial investigation."[71]

Such an inquiry was impossible, however, given the political minefields through which it had to be negotiated. The hints dropped by Bontecou and Tamm make eminent sense when considered in terms of (1) the long-term political rivalries in Tennessee and the centrality of the competing Nashville newspapers in this rivalry, (2) the renewed intensity of the competition after New Dealer Silliman Evans became owner and publisher of the *Tennessean* in 1937, and (3) the larger power struggle underway in the country in 1946 and the primary election campaign that unfolded within it in Tennessee at the time of the grand jury hearing. Busy CRS lawyers might have little understanding of the intricacies of Tennessee politics, but federal officials there were not only acutely aware of them but completely enmeshed within them.

LONG-TERM POLITICAL RIVALRIES

At the turn of the century, Major Edward Bushrod Stahlman, owner and publisher of the Nashville *Banner*, and Colonel Luke Lea, owner and publisher of the Nashville *Tennessean*, occupied the same side of the factional fence in Tennessee Democratic politics. Both were Independents, as opposed to Regulars, and both supported Prohibitionist candidates. As late as 1912, both had endorsed Woodrow Wilson for president, but this affiliation was about to come to an abrupt end. In 1911, Mississippi native and Memphis lawyer, Kenneth Douglas "K. D." McKellar had run successfully for the U.S. House of Representatives. In 1915, he entered the Democratic primary in Tennessee's first popular election for U.S. senator. In this campaign, he was considered a distant third. Frontrunners were former governor Malcolm Patterson and Luke Lea, who had been chosen senator the same year McKellar went to the House by a combination of Independent Democrats and Republicans (known as Fusionists). Patterson and Lea delivered knockout blows to one another, however, and McKellar not only came out on top in the first primary but won the runoff against Patterson as well, a victory tantamount to election in this overwhelmingly Democratic state.[72]

Stahlman had opposed Lea in the primary, and he had good reason to oppose him thereafter. Already a keen rival of Stahlman in the newspaper business and a flamboyant character who at the end of World War I led his military unit in a madcap effort to capture Kaiser Wilhelm II, Lea caused the major considerable embarrassment when he attempted during the war to have him deported as an alien![73] Thereafter, their rivalry intensified. As Stahlman's great-granddaughter Mildred Stahlman explained: "The publisher of the *Tennessean* and my great-grandfather were tremendous political enemies and they considered that real animosity—family animosity and personal animosity and political animosity—and I was raised [to believe] that that family was the devil with horns."[74] Similarly, longtime newspaperman Ralph McGill recalled that when he worked for Stahlman in the early 1920s "all but the more timorous reporters kept loaded pistols in their scarred old desks. . . . Legend had it that one day the Leas would come surging up the stairway with revolvers drawn and the shooting would begin."[75]

Rescued by McKellar during the alien gambit, Stahlman became a staunch proponent of the senator, although they assumed opposing positions when McKellar supported women's suffrage, an issue the conservative newspaper owner could not endorse. Stahlman and his grandson and successor James Geddes Stahlman (Mildred's father, who became publisher of the *Banner* after his grandfather's death in 1931) continued to endorse the senator in every election until his final one in 1952, and they were vociferous in their partisanship. As McGill explained, "The Major's style was to walk right out of his corner when the bell ran and throw his Sunday punch." He taught his grandson well.[76]

Throughout the 1920s, Lea's faction reigned supreme in state government, but the publisher's personal, speculative fortunes began to unravel with the Wall Street crash in 1929. A year later, a bank in which he had an interest closed; it had contained state deposits totaling over $3 million. This and other disclosures discredited Lea's political organization as well as himself, and Edward Crump, who had by this time consolidated his power in Memphis, saw his "reform" candidate, Hill McAllister, become governor.

At the same time that Crump forces triumphed in Tennessee, Democrats won at the national level, and McKellar "gained access to a large store of patronage." Building on support in Memphis-anchored Shelby County and neighboring counties in West Tennessee and in Republican counties in East Tennessee to which he could dispense state and federal jobs, Crump and his Washington ally McKellar, with the consistent support of Stahlman and his newspaper, dominated Tennessee politics for the next sixteen years. Meanwhile, Lea and his son entered prison in North Carolina on conspiracy charges in 1934, and the *Tennessean*, headed by caretaker Lit Pardue, went into receivership.[77]

SILLIMAN EVANS AND RENEWED COMPETITION

Three years later, Texas reporter and Washington politico Silliman Evans purchased the paper from Pardue. Although there existed no "well-disciplined core of opposition" to Crump, the *Tennessean* and its new owner came to play "no mean political role" in the antiorganization forces. Not only was the newspaper "a consistent and strident critic of Crump," but Evans also participated in the selection of anti-Crump candidates and played a very influential role in planning and financing their campaigns, including those of Edward Ward "Ned" Carmack Jr., who ran against Senator A. T. "Tom" Stewart in the 1942 Democratic primary and against McKellar in 1946. Whether the *Tennessean* guided or simply voiced the views of its readers, its circulation area roughly coincided with the vicinity voting anti-Crump, and, according to contemporary analyst V. O. Key Jr., the newspaper played "a role of unusual significance in state politics."[78]

A friend as well as a former employee of Amon Carter, owner of the *Fort Worth Star Telegram*, Evans was tied closely to a cadre of men from his home state who were prominent New Dealers. They included John Nance Garner, Roosevelt's running mate in 1932; Sam Rayburn, congressman and later speaker of the House; and Jesse Jones, head of the Reconstruction Finance Corporation. Additionally, Evans had a personal—and personable—relationship with President Roosevelt himself.[79]

Schooled in the reformist tradition of Carter and an ardent proponent of the New Deal, Evans attacked the Crump organization in a variety of ways. He campaigned boldly for the establishment of a state civil service and, with even more import for the grand jury hearing in 1946, he exposed and ended "rackets among justices of the peace and *state-highway police*." Also in conjunction with his astute, free-spirited editor, Jennings Perry, he launched an all-out offensive against the poll tax, a "pernicious" device designed, in the words of Evans's son, "to maintain a power base for those that were able to control the election."[80]

Although Crump was the main target of Perry's political invective, McKellar came in for his share as well. He was especially denounced by the editor when poll tax measures were filibustered to death by southern senators in 1942 and 1943. In the first debate, wrote Perry, "McKellar waddled up and down the empty Senate aisles behind his pampered little middle"; in the second, he "rose to a point of personal privilege and . . . called everybody bad names."[81]

The poll tax not only brought to office "reactionary elements of the state in which the instrument is employed," Perry continued, but also it gave those elements "commanding posts in the committees of Congress" and "extraordinary power in federal government," because influence "in the national legislature is the achievement of simply staying in office." Again, McKellar served as a useful example:

> Senator K. D. McKellar of Tennessee, pinched upward through the years by the simple escapement of seniority, pontificates as acting-chairman and ranking member of the Appropriations Committee and sits next to Byrd in authority on the Rules Committee: afflicted with innumerable petty prejudices and touchy vanities, aged, sour-tempered, narrowminded, and irrevocably tied to the antidemocratic machine of Boss Ed Crump, he has withal more power over legislation, and hence over government, than any other member of the American Legislature.[82]

In addition to the fight waged by Evans and Perry against the poll tax, McKellar emerged as a special target of the *Tennessean* "because of his incessant attempts to make the non-political TVA a patronage plundering ground."[83] Furious at the newspaper's attacks, Tennessee's senior senator had one of Crump's most vitriolic verbal assaults on Evans published in the *Congressional Record*.[84] From the floor of the Senate, he charged that the *Tennessean* was filled with "dirty, venomous, corrupt and most damnable falsehoods," and he denounced the newspaper's publisher as an "assassin of character." Still unsatisfied, McKellar demanded—and got—a Senate investigation of Evans's acquisition of the *Tennessean*. It occurred in November 1945, just five months before the Nashville grand jury hearing commenced.[85]

Although the senator failed to prove his accusations, his fury at Evans remained at such an intense level that he punched the newspaper owner in the face two years later when he encountered him in his Washington hotel.[86] Equally revealing, as late as three days before the grand jury hearing on the Columbia incident, Crump was still pondering whether or not McKellar should, as part of his 1946 reelection bid, further attack the publisher's acquisition of the *Tennessean*. Crump also harshly denounced Evans once again in a personal communication in April of 1946.[87] Given these circumstances, it is understandable that Elmer Davies deduced that Evans's friends had launched a counterattack in the form of a grand jury hearing and were out to undercut the senator's bid for reelection.

In his denunciation of the newspaper owner, Crump predicted that "Senator McKellar will be elected by a tremendous majority next August, which is a horrible thought for you." The Memphis boss was much less sanguine about the senator's chances, however, than he appeared in this communique. Near the end of March, he telegraphed McKellar the following advice: "[Ned] Carmack will put up a hard campaign speaking everywhere[,] therefore let's not overlook a single bet." Undoubtedly, Crump was remembering the Senate campaign four years earlier. In that contest, Carmack, whose father had been a U.S. senator and then an editor for Luke Lea at the *Tennessean* before he was gunned down in 1908 in the streets of Nashville by his political foes, held a commanding lead over Tennessee's junior senator until the Shelby County vote was added. The *Tennessean* candidate would in fact have won the election had Crump not delivered 86 percent of Shelby's 50,000 votes for the incumbent Stewart.[88]

Moreover, in 1946, Crump was worried about "a large soldier vote" and about "the negro vote." "The Northern negro papers are against Senator McKellar because he is against FEPC," he commented. Even more than either of those constituencies, Crump was concerned about the CIO. "Right here in Memphis the CIO may give us a fight we have never had before," he brooded. "We just don't know about it at the present time and the same things exists [*sic*] in the other cities." Although Crump acknowledged that "there is a terrible feeling among many against the CIO throughout the country and in the cities," he continued to obsess about it, worrying, "At the same time it existed back there when Roosevelt ran [in 1940 and 1944] and he was buddying with them everyday."[89]

THE LARGER POWER STRUGGLE AND THE
PRIMARY BATTLE OF 1946

Crump's concerns reflected the larger power struggle between business and labor that was intensifying in the wake of the war, as each side attempted to set the demobilization agenda and to ensure acceptance of its vision of "Americanism." Throughout the 1920s, notes historian Elizabeth Fones-

Wolf, the conservative, business perspective—with its emphasis on "social harmony, free enterprise, individual rights, and abundance"—had held sway. As the Depression deepened, however, the corporate view lost influence and prestige, and workers increasingly embraced a vision of Americanism that emphasized "economic equality, social justice, and human rights." They especially had in mind "the right to a decent wage and to security from poverty, ill health, unemployment, and old age." With these goals— and as the New Deal gathered momentum—workers looked increasingly to the federal government, not to private enterprise, for protection and assistance. Although business's image improved somewhat during the war, as high production levels were achieved, surveys conducted as servicemen returned to veteran status indicated that they continued to believe that government, not business, should solve most of society's problems.[90]

The heart of the liberal-labor postwar legislative program was a Full Employment Bill, and this measure attracted not only the AFL and the CIO but a broad coalition that included the NAACP and the National Farmers Union. Having formed a political action committee (PAC) in 1943, having allied itself closely with New Deal Democrats since its inception, and possessing a more leftist orientation than the AFL, the CIO in particular appeared poised after the war to use the political process to achieve labor's goals. Not surprisingly, the CIO served as the main target of pro-business conservatives and moderates, who attempted to reestablish the pre-Depression view of Americanism and the image of themselves, not the federal government or organized labor, as society's chief arbiters.[91]

A businessman himself, as well as an astute politician and an emphatic foe of the CIO, Ed Crump set out in conjunction with McKellar to craft a campaign that appealed especially to business and that smeared the CIO and its PAC, as well as the FEPC, as "communistic." Editing a diatribe McKellar had fashioned against the chairman of the Memphis CIO-PAC, Crump informed the senator, "I cut out where you enumerated some of the things you have voted for [such as the 65-cent minimum wage bill]. None of the business people like those things and I believe the letter reads just as good without them." He added, "I cut out where you said you felt sure that the American Federation of Labor will be for you. We think it is well for you to deal strictly with the CIO in your letter."[92]

In addition to reworking this communiqué, which was given extensive publicity, Crump advised McKellar to "talk . . . a little about the CIO and Communism" in statewide radio addresses and to say "CIO, directed from New York and Washington" whenever he mentioned the organization. "That shows long distance interference," he explained.[93] The Crump forces also encouraged the senator in repeated telegrams to find out whether "the man who is now in Memphis directing the smear campaign from there, and writing stories for the Tennessean under the guise of a staff correspondent [Louis Gordon, head of the Capitol Speakers and Writers Bureau in Washington, D.C.]" was the same person identified as a Communist from Maine by Martin Dies's House Un-American Activities Committee. A Memphis ally of Crump's thought it "a golden opportunity to actively identify the Communists with the campaign against us," while Crump himself crowed, "If you get the information on Gordon the communist in Maine, [Silliman] Evans' neck will go off."[94]

Ironically, Crump had McKellar omit from his response to the CIO a rhetorical denial that he was "a Russian"—and with it an allusion to James Dombrowski, whom the senator obviously thought fit this category—because such a reference might "incur the enmity of a lot of Jewish people in the cities." Nevertheless, during the campaign the Shelby organization blasted away at the SCHW as "a notorious Communist-front outfit," and McKellar declared in private correspondence that he was "bitterly opposed to Dombrowski and everything he stands for." The senator also applauded Crump's "hanging Silliman Evans and the Tennessean on to Carmack" in the additions the Boss made to his letter. To these enemies, McKellar added a few of his own. In replying to a Knoxville judge, he proclaimed: "No sir, I never fought TVA in my life. . . . [TVA Head David] Lilienthal is a scoundrel and a falsifier, who is kept in office by Mrs. Franklin Roosevelt, Walter White, the colored leader, Justice Frankfurter, and Sidney Hillman [chairman of the CIO-PAC], so I am advised."[95]

Fervently anti-Communist, anti–New Deal, and anti-labor, James Geddes Stahlman—always "Jimmy" to the more senior McKellar—was well positioned philosophically to do battle in behalf of the Crump forces in the 1946 primary, and he carried on the fight with his usual gusto. As early as January, a *Banner* headline screamed, "SCHW Called Instrument In Hands of Communists." Privately the newspaper publisher lambasted members of the CIO-PAC as "subversive bastards," and in his front-page column "From the Shoulder," he linked the "Communist-dominated CIO" not only to "The Communists" but also to "The FEPC, The SCHW, The Farmers' Union Or the pink fringe Who would like To Carpet-bag Tennessee again." "Once is enough," he added, and closed with the exclamation, "It's McKellar and McCord ALL THE WAY!"[96]

In short, by the time the grand jury met, Crump, McKellar, Stahlman, and their cohorts had clearly defined all of the groups and individuals supporting the inquiry into the Columbia incident as a solid phalanx of political enemies. They undoubtedly noted that Eleanor Roosevelt raised money for the effort as she cochaired the NCJC. They believed, not entirely incorrectly, that Walter White and the NAACP, James Dombrowski and the SCHW, the CIO, and the Communists had mobilized public opinion to such an extent that they induced Tom Clark to instigate an investigation. They probably knew that Justice attorney A. B. Caldwell had clerked for John Nance Garner, Silliman Evans's old Texas buddy and New Dealer, and that Eleanor Bontecou not only had the trust of civil rights organizations but had also authored a major critique of the poll tax. Together with John Kelley, Caldwell and Bontecou had come to Nashville at the behest of Harry Truman, a president that Crump and Stahlman would abandon in favor of Strom Thurmond in 1948.[97] Most telling of all, the only persons who had seen state troopers destroying property in the Bottom and who could identify at least some of them were reporters and photographers from the Nashville *Tennessean*!

In fact, liberals did not hold the same views as Communists. They did not even possess the same opinions within their own ranks in regard to African Americans. Still, all of those involved shared the broad vision of Americanism forged among workers during the New Deal and the war, and many had overtly opposed the Crump organization. This was what McKellar and his associates discerned, and from there it was but a scant step to the belief that the grand jury hearing was politically motivated, a notion that had no support in the extant evidence.

Because most white Tennesseans did not place African American interests high on their list of priorities, it is difficult to know whether indicting state troopers for excesses in Columbia would have reflected negatively on McKellar and McCord. Nevertheless, this was the lens through which Crump forces viewed the hearing. The meshing of their political perspective and their racist proclivities was fortuitous but not essential for them to carry on the fight as they did.

Their view was succinctly epitomized in a cartoon sent to McKellar after the hearing ended. It showed grouped together Eleanor Roosevelt, James Dombrowski, Sidney Hillman, a reporter with the label "Communist Press" in his hat, and, underscoring Ralph Ellison's leitmotif, an African American with NAACP on his shirtsleeve but with his face shielded so that he had no identity. All had hand pumps and were vigorously blowing up a large balloon labeled "The Columbia Incident." Looks of surprise, chagrin, and despair appeared on their faces; a large tear rolled down Mrs. Roosevelt's cheek, as the balloon exploded with a loud "POW!" The caption at the top of the page read "Punctured by The Federal Grand Jury."[98]

"Based on everything I have always heard," John Seigenthaler asserted recently, the grand jury hearing "went absolutely nowhere because . . . K. D. McKellar said, 'We're not going to have any of *that*.'" Seigenthaler may be right, but McKellar did not have to intervene directly in the affair. He had in Elmer Davies a trusted friend whom he had not only recommended as a federal judge but had supported vigorously when his nominee was challenged.[99] For his part, Davies was known "among his political friends and colleagues" as one who would "go to the bridge with you." Additionally, the judge may have had his own ax to grind, since both the national NAACP and the local Nashville branch, as well as the Tennessee Federation of Labor, had opposed his nomination.[100] Certainly he shared the perspective of his political associates when it came to liberals and leftists.[101]

Ironically, despite the belief of McKellar and his allies that the Nashville hearing had been instigated by his political enemies in an effort to defeat him, the proceeding served him and other conservatives well. In the 1942 Democratic primary in Maury County, Ned Carmack amassed 4,054 votes; incumbent Senator Tom Stewart, only 504. In 1946, McKellar outdistanced Carmack in the same locale by a margin of 1,734 to 1,441. Statewide—in marked contrast to the 1942 primary—McKellar defeated Carmack so handily that he needed no votes from Shelby County for his victory.

This turnaround was by no means directly attributable to the grand jury hearing, not even in Maury County. However, the Nashville proceedings provided the Crump organization with an opportunity to link disparate oppositional elements with one another and with Communism in a highly visible setting just at the time the Crump cronies were fashioning their primary campaign. Indeed, it may have helped the Crump group to forge these elements into a single foe in their own minds. Certainly, it provided the chance to connect these liberal elements together in the eyes of others.[102] The hearing also gave conservatives the chance to pillory leaders like Sidney Hillman and James Dombrowski at the end of a war that had imparted momentum to their organizations.[103] In short, politics not only strongly influenced the course of the grand jury hearing, the hearing itself had important political ramifications.

As Charles V. Hamilton noted in the early 1970s, "while the [federal] judge is not expected to *perform* politically, it is quite clear that the jurist is a part of the political process." J. W. Peltason put it in more expansive terms as he explained the role of southern federal judges in school desegregation cases: "the judge must make more than a legal decision; he must make a political decision in the broadest . . . sense. He must choose between competing concepts of the public interest."[104]

In making a strong stand against the advocates of black Maury Countians, Judge Davies probably acted largely in the narrow, partisan sense, but in doing so, he endorsed the wider view of Americanism espoused by Crump, McKellar, and their political associates, a stance with which the upper-middle-class judge himself agreed. In behaving in this fashion, Davies was more the rule than the exception. As Kenneth N. Vines wrote in his epilogue to Peltason's 1971 study:

> The record of failures and segregationist decisions in the southern courts shows that the Supreme Court critically *underestimated* the strength and persistence of judges' alliances to the southern region.
>
> The Court *overestimated*, on the other hand, the functions of the judicial values of "independence" and rational legal thinking in overcoming the segregationist point of view and identification with the local community. . . . Many opinions and attitudes of southern judges indicated that legal values, such as respect for higher court orders and precedents and independence of public opinion, were not strong enough to overcome local prejudices.[105]

The Nashville hearing makes explicit the politicized nature of those "local prejudices," and it serves as a reminder that disciplining police officers is as much a political act as policing itself. Although African Americans and their white allies had garnered enough strength by the end of the war to give pause to the president of the United States, the attorney general, and the FBI director, they remained a relatively insignificant part of the constituencies—and the concerns—of most southern officials, whether federal or state. Their outsider status, more than anything else, determined the course of events in the spring of 1946.[106]

7

OUTSIDERS AND
THE POLITICS OF
JUSTICE

A native of Culleoka who was deeply incensed at the negative publicity his community was receiving, Judge Joe M. Ingram proved no more impartial in the trial that occurred in Lawrenceburg than had his predecessor, Judge Davies, in the grand jury hearing. Time and again Ingram acted in concert with the prosecution, and as happened so often in cases involving African Americans accused of crimes against whites, he seemed to assume the guilt of those on trial and to pursue "speed" as a main objective.[1] Yet the outcome of this case differed markedly from that of the grand jury hearing, with the defenders of black Maury Countians scoring an enormous victory. This chapter explores the reasons for this dramatic turn of events.

Although conservatives, like liberals in the earlier proceeding, did contribute to their own demise in the Lawrenceburg trial, liberals triumphed largely because of their own efforts. Unquestionably, the national office of the NAACP played an important role in this campaign—raising money for the defense, mobilizing lawyers in Tennessee, and sending Thurgood Marshall to map strategy and assist as the initial maneuvers in the case commenced in the spring. Marshall's illness, however, left the trial itself in the hands of Leon Ransom, recent dean of Howard University Law School, and the two attorneys in Tennessee, Z. Alexander Looby of Nashville and Maurice Weaver of Chattanooga. Looby and Weaver in particular carried the day.[2] Though Marshall tried first to get the case postponed and then to procure another attorney from New York, neither he, nor anyone else from the national office, could have done a better job.

The success of the defense attorneys and the loss by the prosecution lawyers were very much related to their insider-outsider status within the white and black communities, the legal establishment, and the criminal justice system itself. Ironically, in this trial, certain outsider attributes of Looby and Weaver, and of the jurors they chose, served their clients well.

THE PROSECUTION AND ITS CASE

For Tennessee's district attorney general (then called attorney general) Paul Bumpus, the Columbia case was clear-cut. On the basis of "some prearranged plans," African Americans gathered in "Mink Slide" at the behest of their leaders: James Morton, Julius Blair, and Blair's sons Saul and Charlie. Having "commandeered" a public street, they attempted to "lure" whites into the vicinity. When their remarks to the police and the sheriff failed to achieve this objective, they acted in a way certain to entice white Maury Countians into their vicinity: they shot out streetlights. When four of the town's six policemen, who were clearly identifiable from lights located at the intersection of East Eighth and South Main Streets, walked into the area, the men gathered in front of Saul Blair's barbershop shot the officers, wounding Will Wilsford very seriously. The charges were as straightforward as the crime: the alleged leaders were charged with inciting others to attempt murder in the first degree, the followers with attempted murder in the first degree.[3]

In the Bumpus scenario, previous lynchings within the community were deemed irrelevant. Hugh Shelton Sr., a private attorney who assisted Bumpus, went so far as to argue before the jury that references by the defense to lynchings "that happened nineteen or thirteen years ago" were an attempt "to divert your mind from the real issues of this lawsuit." Bumpus actually labeled the gathering of *African Americans* in the Bottom as an "attempted lynching." Both demanded conviction of the defendants because they had allegedly shot Wilsford while banding together for an unlawful purpose: the takeover of a public street![4]

In retrospect, one wonders how the attorney general could have so easily—and so persuasively in his own mind—wrenched this case from its social moorings. Why did he base it on a narrow, legalistic argument that obviously did not ring true to the jury? In part, Bumpus was forced to employ the street-seizure line of reasoning because he had no physical evidence connecting any of the defendants to the shooting of Wilsford.[5] Even more important, his decision resulted from his legal training and from his immersion in a segregated white establishment that had little knowledge or understanding of the African American community. Bumpus's perspective influenced not only his perception of the case and of the African

Americans allegedly involved but also their response to him. In the end, then, the legal lens through which the Attorney General viewed the case and his position *within* the white establishment and *apart* from African Americans, including the Bottom's leaders, contributed significantly to his losing the case.

To an extraordinary extent, the professional elite—corporate lawyers and university law professors—have shaped the values and approaches of attorneys throughout the U.S. since the turn of the century. "The words and deeds of bar leaders tell us things worth knowing," legal historian Jerold Auerbach has observed, "about those who were empowered to speak for the legal profession and about a profession that permitted so few to speak for so many."[6]

As law was professionalized in twentieth-century America, form was divorced from substance, and lawyers were taught to focus on solitary parties in discrete cases. "The legal mind" according to Thomas Reed Powell of Harvard, was "one that could think of something that was inextricably connected to something else without thinking about what it was connected to."[7] As a man who recently distinguished between discrimination and segregation on the grounds that if "discrimination" is "the right term" in referring to African Americans, "the whites were also being discriminated against, for they were segregated from the blacks just as much as the other way around," Bumpus was especially suited intellectually for legal formalism. At the same time, his eleven-month apprenticeship with an attorney in nearby Lebanon, Tennessee, and his service first as a lawyer in private practice and then as assistant district attorney general and attorney general for fifteen years, undoubtedly reinforced his personal proclivities. "Courts . . . care little for the social setting of conflict," Auerbach observed. "They empty a dispute of its social content." This was Paul Bumpus's forte.[8]

Bumpus's refusal to acknowledge any connection between previous lynchings in Maury County and black actions on the 25th went beyond personal penchant and legal education, however. First, as an official committed to the maintenance of the status quo and as a champion of southern honor and traditions, the attorney general simply could not admit the lynching fears of black Maury Countians, even to himself, without acknowledging problems in the *structure* of southern race relations. Second, his social location in a white caste that interacted, for the most part, only superficially with African Americans, rendered him incapable of even *fathoming* their concerns, while World War II heightened his misconceptions.

As Channing Tobias explained to the PCCR as it discussed the mob violence issue:

What concerns me is that somehow or other we have to get back to the cause underlying these attacks upon particular groups of people, minority groups. I think the chief cause is the cheapening of the personality [status] of these groups through practices of discrimination that go unchallenged. A man is lynched because the people in the community realize that it doesn't cost as much to do him to death as it does a representative of a group whose personality is up to par. Therefore, he is the easy victim. . . .

I don't see how we are going to be able to take care of the rank and file who are kept cheap in that way because they, as someone has expressed it, are second-class citizens. We have a double standard . . . in American life. . . .

So it seems to me that . . . in order to get after the right to live . . . we have got to get after the right of every citizen to be on equality with every other citizen in those basic rights like education, those things that involve life, like jobs, and everything of that sort; that if we are going to do a thorough job and not a superficial job, we won't just be thinking in terms of an added statute that in an emergency might take care of a situation, but of our total structure as it affects minority groups.[9]

Southern white authorities, whether state or local, simply could not take this step. Instead, they maintained that race relations in their region were especially harmonious and that problems were caused either by a small group of malcontents among both races or by outsiders. In support of this perspective, they often pointed to friendly personal relations between individual black and white southerners. For these reasons, Bumpus told the Lawrenceburg jury:

[T]here is not the prejudice in the South against colored people . . . that exists in other sections of the country. . . .

The Southern people have always gotten along with colored people as a whole. Of course there are individual cases of trouble, but the Southern white people and the Southern colored people as a racial proposition would never have any trouble if these outside carpet-baggers would stay at home and attend to their own business.

The attorney general then waxed euphoric about "an old Negro woman who looked after me" and for whom "I shall continue to thank Almighty God for the lullabys she once sang . . . as long as the breath stays in my body, as long as my lips can respond to the devotion of my soul."[10]

For people like Bumpus, however, World War II added a new worry. As a

white southerner who had just witnessed the growing sense of personal efficacy among Africans Americans, he believed that "the blacks were deeply
saturated with the feeling that if they were good enough to endure the hard-
ships of military service during the war they were also good enough to associate with the whites in schools, cafes, and on all levels." In a sense, he was
not wrong, but the attorney general, like many whites, attributed a degree of
aggression and militancy to African Americans that was all out of proportion
to the changed state of affairs, especially when applied to middle-class
leaders like Morton and the Blairs. To Bumpus, a staunch supporter of
segregationist candidate Strom Thurmond in 1948, black actions on the
25th constituted an "uprising," and he argued in Lawrenceburg that black
Maury Countians attempted to "lure" whites into the East Eighth Street
vicinity "in order that they could snuff out the lives of some white people."[11]

At the same time that Bumpus envisioned black aggression in the Bottom, he attributed the channeling of this belligerence to East Eighth's
Street's proprietors. Well aware of the participation of black Columbians at
the ballot box and especially of the leadership role played by Morton and
the Blairs in organizing it, he, like other local authorities, was much more
willing than state officials to ascribe autonomy to them in instigating the
affair. Indeed, he was so convinced of their culpability that he never even
called them in for questioning!

The disparate opinions of Bumpus and of state assistant attorney general
Ernest F. "Jack" Smith on the origins of the alleged insurrection appeared in
their questioning of James "Digger" Johnson at the jail in Columbia. The
most striking aspect of their interrogation of the 29-year-old poolroom operator, however, was not their *differences* but the inability of *both* men to *hear*
what Johnson had to say, though they went to extensive lengths to insure
procedural fairness and thereby the future admissibility of his testimony in
court. In the end, their failure to understand Johnson—and the way that they
were manipulating him—led them to indict East Eighth Street's leaders, as
well as its customers, on very serious charges that they could not substantiate. Equally important, it demonstrated the enormous chasm between
blacks and whites that slavery originated and segregation perpetuated.

In questioning Johnson at the jail, the attorney general led off by saying,
"tell us what you know," but when the young man replied, "There was a
bunch of boys out there in the street with guns in their hands," Bumpus
leapt almost immediately to the question "Was Sol Blair there?" Initially,
Johnson shielded the Bottom's proprietors and their patrons, but the poolroom operator was vulnerable to pressure.[12] He had been selected as the
initial suspect for questioning because he had a criminal record, and the

sheriff believed they could obtain information from him. Additionally, highway patrolmen had taken from him a .32 caliber pistol at the time of his arrest, and his place of business was "right in the center of this disturbance." Johnson already had served time in the penitentiary, and Bumpus stated openly during the course of his examination: "He was down there with a gun himself and I think he is guilty as hell."[13]

Johnson also possessed latent anger and jealousy toward the Blairs and Morton that his interrogators could tap. Two-thirds of the way into his two-hour grilling, he exploded with his statement that "Blair and James Morton, they got other people, you know to do like they wanted them to do." Though even at this juncture he continued to insist that Saul Blair feared "it was going to be a mob down there," he also covered for himself by emphasizing that he did not believe such a claim. Smith leapt at this assertion, getting the prisoner to admit that he had never harmed a white person and that no white person had ever harmed him. When Johnson was asked whether he had inquired "who they were going to mob and who they were going to hang," he said simply, "No, they just called a meeting."[14]

For the first time, authorities heard a statement that conformed with their own view of the situation, and they pounced on it, asking questions as they believed events had unfolded. Smith, in keeping with the orientation of state officials, inquired about outside influences: "They were phoning people, weren't they?" and "They phoned some people out of town?" Though Mt. Pleasant and Fayetteville, Tennessee, were the only two telephone destinations that Johnson could generate, Smith persisted, "And wasn't it sort of a plan to get the[m] organized and attack the white people? Wasn't that the sort of a plan?" Johnson would say only, "I know he told all them to get guns," but the investigators scarcely heard him. They were hot on the trail of those who attended the alleged meeting, a gathering the FBI later determined had never occurred.[15]

Ironically, Sheriff Underwood played a strategic role in obtaining information from the prisoner. At the outset of the interrogation, he assured Johnson, "They wont [sic] hurt a hair of your head." As the inquiry proceeded, he offered him a cigarette. He also prodded Johnson with the names of specific individuals. Excitedly, Bumpus and Smith urged Underwood on in his questioning. "Give him another name," the attorney general demanded, while Smith pushed, "Let's get another name, Sheriff. He is willing to tell it while you are here. I think he wants to." "We are trying to help you and want to help all the colored people and don't want none of them killed," Underwood explained to the man who would lie dying in a pool of his own blood in the adjoining office within less than four hours.[16]

As Johnson answered officials' queries, they continued to read more into his responses than was actually there. At the same time, they coaxed him along with assurances that they believed he had nothing to do with events on the 25th, a step they were unwilling to take as long as his testimony failed to meet their expectations. From questions about the purported meeting at Morton's, Underwood moved on to ask about other gatherings in the Lodge Hall. Although Johnson replied, "Oh, they have meetings pretty often but there is nothing to any of them," Smith pressed again on the outsider issue, asking whether "any outside people, outside of the county" attended any of these gatherings. "They do over at James Morton's place. . . . They have got a club," Johnson answered. "But I mean anybody from Chicago or any places like that—Louisville?" Smith demanded. "No sir." "What is the name of that club?" "Elks' Club," Johnson replied.[17]

While Smith strove to uncover outside agitators and Communist conspirators, Bumpus pursued the agenda he believed black proprietors had in mind in their alleged uprising—the adjudication of long-standing grievances made more explicit by the recent war and the Stephenson-Fleming fray. Almost fifty years after the trial, the attorney general maintained, "I can understand their position." Then, as long after, he believed that black Columbians were unhappy with segregated public facilities, that the war had intensified their frustration, and that their grievances prompted the shooting of the Columbia police.[18]

To this end, Bumpus asked Johnson whether "Julius Blair has got the idea that he ought to associate with white folks" and whether Johnson had "heard him do a lot of talking like that." He also inquired about the refusal of the Bottom's patriarch to attend "the picture show because they make him go through the colored entrance" and whether his sons and James Morton followed the same practice. Eventually, after considerable guidance, Johnson offered this assessment: "There wouldn't have been that trouble if it hadn't been for Sol and James Morton. If it hadn't been for them two niggers we wouldn't have been in it." As the version of events that Bumpus anticipated unfolded, the attorney general interjected: "I think you are telling the truth now, Jigger [sic]. Of course, that is the idea that we had all the time."[19]

Although Johnson's death precluded his appearance as the State's "star witness" at the trial, and further investigation by the FBI failed to substantiate *any* of his claims, local and state authorities continued to give undue weight to them. Smith relied on them in his report to the governor, and Bumpus admitted to the FBI that Johnson's remarks were "the only definite information which was uncovered to substantiate his [personal] belief that there had been some prearranged plans among the negroes to congregate in Mink Slide with arms in the event there was any indication of racial trouble."[20]

At the outset of his interrogation, Johnson was told that he had "a constitutional right" and did not have to talk unless he wanted to. He was reminded that if he did make a statement, it could be used against him if he had committed any crime. Underwood explained, "We are not promising you anything and we are not threatening you."[21] When J. Walter Griffin entered the room, the prisoner was asked if he objected to the police chief's presence. As the poolroom operator was being questioned, no one struck him or abused him in any way. Yet despite these precautions, Johnson's interrogators did not hear an accurate account of developments in the Bottom on the 25th. Instead, they selectively pieced together fragments of information that corresponded to the preconceived version of events that they carried with them into the examination room. As Johnson's scenario grew closer to their own, they believed him.

Local and state officials misheard Johnson in part because, like many southern whites, they held sinister notions of African Americans that were channeled by the war into expectations of conspiracies and rebellions. They also misheard him because they did not share the same, horrendous perception of mob violence that black southerners did. The chasm built up through years of separation and estrangement was too wide. Lynchings did not hold the same meaning for perpetrators as for victims. This was, above all, the central message of Johnson's interrogation. The body of Cordie Cheek lying crumpled in a rumble seat simply did not resonate the same on both sides of the racial divide.

As representatives of the criminal justice system, officials like Bumpus and Smith had a special obligation, not just to the police or the victim but to an abstract principle of equity. In 1935, the Supreme Court held that "the interest of the prosecutor is not that he shall win a case, but that justice shall be done."[22] While "the defense attorney's job is to defend his client," the executive secretary of the North Carolina Conference of District Attorneys recently explained, "The District Attorney's job is more difficult. He has multiple clients: the State, the victim, and an intangible concept of justice. These interests often come into conflict and it is his responsibility to balance them."[23] Yet with authorities arrayed on one side of an expansive, enduring racial cleavage and alleged offenders on the other side, it was very difficult, if not impossible, to achieve balance.

To make matters more complicated, the abstract legalism so readily embraced by professionals like Bumpus legitimized their racial orthodoxy in their own eyes. A man who eschewed mob violence, the former attorney general firmly believed that he never discriminated against African Americans in carrying out his official duties. Scrupulously maintaining all the forms of procedural fairness during interrogations (even while selectively hearing the testimony of unreliable witnesses), emptying a case of its social content by separating the fears and subsequent actions of black Americans from a long tradition of white aggression and dominance, and treating their alleged infractions as discrete events—all these actions bespoke *objectivity* to the district attorney. In his view of the situation, he was upholding the highest precepts of law and justice. Yet the confines of his approach were so narrow that those outside the system—in class terms, but more especially in racial terms—were rarely served.

Not surprisingly, these forms of interaction between blacks and whites had grave, long-term implications for African Americans and their relationship with the criminal justice establishment. As Auerbach has explained in regard to attorneys generally: "My point is not that lawyers have been more prejudiced than other Americans. It is, instead, that bias in the legal profession has had particularly serious consequences in a society that depends so heavily upon the legal profession to implement the principle of equal justice under law and, simultaneously, to harmonize law with social change."[24] What was true for lawyers was even more applicable to district attorneys. Bumpus's actions in the Columbia case did nothing to improve relations between the criminal justice system and black Maury Countians, though ironically, his steps did inadvertently help achieve the freedom of those on trial in Lawrenceburg.

Bumpus's failure to interview the Bottom's leaders and his overreliance on a misunderstood version of Digger Johnson's testimony, resulted not only in his losing his best chance for gaining any real understanding of events on the 25th but also for fashioning indictments more in keeping with the confusion of the moment, indictments that he might have been able to sustain. Tennessee's statute for attempted murder, for example, required "felonious intent." To achieve conviction, one had "to establish deliberation, malice, and premeditation on the part of the defendant." In contrast, a statute for "malicious shooting" necessitated only that it be shown that the act was "unlawfully *or* maliciously" perpetrated. By going for the maximum charge, Bumpus significantly increased his burden of proof, an approach that did not work before a jury looking for concrete evidence.[25]

The attorney general's actions also intensified interclass solidarity among black Maury Countians and affected the credibility of both prosecution and defense witnesses in a way that contributed to the State's loss. Not unexpectedly, given the long-standing, adverse relationship most African Americans had with the criminal justice system, they shared a strong sense of solidarity with one another—"a solidarity," in Gunnar Myrdal's words, "against the law and the police."[26]

Yet unlike their customers, black proprietors had some reason to cooperate with authorities. Although Morton and the Blairs were well aware of the problems their patrons faced in dealing with the criminal justice establishment, they, after all, helped elect officials like Bumpus and Underwood, and they had on occasion gotten some relief in the courts. James Morton, for example, had once won a suit against a white man, who subsequently served a prison term.[27]

Not surprisingly, however, Bumpus's adamant belief in the complicity of East Eighth Street's business owners in the shooting of Wilsford, coupled with the harsh charges that he levied against them, further solidified their ties to the men who frequented their establishments. At one point in the trial when the defendants had been out of work for a considerable length of time, Julius Blair gave each money. Even more indicative of their orientation, the Bottom's leaders refused to name a single individual on the street the evening of the 25th, though they were grilled again and again on the issue while on the witness stand in Lawrenceburg. "I can't recall them," "I didn't pay no attention," "I don't generally keep up with names when I see them in the evening," Saul Blair stubbornly insisted. As usual, however, his father proved most intrepid before officials. "How many Negro men did you see in Mink Slide that night?" the attorney general asked the elder Blair. "I wouldn't know," Blair responded and, in an obvious reference to the claims of white leaders about the age of mob members, added, "Most of them were teen-age boys."[28]

The refusal of white authorities to seek the perspective of East Eighth Street's proprietors on the February events and their subsequent indictment of them made officials' estrangement from all African Americans quite acute. Sheriff Underwood estimated that seventy-five people were questioned about the police shootings. Yet in court only seven witnesses identified anyone on the street that evening, and all presented problems for the prosecution.[29] In contrast, defense witnesses proved an enormous asset, in no small measure because of the inclusion of middle-class leaders among the defendants and because of the friends and associates who testified on their behalf.[30]

In the end, the dramatic differences between African Americans who testified for the defense and for the prosecution mattered. As Leon Ransom reminded the jury:

NAACP defense counsel and five of the African Americans taken into custody by the Highway Patrol: seated left to right, Attorney Maurice Weaver, Julius Blair, and Attorney Z. Alexander Looby; standing left to right, James Martin, James Morton, Charlie Blair, and Saul Blair. Note the middle-class dress and demeanor of all of the accused. (Courtesy of NAACP)

> Do you think Julius Blair went out there and got the Defendants . . . and said, "Look fellows, get your guns and the first time the police come down in this place you shoot them with the intent to kill." It is ridiculous. You have observed Julius Blair, you know he is not that type of man. . . . Do you think James Morton, a man who has a business which he is trying to develop, a thriving business is deliberately going out and invite these five men and others to go commit a crime? The men aren't built like that.

The jury agreed. Juror James Siegel Davis recently described Julius and Saul Blair, along with James Morton, as "the business, reliable characters in the black community." On the other hand, to Juror Jesse Bradley, prosecution witness Mamie Fisher was "just a streetwalker." "I wouldn't believe nothing she said, no way," he commented.[31]

Other factors figured in the decision of the Lawrenceburg jury. NAACP attorneys played an indispensable role that went beyond the selection of defense witnesses and the successful cross-examination of those appearing for the prosecution. The change of venue they obtained and the jurors they ultimately reached were critical. Still, the prosecution contributed to its own demise by bringing the indictments, and building the case, as it did. The proclivity of Bumpus and his associates for narrow, legalistic interpretations, and their failure—or inability—to *hear* the words of black Maury Countians, and to consult with their leaders, proved decidedly inimical to the prosecution's interests.

THE NAACP AND ITS ATTORNEYS

If local and state officials were hindered by their position *within* the legal profession, the criminal justice establishment, and a white caste generally, Looby and Weaver were set free by their *outsider* relationship to these same entities. Intellectually astute and well trained, both could use legal procedures very effectively, but their backgrounds and experiences allowed them to move beyond traditional boundaries in important ways.

An African American with West Indian roots, Looby encountered apartheid in the American South as a newly minted, Ivy League–trained attorney. Because of this situation, he possessed a commitment to the civil rights movement all of his adult life, which freed him from the formalistic, case-by-case approach of so many of his colleagues. At the same time, Maurice Weaver, a white southerner who was already something of a maverick in personal style as well as in his work as a labor lawyer, was affected by the war in a way that released him from white racial shibboleths and made him a passionate defender of equal rights. Together, the reserved African American and the ebullient white southerner scored an enormous victory. Jointly they demonstrated the necessity of going beyond profession, caste, and class to achieve justice for the underdog in the 1940s.

"A poker-loving crusader" who "quotes the classics like a highbrow" and "defends pawn shop operators with the low-brow admission that 'I've gone there myself,'" Zephaniah Alexander Looby—known as Z. Alexander or simply Looby—was born on Antigua, "a flyspeck of an island" in the British West Indies. When he was too young to recall, his family moved to the island of Dominica. At age 6 or 7, he lost his mother, who died in childbirth; at 15 he lost his father. Most of the inhabitants of Dominica were black, and they worked in the fields growing crops such as cacao, nutmeg, sugar, bananas, cotton, and arrowroot. Though his own father had "operated a few fishing boats," Looby never remembered "seeing much in the way of money." Still, a passionate reader who "never was much good at cricket" and who "from the very first showed an alarming ineptitude for music,"

Looby attended high school, where he received a much better education, he later told his wife, than he would have gotten in the United States.

Faced with the prospect of going into the fields at his father's death, Looby signed on as a cabin boy with a whaling ship bound for the U.S. In 1914, in New Bedford, Massachusetts, at the age of about 16, he jumped ship. "Broke and bedraggled," he set out to become "an American citizen and a lawyer," a career he had wanted to pursue since frequenting the magistrate's court in Dominica as a lad. While working in a variety of jobs that included a yarn mill, a restaurant, and a bakery (where he burned his right arm so badly that he carried scars from his elbow to his wrist throughout his life), Looby finished high school in the last high school class to matriculate at Howard University and completed college there as well. He then went on to receive his law degree from Columbia University, and in 1926 a doctorate in law from New York University.[32]

With his naturalization process still incomplete in 1926, Looby "swallowed his apprehension about coming South" and joined the faculty at Fisk University in Nashville. At that time, he later explained, "the cream of employment" for a black American was "in and around the schools." In 1928, he was admitted to the Nashville Bar, but a short time later, when "something happened with the salary business" at Fisk, he headed for Memphis with a friend to practice law. Looby remained in Memphis about three years, "But I wasn't willing to pay the moral price Mr. Crump demanded of attorneys there," he recounted. "However, I met my wife who was a school teacher. The trip was well worth it," he added. Returning to Nashville, Looby set up his own law practice, though like many black attorneys who found survival difficult, he continued to teach courses at Fisk in the 1930s and 1940s as well at Tennessee Agricultural and Industrial College and at Meharry Medical College.[33]

One of an exceedingly small number of African American lawyers in the country and member of an even more restricted pool in the South that had been shrinking steadily since 1910, Looby entered a harsh world.[34] Though well-educated, he faced discrimination both inside and outside the courtroom. When he received his first paycheck and went into town to buy a bathrobe and a hat, he remembered: "I learned something that day. While I was in the store, spending my money, I was treated with respect. But when I stepped outside, it was as if I didn't exist."[35]

Although never himself barred from appearing in court, Looby knew of black attorneys who were. Members of the court, including judges, routinely used the terms "darkie" and "nigger." The problem was twofold, the Nashville lawyer explained: "Whites didn't respect you and Negroes didn't think you could adequately represent them."[36] In addition, as Auerbach explains, opportunities for entering established law practices were limited, since whites usually would not hire a black attorney and black firms could not afford to do so. Like Looby, then, most young black lawyers "were shunted into solo practice," where they competed with other black attorneys as well as with white lawyers "for minuscule retainers from an economically disadvantaged clientele." "Indeed, failure often provided the only escape from sustained professional hardship."[37]

The 1920s, however, portended changes in the way many black attorneys viewed themselves and their relationship to their communities. Lawyers like Looby, "an . . . elite within the black bar" whose members were trained at some of the finest law schools in the country, emerged in this decade. Auerbach describes how "the precedent of black lawyers engaged in legal defense work" was also established in the wake of race riots in Chicago and the District of Columbia in 1919. In 1925, the National Bar Association (NBA) was founded by black attorneys who had been refused admission into the American Bar Association (ABA). According to its charter, the NBA was designed "to strengthen and elevate the Negro lawyer in his profession and in his relationship to his people." The twenties were also "crucial for the development of black cohesiveness," as African American attorneys shared with other black urbanites the rising consciousness that accompanied "the horrors of the postwar riots, the excitement of Marcus Garvey's black nationalist crusade, and the creativity of the Harlem Renaissance."[38]

Within this intellectual, social, and cultural ferment, some young black lawyers began to speak of a new role for themselves and their colleagues. Among the first was Raymond Pace Alexander, a 1923 graduate of Harvard Law School, who proclaimed: "We owe the law more than merely using it as a means of making a livelihood. We owe to our people, who, more than any other people are in need of our services, a duty to see that there shall be a quick end to the discrimination and segregation they suffer in their everyday activity."[39]

At this propitious time, the NAACP began reassessing its legal strategy, and the Howard University Law School inaugurated changes that would place African Americans at the forefront of the Association's new campaign. Charles Hamilton Houston was central to both developments. The only son of a Washington, D.C., lawyer, Houston graduated first in his class at the age of 15 from the M Street school, one of the best black high schools in the country. He went on to Amherst, where he was elected to Phi Beta Kappa and graduated as valedictorian at age 19. Completing college two years before the United States entered World War I, Houston taught English briefly at Howard and then attended the officers training school at Fort Des Moines, Iowa, where he was commissioned a first lieutenant in the Infantry.

After his military stint, Houston entered Harvard Law School, where he became the first African American to serve on the *Harvard Law Review*. While at Harvard, he caught the eye of Felix Frankfurter, who, according to historian Donald Nieman, was "an inspiring teacher, an exacting scholar, an avid civil libertarian," and a strong advocate of public service. After graduating fifth in his class in 1922, Houston studied an additional year with the eminent jurist, receiving his doctorate in law in 1923. He then traveled to Italy and Spain, earning the degree of doctor of civil law at the University of Madrid. From 1924 until 1929, Houston practiced in his father's law firm, though under his own initiative he also taught in the Howard Law School and in 1927 directed a "Survey of the Status and Activities of Negro Lawyers in the United States."

Appointed in 1929 by Howard's first black president, Mordecai W. Johnson, as vice dean in charge of building a three-year, full-time law program, Houston led a drive that culminated in the school's full accreditation by the ABA and the American Association of Law Schools in 1931. Only seventy-one schools in the nation enjoyed the ABA's stamp of approval. In a recent interview, Thurgood Marshall recalled Houston as so "tough" that his students called him " 'Iron Shoes' and 'Cement Pants' and a few other names that don't bear repeating" but said Houston was "absolutely fair," though a stern taskmaster. Marshall recalled losing thirty pounds his first year of law school, "solely from work, intellectual work, studying." The eventual Supreme Court justice entered Howard as a member of a class of thirty; "no more than eight or ten" graduated. In addition to demanding academic excellence, Houston pioneered in civil rights law, and he stressed a broad social role for black attorneys. According to his biographer, historian Genna Rae McNeil, the intrepid attorney told them all: "A lawyer's either a social engineer or he's a parasite on society."[40]

In 1935, Houston left Howard to serve as the special counsel for the NAACP, a position he would hold until 1938, when his protégé, Thurgood Marshall, assumed the post. Already six years earlier, at the deaths of NAACP litigators Moorfield Storey and Louis Marshall, the organization had begun reconsidering its legal strategy. A legal advisory committee had procured $100,000 from the American Fund for Public Service (Garland Fund) in 1930, and Nathan Margold, a Harvard graduate but at the same time, in Auerbach's words, "the prototypical outsider whose social conscience and hunger for opportunity had propelled him into the legal profession," had set out in a preliminary report guidelines for the legal strategy that would culminate in the *Brown v. Board of Education* decision in 1954.[41]

When Houston assumed the special counsel position in 1935, he urged that the Garland grant be used primarily to fight discrimination in education and that emphasis be placed on working with local communities and with black attorneys whenever possible. The latter insured not only that men like Looby would work closely with the Association but also that the fight against racial discrimination would continue long after the Garland fund was depleted. Houston's selection as the NAACP's chief counsel also meant that racial injustice would be fought "by means of a 'carefully planned [program] to secure decisions, rulings and public opinion on the broad principle instead of being devoted to merely miscellaneous cases.' "[42]

To Z. Alexander Looby, Charles Houston "topped them all." He "had no peers." Like Houston—who believed that in addition to being a social engineer, a black lawyer should act as a "business adviser . . . for the protection of the scattered resources possessed or controlled by the group"—Looby taught economics as well as business law at Fisk. Also in the tradition of Houston, he founded the Kent College of Law in Nashville in 1932 "with the express purpose of training colored men and women for the profession of law," but it was above all in civil rights litigation that Looby worked with the NAACP and that his efforts most closely resembled those of his hero.[43]

From the time he arrived in Nashville in 1926, the young attorney was involved in civil rights cases, especially those related to the systematic exclusion of African Americans from juries, an issue that Looby insisted he pioneered. A lifetime member of the NAACP and in the 1940s of its National Legal Committee, Looby worked with Houston and Marshall in their campaign to end discrimination in education. Specifically, he represented a Franklin County couple in their attempt to have their son admitted to the University of Tennessee's School of Pharmacy in 1937, and in 1942 he launched a teacher salary equalization suit in Nashville.[44]

Though he considered the Columbia litigation "his biggest civil rights case," Looby also initiated actions, both as a lawyer for the NAACP and as a member of the Nashville City Council, that led to the integration of the Nashville and Davidson County schools; the Clinton, Tennessee schools; several local restaurants and public golf courses; and even visiting hours at Nashville's landmark Parthenon. In 1960, Looby and his partner Avon Williams handled much of the defense for the first round of students arrested and tried for sit-ins in downtown stores. "Under his stress . . . every Negro lawyer in that city joined together," student demonstrator and later

SCLC staff member C. T. Vivian remembered. "I have seen lawyers just unmercifully bleed black people who were fighting for their bare living rights," he continued, "But here, under Looby . . . I think it was 13 banded together, fought our cases for nothing." Indirectly, Looby's participation in the student cases produced Nashville's largest civil rights march. This occurred when, in retaliation for his involvement with the students, the attorney's house was firebombed. In response, 2,500 people marched to City Hall demanding an end to violence and intimidation.[45]

"The generation of black civil rights lawyers who came of age in the 1930's forged an identity for themselves in the process of litigating equality for their race," Auerbach observed, and he continued: "Like Jewish lawyers who found opportunities in New Deal agencies that did not exist in private practice, these black lawyers fulfilled their aspirations with a commitment to the cause of civil rights. No longer was law practice a tenuous means of earning a living for black lawyers; it had become a mission of consuming social and personal significance."[46]

Unquestionably, Looby possessed personal qualities that helped explain his involvement with the NAACP and its civil rights campaign.[47] Yet in conjunction with his personal traits, his participation in a national civil rights campaign shaped him and his approach to law in ways that contributed significantly to his success at Lawrenceburg. "Looby's work is his life," journalist George Barker observed, while like his model, Charles Houston, "education and litigation were his instruments for social change."[48]

An Episcopalian and a Republican who supported Dewey in 1948, Looby was not a revolutionary. "When you break a door down, you injure the whole house," he asserted, and he proclaimed in a 1967 interview that he much preferred "the civilized group" of early 1960s demonstrators to "this black power group." But as a black civil rights lawyer, the Nashville attorney insisted on respect for his clients as well as himself, and he won both in the Lawrenceburg courtroom. At a dinner honoring him just after the fall trials, he explained that he "did not and never does go into a trial in the role of a 'Negro lawyer' nor put his client in the role of a 'Negro client'. . . . colored lawyers must make their fights as American lawyers and contend for every right the Constitution guarantees a citizen even when defending the humblest of colored citizens."[49]

In Lawrenceburg, Looby put this dictum into practice as he demanded that Judge Ingram instruct the attorney general "who is a Public Official and being paid by the Tax Payers, to at least exhibit some respect to these people." When Bumpus referred to defense witness Marcia Mayes as "'this nigger' woman," Looby again appealed to the judge: "I resent his language, and ask the Court to instruct him not to use that language in Court." "The Jury understands what I mean to say," Bumpus responded offhandedly, to which Looby shot back: "It is not a matter of what you want the Jury to understand. I object to it." Yet even this move was undoubtedly calculated, for, as African American Judge A. A. Birch recalled, everything Looby did "was done deliberately and to prove a point." However, Birch also noted: "I think Looby was very careful when selecting those occasions on which he said, 'Don't call my client Sally cause you don't know her, Judge, you call her Miss or Mrs.' I mean that's fine and it works sometimes, but there are times when discretion calls for you not to do that because of the stakes involved, so I think Looby sort of had a good feel for that."[50] In Lawrenceburg, Looby obviously read his jury well. Juror James Davis recently avowed: "Now the black attorney, Z. Alexander Looby, now he deserves lots of credit. . . . he was a gentleman that we respected."[51]

Looby's involvement in the civil rights campaign also gave him valuable legal experience that served him well in the Columbia-Lawrenceburg proceedings. As Thurgood Marshall explained: "Dr. Looby . . . has been the 'Rock of Gibraltar' around which the splendid defense of these cases has been carried on. He has never waivered [sic] an inch and has worked unceasingly day in and day out not only on the trials themselves but has been the one who has been responsible for preparation of the law of Tennessee on these cases and has had the responsibility of preparing all of the technical papers necessary to assure that the cases will not be lost on any technicalities."[52]

Most importantly, Looby's role as a civil rights attorney informed his overall approach to the case. To him, the Columbia affair was not an isolated incident involving the takeover of a public street and the shooting of a police officer but part of a large crusade dedicated to extending black rights and ending mob violence. For this reason, he not only worked with Marshall and Weaver in challenging the racial composition of the grand jury, but he also convincingly framed his response to the indictments in terms of self-defense, a position that Weaver too was able to embrace wholeheartedly because of his status as an outsider to mainstream white society.

Looby heard what the defendants had to say and he understood their concerns because he was part of the African American community, but he was able to translate their fears into a convincing plea because he was legally well trained and because he did not divorce form from substance. For Looby, the case could be seen *only* as part of a larger historical and social pattern. In short, he viewed it as he did because he stood in opposition to certain aspects of legal formalism in a way that the prosecution, entangled in both legalisms and a white establishment, could not do. Furthermore, Looby managed to reach jurors who saw his portrayal of events as quite convincing and who were willing to act on their convictions.

If Looby was freed from certain reigning legal precepts by his civil rights commitment, Maurice Weaver stepped outside white racial orthodoxy via an enhanced sense of racial egalitarianism, which he experienced during his military service. Like Looby prior to his engagement in the civil rights campaign, the Chattanooga attorney was in certain ways already predisposed toward the direction he took, but the war and its idealistic rhetoric made a difference. Weaver's altered racial perspective resulted in his pursuing the acquittal of the Lawrenceburg defendants with a passion and a vigor, born of a belief in racial equality, that distinguished him from the southern white attorneys who usually took NAACP cases. In turn, his efforts very successfully complemented those of Looby.

Weaver was by no means the first white lawyer to defend African Americans in behalf of the NAACP. Even in the Deep South, the Association found white attorneys willing to take some of its cases. Whether southern or nonsouthern, most of these individuals were preeminent within their communities and were graduates of some of the nation's best law schools. As scholars August Meier and Elliott Rudwick explain, this was especially important in the South, because the organization had to find legal counsel "whose standing was so impeccable within their communities that they could undertake such work without serious criticism or harm to their practice."[53]

The willingness of white attorneys to take NAACP cases did not mean, however, that they were progressives or liberals or even that they agreed with the Association's broad program. In fact, according to Meier and Rudwick, most "were essentially conservative men, characterized by a degree of noblesse oblige toward blacks, or by a conservative's concern with due process, law and order, and the protection of an individual's constitutional rights." Thus, a well-to-do southern white lawyer might take a case in an attempt to guarantee an African American accused of a serious crime a fair trial, "a position with which even highly conservative lawyers often agreed." Yet this same attorney did *not* support an end to disfranchisement and segregation, and concomitantly, he did not adopt the no-holds-barred approach that Weaver used so effectively in the Lawrenceburg case.[54] In fact, many southern white lawyers seemed to feel that justice had been served when their clients averted the death penalty and instead received life in prison, a position that neither Weaver nor Looby ever accepted.

In his personal style, his politics and legal practice, and most important of all, in his attitudes toward black Americans, Weaver differed from the white lawyers who usually participated in NAACP cases, and in the Lawrenceburg trial, these differences mattered. Born in 1911 in Evensville, "a little whistle stop in Rhea County" in southwestern Tennessee, the young attorney grew up in the small town of Soddy, just north of Chattanooga. A 130-pound "hotshot," Weaver liked to drink and party in a manner very similar to Silliman Evans and others wedded to behind-the-scenes, political cavorting.[55]

This orientation was important because it made the young lawyer much less concerned about appearances than was the case with most members of the middle class and thereby enabled him to thumb his nose at racial conventions in a way that few white southerners were bold enough to do. Weaver's jaunty style also rendered him impervious to criticism from whites, even when it grew menacing. "Neither violence nor the threats of violence had the slightest effect upon the young Tennessean," Walter White noted, and he added: "It was my impression that Maurice reveled in the danger as did Z. Alexander Looby."[56]

In addition to his personal characteristics, Weaver's politics and his legal work set him apart from most southern white attorneys and oriented him positively toward the message of equality that the war would convey. Remembered by his law school friend and former roommate, Laurent Frantz, as "a good-natured, genial, rather politician-type progressive and prolabor New Deal Democrat," Weaver did some work for the CIO following his graduation from the University of Tennessee Law School in 1935.[57]

The young attorney's work with organized labor, like his personal style, predisposed him toward the radical line he would adopt in 1946. As Auerbach noted, labor law in the 1930s, much like civil rights law at that time, was used as "'a weapon, as a tool in the service of the movement for social change'"; disparaged and sometimes harmed physically, labor lawyers evinced a commitment that "molded their lives and careers." Further, Auerbach reported, "Long after labor militancy had subsided into business unionism, labor lawyers retained a distinctive identity shaped by their Depression experiences." "These veterans remained," he added significantly, "'partisans of the underdog.'"[58]

Still, if Weaver, as Frantz recently remembered him, "was for a better break for the underdog, which certainly included blacks, . . . racial injustice did not have for him, at least in law school days, the kind of central focus which it had for the [Communist] Party, or for many people later during the Civil Rights struggles." Following the war, however, Weaver's racial awareness clearly heightened. As African American Professor A. F. Dixon of

Chattanooga explained to Walter White in March 1946: "Maurice Weaver has meant so very much to me and to our cause in general."[59]

Without a doubt Weaver delved wholeheartedly into the defense of black Maury Countians. Following the hearings on the pleas of abatement and the change of venue in the spring and summer of 1946, the Chattanooga attorney charged around the countryside procuring affidavits in an effort to shift the trial from Lawrenceburg to Nashville. Revealingly, he approached African Americans first in order to learn which whites might be amenable to his goals; *then* he went to local whites. He also secured 250 affidavits from blacks themselves.[60]

Weaver further distinguished himself from other white southern lawyers who took NAACP cases by boldly attacking the solidly entrenched system of segregation through words as well as deeds. Thus, not only did he assert during the pleas of abatement hearing that "a 'vicious' segregation of races" prevented black Maury Countians from being called for jury service because "they might be compelled to spend the night . . . [or] forced to eat in the same restaurant with white jurors," but also he attacked discrimination head-on in the Kennedy-Pillow trial, telling the jury, "prejudice doesn't have to be so violent you want to lynch somebody, it can be so insidious that it renders one incapable of rendering justice."[61] Additionally, Weaver broke the southern white taboo against employing courtesy titles for African Americans, by consistently using "Mr." and "Mrs." in addressing black witnesses, and he slyly asked African American agricultural extension agent George Newbern if he had ever competed against Lynn Bomar during the five years Newbern played football at the all-black Tennessee Agricultural and Industrial College in Nashville.

Finally, the attorney allied himself totally with the defendants and the other defense lawyers, spending time in the Bottom, where he discerned very quickly that blacks there did not like the term "Mink Slide," interviewing all of the more than one hundred men who were jailed, addressing NAACP fund-raising rallies, accompanying Marshall and Looby to the national NAACP convention, and traveling back and forth between Nashville and Columbia, and later Lawrenceburg, together with Looby in Looby's automobile.[62] So closely did the young attorney identify with black Maury Countians that he referred in his closing argument to "our people," though he quickly adjusted the phrase to "our clients."[63]

Unquestionably, Weaver's participation in the Columbia case promoted his wider involvement with the NAACP and intensified his commitment to civil rights.[64] Yet the war also had affected his perceptions. While Bumpus railed in his closing argument against outsiders who "like the filthy, loathsome birds of prey they are . . . swooped upon Tennessee's tragedy" and Looby depicted a technological, though God-ordered, world where "time and space have been annihilated" and "we have got to learn to live together," Weaver chose the recent war as the grounds for his rhetorical appeal. The attempt by the State to prosecute those on trial in Lawrenceburg reminded him of Lidice, he said, where Nazis "took a whole Czech village and wiped it out to make an example for all people in Czechoslovakia." The young attorney also noted that "just about forty-eight hours ago history was made in the world upon the ending of the Nuernburg [sic] Trials," and he urged jurors to consider the important historical role they could play by proclaiming "that the principles of law and the rights declared under our Constitution . . . will remain with us."[65]

In his most fervid plea, however, Weaver turned to the brotherhood exhibited in recent combat:

> Gentlemen of the Jury, in the last great war that we fought, Negroes and whites fought side by side on land, on sea, and in the air. In that last great war when a man lay dying on the battlefield, did his blood run black or did it run American red? It ran American red, and he defended for us the ideal that you are here today to defend. A man who was dying and gasping with his hands digging in the ground in his last agonizing suffering was not asked by the Almighty as he ascended having defended the thing he believed to be sacred whether he was a Negro or whether he was a white man.

To the Kennedy-Pillow jury, he thundered: "a Negro man, his blood gushing from his arteries . . . died so that there would exist no race prejudice in this country and so we could have Jurors who could sit here and give equal and exact justice to all men irrespective of race, creed, or color."[66]

In his allusions to World War II, Weaver resembled other liberals of the day. In his changed racial perspectives, however, he stood among a small minority of white servicemen. This does not mean that the war had no transforming *potential* or that some white veterans were not amenable to the kind of racial appeals that Weaver made. Still, in a survey conducted by Samuel Stouffer and his colleagues immediately after the war, only 15 percent of American soldiers attempted to define the war in moral terms. Even more significant, the study's detailed statistical analysis of the American soldier revealed that "men's acceptance of the war depended primarily on excluding from consideration everything but the immediate events surrounding America's entry into the war. . . . once their attention strayed to what had gone before or would come after, most men found themselves without a consistent rationale by which to justify the war."[67]

Weaver obviously changed in part because of the type of military experiences he had. While a number of white servicemen, including southerners, always related reasonably well to African American soldiers, those who shifted their attitudes the most were the ones who fought alongside blacks.[68] Although Weaver's branch of service, the U.S. Navy, did not achieve parity with the Army in its induction of black servicemen until the end of 1944, Weaver clearly served with African Americans, and it made a strong impression on him. As he explained to the Lawrenceburg jury: "I served on a mine sweeper in Normandy and Southern France and Okinawa, and I know that some of those boys fighting on that ship alongside me were Negroes, and they fought courageously defending the idea that people are free and they were assured . . . that all people are free and can enjoy the full benefits and the right to live happily and peacefully."[69]

Thus Weaver's military service bonded with his personality and his experiences as a labor lawyer to produce a transformation in his racial thinking, which was brought to full flower by his efforts in behalf of the NAACP. In turn, his bold personal style, coupled with his newfound passion for civil rights, produced spirited cross-examinations and courtroom confrontations in which the young lawyer challenged every segment of the criminal justice apparatus, from the police to the judge and district attorney. Weaver also pursued the lynching issue as ardently as Looby did.[70]

Weaver's behavior not only demonstrated the intensity of his commitment to equal rights, but also it contributed significantly to the defense's success. Because of his tenacity in the courtroom, Weaver absorbed some of the ferocity that the judge and prosecuting attorneys, as well as white spectators, would have directed at Looby and the other black lawyers in the case.[71] More significantly, he obtained important admissions from the witnesses that he so vigorously queried.[72] He also elicited from Police Chief Griffin a very positive assessment of the Blairs and Morton.

Not only was Weaver effective alone, but he worked very well in tandem with Looby. Weaver's aggressive style both highlighted and complemented Looby's more low-key approach. "Now the hotshot of those three was this little white attorney from Chattanooga," juror Davis remembered.

The two lawyers also worked successfully together because of their respective races. As a white lawyer, Weaver was able to acquire information the morning following the Patrol raid from Sheriff Underwood that a black attorney would have found difficult, if not impossible, to obtain. In turn, Looby used Weaver's transcript very effectively in cross-examining the sheriff.[73] Additionally, the two lawyers were able to grill witnesses of their own race in ways that played well with the jury.[74]

The defense attorneys got their points across. Juror James Davis wrote recently that following the Stephenson-Fleming fight "blacks gathered in their business section about 2 city blocks south of the public square and whites gathered on the City's public square." He continued: "The City police went to the Black section to investigate and one was shot in the Buttox [sic] with what looked like shotgun pellets (He was not injured seriously as the picture shown to the Jury indicated[)]. But this incident evidently caused a lot of individuals on both sides to arm themselves. . . . It was said that a Black had been hung out a window on the Public Square in prior years. Columbia was ripe it seemed for just such a thing to occur."[75]

During the Columbia affair, Donald Jones of the NAACP described Weaver as a "jewel," while Walter White "variously pictured" him "as a Clarence Darrow, Sir Galahad, and an Eisenhower." Looby's wife, Grafta Looby Westbrook, remembered him as "good for the cause"; Charles Houston asserted that he "demonstrated the finest courage and loyalty to civic and professional ideals throughout the entire case." The Chicago *Defender* called Weaver's "courageous performance . . . as gratifying as the acquittal of the 25 defendants" and concluded: "Mr. Weaver brought a new concept of the manner in which Southern white attorneys should handle the defense of their Negro clients." A Chattanooga African Methodist Episcopal minister declared simply: "He has a magnificent obsession for social justice."[76]

Weaver became a formidable opponent of the state in 1946 precisely because his "magnificent obsession" sundered him from conventional white racial thought and thereby enabled him to challenge the criminal justice establishment very effectively. Together, though in different ways, he and Looby stood apart from reigning ideology, and their respective, outsider positions—to legalism and to white racial orthodoxy—furthered their cause.

Their effort would not have succeeded, however, in just any place before any jury at any time in southern history. Though initially horrified that the trial had been moved to Lawrenceburg rather than Nashville, the lawyers discovered that the location they secured, and the jurors they reached, were critical to the positive outcome they achieved. It is to this last piece of the puzzle that we now turn.

LAWRENCEBURG AND ITS JURORS

When Judge Joe Ingram announced on the second day of the change of venue hearing that the trial would begin in Lawrenceburg on August 6, Looby and Weaver were appalled. "It is a part of the defendants' feelings that if any race hatred and prejudice exist in Maury county it is doubly so in Lawrence county," Weaver explained as he commenced his whirlwind of activities in preparation for a second change of venue proceeding. Meanwhile, Looby worried about Lawrence's sparse black population, about the provincialism of small towns in comparison to large cities generally, and about the extent to which the prosecution lawyers were already well-known in the community. After all, Paul Bumpus had long practiced before the court in Lawrenceburg and his assistant, William A. "Bud" Harwell, was a native son, a situation "which places us at a disadvantage," Looby believed.[77]

At first glance, the concerns of the defense attorneys appeared well-founded. As in Maury County, most African Americans in Lawrence occupied the lowest rungs of the economic ladder.[78] Additionally, fifty-five black Lawrence Countians completed affidavits saying they did not think a fair trial could be obtained in their community. According to "one court room hanger-on," signs had at one time appeared in some parts of the county which read: "Niggers read and run. If you can't read, run anyhow." Similarly, juror James Davis, who was 30 years old in 1946, recalled that as a child, he had seen signs "on the highway going north or south" which read "Nigger don't let the sun go down on your head." The preference by everyone, including "the court officer," for the floor rather than the numerous spittoons located around the courtroom also suggested a certain poverty of place that seemed to bode ill for the defendants.[79]

Yet Lawrence County's position on the economic margin of southern society offered advantages to the defense that were not immediately apparent. A "highland rim" county, where farming was much more difficult than in Middle Tennessee's "heartland," Lawrence's economy was not, and never had been, as dependent on African American labor as the economies of counties in plantation regions or in communities like Maury with its lush bluegrass vicinity.[80] Thus, though the limited presence of African Americans in the community worried Looby, their small number and their lack of centrality to the economy meant that white leaders there were not, and had never been, as concerned with the issue of race—and labor control—as those in neighboring Maury County. Neither had they engaged in mob violence or shrill racial rhetoric.[81] In short, with commercial farms that were far less valuable than those in Maury County, Lawrence County lacked a vibrant plantation tradition and a wealthy elite with Old South pretensions and concerns.[82]

The different orientations of officials from the two counties appeared in the closing addresses of the prosecution. While Columbia lawyer Hugh Shelton was disparaging toward black defense witnesses, as well as toward the defendants themselves, and Paul Bumpus ranted at both the renegade Weaver and the "carpetbaggers" who had dared interfere in Columbia's affairs, Lawrenceburg native Bud Harwell delivered evenhanded remarks. More importantly, he placed the responsibility of resolving conflicting testimony and reaching a decision solely in the hands of the jurors themselves: "I beg of you again in making these closing statements, that to just give this case your calm and cool and deliberate consideration, try it like twenty-five Lawrence County people being tried, and I think those who know me know that is exactly the way I feel about it, and then render your verdict fairly and impartially and let the chips fall where they may."[83]

In short, Harwell gave jurors license to follow their own inclinations in a way that neither Shelton nor Bumpus did. Other Lawrence County authorities also gave their tacit approval to such a course of action by roundly condemning the transfer of the trial to their community. Ultimately, the anger of the local establishment led NAACP publicity director Oliver Harrington to conclude that "one reason for the surprise verdict was the jury's very strong dislike for Judge Ingram and Paul Bumpus for bringing the trial to Lawrenceburg."[84]

Still, though local authorities helped create an environment in which a not guilty verdict was possible, it was above all Harwell's stance that impressed jurors. Forty-three years after his closing remarks, juror James Davis remembered and applauded them. "Yes, we knew where it was going," he recalled, and he continued: "We had talked about it. There was going to be, you know, acquittal. But when this day came and everybody had to stand up there—-and now Bud Harwell was the first to stand up and make his plea, and he said '. . . Take the law, use the law and evidence and let the chips fall where they may.' And that's the way he—That's the way he is, and we all appreciated that. He gave the facts and that's what he said."[85] As the jurors stood one by one and the "not guilty" verdicts rolled in, only one person rose from the prosecution table to shake hands with the defense counsel: Bud Harwell.

If Lawrence County's topography resulted in a white establishment that was less affluent and less preoccupied with the issue of race than that in counties like Maury, it also produced a more diverse population than one might expect in a community situated on the periphery of the economic mainstream. Just five years after the Civil War, German Catholic families began arriving in the community, and three parishes endured: Lawrenceburg, "the Mother parish"; Loretto, the second largest town in the county; and Saint Joseph. Refugees from Alsace-Lorraine who had settled briefly in Cincinnati, the original members of the German Catholic Tennessee

Homestead Association had been able to purchase 25,000 acres in the Lawrence vicinity precisely because "it was all wild and barren" and thus "sold cheap."[86]

Though noticeably different from the earlier, generally Protestant settlers, the Germans of Lawrence County—with their Catholic churches, priests' houses, schools, and convents—proved a welcome addition to the community. Not only did the 350 families who initially settled in the county seat enhance the size of the sparsely populated town, but as skilled artisans, they also provided essential services. As a group, these immigrants and their descendants—who were invariably labeled "thrifty" by county chroniclers— clearly demonstrated to the Protestant majority that having a discernible minority within its midst did not automatically yield negative consequences. Juror Frank Kersteins, a 62-year-old carpenter and Roman Catholic scion of these early settlers, undoubtedly reinforced this point to other jurors. Equally significant, as a man who declared that he "would try the case on 'the law and evidence,'" he may well have contributed an additional measure of tolerance to the deliberative body.[87]

If German Catholics had long enhanced the diversity of Lawrence County, another, even more distinct group arrived in the community during World War II, and again, as had been true with the Catholic minority, the local topography played an important role in this development. In January 1944, three Orthodox Amish families relocated in Lawrence because they were interested in diversified farming and were unhappy with "the local type of agriculture" in southern Mississippi, where they had been living. That fall, they were joined by other Amish settlers who moved into the area from Wayne County, Ohio, probably for similar reasons. Thus, just two years before the trial, Lawrence residents had to adjust to a strikingly premodern group of people who rode around the streets of Lawrenceburg in their horse-drawn buggies, the women in shawls rather than coats and in caps covered by bonnets, the men with long hair and beards. Though the newcomers initially "caused many curious looks," they were described later as "well respected," and they probably were, or at least they were tolerated, for in 1947, a group of Reformed Amish from Indiana joined their Orthodox brethren in the community.[88] In short, the location of the county on the rim of the southern economy did not translate into an isolated or homogeneous populace. Instead, austere farming conditions resulted in greater religious and cultural diversity than existed in a more prosperous county like Maury.

Not only did Lawrence residents have models of diversity before them, they also had images of African American farmers as almost exclusively landowners rather than tenants and of whites as tenants as well as owners.[89]

The small number of blacks living in Lawrence County meant too that they intermingled with whites more freely than in locales where their larger numbers resulted in separate establishments and stricter segregation. As a *Pittsburgh Courier* correspondent explained: "Colored and white spectators sat together in the courtroom. They swapped opinions and used the same toilets."[90] These arrangements were important, for as noted jurist A. Leon Higginbotham Jr. recently explained: "When courthouses in the southern United States maintained segregated restrooms, cafeterias, and spectator sections in courtrooms . . . they sent a symbolic message that legitimated, reinforced, and perpetuated the segregation that was a way of life in the post-*Plessy* South and helped to justify the ideology of racism underlying its existence and enforcement."[91] Thus, while racism was alive and well in Lawrence County, the parameters guiding individual thoughts and actions were far wider than in a hierarchical, plantation setting or even in a wealthier diversified farming region with a sizable black population and strong Old South proclivities like Maury.

To ensure jurors who would be most favorable toward their clients, defense attorneys needed to reach to the edge of this marginalized community, and once there, they had to be highly selective. Getting to the perimeter was important because men on the margin possessed no paramount need to uphold either appearances or the status quo. As Davis and the Gardners had discovered in their study of Natchez, some lower-class whites related well to both lower- and middle-class blacks in urban and rural settings. "Middle-class whites, on the other hand, even though living near Negroes, never developed neighborly relations and were generally antagonistic." Similarly, historian Guion Griffis Johnson asserted that while the "planter class" was "tolerant of the Negro . . . although quick enough to exploit his services" and the white middle class "remained the black man's implacable foe. . . . The poor whites—the landless, unskilled laborers— reacted toward the Negro in a variety of ways." "Some," she added, "apparently had little, if any antagonism toward the black man, while others bitterly resented his presence in American society."[92]

Davis and the Gardners also found instances where less affluent whites accorded upper-class blacks the same cordial treatment that they gave to upper-class whites. "It appears, then," they concluded, "that whites sometimes ignored minor aspects of caste etiquette and, both consciously and unconsciously, followed correct class, rather than caste, behavior in relation to upper-class Negroes."[93] Even more revealing, a five-city survey conducted during World War II discovered that "educated [white] people, both in the North and South, have a significantly lower opinion than do the un-

Left to right: Defense attorneys Z. Alexander Looby, Maurice Weaver, and Leon Ransom question one of the many potential jurors that they queried during jury selection for the Lawrenceburg trial. (Courtesy of NAACP)

educated of Negroes' ability to learn." Equally significant, although southern whites with only a grade school education were slightly more opposed than their better educated brethren to blacks being trained during the war as pilots, bombardiers, and navigators—that is, positions to which they themselves could not aspire—they were less insistent on attending separate training schools or serving in separate combat or ground crews.[94]

This is not to suggest that raw, unadulterated prejudice did not exist among poor whites. But it does indicate less uniformity among poorer whites in their relations with African Americans than among the more affluent. This, in turn, meant greater potential for fair and equitable treatment from poor white jurors if the selection process were sufficiently meticulous. Here, above all, the perseverance and commitment of Looby and Weaver paid off.

For five arduous weeks, jury selection ground on. When the process was completed, over 700 veniremen had been called, from which 12 plus an alternate had been chosen. All were white; most were native Tennesseans and farmers; none were wealthy. The eldest at 73, John Pigg entered the jury box "wearing faded blue overalls." A farmer and Missionary Baptist, 64-year-old A. J. Jordan also "squirmed in his high-front bib overalls." Sixty-year-old Wash King was a farmer and janitor at a nearby country school; earlier, he had mined coal in Alabama. As noted, Frank Kersteins worked as a carpenter, as did 30-year-old James Siegel Davis. Raymond Dunn, the thirteenth and alternate juror, was a truck driver. The foreman and probably the most prosperous member of the jury, 50-year-old Herbert Patterson, was a country storekeeper. The limited financial means of the jurors was graphically demonstrated as they enjoyed "the comfort of their squeaking swivel chairs," furniture that was "distinctly novel to many of them." It was also seen in their "shy and somewhat embarrassed" demeanors as defense attorneys and defendants alike rushed to clasp their hands at the trial's conclusion.[95]

Although once Judge Ingram took over the questioning of the veniremen some were queried so briefly their racial views were unknown, there were encouraging signs among most. While Jordan said that he did not "know enough about the Ku Klux Klan to say anything for or against it," he added that he did "not subscribe" to its "principles of race hate." King, a former member of the United Mine Workers of America, proclaimed that he "believed in the principle of Negro and white unity in the trade union movement." Davis, who sat next to King in the jury box, said he had "no racial prejudice against Negroes and . . . would base his verdict on the 'evidence.'" Kersteins also maintained that he "would try the case on 'the law and evidence.'" John Pigg, who lived in Illinois until he moved to Lawrence County at the age of 15, stated "They (Negroes) have as good rights under law as white people." Similarly, 29-year-old Jesse Bradley asserted, "I can give them (the Negroes) a fair and impartial trial," as did 58-year-old farmer J. J. Cleveland and 53-year-old Arthur J. Pollock. In short, the diligence of Looby and Weaver yielded positive results as three-quarters of the jurors were on record as disavowing prejudice and asserting the rights of African Americans to a fair trial.[96]

Most important in the verdict, the economic location of the jurors on the perimeter of a marginalized community meant that they were little swayed by shrill regionalism or Old South romanticism. At the same time, they had just been through a war saturated with democratic rhetoric. Thus, while Maurice Weaver's appeal to universal rights made some sense to them, sitting there in their bib overalls, enjoying the novelty of their swivel chairs, they felt little connection to Paul Bumpus's blast at "the filthy, loathsome birds of prey [who] . . . swooped upon Tennessee's tragedy," and his high-flown appeal "in the name of a chivalrous manhood and a pure and precious womanhood." "We had never heard anything like that," James Davis reflected. Similarly, Vincent Sheean concluded that jurors had "no real use for the kind of racism and sectionalism that flowered so luxuriantly in that courtroom."[97] As Davis explained further:

> We had decided that the state didn't have anything. We know there was a conflict, there was a war. Both sides, one building up down in Mink Slide, and the other up . . . around the courthouse. . . . But the only solid proof they had was a photograph of an officer's fanny, turned up . . . with his pants down, and some speckles in his bottom. Of course we knew somebody hit him with buckshot but it could've been anybody. . . . we were all of the same opinion that they didn't have *enough*. These things *might* have happened. It was kind of a fairy tale as far as we were concerned. It wasn't real because they couldn't produce any concrete evidence, and that's the law.[98]

Then, as now, juror Jesse Bradley reasoned simply that if twenty-five men had shot at a policeman with the intention of murdering him, they would have killed him![99]

No one demonstrated better than Bradley the concatenation of views held by some poor whites that could bode well for African Americans on trial. Though he was the youngest juror at 29, by the time the trial occurred, he and his wife and two children had already moved from Lawrenceburg, where they farmed; to Columbia, where Bradley worked in construction for his niece's husband; and back again to Lawrence County. At the time he was called for jury duty, he was working in downtown Lawrenceburg in a blacksmith-welding shop in "the old Hitch Yard."

For Bradley, the word "nigger" comes easily, but his use of the term belies a profound belief in equity before the law and a kind of rough equality with African Americans that translated into respect, and even deference, before middle-class leaders like James Morton and Z. Alexander Looby. A man who liked to drink as Weaver did but "couldn't afford it like he could," Bradley was far removed from the establishment, even in Lawrenceburg, and he had a healthy skepticism for its members. At the same time, his position on the lower rungs of the socioeconomic ladder not only resulted in his respecting and liking middle-class African Americans like Morton and Looby, but also it meant that he worried little about appearances. Was he concerned when the verdict was rendered that there might be trouble, he was asked recently? "Oh no," he replied, "In fact . . . I didn't much care if there was."[100]

A couple of years after he first moved to Nashville, defense attorney Looby was struck by an automobile that pulled out of a sidestreet as he was driving down Fourth Avenue. As he explained further: "The police showed

Several of the jurors in the Lawrenceburg courtroom. Jesse Bradley is the first person on the left in the second row. (Courtesy of NAACP)

up and were all ready to arrest me when an elderly white man who had witnessed the accident came to my defense. 'This nigger is innocent,' he told the police, 'and I'll come to court tomorrow and testify for him.'" "Now, I didn't especially appreciate being referred to that way," Looby added, "but I wasn't going to quibble about words when the man's intentions were so good!" Looby might have made a similar statement about Jesse Bradley—and about his compatriots on the Lawrenceburg jury in 1946. Men whose lots in life were not easy ones, they "administered justice," as Bradley summed it, "just about as good as we could."[101]

According to Will D. Campbell, a Baptist clergyman and white, southern civil rights activist who also ministers to Klan members,

the redneck is probably the least racist of any group in white American society. . . . because racism is not an attitude, a prejudice, a matter of bigotry. . . . [It] is the condition in and under which we live. It is the structures in which we live and move and have our being. . . . It just has to do with being white within these structures. . . . Yet there continues to be less real racism in redneckism because the redneck participates in our society from a base of considerably less power than the rest of us.[102]

In a sense, the argument made by Campbell applied to the Lawrenceburg jurors, for they dwelled on the edge of the structures of power—political, economic, and social. But as their statements and actions indicate, their location on the edge of a community, peripheral to the southern economy and characterized by both cultural diversity and high rates of black land-ownership, did not simply limit their input into a racist society. Instead, it affected their basic perceptions of African Americans and in that way, facilitated their decision.

The timing of the trial—just as the war ended and before anti-Fascism was sublimated to anti-Communism—undoubtedly aided the defense, but complex relationships between class and race and between insiders and outsiders are also important keys to understanding the verdict.[103] Leaders, with vested interests in the status quo, have little inclination to change. To members of the middle class, appearances and respectability matter. For these reasons, neither group is inclined to assist or to fraternize with a submerged minority. In contrast, those who worry least about upholding the status quo or appearances are most likely to manifest a rough equality with African Americans—sometimes as friends, more often as enemies. The defense team of Looby and Weaver secured the verdict they did not only because they were outsiders, professionally and racially, but also because they selected as jurors a group of men who were outsiders in social and economic terms. The verdict they achieved was notable because of its rarity, then as now.

CONCLUSION

"Prevented lynchings function as 'historical counterexamples' to completed lynchings and, as such, are analytically indispensable to the analysis of lynchings," scholars Larry J. Griffin, Paula Clark, and Joanne C. Sandberg recently observed.[1] In keeping with this observation, the failed lynching in Maury County in February 1946 tells us much about the lynching phenomenon and its demise. It also reveals a great deal about the evolution of black-white relations since the Civil War and about the impact on those relations of a war that permeated American society more than any other in the twentieth century.

Additionally, the actions of law enforcement officers and the legal proceedings that flowed from the attempted lynching indicate much about the relationship between African Americans and the criminal justice system at a time when disfranchisement and legal segregation had been in place for half a century. Though both would be dismantled within the next two decades, understanding their implications when they had reached their zenith sheds a great deal of light on the difficulties that black Americans faced in dealing with the criminal justice apparatus. It also helps explain the continued problems that they confront, and the suspicions that they harbor, toward that system.

Averted lynchings were not uncommon in the American South, at least by the 1920s and the 1930s.[2] Nor was it unusual for law officers to play an important role in such events. Most lynchings, however, were avoided when a sheriff or his deputies forcibly dispersed a mob, spirited the potential victim away to a safer jail, or called in the National Guard or state militia to protect a prisoner. The avoidance of a lynching in Maury County was significant, in part, because the sheriff protected his prisoners by turning them over to African American leaders. This action represented not only a departure from the way law officers who protected a potential lynch victim usually operated in the South but also a definite shift from earlier events in Maury County, when the sheriff and his deputies either acquiesced or actively participated in mob killings.

The formation of a different political matrix undergirded the changed relationship between the Sheriff and black Maury Countians, and while this alteration did not signify a widespread change throughout the South, it did occur on occasion in other communities following the war.[3] Equally significant, the altered relationship points toward the extent to which the safety of any group in a democracy is intimately related to politics and the distribution of power, a fact that many civil rights advocates, including the NAACP, clearly perceived as they made voting a top priority in the 1930s and 1940s.

Sheriff Underwood's release of his prisoners to black leaders, however, represented only the first step in James Stephenson's journey to safety. The determination of local black businessmen to protect their charge by arming themselves, whisking Stephenson out of town, and forcefully confronting the police and sheriff, represented the next important phase of the event. Black proprietors were joined in this stage by their customers, who comprised an even more militant component of the coalition.

This phase of the averted lynching pointed toward an evolutionary process that had occurred over the course of the twentieth century as black proprietors shifted from white to black clienteles and black business districts blossomed in towns and cities across the nation. As the owners of these businesses protected and disciplined their customers, they developed a rough side that was atypical of most members of the black bourgeoisie.

At the same time, by remaining firmly grounded in the middle class themselves, black proprietors were in a position to call attention to the problems of their working-class customers. Mistreatment by law officers of the patrons of "nightspots" in Columbia, South Carolina, in 1941 and in Nashville, Tennessee, in 1943 produced organized campaigns by religious and business leaders for full-fledged military investigations and for the assignment of black officers to black business districts.[4] As in Maury County in 1946, the owners of the establishments in which the abuse occurred played no small part in calling attention to the problems. Along with two ministers, the most aggressive spokesmen in the South Carolina case were the owners of the Blue Palace Cafe, the site of many of the police infractions.[5]

Though often conceived by scholars as accommodationists, black entrepreneurs could aggressively confront whites who threatened their community. As in Columbia, racial confrontations in East St. Louis in 1917 and in

Tulsa in 1921 illuminated not only the multifaceted roles that proprietors played in their communities but also the militancy with which they were imbued.[6]

The aggressive posture assumed by black leaders in Columbia is noteworthy in part because proprietors there succeeded in getting James Stephenson to safety. Their fate in the aftermath of the police shootings, however, reveals both sharp limits to their power and their vulnerability to the criminal justice system, despite their middle-class status and the respect that they ostensibly had from influential, local white people. Most significant of all, the actions of Columbia entrepreneurs offer insights into the guardianship role that black businessmen increasingly assumed within their communities as the twentieth century progressed and law officers failed in their obligations to black citizens, into the militancy with which they were endowed, and into the overtly aggressive stance that they could assume when whites threatened or invaded their communities.

Still, while black proprietors could become aggressive defenders of their communities, they were not usually in the vanguard of civil rights organizations.[7] These posts were instead occupied by middle-class professionals such as physicians, lawyers, ministers, and newspaper editors.[8] Thus, while Julius Blair initially inquired about procedures for establishing an NAACP chapter in Columbia, it was the Reverend Calvin Lockridge, and later his brother the Reverend Raymond Lockridge—not Blair's businessmen sons, Saul or Charlie—who nursed the organization along.

Nevertheless, the decision by businessmen to take up arms in defense of James Stephenson altered their image in the local white mind and improved the treatment that whites accorded them. It also engendered pride in the participants themselves, as well as in other African Americans in Maury County. Raymond Lockridge recalled that prior to the "riot," whenever he worked for whites, they gave him something to eat on the back porch; afterwards, he either ate with them or at their table when they had finished. Similarly, Addie Blair Cooper, who worked in a downtown department store as an elevator operator, noted that after the fray whites began to treat blacks "with just a little more courtesy."[9]

In 1951, when journalist Carl Rowan visited Columbia in search of material for the work that later became his 1952 book *South of Freedom*, he discovered well-worn copies of Nashville newspapers detailing the confrontation of five years earlier in Saul Blair's barbershop. In response to Rowan's inquiries regarding the affair, Blair responded: " 'You just tell them that before the riot Columbia was a hell-hole, but that we've got a good city now. Used to be that when a Negro went in a store uptown the clerks didn't see him until he started to walk out. Then they *might* offer to serve him. You go in now and ask for a pair of galluses and those clerks will button 'em on you.'"[10] As Rowan traveled deep into the Maury County countryside, he visited the home of 90-year-old Henry Clay Harlan, the grandfather of lynching victim Henry Choate. When Harlan's wife admonished her husband not to talk about the details surrounding their grandson's murder, Harlan responded: "There won't be no more trouble. . . . No, there ain't gonna be no more trouble. That's the one thing I learned from 1946. They know now that Negroes have guts. The Blairs and Mortons was the first Columbia Negroes ever to stand up like men. Blood was shed, but it paid off. I dare as to say times has changed. A colored man used to not have the chance of a sheep-killing dog. But 1946 changed that."[11]

Like black businesses described by scholars throughout the twentieth century, those in Columbia were typically small operations that originated with little capital, served an overwhelmingly black clientele, and were run by their owners.[12] In comparison to the wealth of the white elite, that of black leaders was modest.[13] But black entrepreneurs should be considered in terms other than their relative position to whites. "Firm" and "fiery" in temperament and willing to resist white intrusion forcefully under certain conditions, members of the black middle class themselves and thus positioned to forge both inter- and intraclass coalitions in behalf of their clients, and men of "peace and quietude" who had the respect and ear of a number of white officials, Columbia proprietors played a strategic role within their community that went well beyond dollars and cents.

Even more than East Eighth Street's proprietors, the patrons of their establishments were willing to use force to protect James Stephenson, and they resorted to it when they thought that whites were invading their vicinity. These defenders were part of a larger pattern of an increased sense of entitlement and personal efficacy generated among African Americans by wartime conditions. Women, as well as men, had their notion of possibilities raised, and this included some of those lowest on the nation's economic chain, as domestic workers and tenant farmers found greater room to maneuver.

In the immediate aftermath of the war, some black southerners not only resisted white aggression with arms, as in Columbia, but they also openly expressed contempt for revival efforts by the Ku Klux Klan. As Klan specialist David Chalmers explained: "Jeers and laughter, from Negro as well as white, greeted many a Klan speech, parade, and cross burning. In Greenville, Georgia, Negroes lined the road for a Klan parade; giggling children drumming on kitchen pots and pans followed the marchers and an old woman called out to Klansmen, 'Send us your sheets, white folks, we'll wash 'em.'"[14] Blacks in southern cities in particular expressed less fear of the Klan than their counterparts in the southern countryside, and urban areas were the scenes of most of the efforts to revitalize the organization.[15]

The timing of black resistance to white encroachment was important because it occurred just as organized white violence seemed on the verge of expanding. This does *not* mean that black southerners were spared suffering at the hands of whites following the war, but it does mean that black defiance merged with other factors in curbing the dramatic expansion of extralegal white terrorism. Especially important among these factors was the migration of large numbers of blacks *and whites* out of the rural South.

If World War II imparted such militancy to African Americans, especially to soldiers, why did a direct-action, mass-participation challenge to Jim Crow not appear until the mid-1950s and not accelerate until the 1960s? Part of the answer to this question lies in the kind of campaign that was carried on throughout the South during the 1940s. The destruction of segregation was not the issue. Obtaining the franchise was, and black veterans played an important role in African American attempts to register to vote.[16]

During the war, being a part of a military unit encouraged a group response to racial problems. After the war, however, this platform disintegrated. Even though black veterans' associations existed, their main goal, like that of white veterans, was meeting individual needs and not tackling structural problems. Additionally, while the Ku Klux Klan did not reach the size its supporters would have liked, terrorism was still a problem for individuals. Thus, a black former soldier in Greensboro, North Carolina, confided in 1951: "Truly I am a graduate of the university of hard knocks. Served four years in the armed forces, World War II. Therefore boldness is my twin brother. However, I am married now, two small children, expecting a third. . . . I must try to be careful."[17]

When black veterans had a chance to join a group effort, their militancy grew palpable, just as it did for students on college campuses and among members of church congregations, civic associations, and civil rights organizations in the 1960s. World War II veterans Amzie Moore and Aaron Henry and their involvement with the Student Nonviolent Coordinating Committee, Medgar Evers and the NAACP, and Hosea Williams and the SCLC represent high-profile cases of this phenomenon at work.[18]

Finally, black soldiers, like most white ones, returned home with a strong desire for personal advancement.[19] Some undoubtedly achieved their goal, but for many the struggle was a disheartening, uphill battle. Though the

Servicemen's Readjustment Act of 1944 (GI Bill) made no distinction by race, institutions and agencies that had a separate and thoroughly racist past administered it. For this reason, the GI Bill's equal educational opportunities became mired in separate, and very unequal, southern school systems, and the route that many white veterans took to higher level jobs was less available to their black brethren.[20]

It should be no great surprise then, that, as the South acquired a more industrialized, mechanized, high-wage economy in the aftermath of World War II, the faces of its workers grew increasingly white and its overall black population increasingly dwindled. Especially the high reenlistment rate among black soldiers during the year following the war reflected the gloomy prospects that awaited most of them upon their return home.[21]

The job situations of the veteran-defenders of James Stephenson mirrored the problems that black soldiers encountered, particularly when they returned to small towns and rural areas in the South. Among the twelve arrestees who were veterans and who appeared in the Lawrenceburg trial as either defendants or prosecution witnesses, only three mentioned employment, and they worked as unskilled laborers. As late as 1948, Milton "Toady" Johnson listed no occupation at all.

Leonard Evans in particular demonstrated the limited impact that the war could have on job opportunities. The 25-year-old Evans had been born in White County on the eastern edge of Middle Tennessee. He had moved to Columbia around the age of 10. In October 1942, Evans entered the Army. Although he had gone to school only as far as the seventh grade, he rose in service to private first class and became a squad leader with an engineering battalion. He also spent considerable time abroad, serving in the European, African, and Middle Eastern theaters. At the time of the Lawrenceburg trial, he was studying carpentry and supporting himself by working as a janitor at the Columbia Military Academy. Prior to his entry into the Army, Evans had worked as a porter at Kaufman's, a ladies' dress shop in Columbia. After three years in the military, holding the responsible position of squad leader and serving abroad, and taking a course in carpentry, in 1948 Evans was working at Holman Nash, an automobile brake service company—as a porter. He continued to rent a home at the same location as prior to the war, in the Macedonia section of Columbia.

The restricted options of Maury County veterans reflected not only the disparities of the GI Bill for African Americans but also a shrinking economy that no longer needed all of its workers. The last hired, black Americans were the first fired as postwar cutbacks began and as federal officials from

1946 forward began emphasizing the stabilization of purchasing power rather than jobs for all workers. By the early 1950s, job prospects for African Americans were abysmal even in northern cities, and along with the jobs went much of the sense of personal efficacy that blacks had experienced as a result of full employment in the 1940s. Instructively, economic growth was not large enough to affect African Americans again until the 1960s—that is, at the time that the civil rights movement burgeoned.[22]

In contrast, many whites, veterans as well as nonveterans, experienced considerable job mobility in the postwar years. One of the central stories of the white South since the war has been the expansion of the middle class, a phenomenon that Hollywood has rarely noticed but one on which the publishers of *Southern Living* magazine have capitalized as they targeted newcomers to the middle ranks as their primary readership.[23]

With economic, and often geographic, mobility, many white southerners began to eschew participation in extralegal, crowd violence against African Americans, whether in the form of a mob, the Klan, or a riot. Some had undoubtedly always recoiled at such actions, but because they lived in tight-knit rural communities, they had remained silent in the face of lynchings and Klan activity in particular. After the war, former farmers and their offspring were freer to follow their own inclinations. Even more important, as newcomers to an expanding middle class, most were simply too busy getting ahead and achieving respectability to worry about monitoring black behavior.

How did public officials respond to changes initiated by the war? Did they continue to emphasize control, rather than protection, of black citizens as white agrarian enclaves disintegrated and as African Americans shifted from the nation's largest rural minority in 1940 to its largest urban minority in 1960? The evidence suggests that they did, at least initially, and that police encounters with African Americans grew more, not less, likely as black citizens situated themselves in the nation's cities.

The reasons for the continuation of older patterns lay in the central role played by politics in the operation of the criminal justice system and in the legacy provided by a society that had long disfranchised and segregated its African American minority. This does not mean that there was no room for individual initiative—the disparate behavior of State Guard Commander Dickinson and Highway Patrol Chief Bomar illustrated clearly that personal styles and proclivities mattered. However, support for Bomar by state authorities illumined not only their preferences but also the racial provincialism within which they were mired and, in turn, the very limited parameters of the electorate that chose them. These factors influenced both the behavior of the police *and* efforts to discipline them.

Though forces for change gathered momentum during the war, those representing the status quo gained the upper hand in the years immediately following.[24] Civil rights advocates would rebound, but their victories would not be nearly so thorough, some scholars argue, as they might have been if leftists had not been purged from their ranks by the effective manipulation of Cold War fears by southern conservatives.[25] At minimum, the interracialism and success of Maury County's International Union of Mine, Mill, and Smelter Workers, coupled with the effectiveness of the no-holds-barred approach of Maurice Weaver, raise intriguing questions about the *potential* of a more radical and grassroots appeal for racial change in the postwar South. Certainly, however, southern authorities had little reason to initiate it.

In probing the relationship between politics and the criminal justice system, this study highlights the very important role played by the Highway Patrol as a mechanism for social control in the South. A phenomenon that manifested itself in both labor and racial affairs, the very close connection between southern governors and state troopers was by no means confined to Tennessee or to the 1940s. One of the most dramatic illustrations of this point was the behavior of George Wallace's Highway Patrol chief, Al Lingo, and his Alabama state troopers in both Birmingham and at the infamous Edmund Pettus Bridge in the 1960s.[26]

Examination of the relationship between politics and the criminal justice system has amplified not only the important control function of state highway patrols in the South but also the ways in which institutions and institutional ties formed during the Jim Crow era had racial implications even when they were not specifically designed for that purpose. These included the close association of the FBI with local and state police and the intimate affiliation of FBI agents with members of the U.S. Attorney's Office. Both the FBI and the U.S. attorney in turn were extremely close to state-based federal officials—that is, judges and senators. Like these patterns of association, the central role of interviewing in the FBI agent's job represented an institutional development that had negative repercussions for efforts to discipline state patrolmen and for black Maury Countians who suffered at their hands, though neither were designed with that goal in mind. Instead, the exclusion of black southerners from politics and politicians' concerns produced these unintended—and easily overlooked—effects.

One of the most pronounced demonstrations of the impact of segregation on public officials was the inability of District Attorney General Paul

Bumpus and Assistant State Attorney General Ernest F. Smith to hear James "Digger" Johnson when they interviewed him, even though in procedural terms they acted correctly. Their failure and the way that they in turn structured their investigation and case was undoubtedly the kind of situation that the National Minority Advisory Council on Criminal Justice had in mind in 1982 when it wrote: "After a careful review of the current operations of the criminal justice system and the racial configuration of its personnel . . . the Council urges vastly increased participation of blacks in the operation of the criminal justice agencies in all its phases and at all levels. It is essential that more blacks occupy decisionmaking positions and that they are granted the necessary resources and support to perform their task."[27]

Finally, the state trials emanating from the Columbia episode, especially the one in Lawrenceburg, illustrated two important points. First, it underscored the reality that whites who came closest to relating on an equitable basis with African Americans in the South were among the region's poorest. Middle-class whites, including members of the lower middle class, were simply too concerned with appearances and respectability to fraternize with a disparaged minority, while the upper class was too far removed from it socially and economically to relate on an equal basis. Poor whites, on the other hand, demonstrated far more variability in their relations with blacks. Highly sensitive to "appropriate" black behavior and reared in a violent culture, less affluent white men readily joined together to attack African Americans; at the same time, some whites in similar economic circumstances were neighborly with them and even respectful toward members of the black middle class.

Z. Alexander Looby and Maurice Weaver capitalized on the greater variability among marginal whites toward blacks by working long and hard to reach the most favorably disposed in this group. They were aided in their efforts by the movement of the trial to a marginalized community where blacks were few in number and local leaders had little reason to rigidly enforce racial domination. They were also helped not only by the occurrence of the trial at a time when World War II had just ended and the Cold War was only beginning to gather momentum but also by their own outsider orientations to the legal profession and the white racial consensus of the 1940s.

Without question, the greatest surprise in the Lawrenceburg case—and the component least likely to be emulated in other parts of the South, or in the nation for that matter—was the jury's decision to free twenty-three of the twenty-five men accused of seriously wounding a white Columbia police officer. Even today, juries are far more likely to punish offenders severely in capital cases if the victim is white, while, aside from alleged assaults on white women, nothing has traditionally aroused the ire of white southerners more than an attack by a black man on a white law officer.[28]

The jury's unprecedented verdict, however, probably played differently on opposite sides of the racial divide. To whites who were supportive of African Americans, the acquittal was inspiring and provided hope for the future. For this reason, Maurice Weaver jubilantly slapped Julius Blair on the knee when it was announced and shouted, "This makes a man proud to be an American!"[29] Even northern journalist Vincent Sheean described the decision as "the kind of thing that makes us realize the full splendor of our destiny as a nation," and he went on to conclude: "This is primarily a Southern problem and the intrusion of any element from the other parts of our society is likely to make things worse rather than better. . . . The Negroes have a long, hard row to hoe, but those who wish to help them will have to learn how to appeal to the good will of Southern white men, our brothers and our fellow citizens, who have so magnificently proved their mettle by this verdict."[30]

In a display of similar sentiment, whites who empathized with African Americans thrilled almost twenty years later to Harper Lee's fictional account of Atticus Finch's courageous defense of Tom Robinson in *To Kill a Mockingbird*. (Robinson, of course, still died in an ill-fated escape attempt.) Three decades after the publication of Lee's novel in Monroeville, Alabama, the town on which it was based, a Harvard-trained black attorney, Bryan Stevenson, tried to free another black man, Walter "Johnny D." McMillian, from death row in the murder of two white teenagers. In the process, Stevenson offered a very different and revealing assessment of Atticus Finch:

> The reason I dislike that book is because it contributes to the "invisible legacy" [of African Americans]. What did Atticus Finch do to change his community? The Tom Robinsons of the world, and the black community from which he came, were still left in the margins. It doesn't change things because there is one white Atticus Finch out there ready to represent you, willing to stand up against the other whites. It may make you *feel* better to believe there is someone out there like Atticus Finch, but it didn't keep Tom Robinson from being killed.
>
> The problem is that too many people in the justice system define their contribution as being like a modern-day Atticus Finch. Well, that is not enough! What you should care about is creating a society and a legal

system where people are not forced to have an Atticus Finch represent them, where people who do not have enough money or who are black or who are not well educated do not have to be in a position where they pray for an Atticus Finch to step forward.

What I am talking about is the next level up from *To Kill a Mockingbird*, a higher level where what Atticus Finch did is not seen as extraordinary but as normal—the everyday way that things should be done. That is the level where the people in the margins are made part of the entire community, and that not only benefits the invisible people but also the community. It makes for a better community because it makes for real justice.[31]

As Julius Blair silently "nodded his white head in accord" with the Lawrenceburg jury's verdict, he undoubtedly felt pleased with the outcome. Yet, as he returned to the Bottom to observe the overzealous policing and arrests in the wake of the acquittal—not to mention the difficult economic circumstances in which most of his customers continued to live—he too must have wondered at a system that seemed so little changed by that decision. When would justice become so routine for African Americans that it did not require extraordinary measures and elicit elaborate praise? That was the central question posed by the Lawrenceburg verdict.

In a larger sense, the state trials, along with the Highway Patrol's invasion of the Bottom and the lack of indictments by the federal grand jury, pointed forward—to issues related to the unequal *enforcement* of the law that so concerns African Americans and their liberal white allies today. In contrast, the averted lynching from which these proceedings emanated hearkened backward—to the problem of unequal protection, or *non*protection, of African American citizens from lawless whites. Though both areas of concern existed before and after World War II, the war accelerated the shift in emphasis by propelling black and white citizens out of the rural South.[32]

The Columbia episode highlights this change and demonstrates the role of everyday people in effecting it. Most did so quite unconsciously as they made individual decisions in thousands of households across the South to try to improve their own lives and those of their families and their progeny. Some, like black Maury Countians, very consciously stepped forward to offer protection to their brethren. In doing so, they revealed resilience and courage, nurtured by personal and communal ties and brought to fruition by the horrors of previous mob actions and the necessities of war.

Veteran Clarence Brown offered a fresh glimpse of that fortitude as he conversed recently in his modest frame home beside a country highway not far from the rock quarry from which he is retired. After reminiscing about the Stephenson affair and his role in it, Brown was asked what he would do if he were a young man and something like that happened again. "Oh," he said with a half smile and a faraway look in his eyes, "I 'spect I'd be in it."[33] As Arthur Raper declared two decades ago, "Crisis—there's strength in it."[34]

NOTES

Abbreviations

ARP	Arthur Raper Papers, University of North Carolina at Chapel Hill
AU	Atlanta University, Atlanta, Ga.
BAE	Bureau of Agricultural Economics
CMC	Crump-McKellar Correspondence, Memphis Public Library
CRDP	Civil Rights Documentation Project, Howard University, Washington, D.C.
FBI	Federal Bureau of Investigation Case 44-1366, Sections 1–6
FGJ	Federal Grand Jury Records, Vols. 1–11, 14, author's personal collection, Raleigh, N.C.
JMDP	Jacob McGavock Dickinson Jr. Papers, TSLA
LC	Library of Congress, Washington, D.C.
MCPL	Maury County Public Library, Columbia, Tenn.
MPL	Memphis Public Library, Memphis, Tenn.
NA	National Archives, Washington, D.C.
NAACP	National Association for the Advancement of Colored People
NCJC	National Committee for Justice in Columbia, Tennessee
OAH	Organization of American Historians
PCCR	President's Committee on Civil Rights
RG	Record Group
RMP	Robert Minor Papers, Columbia University
SRC	Southern Regional Council
TL	Truman Library, Independence, Mo.
TSLA	Tennessee State Library and Archives, Nashville
TT	Trial Transcript, *State of Tennessee v. Sol Blair, et al.*, 10 vols. and arguments, author's personal collection, Raleigh, N.C.
UNC	University of North Carolina at Chapel Hill
ZALP	Z. Alexander Looby Papers, Fisk University, Nashville, Tenn.

Introduction

1. Griffin, Clark, and Sandberg, "Narrative and Event," 25, 29.

Chapter One

1. This account of Gladys Stephenson's problems in getting her radio repaired and the confrontation that ensued between James Stephenson and William Fleming is pieced together especially from the testimony of LaVal A. LaPointe and William F. Fleming in Federal Bureau of Investigation Case 44-1366, Section 1 (hereafter cited as FBI 1) and from testimony of LaPointe, W. Fleming, Gladys Stephenson, James Stephenson, and J. Walter Griffin before the federal grand jury in "Columbia, Tennessee, Investigation Before the United States District Court Grand Jury of Tennessee, Beginning April 8, 1946," vols. 1 and 2 (cited hereafter as FGJ 1 and FGJ 2). Also used were the testimonies of Mrs. Joe McCall, Mrs. James McCall, LaVerne Bryan, Evelyn Watkins Sowell, and John Fleming Sr., FBI 1.

2. Quotations from LaVal A. LaPointe, FBI 1:7–8.

3. Gladys Stephenson, FGJ 2:136–37.

4. Quotation from Laverne Bryan Brown, FBI 1:14.

5. James Stephenson, FGJ 2:162.

6. FBI 1:18, 11. Stephenson's welterweight boxing career is mentioned in Ikard, *No More Social Lynchings*, 14.

7. FGJ 2:132 and FGJ 1:76.

8. Although Gladys Stephenson denied that she lunged at Fleming with a piece of glass, not only LaPointe but two customers and a store clerk described the same incident to FBI agents. See Mrs. Joe McCall, Mrs. James McCall, and Laverne Bryan Brown, FBI 1:12–15.

9. LaPointe, FBI 1:10.

10. James Stephenson, FGJ 2:165.

11. Quotations from J. Stephenson, FGJ 2:165, and G. Stephenson, FGJ 2:139. See also Griffin, FGJ 2:227, and LaPointe, FGJ 1:80.

12. FGJ 2:171–72.

13. For John Fleming's activities on the square and his "fainting," see W. B. Twitty, "Special Report on Columbia, March 26, 27, 28," 2–3, SRC Papers, UNC.

14. TT 10:2043–44.

15. TT 8:1533.

16. Saul Blair, FGJ 7:960. Saul Blair's name was spelled both "Saul" and "Sol" in the official records. He was actually named Saul Wilkins Blair in honor of his maternal grandfather Saul Wilkins.

17. May 10, 1946, Report, FBI 4:9–10.

18. Although Underwood later claimed that he had not made such a statement, Saul Blair recalled it on the witness stand in Lawrenceburg, and the sheriff himself told the FBI he had said it. Saul Blair, FGJ 7:962; and FBI 1:35.

19. FGJ 7:1002.

20. FGJ 2:279.

21. James Morton, FBI 1:85; Calvin Lockridge, FBI 1:109; Bernard Stofel, TT 2:185; and Underwood, FGJ 2:280–81.

22. Calvin Lockridge, FBI 1:109; Underwood, FGJ 2:280; Underwood, TT 3:444.

23. Lockridge, FBI 1:108; and Reeves, TT 6:1087–88.

24. Saul Blair, TT 8:1625; Julius Blair, TT 8:1533; Thomas William Neely, TT 10:1919; and James Stephenson, FGJ 2:206, 187.

25. The account of the trip to Nashville is pieced together from Saul Blair, TT 8; James Stephenson, FGJ 2; and Thomas William "Tommy" Neely and George Nicholson, TT 10. The reference to "Mr. Chapman" appeared in Neely, TT 10:1922.

26. Neely, TT 10:1923.

27. Saul Blair, TT 8:1628.

28. Eventually, like most black veterans who chose northern cities when they left the South, James Stephenson settled in Detroit. There he reared a family and worked in an automobile factory and as a shipping clerk for a graphic arts company. His mother and grandmother joined him. Gladys died in March 1987 at the age of 87; his grandmother, Hannah Peppers, died four months later at the age of 100. Stephenson continues to enjoy bowling, playing baseball, and most recently, golf. Ikard, *No More Social Lynchings*, 139.

29. Prosecutors in the Lawrenceburg trial asserted that the Stephenson-Blair party left town after several city policemen were shot, but neither the FBI nor the federal grand jury made this claim.

30. FBI Report 1:35–36.

31. Blair believed that Denton fed the flames of rumor, and he saw much significance in a crowd's gathering on the street in front of his office. See Julius Blair, FGJ 7:1026–28, 1030.

32. FGJ 3:446–47.

33. Though Underwood maintained at the federal grand jury hearing that only twenty or thirty came to the jail, he had put the group at fifty in his initial conversation with NAACP lawyer Maurice Weaver; Constable Homer Copeland, who appeared at the door with Underwood, also estimated that fifty were there. The Kelly quotation appeared in Homer Copeland, FBI 1:61, though Kelly was identified as having asked the question in Underwood, FGJ 2:284. The other quotations in this paragraph appeared in Underwood, TT 3:429.

34. Several of those attending the meeting testified at the later state trial about James Morton's arrival and his warning. Agricultural extension agent George A. Newbern in particular noted his excited state (Newbern, TT

9:1773–4). The quotations in this paragraph appeared in Morton, FGJ 6:827, and Julius Blair, TT 8:1535–36.

35. Julius Blair Testimony, TT 8:1536.

36. Griffin, FGJ 2:235.

37. Griffin, FGJ 2:238; Collins, TT 6:1154; Wilsford, TT 1:80; and FBI 1:42.

38. Underwood, FGJ 3:379.

39. The account of keeping whites out of the Bottom, including the quotations in this paragraph, appeared in both FBI 1:46 and FGJ 3:378–79.

40. Lynn Bomar, FGJ 4:543.

41. This episode and the quotations in this paragraph and the following one appeared in J. W. Barker, Lt. Col., Infantry, Inspector General, to The Commanding General, 2nd Infantry Brigade, "Report of Armory Incident, Columbia, Tennessee," 15 April 1946, JMDP, TSLA. It is also described in Dickinson to The Adjutant General of Tennessee, "Supplement to Recommendations Relative to the Tennessee State Guard," 12 March 1946, 2–3, JMDP, TSLA.

42. Although neither man would admit their reason for going toward East Eighth Street on the night of February 25 to the federal grand jury that met in April, neither denied carrying the gasoline with them, and Beard earlier confessed all to the FBI. See esp. James Beard, FBI 1:56–7. The quotation appeared in Claude, FGJ: 4:668.

43. *Nashville Banner*, February 26, 1946.

44. FBI 3:60.

45. Dickinson to The Adjutant General of Tennessee, "Report on Tour of Active Duty," March 8, 1946, 2, JMDP, TSLA.

46. The emphasis is Dickinson's. Note placed in *Journal*, Second Brigade Task Force, Columbia, Tennessee, February 26, 1946, JMDP, TSLA.

47. Kingcaid, FGJ 6:771. Journalists representing the *Nashville Tennessean*, the Associated Press, and the United Press had gathered at a circulation office maintained in Columbia by the *Banner* and the *Tennessean*, and they were trying "to get the negro side of the case . . . so everyone would get a fair hearing." John Thompson, Associated Press, FGJ 7:1082.

48. The account of the arrests at Morton's appeared in Mary Morton, TT 10:2010–15, 2035–40; Marcia Mayes, TT 9:1857–59, 1882–85; Lynn Bomar, FGJ 3:470–76, FGJ 4:531–38, and TT 7:1205–6, 1212–36; John A. Kingcaid, FGJ 6:772–82; John Thompson, FGJ 7:1083–87, 1101; and James Morton, FGJ 6:837–46. Scattered references also appeared in the FBI reports. The quotations in this paragraph appeared in James Morton, FGJ 6:844, 841.

49. The quotations regarding the patrol and their behavior appeared in James Morton, "Stenographic Notes taken at Committee Meeting, March 4th, re situation at Columbia, Tennessee," Attorney Fyke Farmer presiding, 10, NAACP Papers, LC; and James Morton, FGJ 6:844–45. The account of the "ransacking" of the house appeared in Walter S. Hurt Jr., Editorial Staff, *Tennessean*, May 10, 1946, Report, FBI 4:11. Quotations regarding the state of

the women appeared in John Thompson, FGJ 7:1084–85. William Dawson mentioned that he was struck in William Dawson Garber, FBI 1:146.

50. Dickinson, FGJ 5:692.

51. The Guard plan was described in Dickinson, FGJ 5:678–88; quotations appeared on 678 and 686.

52. *Tennessean*, February 27, 1946.

53. The quotation about Wilson's repeatedly pushing the armed men back appeared in John Thompson, FGJ 7:1089–90, the rest in the *Tennessean*, February 27, 1946.

54. Dave White, *State of Tennessee v. William A. Pillow and Lloyd Kennedy*, No. 4720, Columbia, Tennessee, November 15, 1946 (hereafter cited as *Pillow-Kennedy*), 3:671; Ray Austin, 3:620; and J. J. Underwood, 3:743, both in *Pillow-Kennedy*. For the amount of ammunition fired into the shop, see Maurice Weaver Summation, 4:965, and White, 3:682–83, also in *Pillow-Kennedy*.

55. The quotations appeared in William Pillow, *Pillow-Kennedy*, 4:837. For Kennedy's description of abusive treatment at the hands of the highway patrol, see Kennedy, *Pillow-Kennedy*, 4:791–94.

56. Jackson, FGJ 8:1277, and Evans, FGJ 11:1899.

57. Smith, FGJ 11:1739, and Jackson, FGJ 8:1278.

58. Jackson, FGJ 8:1278; Smith, FGJ 11:1741, 1748. For Smith's insistence that Blackwell had his hands up and that he saw no gun, see FGJ 11:1752–54.

59. W. Edward Clark, FGJ 6:909–10.

60. Several of those taken to jail mentioned yells of this nature by patrolmen. This particular quote appeared in Leonard Evans, FGJ 11:1906.

61. Dooley, FGJ 11:1842; Porter, FGJ 11:1852; Evans, FGJ 11:1900; and Clark, FGJ 6:911–12. Clark had worked for the *Tennessean* but in 1946 was employed as a photographer for *Life* magazine. Among the many events he photographed was the Emmett Till lynching in 1955.

62. Clark, FGJ 6:913, and Luther Edwards, FGJ 11:1697.

63. John Thompson, FGJ 7:1094; Dickinson, FGJ 5:739; Saul Blair, FGJ 7:979–80.

64. Julius Blair, FGJ 7:1013.

65. Mary Morton, FBI 3:189; Clark, FGJ 6:921, 926; M. E. Tilly to Guy B. Johnson, "Re: Columbia, Tennessee, Incident," March 8, 1946, 10, SRC Papers, UNC; and James Morton, FGJ 6:861–65.

66. Twitty, "Special Report on Columbia," 7. SRC Papers, UNC. For the admissions of guardsmen, see FBI 3:128–31.

67. *Tennessean*, February 27, 1946; and *Columbia Daily Herald*, February 26, 1946.

68. Mary Morton, TT 10:2014–15; M. Smith, "Racial Confrontation in Columbia, Tennessee, 1946" (M.A. thesis), 21; and Looby Comments, "Stenographic Notes," 1, NAACP Papers, LC. Mary Morton also mentioned this phone call in a talk she made on behalf of the NAACP in Washington, D.C., at

the Asbury African Methodist Episcopal Church on April 7, 1946. See "Tennessee Victim's Wife Addresses D.C. Audience," April 11, 1946, NAACP Papers, LC.

69. Muriel Standard to Mr. White, *Memorandum*, February 26, 1946, and "Stenographic Notes," 2, 1, NAACP Papers, LC. See also A. F. Dixon to Walter White, March 21, 1946, and *What Happened at Columbia, Tennessee, Beginning February 25, 1946*, a report of an investigation by Maurice Weaver, attorney-at-law of Chattanooga, Tennessee, and Navy World War II veteran; and Z. Alexander Looby of Nashville, Tennessee, member of the National Legal Committee of the NAACP, NAACP Papers, LC.

70. Weaver was labeled "the CIO attorney" by Mrs. M. E. Tilly in her report to the Executive Committee of the Jurisdiction Women's Society of Christian Services—the Conference Presidents and Secretaries of Christian Social Relations, "The Columbia, Tenn. Tragedy," 1, SRC Papers. He participated in the first Southern Conference for Human Welfare as "a spokesman for the Legislative Committee." A. F. Dixon to Walter White, March 21, 1946, NAACP Papers, LC. The other quotations in this paragraph appeared, respectively, in "Stenographic Notes," 2, NAACP Papers, and Weaver, FGJ 8:1332.

71. Julius Blair, FGJ 7:1011–12. The retort about the white lawyers is also mentioned in Weaver, FGJ 8:1334, and in "Stenographic Notes," NAACP Papers, LC, p. 6.

72. "Transcript of Investigation Taken at Columbia, Tenn. on February 27th and 28th, 1946, in Regard to Racial Disturbance" (hereafter "Transcript of Investigation"), 13, 15, RG 29, TSLA.

73. The term "star witness" was used by Underwood in an interview with an FBI agent. See May 17, 1946, Report, FBI 4:4.

74. The terms "Board of Inquiry" or "Board of Investigation" were frequently used by the NAACP; see, for example, "Stenographic Notes," 6, NAACP Papers, LC. For the quotation about Johnson's father making his bond, see Underwood, FGJ 2:340.

75. FBI 1:67.

76. Officers insisted that Gordon fired a shot that grazed Darnell's arm, though this seems unlikely if, as authorities also maintained, the guns stacked in the jail office were unloaded and the one that Gordon seized had been taken from the home of a local white woman. Either the gun was in fact loaded or Darnell was wounded, as SRC investigator W. B. Twitty speculated, by the highway patrol when they blazed away at Gordon and Johnson. Officers tried to argue that Gordon had a bullet in his pocket that fit the gun that he was able to retrieve from the stack in the office, load, and fire! On the jail murders, see especially FBI 1:66–82. Twitty's remark appeared in "Special Report on Columbia," 6, SRC Papers, UNC.

77. Napoleon Stewart, FBI 1:71–73; Jackson, FGJ 8:1289; and Lynn Bomar, FGJ 4:503–4.

78. Newspaper clipping entitled "Negroes Brought to Nashville," SRC Papers, AU.

79. "Stenographic Notes," 13, NAACP Papers, LC.

80. The petition for writ of habeas corpus and release of prisoners is described in the *Daily Herald*, March 2, 4, and 6, 1946; the quotation by Weaver appeared in the black-owned *Nashville Globe*, March 8, 1946.

81. The mayor's March 3 speech was reprinted in the *Columbia Daily Herald*, April 30, 1946.

82. To write the broadside, James Dombrowski, the executive secretary of the association, turned to Laurent Frantz, a recently discharged Navy vet and the unemployed husband of Dombrowski's assistant, Marge Gelders Frantz. Ironically, Frantz, a Tennessee lawyer who had been a member of the Communist Party since 1937, was never called before the federal grand jury that met in Nashville in the spring of 1946, while Dombrowski, who was never a Communist, was "given a lengthy and uncomfortable grilling." Laurent Frantz to Gail O'Brien, January 20, 1991, in author's possession. Frantz's involvement in the creation of the pamphlet is also described in Adams, *James A. Dombrowski*, 159.

83. Guy Johnson interviews, February 22, 1988, and July 12, 1989.

84. This term was used by Zangrando, *NAACP Crusade*, 173.

85. Five teams that included a defendant and a representative from the national office were scheduled to travel to forty-nine branch meetings "in an area extending along the eastern seaboard from Boston, Massachusetts, to Roanoke, Virginia, and reaching as far west as Minneapolis, St. Paul, and Kansas [City]." Although Gladys Stephenson spoke in Detroit and Mary Morton in Washington, neither were members of the speaking teams as was originally planned. Instead, the teams included Julius and Saul Blair, Calvin and Raymond Lockridge, and James Bellanfante, a man who, Looby warned, "likes to talk and will have to be held in check." "Press Releases," June 1946–47, and Looby to Madison Jones, April 19, 1946, NAACP Papers, LC.

86. The star-studded cast of the National Committee for Justice in Columbia, Tennessee, included, among others, Roger Baldwin, Edward Bearnays, Mary McLeod Bethune, Charlotte Hawkins Brown, Albert Einstein, Edwin Embree, Marshall Field, Frank Porter Graham, Oscar Hammerstein II, William H. Hastie, Helen Hayes, Langston Hughes, Harold Ickes, Charles M. LaFollette, Sinclair Lewis, Joe Louis, Henry Luce, Wayne Morse, Adam Clayton Powell Jr., A. Phillip Randolph, David O. Selznick, Artie Shaw, Lillian Smith, and Arthur Spingarn.

87. *Tennessean*, April 9, 1946.

88. *Report of Grand Jury in the Matter of the Racial Disturbance at Columbia, Tennessee, in the District Court of the United States for the Middle District of Tennessee, to the Honorable Elmer P. Davies, Judge of the United States District Court*, FBI 6; a verbatim copy of this report appeared in the *Memphis Commercial Appeal*, June 16, 1946.

89. The transcripts of the plea of abatement hearing, including the testimony of all black witnesses and the subsequent change of venue hearing, appear in *State of Tennessee v. Sol Blair*, 4. They are housed in the state supreme court building in Nashville with the transcript of the Kennedy-Pillow trial. The actions of the defense in the case, including the number of black witnesses who testified, are succinctly summarized in "Memorandum to Office on Columbia: Copies for WW [Walter White], Carter, and Harrington from TM [Thurgood Marshall]," June 12, 1946, NAACP Papers, LC.

90. When Whitthorne served as a magistrate between 1898 and 1901, Monroe Campbell, a black justice of the peace, frequently placed his own name on the jury list and served many times. Such a practice became impossible after 1913, however, for even if black magistrates had endured—which they did not—a new law placed jury selection in the hands of three jury commissioners, rather than the justices.

91. Though this agreement fell short of what defense lawyers had hoped to achieve, they were finding it increasingly difficult to procure witnesses. *Tennessean*, June 5, 12 (quotes), 1946.

92. *Tennessean*, May 29, 1946.

93. Ibid., June 14, 1946.

94. Ibid., June 11, 1946.

95. Owen, who spoke in early May with the FBI about coworkers who were allegedly in the mob on the 25th, subsequently fled Columbia for fear of his life but had returned by 1948.

96. *State of Tennessee v. Sol Blair*, 4:480. The editorial had appeared in the June 22nd edition of the *Daily Herald*.

97. *State of Tennessee v. Sol Blair*, 4:485.

98. Ibid., 4:487.

99. The quotations appeared in "Storm Brews over Trial Shift to South Tennessee," NAACP Papers, LC; and *Tennessean*, August 7, 1946. For other specifics in the paragraph, see *Tennessean*, July 10, 13, 1946.

100. "Storm Brews over Trial Shift to South Tennessee," NAACP Papers, LC.

101. *Tennessean*, August 17, 1946.

102. Underwood himself used the term "mob," while police officer Sam Richardson referred to "mob talk." Weaver, TT, "Closing Argument," 2326; and Richardson, TT 2:322–23.

103. Griffin, TT 2:385, and Underwood, TT 7:1421.

104. Underwood, TT 6:1025.

105. The testimony of the high school students appeared in TT 5:875–912, the quotation on 5:879.

106. Police officer Bernard Stofel, for example, noted that he "didn't count" those behind them, while police officer T. Frank Collins observed that his compatriot, George Reeves, was on the corner of South Main and East Eighth "pushing people back." Stofel, TT 2:243; and Collins, TT 6:1172.

107. Sheean had written that the safety commissioner was "a stout, ruddy man with a bald head and an irascible temper, who appeared to resent being in the court at all," and that he offered evidence about knocking Napoleon Stewart down and putting "his foot on the boy's neck . . . with the most truculent zeal, his face bright red and his eyes darting about the courtroom as if to defy anybody to object." For Sheean's remarks, see "A Social Question Outlaws Law," *New York Herald Tribune*, October 1, 1946; for descriptions of the encounter, see *Tennessean* and *Banner*, October 4, 1946.

108. TT, 5:843, 845, and 800–801.

109. Bullock had met Gentry, McKivens, and Fisher at the Ritz after the police were shot. All had headed in the direction of Mt. Pleasant but had to turn around when Bullock's car "started running bad." At that point, Bullock and his cohorts encountered the TVA guards and constables sent by Bomar to prevent "car loads" of blacks from getting from Mt. Pleasant to Columbia. The men fled the car; Fisher stayed behind and was arrested. Bullock, Gentry, and McKivens claimed they ran into a nearby cornfield when the police began shooting at them; the law officers alleged the men hid in the field and shot at them.

110. TT, "Closing Argument," 2286.

111. Ibid., 2288.

112. They included, among others, James Morton's wife, Mary; Meade Johnson's wife, Sally; and Henry Sellers, a neighbor of the father of defendant William "Moot" Bills and the only white defense witness.

113. TT, "Closing Argument," 2313.

114. Ibid. 2342, 2343, 2354–55.

115. Ibid. 2366, 2367, 2371–72, 2374.

116. Ibid., 2388–89.

117. Ibid., 2397–98.

118. Ibid., 2397, 2396.

119. TT, "Closing Argument," 2421, 2406, 2409.

120. Ibid., 2455–58. The quotation about Bumpus's demeanor appeared in the *Norfolk Journal and Guide*, October 12, 1946.

121. TT, "Closing Argument," 2459.

122. Ibid., 2460.

123. Unfortunately, the judge's written charge to the jury was filed in a volume separate from the others in the trial transcript and was not included in the material I received from General Bumpus. The quotations in this paragraph and the summary of the judge's charge appeared in the *Norfolk Journal and Guide*, October 12, 1946.

124. TT, "Closing Argument," 2462, 2464–65.

125. All the quotations in this paragraph appeared in Robert M. Ratcliffe, "Democracy Wins in Dixie Court," *Pittsburgh Courier*, October 12, 1946. The ellipses dots are in the original article; they do not signify omissions on my part.

The fact that many in the courtroom were family members of those on trial appeared in *New York Times*, October 5, 1946.

126. The quotations in this paragraph appeared, respectively, in *Norfolk Journal and Guide*, October 12, 1946; "Telephone Conversation between Ollie Harrington and Mr. White from Nashville, Tenn., October 5, 1946," NAACP Papers, LC; Ratcliffe, *Pittsburgh Courier*, October 12, 1946; and TT, "Closing Argument," 2466–68.

127. The quotations in this paragraph appeared in "Telephone Conversation between Harrington and White," October 5, 1946, NAACP Papers, LC; and *Pittsburgh Courier*, October 12, 1946.

128. Z. Alexander Looby, Maurice M. Weaver, and Thurgood Marshall, in *Lloyd Kennedy v. State of Tennessee*, "Statement of Case, Assignment of Errors, Brief and Argument," 33, Tennessee State Supreme Court; and *Tennessean*, November 15, 1946.

129. *Pillow-Kennedy*, 4:941.

130. Nat Tipton, Assistant Attorney General, "Reply Brief for the State," in the Supreme Court of Tennessee at Nashville, December Term, 1946, 7.

131. Kennedy was taken into custody briefly by the sheriff following the state supreme court decision, but Looby said he expected to get another bond "just as soon as we can get action on our stay of preceding." Looby to Thurgood, June 26, 1947, NAACP Papers, LC.

132. The total time served by Kennedy is difficult to discern from extant sources, but Marjorie Smith insisted it was four months. See M. Smith, "Racial Confrontation," 50.

133. This episode is recounted in many places, most recently by Marshall himself in a "Tribute to Thurgood Marshall," presented by the Congressional Black Caucus, Eighteenth Annual Legislative Weekend, shown on PBS, September 14, 1988. The details in this account appeared in a letter written by Marshall to the Justice Department and are quoted in White, *A Man Called White*, 319–20.

Chapter Two

1. W. Carter, "Negro Main Street," 237.

2. Greater residential segregation and the movement of wealthy whites from the heart of the city to its periphery affected market conditions in some locales, while large-scale immigration from southern and eastern Europe produced keen competition for jobs as barbers, hotel waiters, and similar positions in many northern cities. In addition, many African Americans who came of age in the 1890s were determined that they would enter no trade that involved serving whites.

3. Edmund, a Maury County slave who was owned by an estate and await-

ing assignment to a new heir, declared himself free in the summer of 1862 when the federal army came through. Departing with the soldiers but recaptured and held in jail in May 1863, he persisted "'in his determination of returning to the Federals and . . . repeatedly expressed his intention of doing so.'" More prevalent signs of impinging freedom included "disobedience and refusal to work." Ash, *Middle Tennessee Society Transformed*, 115, 117.

4. After growing cotton in the very early years of settlement, most Middle Tennessee farmers had turned to general agriculture by the mid-nineteenth century. Although the Civil War destroyed much of the livestock in the region, agriculturalists made their way back to grain and livestock by the turn of the century. Tobacco further edged out cotton in the 1920s, when the boll weevil struck. By 1934, federal compensation for cotton allotments in Maury County totaled a mere $1,000. In contrast, compensation for wheat stood at $10,000; tobacco, $75,000; and corn-hog, $130,000. General farming in the prewar era and the impact of the Civil War on livestock are described in Ash, *Middle Tennessee Society Transformed*, 16–17, 188–89, while the predominance of general farming in the late nineteenth century through the mid-twentieth is discussed in Shannon, "Social and Economic History of Columbia Reservoir Area," TSLA. The figures for 1934 appear on 87.

5. In Maury County, 55 percent of the black farmers owned their land in 1910, a figure slightly higher than the 50 percent rate in other Upper South states and considerably higher than the 19 percent who owned their land in the Lower South. Maury County rates were calculated from U.S. Census Bureau, *Thirteenth Census: 1910, Agriculture*; rates for the Upper and Lower South appear in Schweninger, *Black Property Owners in the South*, 176.

6. Lamon, *Black Tennesseans*, 114.

7. Brundage, "Southern Black Responses to White Violence" (OAH paper), 21–22.

8. For the new interest among post–Civil War planters in the fertilizer industry, see Wright, *Old South, New South*, 45–46. The Maury County story appears in Lamon, *Black Tennesseans*, 133–34.

9. Black residents numbered 2,518 in 1870, whites 2,320. U.S. Census Bureau, *Ninth Census: 1870, Population*.

10. Ash, *Middle Tennessee Society Transformed*, 253.

11. Quoted in ibid., 213.

12. Dwyer, "Social and Economic History of Columbia Reservoir Area," 154, TSLA.

13. In 1940, most black men (69 percent) in Maury County farmed or toiled as nonfarm laborers, largely in the phosphate operations and, second most commonly, in nondomestic service positions. This figure was higher than the national average of the African American males who worked in these types of jobs (62 percent). On the other hand, only 4 percent of the black men in Maury County in 1940 (5 percent nationally) were in professional, semiprofes-

sional, proprietorship, sales, and clerical positions. Among African American women in Maury County, 88 percent were service workers (compared to 70 percent nationally), with 79 percent engaged as domestics. Despite some improvement in opportunities and wages during the war, median black incomes in the county and town were just over half of the median for all Maury County residents at midcentury. County figures taken from U.S. Census Bureau, *Sixteenth Census: 1940, Population* and *Seventeenth Census: 1950, Population*; national averages from the Department of Industrial Relations, National Urban League, "A Memorandum on the Problem of Counselling Negro Veterans," 2, Hastie Files, RG 107, NA.

14. In 1940, over 90 percent of the black labor force in Maury County, male and female, was employed. The figures for 1950 were even higher than those for 1940, although a smaller number of people were actually working, because of the large outmigration that occurred during the war decade. Figures for Columbia were comparable. U.S. Census Bureau, *Sixteenth Census: 1940, Population* and *Seventeenth Census: 1950, Population*.

15. Quoted in Dwyer, "Social and Economic History of Columbia Reservoir Area," 157, TSLA.

16. Shannon, "Social and Economic History of Columbia Reservoir Area," 109–10, TSLA; and Ash, *Middle Tennessee Society Transformed*, 214.

17. Dwyer, "Social and Economic History of Columbia Reservoir Area," 157, 176, TSLA; and Ash, *Middle Tennessee Society Transformed*, 215.

18. Dwyer, "Social and Economic History of Columbia Reservoir Area," 156, 157, TSLA; and Ash, *Middle Tennessee Society Transformed*, 215.

19. Dwyer, "Social and Economic History of Columbia Reservoir Area," 165–68, TSLA.

20. Ibid., 154.

21. The establishment of the first school is described in Dwyer, "Social and Economic History of Columbia Reservoir Area," 153, TSLA; Ash, *Middle Tennessee Society Transformed*, 141 (quotation); and in the typescript "Ku Klux Klan in Maury County," 1, MCPL. According to the Klan typescript, "enraged citizens descended upon him [Jordan], broke up the school and cowhided the teacher."

22. Schools, the Freedmen's Bureau, and Loyal Leagues are woven together again and again in the thirty-seven-page apologia for the Klan in Maury County. See "Ku Klux Klan in Maury County," MCPL.

23. Columbia *Herald*, August 20, 1869, reported in "Ku Klux Klan in Maury County," 32, MCPL.

24. When a modified civil rights bill was passed by Congress in 1875, it did not require integration of schools and cemeteries. Dwyer, "Social and Economic History of Columbia Reservoir Area," 153, 160, TSLA.

25. Herbert Johnson interview, May 16, 1992.

26. Comparable figures for Birmingham, Alabama, were 5.9; for Chicago

and Detroit, 7.8 and 7.6, respectively. Five Cities Survey, Minorities—Negro—Negro Opinion Study, OWI-Alphabetical Files, Box 22, n.p. Nash Papers, TL. Figures for Columbia appear in the U.S. Census Bureau, *Seventeenth Census: 1950, Population*.

27. While all-black Baptist and Presbyterian churches in Maury County dated from the 1840s, after the war their numbers greatly expanded and African Methodist Episcopal churches joined their ranks. Ash, *Middle Tennessee Society Transformed*, 211; and Dwyer, "Social and Economic History of Columbia Reservoir Area," 151, 156, TSLA.

28. The organization of the Elks Club is described in detail in FBI 4:58.

29. The Royal Duke Club is described by Lee Andrew and Early Shyes in FBI, 4:38–39.

30. Jones, "The Columbia, Tennessee 'Race Riot' " (M.A. thesis), 4.

31. All these figures were calculated from the *Columbia Tennessee City Directory*, 1942, Vol. 2, Chamber of Commerce, Columbia, Tenn.

32. Lt. Col. Samuel Lapham and Major Moffatt C. Bonner, "Report of investigation of alleged 'Dangerous Incident' or riot, occurring in Nashville, Tenn. on April 3, 1943," RG 407, 110, NA. For a similar division in Raleigh, North Carolina, see W. Carter, "Negro Main Street" (Ph.D. diss.), 170.

33. In 1946, Julius Blair owned eight pieces of property, which carried a tax evaluation of $4,900. James Morton, who had seven pieces of real estate and $2,000 in personal property, had a slightly higher assessment of $6,200. Meade and Sallie Johnson, with fourteen pieces of property and an assessment of $5,300, ranked between Blair and Morton. On a smaller scale, Saul Blair owned two pieces of property, together valued at $700. Charlie Blair had one piece worth $150, and Calvin Lockridge owned one worth $300. The Maury County tax lists of 1946 carried no racial designations. I compared the names of over 200 black property owners who testified at the trial with the names on the lists. I found no black Columbian who owned more property than James Morton.

34. Blair, TT, 8:1560–61.

35. Ibid., 8:1561.

36. Among the defendants, Robert "Bob" Gentry shined shoes at Saul Blair's barbershop; "Papa Lloyd" Kennedy worked as a porter at the same establishment and often slept in the back at night; and John Lockridge worked for James Morton, assisting him around his home and funeral parlor.

37. The propensity toward violence among many southern, and indeed American, men was by no means a phenomenon unique to African American culture. The quotations cited here were by Ronald Ryan, February 3, 1990, but the nature of the Bottom was described by many interviewees.

38. For a detailed account of the problems involving the lightness with which black areas were policed, see Reginald S. Matthews, "Racial Situation in the Hampton Roads Area," a report sent by Wayne E. Homan to Chief of Transportation, Army Service Forces, January 11, 1945, RG 107, NA.

39. Addie Blair Cooper interview, February 3, 1990; Mayes Testimony, TT 9:1850; and Flippen's Testimony, "Transcript of Investigation," 125, RG 29, TSLA.

40. Interviews with Ronald Ryan, Pat Martin Bowman, and Addie Blair Cooper, February 3, 1990.

41. J. Blair, TT 8:1527–28.

42. Cooper interview, February 3, 1990.

43. Walter Weare makes clear both the pivotal role of Merrick in the founding of the company and the importance of Merrick's work as a barber in his business education. Weare, *Black Business*, 29–37. Herndon is mentioned in Meier and Lewis, "History of the Negro Upper Class," 131.

44. TT 8:1528.

45. Lamon, *Black Tennesseans*, 141.

46. James Johnson, "Transcript of Investigation," 83, RG 29, TSLA. The quotations in this paragraph are from Saul Blair, TT 8:1640.

47. Lockridge interview, July 31, 1989; and Ryan interview, February 3, 1990.

48. Bills interview, FBI 1:133.

49. FBI 4:51.

50. Jones, TT 9:1723; and Blade, TT 10:1993–94.

51. TT 9:1742; and Bowman interview, February 3, 1990.

52. Julius Blair wrote on the back of this invitation a brief note to Madison Jones of the NAACP. Blair to Jones, February 7, 1947, Branch Files, NAACP Papers, LC.

53. Newbern interview, February 3, 1990.

54. Ibid.

55. Johnson testimony, "Transcript of Investigation," 59, 71, RG 29, TSLA.

56. Blair, TT 8:1570.

57. Ibid., 8:1569–71.

58. Fleming interview, July 29, 1989.

59. Arthur Raper, "Kidnapped and Lynched," December 28, 1933, 3, RMP.

60. Minor, *Lynching and Frame-Up*, 19–20.

61. D. Carter, *Scottsboro*, 134.

62. FBI 4:44.

63. The account of Choate's lynching is pieced together from accounts in the *Nashville Banner*, November 12, 14, 20, 1927; Minor, *Lynching and Frame-Up*, 21–25; and Rowan, *South of Freedom*, 46–49.

64. Rowan, *South of Freedom*, 48.

65. *Nashville Banner*, November 20, 1927, 6.

66. Lockridge interview, July 28, 1989.

67. Robert Minor asserts that a rope hung for a lengthy period from a courthouse located elsewhere (*Lynching and Frame-Up*, 25). For a very insightful discussion of the ways scholars can learn about the meaning imparted to events by the transposition of "facts," see Portelli, *Death of Luigi Trastulli*, chap. 1.

68. This story of Cheek's lynching was pieced together from the following sources: "Data Regarding the Lynching of Cordie Cheek," a thirteen-page, single-spaced typescript prepared by Scarritt College professor Dr. Albert E. Barnett and Barnett's "Summary of Events Relating to Lynching of Cordie Cheek"; "Kidnapped and Lynched," a three-page typescript by Arthur Raper; "Cordie Cheek Lynching," a six-page, single-spaced typescript by Dr. Thomas E. Jones, president of Fisk University; and a number of affidavits, most of which were probably collected by Jones and Barnett as they prepared for a third grand jury hearing in their final effort to bring Cheek's lynchers to justice. These documents demonstrate the care with which Jones, Raper, Barnett and others collected information as they sought to get Cheek's killers indicted. This is important because it makes the data they gathered very credible. All of these materials are in Box 13, RMP.

69. Jones, "Cordie Cheek Lynching," 3, RMP.

70. Ibid.

71. Although Arthur Raper termed the fight "indecisive," both Jones and Barnett reported that Henry Carl was "worsted." There is also some disagreement in the written accounts about the timing of the fight. Raper placed it on the day of Henry Carl's accusation against Cheek regarding his sister, but Barnett's account makes that unlikely. Jones stated simply that there was a fight and that Henry Carl made his accusation on the 16th "to get even." Raper, "Kidnapped and Lynched," 2; Barnett, "Data Regarding," 1; Jones, "Cordie Cheek Lynching," 3; and Barnett, "Summary of Events," 3, all in RMP. A copy of the latter document is also in Costigan Papers, University of Colorado.

72. The quotations appeared in Barnett, "Summary of Events," 3; and Jones, "Cordie Cheek Lynching," 3, both in RMP.

73. The description of the mob's visits appeared in the "Fate Cheek Interview," RMP.

74. Barnett, "Data Regarding," 2, RMP.

75. Ibid., 3. Cheatham detailed these events to Barnett and Jones on Friday, July 13, 1934, during their initial visit to Columbia.

76. Sheriff Bauman stated to Barnett that the Cheeks were "too terrified" to report the abduction, while Jones and Raper found them "very much frightened" and hesitant to talk three days following Cheek's murder. Jones, "Cordie Cheek Lynching," 2; and Barnett, "Summary of Events," 2, both in RMP.

77. Cheek's abduction from his uncle's residence is pieced together from Raper, "Kidnapped and Lynched," 1–2; Jones, "Cordie Cheek Lynching," 2; and the affidavits of Rush Cheek, Leona Cheek, Jackson Cheek, Hilary Cheek, and Dixie Stones, Leona Cheek's niece; all sources in RMP. The quotations are taken from Jones and statements by Rush and Leona Cheek.

78. Barnett, "Data Regarding," 10, RMP.

79. For a vivid description of the difficulty in reaching the Harlan farm, see Rowan, *South of Freedom*, 46–47.

80. The son of a farmer who owned his own land in Chapel Hill, Tennessee, James Garrett, who was about 18 or 19 years old in 1933, was forced to stop the truck he was driving and view the lynching. Barnett noted the clear view that Garrett had of the scene, even though the young man remained inside the vehicle.

81. Raper noted that a man who was picked up along the road two days after Cheek's killing mentioned that he knew it was going to happen but did not know it had occurred. Barnett recounted a similar incident. The quote appeared in Raper, "Kidnapped and Lynched," 2; see also Barnett, "Summary of Events," 3, RMP.

82. The quotations about the cars and the composition of the crowd appeared in "Interview with James L. Garrett, Chapel Hill, Tennessee, Evening, January 10th, 1934" (hereafter "Garrett Interview"), 3–4, RMP. This interview was probably conducted by Jones. The Fisk University president mentioned interviewing Garrett early in January, and he noted that Garrett was interviewed by others some months later. Always, Garrett told the same story. Jones, "Cordie Cheek Lynching," 5, RMP.

83. "Garrett Interview," 3, RMP.

84. Castration is mentioned in the "Garrett Interview," but this quote appears in Jones, "Cordie Cheek Lynching," 5, RMP.

85. "Garrett Interview," 4, RMP.

86. The "pleased by their manner" quote appeared in "In Re: Cordie Cheek. Statement of Rush Cheek," 2, RMP. The other details of Cheek's arrest are confirmed in statements of Rush Cheek, Leona Cheek, and Jackson Cheek. Jackson Cheek, who had grown up in Maury County, readily recognized Austin Harlan and his compatriot Gerald Hawkins, who was also from Columbia. Jackson Cheek's obvious fear and agitation when he ran into Harlan at the third grand jury hearing in August 1934 was also an indicator of his knowledge of the constable's identity. See Barnett, "Data Regarding," 12, RMP.

87. Unfortunately, it is unclear whether these remarks were delivered before or after Cordie's death. If they came before, they appear a warning by Denton to Cheek; if they came afterwards, they seem an effort on Denton's part to protect the lynchers. Fate's response that Denton had been his friend "up till this" does not clarify matters, since it could be a reference either to Cordie's jailing or to his death. "Interview between Fate Cheek . . . and Mrs. Thomas E. Jones," 1, RMP.

88. Although the identity of this person is made clear in numerous documents in the RMP, I have chosen for the only time in the manuscript to use a pseudonym. I did this because the man's descendants still reside in Maury County, and I had no opportunity to interview them. The important point for the discussion here is that this alleged murderer held in 1933, and continued to hold in 1946, an official, prominent position in county government.

89. Allen had earned money for the Nashville deputy on various occasions

by leading Pugh's bloodhounds, though whether in search of game or fugitives is unclear.

90. The identification of those involved in Cheek's abduction and murder was checked and rechecked by those seeking indictments. Especially Barnett described the elaborate efforts made by Jones and himself as they prepared for the third and final grand jury hearing in August 1934. See Barnett, "Data Regarding," RMP.

91. Fate Cheek referred to Ann's elder sister as having a last name resembling Allen's.

92. According to Raper, on the afternoon of the accusation against Cheek, Henry Carl's elder sister and young Ann had quarreled. The next morning the sister and her husband moved out of the household to Columbia. Raper noted also that it was reported that Ann had been molested. Fate Cheek in an interview with President Jones's wife in March 1934 did not mention a move by the couple to Columbia. He maintained instead that Ann had gone to the Denton household after the alleged attack and that when she asked when she could return home, her sister told her she would not be returning, that she had "made enough trouble between her and her husband." Raper, "Kidnapped and Lynched," 2–3; and Fate Cheek interview, March 18, 1934, 3, both in RMP.

93. Jones, "Cordie Cheek Lynching," 3, and Barnett, "Data Regarding," 3, RMP.

94. Both quotations in this paragraph appear in "Interview between Fate Cheek . . . and Mrs. Thomas E. Jones," 2, RMP.

95. Barnett, "Summary of Events," 4, RMP.

96. Goodwin's comment about Denton appeared in Barnett, "Summary of Events," 2, RMP. Barnett also included in this segment of his summary the statement quoted by Raper. The only difference between the two was that rather than "white girls," Barnett's quote said "little girls." All of the quotations from Raper appear in "Kidnapped and Lynched," 3, RMP.

97. Jones, "Cordie Cheek Lynching," 1, 3–4, RMP.

98. Ibid., 1–2, 4.

99. They included a Mr. Cook, a former police officer who was at that time managing the Bethel Hotel in Columbia. This hotel, allegedly the center of bootlegging operations in the county, was owned by Joseph Dedman, the U.S. postmaster in Columbia.

100. B. Kerr, a worker with Henry Carl Moore on the road crew where Moore allegedly made statements about being involved in the Cheek lynching, was out "electioneering" for Governor Hill McAllister when Barnett and Jones tried to interview him in the summer of 1934. At the final grand jury hearing, Kerr defended the lynching of Cheek, saying that was the way they did things in Maury County. Barnett, "Data Regarding," 6, 10, RMP.

101. Jones, "Cordie Cheek Lynching," 4–5; and Barnett, "Summary of

Events," 3, both in RMP. The quotation about the attorney general appears in Jones, 4.

102. Jones, "Cordie Cheek Lynching," 6, RMP.

103. J. D. Hall, *Revolt Against Chivalry*, 240–41.

104. Blair, TT 8:1541.

105. Blair, FBI 4:27.

106. William Bills, FBI 1:133.

107. For the important role that unprotection and underprotection has played in creating mistrust between black citizens and the criminal justice system, see Kennedy, *Race, Crime, and the Law*, 29–75.

108. FBI 4:36, 49.

109. Barnett, "Data Regarding," 9, RMP.

110. Minor, *Lynching and Frame-Up*, 41–42; and Barnett, "Data Regarding," 6–7, RMP.

Chapter Three

1. W. B. Twitty, "Special Report on Columbia, March 26, 27, 28," 6, SRC Papers, UNC.

2. Using a 1980 national sample of black Americans, sociologists Michael Hughes and David H. Demo concluded that *personal esteem* among adults derives from "microsocial relations" involving family, friends, and community (especially church-based social networks) and hence is "generated in micro-processes in the black community that are insulated from institutional inequality." *Personal efficacy*, on the other hand, was very much related to institutional inequality, because "the experience of effective performance" is the most important factor in the development of a feeling of control. Hughes and Demo, "Self-Perceptions of Black Americans," 132, 152–54.

3. Lawrence, "Race Riots," 249.

4. Daniel, "Going Among Strangers," 898.

5. While gains in the white population in Maury County slowed significantly during the war decade (from a 25 percent gain in the 1930s to a 6 percent gain in the 1940s), the change was far more dramatic among the black population, as a 3 percent increase in the 1930s became a 15 percent *loss* in the 1940s. Though black Columbia did not lose population, a 28 percent gain in the 1920s, followed by a 17 percent growth rate in the 1930s, became *no growth at all* in the 1940s. The no-growth rate, however, masked considerable population turnover, as residents from the town departed and rural blacks moved in to take their places. These figures were calculated by the author from the census population schedules of 1930, 1940, and 1950 (U.S. Census Bureau, *Fifteenth Census: 1930, Population*; *Sixteenth Census: 1940, Population*; *Seventeenth*

Census: 1950, Population). The flux in the black population in Columbia was revealed by the city directories of 1942 and 1948 (Chamber of Commerce, Columbia).

6. The number of tenant farmers in Maury County shrank from 224 to 123 between 1940 and 1950, farm laborers from 523 to 350, and domestic workers from 1,113 to 629.

7. Between 1942 and 1943, the increasing sparsity of the labor force pushed up average daily farm wages almost 50 percent across the South (from $1.60 per day to around $2.35), although agricultural wages in the region remained at the bottom of the national wage scale. Arthur Raper, "Race Tension and Rising Farm Wages in the Rural South," October 16, 1943, ARP.

8. "Lowndes County, Georgia," 2, Raper Field Notes, ARP.

9. Raper, "Race Tension and Rising Farm Wages," 1, ARP.

10. Shadow to Department of Agriculture, Baton Rouge, Louisiana, April 29, 1942, BAE Papers, NA.

11. "Coahoma County, Miss.," 4, Raper Field Notes, ARP.

12. U.S. Census Bureau, "Census of Agriculture—Tennessee, 1940," *Sixteenth Census: 1940, Agriculture*; "Census of Agriculture: 1945," *U.S. Census of Agriculture: 1945*; and "Census of Agriculture—Tennessee, 1950," *Seventeenth Census: 1950, Agriculture*. The 1940 census included figures for both 1935 and 1940.

13. Daniel, "Going Among Strangers," 887; and Rowan, *South of Freedom*, 47.

14. "Lowndes County, Georgia," Raper Field Notes, May 1944, ARP.

15. "Coahoma County, Miss.," 5, Raper Field Notes, ARP. For the dilemma as Delta planters themselves saw it, see Woodruff, "Mississippi Delta Panters."

16. Sometimes household workers transferred into mills or other forms of employment. Domestic worker Willie Mae Jackson of Atlanta, Georgia, recalled that she replaced her husband as a tailor at Sears and Roebuck while he was in the army and that she sometimes performed waitress work on weekends because all the waiters were gone. Kuhn, Joye, and West, *Living Atlanta*, 364. Other domestic workers left the workplace altogether, because their husbands or sons made more money through better civilian opportunities or in the military. In Clarksdale, Mississippi, the white agent for the Agricultural Adjustment Administration "complained bitterly" that black women were "loafing around town because they received money from their relatives in the service." Independent of wage work, they refused to pick cotton, take in ironing, or do housework. Daniel, "Going Among Strangers," 895.

17. One exasperated mother summed to the president her frustration over her son's treatment at Camp Stewart, Georgia: "He is being treated worse than your dog Falla!" Laurie Horne to Honorable Franklin Delano Roosevelt, May 26, 1943, RG 407, NA.

18. For the "profane and militant" nature of challenges to the Jim Crow system by black domestic workers on streetcars and busses in Birmingham during the war, see Kelley, *Race Rebels*, 67–70.

19. One woman for whom Stephenson had worked and who had moved away from Columbia telephoned a Columbia friend when she read reports of the "riot" in the newspaper to inquire, "What in the world happened down there?" and added "Gladys never bothered anybody." Cooper interview, February 3, 1990.

20. Minor, *Lynching and Frame-Up*, 4.

21. Gladys Stephenson, FBI 1:25.

22. Mrs. Joe McCall and Mrs. James McCall, FBI 1:13.

23. Laverne Bryan Brown, FBI 1:15.

24. Honey, "Industrial Unionism and Racial Justice," 142.

25. Although the name of the parent company, International Agricultural Corporation, was used in NLRB documents in 1938 and 1939, the name IMCC was used by 1941 and in the subsequent War Labor Board hearing in 1944.

26. Information on local numbers and plant locations were pieced together from materials in the Western Federation of Miners Papers, University of Colorado, Boulder.

27. Shannon, "Social and Economic History of Columbia Reservoir Area," 204–5, TSLA.

28. Calvin Lockridge had worked previously for Monsanto, while at least four of those arrested were current Monsanto employees. One of these men, William "Moot" Bills, who later went on trial in Lawrenceburg, had been employed by the company for seven years. Robert Frierson, who rode in the car with Stephenson to Nashville and helped purchase his ticket to Chicago, was also a Monsanto worker.

29. The CIO's censure of Mine, Mill in 1949 for its alleged Communist ties and its expulsion of the union in 1950 caused hardly a ripple in Mine, Mill's activities in the Maury County region. By the late 1950s and early 1960s, however, the area's high-grade phosphate veins were nearing exhaustion, and the union succumbed with them. By 1963, only Mine Mill's long-time rival, the AFL's International Union of Operating Engineers, remained. It represented all organized chemical workers in the vicinity.

30. "Know the Facts," TO ALL WORKERS—Armour Fertilizer Works, May 31, 1951, Box 145, Western Federation of Miners Papers, University of Colorado, Boulder.

31. Twitty, "Special Report on Columbia," 6, SRC Papers, UNC.

32. Lee, *Employment of Negro Troops*, 266.

33. "TM-10-379, Handbook for the Quartermaster Railhead Company, AG 300.4 (4 Nov. 43)," 15–19, quoted in ibid., 267.

34. Lee, *Employment of Negro Troops*, 267–68.

35. James Stephenson, FGJ 2:161.

36. "Migration of Negroes to the North and Education Have Created New Army Problems," 2 and unnumbered page located between nos. 7 and 8, Attitude Surveys, Box 989, RG 330, NA.

37. Stouffer et al., *The American Soldier*, 1:497–98. This work is a part of a four-volume series that Stouffer and his associates wrote on the basis of the more than 200 surveys conducted during World War II under the auspices of the Research Branch of the U.S. Army Service Forces.

38. The interview with John Orr appeared in Alexander and Ashton, *Maury County Remembers*, 2:376–79, quotations on 377.

39. Ibid., 377.

40. Ibid., 377–78.

41. Ibid., 378–79.

42. Ibid., 379.

43. Lee, *Employment of Negro Troops*, 592.

44. Murray interview, February 5, 1990.

45. Herbert Johnson interview, May 16, 1992.

46. In March 1943, the Research Branch in the Information and Education Division of the U.S. Army Service Forces conducted an extensive survey of attitudes of black soldiers. Although frustrated with segregation, discrimination, and the sense that they were limited in their contributions to the war effort, the men surveyed reported that they were *not* unhappy with their jobs, with their units, or, at that time, with their opportunities in the army. Indeed, in response to questions very similar to those used by sociologists Michael Hughes and David H. Demo in measuring self-esteem in a 1989 study, a full 68 percent said they usually felt that the job they were doing in the army was worthwhile; a staggering 85 percent thought that the men in their company or battery cooperated and worked well together all or most of the time; and an equally high proportion (83 percent) were proud of their unit.

47. Comments by LeRoy Love appeared in the Asheville, North Carolina, *Southern News* and were requoted in an NAACP press release, Hastie File, RG 107, NA.

48. Prattis, "Morale of the Negro," 358–59.

49. Dalfiume, *Desegregation of the U.S. Armed Forces*, 72, 88.

50. Tennessee, along with North and South Carolina, Georgia, Florida, Alabama, and Mississippi made up the Fourth Service Command, while Arkansas, Texas, and Louisiana, along with New Mexico and Oklahoma comprised the Eighth Command. The Third Command included Virginia, as well as Pennsylvania and Maryland. Stouffer, *American Soldier*, 1:550.

51. Millard F. Waltz, Jr., Colonel, Infantry, Commanding, to Adjutant General of the Army, "Headquarters Camp Forrest," June 4, 1943, RG 407, NA.

52. In April 1941, just a little over a year before John Orr and Herbert Johnson arrived at Fort Benning, the body of a black soldier, Private Felix Hall, was found hanging from a tree. Military authorities tried to argue that Hall had

committed suicide, but circumstances, including the victims's hands being tied behind his back, suggested otherwise. An investigation failed to solve the case, but blacks remained convinced that Hall had been lynched, and "a queasy uneasiness among Negro troops . . . lingered." Lee, *Employment of Negro Troops*, 349.

53. Walter White to Robert P. Patterson, Secretary of War, December 31, 1945, 2–3, RG 107, NA.

54. Motley, *The Invisible Soldier*, 39.

55. Orr interview, in Alexander, *Maury County Remembers*, 2:379.

56. Untitled, undated document found in Box 54, Philleo Nash Papers, TL. See also G. Smith, *When Jim Crow Met John Bull*.

57. Herbert Johnson interview, May 16, 1992.

58. Mrs. Hannah Price to Gentlemen, October 25, 1945, RG 407, NA.

59. The quotation, which appeared in the *Chicago Defender*, October 20, 1945, was cited in an untitled, confidential document, RG 107, NA.

60. Collective actions could be prompted by insensitive language and by differential treatment—and outright mistreatment—of black soldiers at the hands of military and civilian personnel, by a lack of support and understanding by white officers, and increasingly, as the war progressed, by the very existence of segregated facilities. These actions assumed many forms: coordinated letter-writing campaigns, physical confrontations, mass noncompliance, and mass actions to integrate base facilities. While violent incidents continued throughout the war, they peaked, as did civilian racial disturbances, in 1943. Quieter collective protests also occurred throughout the war era, but mass noncompliance and overt desegregation efforts involving groups of enlisted men grew more prevalent during the later war years.

61. Especially prescient for the Columbia episode, inspectors of racial tensions discovered, frequently to their own surprise, that "*Southern Negroes of relatively long service often turned out to be the chief complainants in investigations of charges of discrimination conducted during the last half of the war.*" Lee, *Employment of Negro Troops*, 306 (emphasis mine).

62. Although interviews conducted in November and December 1944 were with veterans who were mildly disabled, the findings were in many ways very similar to those discovered in a survey of a cross section of enlisted men who were discharged in July 1945. U.S. Department of Agriculture, BAE, "Veterans' Readjustment to Civilian Life," Study No. 109, Condensed, July 16, 1945, RG 330, NA. For comments regarding African American soldiers, see Campbell C. Johnson, "What the G.I. Bill Means to Negro Veterans," speech delivered to the Conference on Employment Problems of Negro Veterans, June 1, 1946, Baltimore, Md., 5–6, Folder 72, Box 57-4, Johnson Papers, Moorland-Spingarn Research Center, Howard University.

63. Almost half of the returning veterans surveyed in 1944 indicated that they palled around "a little" or "quite a bit" with other veterans, and their level

of endorsement for their own organizations was exceedingly high. U.S. Department of Agriculture, BAE, "Veterans' Readjustment to Civilian Life," Study No. 109, Condensed, July 16, 1945, RG 330, NA.

64. Robert Frierson mentioned to the FBI that "most of the returned negro [*sic*] servicemen in Columbia are members of the Elks Club," while in a recent interview Ophelia Tisby said that she was of the opinion that the Elks Lodge "had something to do with the military." FBI 4:36 and Tisby interview, February 2, 1990.

65. Headed by V. K. Ryan, this organization was sufficiently well known to be included in Michael Carter's survey of veterans organizations that appeared in the Washington *Afro American*, December 22, 1945.

66. Formed the latter part of January 1946, this social club consisted primarily of veterans of World War II. Lee Andrew Shyes and Early Shyes, FBI 4:39–40.

67. Clarence Brown, FBI 1:147; Brown interview, February 28, 1989; Luther Edwards, FGJ 11:1683–84; and Charles C[lifford] Edwards, FGJ 11:1662, 1664.

68. Finkle, *Forum for Protest*, 222.

Chapter Four

1. FGJ 3:379.

2. For a succinct and insightful discussion of these processes at work, see Brundage, *Lynching in the New South*, esp. chap. 8 and epilogue.

3. Zangrando, *NAACP Crusade*.

4. Capeci, "Lynching of Cleo Wright."

5. According to the admittedly incomplete records of the Southern Office of the Anti-Defamation League, fifty-nine bombings occurred in six southern states in 1950–51. Particularly hard hit were Dallas with thirteen, Birmingham with ten, and Atlanta and Chattanooga with several each. "Security of the Person" (1952), 2–3, SRC Papers, AU. For an outstanding account of the racial battles in Chicago over housing immediately following the war and the continued struggle over public facilities in the 1950s, see Hirsch, *Making the Second Ghetto*.

6. On the inability of whites to penetrate large black urban enclaves during race riots, see Tuttle, *Race Riot*; and Capeci and Wilkerson, *Layered Violence*.

7. The term "civil religion" was used by Charles Reagan Wilson in *Baptized in Blood*, but the emphasis on the inclusiveness of this phenomenon is my own.

8. This account is pieced together from recollections by John S. R. Gregory and by Dave F. Gregory and Zack Osborne. Statements by Dave Gregory and Osborne were recorded May 12, 1904. All appear in F. H. Smith, *History of Maury County*, 239–41.

9. Ibid.

10. Ibid.

11. Ibid.

12. Lynching ritual is described in many sources, but it was especially Arthur Raper who noted the "dogmatic assertion that the right person was lynched" in the aftermath of a mob action. Raper, *Tragedy of Lynching*, 8.

13. An 1877 hanging from the third floor of the courthouse of a black schoolteacher, the alleged "ravisher of Miss Templeton," may have commenced as a legal execution; however, a crowd of 1,000 apparently surged forward, seized the victim from the sheriff, and hanged him for fifty-six minutes before he was cut down and laid in the courthouse itself. Dwyer, "Social and Economic History of Columbia Reservoir Area," 164–65, TSLA.

14. Brundage, *Lynching in the New South*, 138, 159.

15. Lieutenant Colonel William Polk owned 5,648 acres along the turnpike, which he divided among his four sons. For descriptions of the Polk family and the Zion Church community, see Turner, *History of Maury County*, 244–62 and 142–59, respectively.

16. One of Polk's four sons, Lucius J. Polk, was one of the most renowned horse breeders in antebellum America.

17. Trelease, *White Terror*, 26–27; the membership figure appears on 29.

18. Ibid., 29–30; both quotations on 29. See also Alcock, "Study in Continuity" (Ph.D. diss.), 233–35; and "Ku Klux Klan in Maury County," 9–10, 26, MCPL.

19. Trelease reports that Fitzpatrick had allegedly set fire to two barns, "although no proof or legal charge was ever brought against him." Alcock indicates that there was "no apparent motive." Trelease, *White Terror*, 29; Alcock, "Study in Continuity," 238–39.

20. Trelease, *White Terror*, 29.

21. Ash, *Middle Tennessee Society Transformed*, 148.

22. Ibid., 148, 150–51.

23. Alcock, "Study in Continuity," iv.

24. Ibid., 231–32.

25. Ibid., 232.

26. Fussell's Klan activities are mentioned in Alcock, "Study in Continuity," 232; and Trelease, *White Terror*, 21. A brief biographical sketch appears in Turner, *History of Maury County*, 283–84.

27. C. R. Wilson, *Baptized in Blood*, 112, 113.

28. The quotations appear respectively in Dwyer, "Social and Economic History of Columbia Reservoir Area," 158; and "Ku Klux Klan in Maury County," 33, MCPL.

29. *Columbia Herald*, August 20, 1869, reported in "Ku Klux Klan in Maury County," 32, MCPL.

30. In 1870, African Americans comprised 45 percent of Maury County's population; by 1950, the figure was 21 percent. Similarly, they constituted 52 percent of Columbia's population in 1870 but only 27 percent by 1950.

31. Turner, *History of Maury County*, 283; and Dwyer, "Social and Economic History of Columbia Reservoir Area," 161, TSLA.

32. F. H. Smith, *History of Maury County*, 354–57.

33. Shannon, "Social and Economic History of Columbia Reservoir Area," 265–66, TSLA.

34. The quotations appear, respectively, in Agnes Meyer, "Columbia (Tenn.) Riot," *Washington Post*, May 20, 1946; and Shannon, "Social and Economic History of Columbia Reservoir Area," 266, 53, 54–55, TSLA.

35. Shannon, "Social and Economic History of Columbia Reservoir Area," 56–79 (quotation on 79), TSLA.

36. Dwyer, "Social and Economic History of Columbia Reservoir Area," 84–86, 97–99, TSLA; and F. H. Smith, *History of Maury County*, 89.

37. Shannon, "Social and Economic History of Columbia Reservoir Area," 100–109, 278–79, TSLA; quotations on 105, 278, 103, 107.

38. Quotations in this paragraph are from, respectively, Dwyer, "Social and Economic History of Columbia Reservoir Area," 87, TSLA; and Shannon, "Social and Economic History of Columbia Reservoir Area," 107, 278–79, and 106, TSLA.

39. Dwyer, "Social and Economic History of Columbia Reservoir Area," 91–95, TSLA.

40. Fiddler William G. Hardison and his son, banjoist Roy Hardison, both of Rock Springs, especially enhanced local pride by gaining spots as regulars on the Grand Ole Opry in 1926. Roy Hardison in particular endured, playing for more than two decades with the Gully Jumpers, "one of the most popular 'old time country bands' in Opry history." Shannon, "Social and Economic History of Columbia Reservoir Area," 128, 69–72, 22–25, 26 (quote), TSLA.

41. Dwyer, "Social and Economic History of Columbia Reservoir Area," 97, TSLA; and Shannon, "Social and Economic History of Columbia Reservoir Area," 132, TSLA.

42. As late as 1907–8, the Maury County school superintendent complained in his official report that "many of our best citizens have patronized and still patronize private schools and are not working for the betterment of the public schools." Shannon, "Social and Economic History of Columbia Reservoir Area," 116, TSLA.

43. Ibid., 113–23; quotations on 119, 123, and 121.

44. Ibid., 119, 124, 126.

45. Initially, local residents manifested very strong reservations toward federal government officials who came to assist during the hog cholera crisis in 1915 and toward those who followed shortly thereafter with the Agricultural

Extension Service. They continued to express similar reservations in the mid-1930s when a county agent tried to introduce techniques to prevent soil erosion. Ibid., 62–63, 69–70, and 88–89.

46. Cell, *Highest Stage of White Supremacy*, 134. Also, for the central role of cities in creating segregation, see Rabinowitz, *Race Relations in the Urban South*.

47. Kin networks even overrode class, and they endured—well into the late 1940s in Orange County, North Carolina. For a careful study of this issue, see Kenzer, *Kinship and Neighborhood*. For a fine discussion of the relationship between isolation, religiosity, and extralegal violence, see Paluadan, *Victims*, 16–23; for the important role of honor in generating a propensity toward violent actions, see Wyatt-Brown, *Honor and Violence*.

48. Hagood, *Mothers of the South*, 178.

49. Ellison, *Invisible Man*; and Murray, quoted in Nathans, *Quest for Progress*, 70.

50. Davis, Gardner, and Gardner, *Deep South*, 50–52; quotations on 51, 57.

51. Fields, "Ideology and Race in American History," 160.

52. Alleged sexual assaults also most often prompted lynchings in the Virginia piedmont, but these were usually private, rather than mass, mob affairs. For an excellent treatment of the geography of lynching, see Brundage, *Lynching in the New South*, 103–39; quotations on 113, 122, 124.

53. Raper, *Tragedy of Lynching*, 6.

54. Ibid., 3, 11.

55. "Popeye" allegedly made a smart remark to Fleming's mother as he strode by the Flemings' yard one day. The next day, Flo awaited him, an air rifle or weapon of some sort in tow, demanding an apology. Flo Fleming interview, July 29, 1989.

56. "Opinions About Inter-Racial Tension," Five Cities Survey, 8, Nash Papers, TL.

57. Odum, *Race and Rumors of Race*.

58. Mr. & Mrs. L. M. Horne to Your Excellency, Franklin D. Roosevelt, August 10, 1942, RG 407, NA.

59. "Minorities—Negro—Negro Opinion Study," OWI-Alphabetical Files, TL.

60. Burran, "Urban Racial Violence," 169.

61. Craig to Honorable Overton Brooks, April 16, 1943, 1–2; R. A. "Bob" Hogin to General Marshall, June 5, 1945; A. Leonard Allen, House of Representatives, to The Adjutant General, April 15, 1943, and Inclosed [*sic*] letter from Mrs. Lizzie Rains, dated April 12, 1943; and "Investigation Concerning Conduct of Negro Soldiers," May 7, 1943; all in RG 407, NA. The emphasis in the quotation from the investigation is my own.

62. In one study of white veterans, almost 40 percent said that they had had no close or sustained contact with African Americans while in the military,

and such a claim "was *significantly* associated with outspoken and intense intolerance toward the Negro." Bettelheim and Janowitz, *Dynamics of Prejudice*, 257 (emphasis in original).

63. Stofel interview, July 29, 1989.

64. "Veterans' Readjustment to Civilian Life," 28, BAE Papers, NA.

65. Bettelheim and Janowitz, *Dynamics of Prejudice*, 143, 149.

66. This is not surprising, for many of the stereotypes whites held about the Japanese—as monkeys, apes, and gorillas, for example—resembled those they held about blacks. Indeed, scientific racism placed African Americans lower on the chain of being than Asians. Also, western whites frequently merged stereotypes of nonwhite groups. Thus, during the U.S. war in the Philippines in the early twentieth century, Filipinos readily became "niggers." On similar stereotyping of blacks and Asians by whites, see Dower, *War Without Mercy*, esp. chaps. 4, 6, and 7.

67. E. T. Hall, "Race Prejudice," 405.

68. Bettelheim and Janowitz discovered that in characterizations of the Negro as a soldier, he was "repeatedly described in terms of his sexual behavior while serving overseas." Bettelheim and Janowitz, *Dynamics of Prejudice*, 134–35. In addition, numerous comments culled by the Army Censorship Branch from letters that servicemen wrote home demonstrated the intense fury with which some white soldiers regarded interracial relationships. See, for example, Base Censor Office #2, "Inter-Racial Relations, 16–31 August 1944," 1 September 1944; and Base Censor Office #3, "Censorship Report for Period 16 August 1944 to 31 August 1944, Inclusive"; both in Box 261, RG 107, NA.

69. Capeci and Wilkerson, *Layered Violence*, 61, 55.

70. John Fleming Jr. interview, July 29, 1989; and Agnes Meyer, "Columbia (Tenn.) Riot," *Washington Post*, May 20, 1946.

71. James Beard, one of the two men who tried to set fire to the Bottom, resembled "irresponsible" auto mechanic Roy "Ross" Scribner and taxi driver and crowd member Ichabod Cox, in that he had worked at a Columbia service station in 1942, operated a small auto repair shop in Mt. Pleasant in 1946, and was a taxi driver in 1948. Moreover, Beard rode into Columbia on the evening of the 25th with a filling station attendant from Mt. Pleasant.

72. In discussing superordinate and subordinate situations, Davis, Gardner, and Gardner used store clerks as their example, but the occupations noted here seem to fit their description. In describing the hat tipping, etc., they specifically mentioned filling station attendants. *Deep South*, 53, 57.

73. James Beard freely admitted to the FBI that he and Borgie Claude "had been drinking throughout the evening" on the 25th, while policeman T. F. Collins reported that when arrested after speeding through the Bottom in a truck, "[Charlie] Andrews was too drunk to use it [a gun] if he had one." Additionally, although auto mechanic Bob Taylor was not arrested on the 25th, he had at Borgie Claude's request stopped working on Claude's truck earlier in

the day when he "got drunk and fell off the fender." Beard Testimony, FBI 1:57; Collins Testimony, TT 6:1183; and Claude Testimony, FGJ 4:672.

74. The relative poverty of some whites in comparison to some blacks in the South, and the jealousy and resentment that these circumstances could produce, is discussed generally in Agnes Meyer, "Columbia (Tenn.) Riot," *Washington Post*, May 20, 1946, and is mentioned specifically in relation to eastern Maury County whites and black Columbian businessmen in Guy Johnson, "What Happened at Columbia," 1, SRC Papers, UNC.

75. FGJ 10:1514.

76. Ira Latimer, FGJ, 10:1513–14.

77. A fact, he disclosed quietly in a recent interview, that he had never told anyone before. John Fleming Jr. interview, July 29, 1989.

78. Although George Tindall described the South as "more campground than arsenal" during the war, he pointed out that "war production increasingly moved southward" (*Emergence of the New South*, 695). Jack Temple Kirby found that the South's industrial capacity increased 40 percent during the early 1940s and "continued strong following peacetime conversion" (*Rural Worlds Lost*, 305). For the crucial role of the war in altering the South's economic direction, see Wright, *Old South, New South*; for its effects on occupational and class structure, see Black and Black, *Politics and Society in the South*, esp. chaps. 1 and 2.

79. A survey conducted by the Army's Information and Education Division indicated that four-fifths of the veterans discharged in 1945 were employed within three months of leaving service. In addition, more were either attending school or planning to do so than had been indicated on the surveys that preceded the end of the war. Similarly, a study by the Veterans' Administration found that within three to four months after discharge about 85 percent were either working at the same job they had before entering service, laboring at a different job, attending school, or "pretty well settled as to what they would do." Two-thirds of these men indicated that they "had been able to carry out their predischarge educational or job plans or still expected to carry them out." "Employment Experience of Army Veterans," RG 330, NA; and Stouffer, *American Soldier*, 2:639–40, quotation on 40.

80. For a thoughtful discussion of the relationship between age, education, and socioeconomic status on the one hand and prejudice on the other, see Bettelheim and Janowitz, *Dynamics of Prejudice*, 14–24. The specific point about class and white views of black intelligence is made on page 23. Principles, implementation, and social distance, including the growing concern among whites at all income levels as the percentage of blacks in the population rises, are discussed in Schuman, Steeh, and Bobo, *Racial Attitudes in America*.

81. Stouffer, *American Soldier*, 2:597.

82. Ibid., 597, 637, 642.

83. In a 1944 study of veterans in five midwestern cities, two out of three of the interviewees talked about African Americans and "unfriendly attitudes were about twice as common as friendly ones." Similarly in their study of the attitudes of 150 white veterans in the Chicago area shortly after the war, Bettelheim and Janowitz discovered that almost half were "outspoken" in their "Anti-Negro Attitudes," while another 16 percent were "intensely" so. Only 8 percent fell into the "tolerant" range. "Veterans Readjustment," BAE Papers, NA; and Bettelheim and Janowitz, *Dynamics of Prejudice*, 134–35.

84. Kirby, *Rural Worlds Lost*, 275–76.

85. Bettelheim and Janowitz, *Dynamics of Prejudice*, 254–56, quotation on 256 (emphasis in original). "Veterans' Readjustment," 33, BAE Papers, NA.

86. Stouffer, *American Soldier*, 2:586.

87. Lawrence, "Race Riots," 254.

88. Stouffer, *American Soldier*, 2:597.

89. John Fleming Jr. interview, July 29, 1989.

90. Hawaii was under martial law at the time Fleming was there, and the provost court was the only one trying both civilian and military cases. Alexander and Ashton, *Maury County Remembers*, 2:149; and John Fleming Jr. interview, July 29, 1989.

91. Twins Fred and Flo enlisted in the Navy in November 1940; Jack William, referred to as "J. W.," joined the Navy two months later, in January 1941; and "Billy," Luther Thomas, and John Jr. were all activated through their National Guard units in February 1941. Although John Jr.'s unit was deactivated just a couple of weeks prior to Pearl Harbor, he was recalled to active duty a few weeks after the attack, in late January 1942. Emmit, the last of the brothers to leave home, joined the Navy when he graduated from high school in the spring of 1941.

92. By far, the most important stream of migration intended by white enlisted men at the war's end was to the Far West, with most headed for the Pacific coast. "4. Expected Pattern of Post-War Migration," 6. Box 992, RG 330, NA.

93. Actually, at the time John Jr. got a job, it was with the Corps of Engineers, Manhattan Engineer District, the forerunner of the Atomic Energy Commission. All of the material presented here on the Flemings appeared in Alexander and Ashton, *Maury County Remembers*, 2:147–49; John Fleming Jr. and Flo Fleming interviews, conducted separately on July 29, 1989.

94. Flo Fleming interview, July 29, 1989.

95. Shannon, "Study of the Social and Economic History of Columbia Reservoir Area," 301–2, TSLA.

96. Brundage, *Lynching in the New South*, 252.

97. Hirsch, *Making the Second Ghetto*. For the community solidarity that characterized these violent actions, see esp. 74–78.

98. Brundage, *Lynching in the New South*, 252.

99. In a 1950 Atlanta University survey, 62 percent of the black teachers and college students from cities across the South indicated that the Klan was active in their communities, while only 28 percent from rural areas indicated that this was the case. Miller and Hill, "Safety, Security," 26, SRC Papers, AU.

100. Belknap, *Federal Law and Southern Order*, esp. 236–51.

Chapter Five

1. In a 1950 survey of black college teachers and students from across the South, 48 percent of the respondents from cities said blacks were beaten when arrested, compared to 36 percent from towns, and 28 percent from rural areas. Miller and Hill, "Safety, Security," 18, SRC Papers, AU.

2. An SRC report noted that no southern state was free of police brutality charges in 1951 and that twenty-six African Americans had been killed by police in Birmingham alone between 1948 and 1951. This compared with nineteen between 1935 and 1940. "Security of the Person" (1952), 3–4, SRC Papers, UNC; and Raper, "Race and Class Pressures," 36, ARP.

3. Raper, "Race and Class Pressures," 52–56, ARP.

4. McKinzie, "Bontecou Interview," 24, TL.

5. A survey conducted at Atlanta University in the summer of 1950 of black teachers, other professionals, and college students from across the South confirmed this point. Although one would expect these middle-class citizens to have had fewer negative encounters with law officers than had members of the black working class, over half rated the police in their communities as "below average" in "intelligence and training," while an additional quarter described them as "poor or very poor" in these respects. When asked about the impartiality of police when a dispute arose between a black person and a white person, three-quarters of the respondents replied that law officers were biased in favor of the white person, and over half described the "justness" of the police as "poor or very poor." Miller and Hill, "Safety, Security," 6–7, SRC Papers, AU.

6. Ibid., 6–7. Just over forty southern cities and towns had black policemen in 1947. Guy Johnson, 76, PCCR Papers, TL.

7. Both men had accompanied police chief J. Walter Griffin to the scene of the fight between James Stephenson and William "Billy" Fleming. FBI 1:29–30.

8. James Stephenson, FGJ 2:165.

9. Williams and Murphy, *Evolving Strategy*, 2.

10. TT 8:1570.

11. The phrasing here is that of Attorney A. O. Denning as he asked Underwood a question, but Underwood agreed this was the substance of the letter. FGJ 3:420.

12. No one demonstrated this phenomenon better than William Gordon. Remembered recently by black Columbian Herbert Johnson as a "fighting Negro," Gordon had once freed a man from jail in order to shoot him, while Sheriff Underwood commented to grand jurors that he would be afraid to say how many times the young man had been in trouble in Mt. Pleasant and Columbia, "fighting over gambling games and so on and so forth." Yet Gordon had been arrested only two times and his sole punishment was a fine for driving while intoxicated. The reason? While Gordon had "quite a reputation among the negroes," the sheriff explained, "among the white people where he was working, he was well thought of. They knew him and he knew them, and they got along fine." It also did not hurt that the farm on which Gordon was born, reared, and continued to work belonged to a local judge. FGJ 3:360 and FGJ 2:341.

13. For the frequency with which this occurred in the South, see Myrdal, *American Dilemma*, 2:551.

14. TT 8:1616.

15. Griffin, FBI 3:187; Griffin, TT 2:383–86; Wilsford, TT 1:108, 112, 113.

16. Griffin, FBI 3:187; Griffin, TT 2:383–86; Wilsford, TT 1:108, 112, 113; Julius Blair, TT 8:1571; and Johnson, TT 9:1695.

17. J. Blair, TT 8:1571; and Griffin, TT 2:383–85.

18. Stofel interview, July 29, 1989. Myrdal makes the point that this pay represented a step up for white unskilled workers but that the job was one looked down on by members of the white middle class (*American Dilemma*, 2:540).

19. Stofel interview, July 29, 1989.

20. Myrdal, *American Dilemma*, II, 540.

21. Stofel interview, July 29, 1989.

22. Ibid. Guy Johnson, director of the SRC, who visited Columbia in 1946 during his investigation, also noted recently that he "didn't find the local law people" believing in a black insurrection, while the testimonies of the police (and all testified) at the Lawrenceburg trial indicated much the same thing. Guy Johnson interview, July 12, 1989.

23. Wilsford, TT 1:113–14.

24. TT 6:1154.

25. TT 1:114.

26. TT 8:1616.

27. Mann, *Unequal Justice*, 163.

28. For an example beyond Columbia, Tennessee, see Krieger, "Investigation of alleged unwarranted assaults," July 30, 1941, RG 407, NA. The file documenting this investigation is very full. It includes Krieger's report, which totals 57 pages, as well as a list of exhibits and numerous other reports and pieces of correspondence.

Like the Columbia, South Carolina, case just noted, a similar situation in

Nashville is very well documented. The file consists not only of the report of an investigation but also of the verbatim transcript of questions and responses of forty-four witnesses, as well as statements and affidavits of others, and a transcript of the trial of Private James Pinkney, an enlisted man who tried to come to the aid of his friend. Lapham and Bonner, "Report of investigation," April 27–May 5, 1945, RG 407, NA.

29. Richardson, TT 1:312; and Stofel, TT 1:261.

30. The quotations appeared respectively in *Pillow-Kennedy*, 1:43, 56–57, 63, 71, 69, and 63.

31. FGJ 3:376–77.

32. The sheriff attempted to contact Clarence Brown's employer so he could make bail for Brown; he passed along Lee Andrew Shyes's car keys to Shyes's mother while the young man was in jail; and he tried to find a hat that Joe Daniel Calloway had lost, bringing him three or four old ones to inspect. Most telling of all, no prisoners were struck while in Underwood's custody. Crowded conditions and poor food were the order of the day in the antiquated Maury County jail, but intentional, physical maltreatment by the sheriff and his deputies was *not* an additional condition that prisoners were forced to endure.

33. Saul Blair quote appeared in TT 8:1637.

34. TT 8:1637; 3:479–81.

35. TT 3:447–49; FGJ 6:849–50; TT 10:2015–17.

36. The statement by Underwood concerning the Lockridges appeared in TT 7:1420–21; the quotation concerning the Blairs and Morton appeared in FGJ 3:429–30.

37. According to one account, the term derived from an earlier era when white bootleggers operated in the vicinity. "Stenographic Notes," NAACP Papers, LC, 3.

38. FBI 1:87 and *Pillow-Kennedy*, 4:888.

39. On one occasion after he was out of office, Underwood used the term "the Slide," but even then, he avoided the detested "Mink Slide." *Pillow-Kennedy*, 3:729. Quotations in this paragraph appeared in FGJ 3:360.

40. This account of Underwood's life is pieced together from FGJ 2:275–76; TT 3:395–96; and J. J. Underwood Jr. interview, July 30, 1989.

41. Underwood, TT 3:473; Calvin Lockridge, FGJ 7:1046; and Underwood interview, July 30, 1989.

42. Calvin Lockridge stated to the grand jury in 1946 that he was born on the farm owned by Underwood's father, while Raymond recollected that the Lockridges knew the Underwoods because "they had a farm out there right next to ours." The younger Lockridge did not know, however, how his father acquired it. For Calvin Lockridge's statement, see FGJ 7:1046; for Raymond's, see Lockridge interview, July 28, 1989.

43. As noted, Underwood was 59 in 1946; Calvin was almost 41 and Ray-

mond was 32. For Underwood's statement regarding his relations with this farm family, see FGJ 3:420–21; Raymond Lockridge's statement is from his July 28, 1989, interview.

44. Underwood opened his butcher store in 1918, the same year that Blair left the square and concentrated all of this financial interests on Eighth Street. For the reference to Blair trading with him, see TT 3:453.

45. Lamon, *Blacks in Tennessee*, 59, 80.

46. Walter Weare has attributed the emergence of the black vote in North Carolina in the 1920s to close elections and a desire on the part of white politicians to use that vote in areas where the black population was not large (Weare, "Charles Clinton Spaulding," 186). Glenda Gilmore, however, argues that black women's protests contributed to greater registration by black men and women in the same decade (Gilmore, *Gender and Jim Crow*, 219–24).

47. This quotation and the point about black activism in Chattanooga and Memphis both appear in Lamon, *Black in Tennessee*, 82.

48. Mayor Eldridge Denham, FBI 1:59.

49. Ibid.; and Guy B. Johnson, "What Happened at Columbia," *New South* 1 (May 1946), 2, SRC Papers, UNC.

50. Beasley Thompson, *Nashville Tennessean* reporter, FGJ 7:1128–29; Flo Fleming interview, July 29, 1989; Albert Wright, FBI 1:107; Denham, FBI 1:59; John Fleming Sr., FBI 1:21. The episode involving Gene Fleming's murder and the death of his alleged killer is also mentioned in Minor, *Lynching and Frame-Up*, 43.

51. The quote regarding support for Underwood among the "negro element" appeared in FBI 4:6, which also makes reference to "every negro pastor in Columbia" working "for the purpose of getting the negro vote solidified . . . to defeat Flo Fleming." The Lockridge quote in FGJ 7:1046.

52. TT 3:453. Black Republicans like Julius Blair often voted in Democratic primaries in Tennessee. See Key, *Southern Politics*, 74 n. 27.

53. Saul Blair said they were discussing the possibility of having Underwood's son run, but all other references were to Underwood himself. FBI 4:9.

54. John Malone, *Nashville Tennessean* photographer, FGJ 7:1163–65, quotation on 1164.

55. The quotations by Malone and Thompson appeared in FGJ 7:1164 and 1125, respectively, but for the entire context surrounding the discussion, see 1162–65 and 1125–26. Flo Fleming, Stofel, and John Fleming Jr. interviews, conducted separately July 29, 1989.

56. Flo Fleming interview, July 29, 1989.

57. Miller and Hill, "Safety, Security," SRC Papers, AU, 10; Maslow Testimony, 38; and Houston Testimony, 121–22, both in PCCR Papers, TL.

58. Lamon, *Black Tennesseans*, 234–35, 238–39 (NAACP petition quoted on 238). The wider involvement of the NAACP in efforts to establish state police forces is noted in Ray, "Contested Legitimacy" (Ph.D. diss.), 23.

59. *Tennessee Defense Force History*, 6–7, author's files; Dickinson to The Adjutant General, "Report on Tour of Active Duty," JMDP, TSLA, 1.

60. FGJ 3:704.

61. FBI 3:60–131.

62. W. W. Hogan to Dickinson, April 21, 1946, JMDP, TSLA.

63. Major General George H. Butler to Dickinson, August 23, 1946, JMDP, TSLA; "Nashville, A Family Town," Public Library of Nashville and Davidson County, and in the possession of Peggy Fleming; and interview with Peggy (Mrs. Swope) Dickinson Fleming, May 17, 1992.

64. Peggy Fleming interview, May 17, 1992; and Butler to Dickinson, August 23, 1946, JMDP, TSLA.

65. FGJ 5:679–80.

66. The only people to confess to the FBI that they pilfered cigars, cigarettes, and candy from establishments on East Eighth Street were two enlisted men in the State Guard. Another took from the Lodge Hall as a souvenir a pennant of the International Union of Mine, Mill, and Smelter Workers.

67. Schott, *Servants*, 25.

68. The quotations appeared respectively in Schott, *Servants*, 7, 12.

69. Ray, " 'A Distinctively American Type of Men' " (OAH paper), 1993, 10.

70. Schott, *Servants*, 10–12; FGJ 3:375; and FGJ 8:1291–92. State Guardsmen also carried Riesen [spelled Rising in FGJ transcript] submachine guns, but the automatic connectors had been removed from them so that they were in fact only autoloading or semiautomatic, that is, one had to pull the trigger for every shot. Dickinson, FGJ 5:722.

71. The first black patrolman was not hired in the Volunteer State until the 1960s, that is, long after black policemen had been added to many urban police forces. The first woman joined the force after 1970, after the women's movement accelerated; she, like the black trooper, was initially assigned to the Drivers' License Division. Martha Remslinger O'Rear interview, May 16, 1992.

72. York, "A Tall Man," 4.

73. Although the Patrol increased to 200 men in 1937, its total stood only at 168 in July 1949 when Safety Commissioner Sam Neal added 76 troopers. Schott, *Servants*, 21, 29.

74. A black-and-white photograph taken at a dinner Flo Fleming hosted at the Ranch House Restaurant when the Patrol was in Columbia attests to the comraderie of the group, to the ceremonial significance of this occasion, and to the stern visages troopers thought appropriate when representing their organization. Flo Fleming interview, July 29, 1989; photograph in Fleming's scrapbook.

75. Of the seventy-two state troopers questioned by the FBI during the course of their investigation, *none* would admit having seen any acts of vandalism in the Bottom. FBI 3.

76. Greg O'Rear interview, February 4, 1990.

77. York, "A Tall Man"; and Wayne Whitt, "Long Career Coming to an End," *Nashville Tennessean*, June 7, 1970.

78. The last duty commenced when a riot broke out at the Pikeville Training School in Bledsoe County, about fifty miles north of Chattanooga. This episode is mentioned and the other wartime duties of the Patrol are described in Schott, *Servants*, 24–27.

79. The Murfreesboro attacks are noted in Lee, *Employment of Negro Troops*, 352, but the quotation appeared in Motley, *Invisible Soldier*, 45.

80. Walter White to Henry L. Stimson, October 3, 1941, and Attachment to White's Letter, September 5, 1941, RG 407, NA; and Lee, *Employment of Negro Troops*, 352–54 (quotation on 352–53).

81. This quotation appeared in Lee, *Employment of Negro Troops*, 354; the escape by Duane Simons and several other members of the 94th is described in Motley, *Invisible Soldier*, 46–49.

82. The Alexandria episode is described in James B. LaFourche to Walter White, January 19, 1942, RG 407, NA. The murder of the black MP appeared in Truman K. Gibson Jr. to Brigadier General B. O. Davis, "Memorandum," 30 June 1943, RG 107, NA, 3, and in an untitled, undated report in the same file. The quotation appeared in the latter document.

83. The quotations appeared in FGJ 11:1692 and Minor, *Lynching and Frame-Up*, 62.

84. FBI 1:3–4, 47, 53; John Malone, FGJ 7:1149; and Luther Edwards, FGJ 11:1697.

85. I am extremely grateful to Robert Lynn Bomar Jr., formerly a resident surgeon at Vanderbilt Hospital, for the very thoughtful, insightful letter he sent to me January 18, 1990.

86. "Lynn Bomar," *Police Reporter*, Clippings File, TSLA.

87. Ibid.

88. Bomar, FGJ 3:479, 478; Robert Bomar Jr. to Author, January 18, 1990; and FBI 4:12.

89. At no time during his sojourn in Columbia did the Patrol Chief attempt to disarm whites, for as he explained to Lawrenceburg jurors: "I didn't want to disarm them, I didn't know what was coming out of Mink Slide." TT 7:1262.

90. "You damn negroes think you are bad"; "You negroes are not as bad as you were last night"; and most revealing, "You all are trying to take this town over." John Porter, FGJ 11:1852; Elmer Dooley, FGJ 11:1846; and Lee Andrew Shyes, TT 4:612.

91. FGJ 6:854, 939–40, 926.

92. Flo Fleming interview, July 29, 1989.

93. McKinzie, "Bontecou Interview," 22, TL.

94. Hogan to Dickinson, April 21, 1946, JMDP, TSLA.

95. Cooper, "State Police Movement," 432–33; Schott, *Servants*, 17–18; Greg O'Rear interview, February 4, 1990; and Noles interview, May 11, 1992.

96. Flo Fleming interview, July 29, 1989; and Noles interview, May 11, 1992.

97. Martha O'Rear interview, May 16, 1992.

98. During Browning's tenure, Jackson—a driver for former governor Prentice Cooper, a personal escort and driver for Governor McCord, and former Nashville division chief—found himself back out patrolling the highways!

99. Actually, Frank Clement, like Senators Albert Gore and Estes Kefauver, was a fresh, young face in Tennessee politics who was more progressive and independent of the Crump machine than other governors between 1932 and 1948, but Crump and *Nashville Banner* stalwart James Geddes Stahlman supported Clement, and he had strong connections with the McCord regime, having served under McCord as attorney for the state railroad and public utilities commission. Even more significantly as far as the Highway Patrol was concerned, the same faction had returned. For a detailed account of Tennessee politicians in the age of transition between Crump-dominated politics and the two-party politics that emerged in 1964, see Gardner, "Political Leadership in a Period of Transition" (Ph.D. diss.).

100. This situation continued, although poll taxes were not cumulative in Tennessee from 1933 forward. They could be expensive, however, because some municipalities levied taxes that were added to the state poll tax. "Summary of Election Laws" and U.S. Department of Labor, "Effects of Poll Taxes," October 26, 1937, Bontecou Papers, TL.

101. Key, *Southern Politics*, 60.

102. In Nashville in the 1940s and 1950s, Robert Lillard spearheaded one faction, Z. Alexander Looby another. One black political leader declared that the officers of the two Nashville groups "would rather go to jail than attend a meeting with each other."

103. Key, *Southern Politics*, 74–75; Gardner, "Political Leadership," Ph.D. diss., 55; Graham, *Crisis in Print*, 5.

104. Meticulous about his name, the governor insisted that he had been named after an old family friend and that it was Jim, not James. "Don't call him 'James'—and he'll be your friend," one journalist reported. Ralph Perry, "Lewisburg Man Without Serious Foe at Any Time," August 4, 1944, McCord Clipping File, MPL.

105. This biographical account was constructed from articles in the McCord Clipping File, MPL. See especially Elizabeth C. Bills, "Lewisburg Citizens Will Miss New 5th District Congressman," August 7, 1942; Ralph Perry, "Lewisburg Man Without Serious Foe at Any Time," August 4, 1944; "Farmboy Jim Nance McCord, Onetime Auctioneer, Raised Tennessee Educational Level," May 23, 1948; and "Death Takes Jim McCord, Two-Term Governor, at Age 89," September 9, 1968. See also Corlew, *Tennessee*, 490.

106. Quotes from Key, *Southern Politics*, 66.

107. Prior to this legislation, a labor union could not be sued as an organization. McCord Clipping File, MPL. For Crump's very hostile orientation to-

ward the CIO and his frequent use of the police against the union in Memphis, see Honey, *Southern Labor.*

108. The quotations in this paragraph appeared respectively in Honey, *Southern Labor,* 48, 165; and Tucker, *Lieutenant Lee,* 125. The change in Crump's approach is discussed briefly in Tucker, 124–26, and in more detail in Honey, 148, 165–70.

109. Honey, *Southern Labor,* 205, 209, 222, 245–46. See also Gardner, "Political Leadership," Ph.D. diss., 26.

110. Tilly to Guy Johnson, March 8, 1946, 1–3, SRC Papers, UNC.

111. Farmer interview, August 2, 1989. Bethune's 1946 speaking tour, including the Nashville visit, is discussed in L. Reed, *Simple Decency,* 100–102.

112. "McCord Shifts, Opposes Truman," March 10, 1948, McCord Clippings File, MPL; and White to Roy [Wilkins?], March 5, 1946, NAACP Papers, NA.

113. White to Roy, March 5, 1946; and Fyke Farmer, "Stenographic Notes," 16, both in NAACP Papers, NA.

114. FGJ 5:705.

115. The quotations in this paragraph all appear in FGJ 9:1405–7.

116. References to "the slide" were made frequently in Smith's testimony before grand jurors; see, for example, FGJ 4:623. The other quotations in the paragraph appeared in "Report of Investigation of Ernest F. Smith, Assistant Attorney General, Concerning Disturbance at Columbia, on February 25–26, 1946," 5, 13, 12, 40, RG 29, TSLA (emphasis mine). For the "Nigger" and "Jigger" references, see FGJ 4:633 and page 9 of Smith's report.

Chapter Six

1. For the emergence of civil rights as a number-one priority among northern white liberals during the war and the immediate postwar years, see Jackson, *Gunnar Myrdal,* 236–38, 274–79. The "acid test" quote appeared in Jackson, p. 237. For the growing focus of the SCHW on racism during the war years, see L. Reed, *Simple Decency,* chap. 5 and 100–102.

2. Zangrando, *NAACP Crusade,* 167–74, 213.

3. The phrase "politics of self-interest" appeared in Sitkoff, *A New Deal for Blacks,* 333. CRS attorney Eleanor Bontecou made the observation regarding the good relations between the NAACP and the more leftist unions, though she did not regard these unions as Communist and was not implying any connection between the NAACP and the American Communist Party. See McKinzie, "Bontecou Interview," 29, TL.

4. Jackson, *Gunnar Myrdal,* 281 (quotations on 240 and 278–79).

5. Krueger, *And Promises to Keep,* 143–44.

6. During the conflict, the Army Inspector General's Office had helped

bring attention to this issue by providing black Americans with a forum to which they could take complaints regarding mistreatment by civilian, as well as military, police in their communities. Additionally, the accelerated migration of African Americans out of the rural South worsened the problem, because official abuse occurred most often in the nation's cities. The race riots of 1943 spotlighted for whites in particular the negative, often physically aggressive orientation of the police toward African Americans. In turn, a greater awareness of the difficulties, coupled with the recognition that national security was at stake, prompted some individuals and organizations to launch formal programs aimed at improving police attitudes and community relations. Although few of these programs were actually implemented, the inauguration of the police-community relations program was important to the Columbia story, because it contributed to a context in which police behavior toward African Americans was very high on the agenda of reform-minded individuals and organizations and thus constituted an issue President Truman and high-ranking Justice Department officials could not ignore. In several of his works, Samuel E. Walker has discussed the changes brought about by the events of 1943 and the police-community relations movement; his fullest articulation appears in "Origins of the American Police-Community Relations Movement." See also Walker, *A Critical History of Police Reform*, 123–24; *Popular Justice*, 197–99; and *The Police in America*, 219–21.

7. *Herald Tribune*, October 1, 1946.

8. Elliff, *U.S. Department of Justice*, 742–44 (quotations on 743 and 742).

9. The conclusion that Clark's liberal position on civil rights resulted more from his office than from the influence of the president was Elliff's (*U.S. Department of Justice*, 211). To look at this issue from a slightly different perspective, however, Hoover biographer Richard Powers reports that FBI Director J. Edgar Hoover allegedly felt "less secure" with Clark than he had with his predecessor, Nicholas Biddle, because Clark "gave Hoover the feeling he made his prosecutorial decisions on the basis of partisan political pressures." Powers, *Secrecy and Power*, 277.

10. The comment by Caudle appeared in Edw. A. Tamm to The Director, May 1, 1946, FBI 2:2; White's statements are in Farmer, "Stenographic Notes," 21, NAACP Papers, LC.

11. Caudle was from North Carolina, Smith from Georgia. The quotation here appeared in Elliff, *U.S. Department of Justice*, 212, but an FBI memorandum also indicated that this was an area of sensitivity, and liberals were aware that they could capitalize on it. See Hostetter to Director, April 30, 1946, FBI 2:3.

12. D. M. Ladd to J. E. Mulford, February 26, 1946, FBI 1; Niles to Clark, March 6, 1946, Office Files, TL; and Clark to David K. Niles, March 22, 1946, 2, Clark Papers, TL.

13. Davies's indictments as reported in the *Nashville Tennessean*, April 9,

1946, were compared with those in the Bontecou Papers, TL. Clark's actions were reported in the *Tennessean*, March 5, 22, and 23, 1946, and summarized in Clark to Niles, March 22 and 29, 1946, Clark Papers, TL. The AG's directive to Frierson, dated March 21, 1946, was released publicly and appeared in a number of places; the copy cited here was in the NAACP Papers.

14. This case involved the 1942 lynching of Howard Wash in Laurel, Mississippi. A jailer and four private citizens were indicted by a federal grand jury, though no guilty verdicts were returned in the trial itself. The quotations appeared in Rotnem to PCCR, 68–69; the Wash case is succinctly summarized in Robert K. Carr to Members of the President's Committee on Civil Rights, June 10, 1947, 10–11, both documents in the PCCR Papers, TL.

15. Actually this was Section 52 (and Section 241 was 51) until 1948, but it is commonly referred to by its subsequent number and not by its 1946 designation.

16. The others were Section 241 (earlier Section 51), which made it a crime "for two or more persons to conspire to injure or intimidate any citizen in the free exercise of the rights guaranteed to him by the Federal Constitution or laws," and Section 444, "the Antipeonage Act." For an overview of the development of these statutes, see Carr, *Federal Protection*, chap. 3; the quotation regarding Section 51 appeared in Wendell Berge, "Civil Rights 'Through the Window of Criminal Statute,' " 4, Bontecou Papers, TL.

17. The implications of the *Screws* decision are discussed in many places. The most accessible is Carr, *Federal Protection*, 105–15.

18. Turner L. Smith, Chief, Civil Rights Section, to PCCR, "Civil Rights Questions in Which Public Has Expressed Most Concern," February 21, 1947, 13, PCCR, TL (emphasis mine).

19. Ibid.

20. Edw. A. Tamm to The Director, May 1, 1946, FBI 2:2.

21. FBI 1:35; FGJ 2:277; and McKinzie, "Bontecou Interview," 26, TL.

22. The quotations in this paragraph appeared respectively in FGJ 2:334, 320; and Underwood interview, July 30, 1989.

23. The NAACP pamphlet described "wooden walls" of "beleaguered [black] houses" that "disintegrated in the face of the hot machine-gun blasts"; "men, women, and children" lying "flattened against their quivering floors"; "screaming children running wildly for their mothers"; and a new type of "klan," wearing "cap and visor, and shining badge" (Oliver W. Harrington, "Terror in Tennessee," NAACP Papers, LC). In a similar though much briefer depiction, the Committee of 100 saw "brute force and blind hatred" as "the sole authority" in lieu of "any sanction of law" (Carl Van Doren to Dear Friend, May 10, 1946, SRC Papers, UNC). The *New Republic* titled its account "Pogrom in Tennessee" (*New Republic*, April 1, 1946).

24. For a comparison of upper-class and middle-class configurations in the South, see Davis, Gardner, and Gardner, *Deep South*, 73–79.

25. This consideration occupied center stage even in the private report submitted by Ernest F. Smith to the State Attorney General (Smith, "Report of Investigation made on February 27–28, 1946 at Columbia, Tennessee," RG 29, TSLA).

26. *Daily Herald*, March 5, 1946.

27. FGJ 3:420.

28. Wright, *Old South, New South*, 198–275.

29. Caldwell commended him on his performance, as did Denning and Foreman J. F. Richardson. No one else received such a compliment.

30. Dickinson, "Report on Tour," 3, and Dickinson to Adjutant General of Tennessee, "Recommendations Relative to the Tennessee State Guard," March 12, 1946, JMDP, TSLA.

31. Dickinson's single, indirect criticism of the Patrol chief came when he acknowledged that he had not mentioned the use of gas to Bomar until troopers were already in the Bottom. When Attorney John Kelley asked "What response did he make?" Dickinson replied aggravatedly, "There was no discussion. He was on his business." FGJ 5:695–96, 729, 734.

32. FGJ 5:723.

33. "Jacob McGavock Dickinson Genealogical Chart," copy given author by Peggy Fleming; and Peggy Fleming interview, May 17, 1992.

34. Supplement to "Confidential letter to The Adjutant General of Tennessee," 12 March 1946, 1, JMDP, TSLA.

35. Ibid.

36. FGJ 5:734.

37. Even as planters benefited from many government programs, they railed against "WPA Projects, Food Stamps and various forms of relief, Government Aid, and Defense Projects" for driving up labor costs (Glen L. Shadow to Department of Agriculture, April 29, 1942, BAE Papers, NA). Hostility toward the WPA (Works Progress Administration) in particular is expressed in many of the reports of the BAE. For the quotations in the text concerning the decline of concern over federal intervention in the South by the late nineteenth century, see Chappell, *Inside Agitators*, 12.

38. In the late 1940s, many upper-class southerners, especially in the Deep South, helped spearhead a growing conservative movement that climaxed in the massive resistance effort of the 1950s. For the dual nature of "neobourbonism" as it revived in the 1940s, see Bartley, *Rise of Massive Resistance*, 31–32.

39. Elliff, *U.S. Department of Justice*, 793.

40. McKinzie, "Bontecou Interview," 39, TL.

41. Ibid., 39.

42. Ibid., 25.

43. J. K. Mumford to D. M. Ladd, April 24, 1946, FBI 2.

44. Lewis, *Public Entrepreneurship*, esp. 116–18, 122, 129; the quotation appeared on 140.

45. Hopton interview, May 18, 1992.

46. FGJ 1:31–32 (emphasis mine).

47. FBI 1:4.

48. "Statement of J. Edgar Hoover, Director, Federal Bureau of Investigation," March 20, 1947, 77, PCCR Papers, TL; O'Reilly, *Racial Matters*, 29–30; and Summers, *Official and Confidential*, 57–60.

49. "Statement of J. Edgar Hoover," 78, PCCR Papers, TL (emphasis mine).

50. In writing about white "Home Owners Protective Associations" in the Los Angeles area that were attempting in 1944 to keep blacks out of their neighborhoods, Agent Royall L. Stauffer referred to the issue as "negro encroachment" and noted that "the negro press continues *to agitate* against restrictive covenants and discrimination." When screening a white person for clearance, Stauffer reported, FBI investigators asked whether the individual "had any Negro friends, or went to Negro people's houses" (Stauffer, "Foreign Inspired Agitation," November 21, 1944, Federal Bureau of Investigation, File 100-14872, RG 107, NA). Similarly, former Farm Security Administration director Will Alexander reported, "whites are often interpreted as of questionable loyalty if they have participated in such events as picketing a restaurant or theater which will not serve Negroes, or if a white personnel administrator gives evidence of sympathy in the direction of equal treatment of Negroes in his employment policies." In short, Alexander concluded, "the very exercise of a civil right becomes a condition for the persecution of that individual in other respects" ("Statement of Dr. Will Alexander, Vice-President, Rosenwald Fund," May 15, 1947, 30; and Alexander, "[Written] Statement before the President's Committee on Civil Rights," 3, both in PCCR Papers, TL).

51. J. Q. Wilson, *Investigators*, 36.

52. Ibid., 127.

53. The dress and conduct that Hoover required of his agents are discussed in numerous works. The quotations here appear in ibid., 26. Southern agents were used in the investigation "in order that there might be no criticism." Mr. Tamm to D. M. Ladd, "Race Riots Columbia, Tennessee," March 2, 1946, Office Memorandum at the outset of FBI 1.

54. The Director from H. H. Clegg, "Racial Violence, Columbia, Tennessee, Civil Rights and Domestic Violence," April 30, 1946, FBI 2:3.

55. Ibid., 3, 4–5.

56. Once he was infuriated when he believed a memo had been in the office for three hours before he saw it; another time, an agent had to fly during the night to get materials from Tennessee to Washington.

57. Hopton produced a summation of the case just two days after he arrived in Columbia, and although the investigation continued for several more days and the FBI report that he filed on March 10 extended to 197 pages, his synopsis mirrored almost word-for-word his initial evaluation. Furthermore,

the extensive work that followed the April 29 grand jury order for additional inquiry did not alter Hopton's original conclusions one iota, though to his credit he resisted shifting to Paul Bumpus's notion of "prearranged plans" among black Maury Countians or to assertions of Communist plots that state officials favored.

58. For the concept of "boundary-spanning devices" and an excellent discussion of them, see Lewis, *Public Entrepreneurship*, 109–23. Quotations in this paragraph appear on 109, 110, and 121. Emphasis on Hoover's states' rights orientation appears in O'Reilly, *Racial Matters*.

59. Underwood used the phrase "very well" when asked how well he knew English, and Griffin indicated a similar familiarity by referring to English as "James." Hopton could not recall the name of the resident agent in Columbia in 1946, but he did not think it was English, although English was one of the agents involved in the case. Hopton interview, May 18, 1992; Jerry Hess, "Tom Clark Interview," Clark Papers, 130–31, TL; K. C. Howe to Mr. Ladd, March 6, 1946, FBI 2; Underwood, FGJ 3:377; Griffin, FGJ 2:241.

60. J. Q. Wilson, *Investigators*, 23–24, 38–39; and Hopton interview, May 18, 1992.

61. Tamm to The Director, April 30, 1946, FBI 2; and Hopton interview, May 18, 1992.

62. Tamm to The Director, April 30, 1946, FBI 2.

63. Lewis, *Public Entrepreneurship*, 122.

64. Quoted in Elliff, *U.S. Department of Justice*, 217.

65. Ibid., 218.

66. "Meeting of the Executive Committee," June 19, 1946, 1–2, NAACP Papers, LC.

67. Davies discussed his membership in the Klan before the Senate subcommittee considering his nomination as a federal judge; see *Nashville Banner*, July 6, 1939. The other quotation in this paragraph is from Seigenthaler interview, May 11, 1992.

68. Carter also added that "Justice [Hugo] Black is perhaps the best example that I can think of whose career on the bench would disprove the theory that a Klansman is necessarily a bad judge." "Memorandum to Mr. White From Robert L. Carter," June 10, 1946, NAACP Papers, LC.

69. Shortly after he assumed office in 1939, Davies had ordered that names be placed in the federal grand and petit jury boxes without regard to race; African American Jasper C. Horne took his seat in 1942. *Tennessean*, April 21, 1942. The comment about Davies being a judicial tyrant is from Seigenthaler interview, May 11, 1992.

70. McKinzie, "Bontecou Interview," 20, TL; and Tamm to The Director, May 1, 1946, FBI 2:2.

71. McKinzie, "Bontecou Interview," 20, TL; Caldwell quoted in Elliff, *U.S. Department of Justice*, 217.

72. Corlew, *Tennessee*, chaps. 22 and 23; and Paul R. Coppock, "For 42 Years, He Was A Man For All Sessions," McKellar Clippings, MPL.

73. Stahlman had immigrated to America with his family in 1853 from the German province of Mecklenburg County. They had settled in what would become Parkersburg, West Virginia. His father had applied for citizenship but died before the process was completed. Stahlman's mother remarried a man who did become a naturalized citizen, but Stahlman had been advised by a Nashville attorney that his own citizenship was "at least doubtful."

When Luke Lea learned the outcome of this investigation, he shared it with the assistant district attorney of Tennessee, a man "who was also on a political side opposed to Major Stahlman." Early in 1918, while visiting New York City with his son and daughter-in-law, Stahlman, dressed in evening clothes and headed for the opera, was arrested by a Secret Service agent as he made his way across the lobby of his hotel! The agent, however, gave the publisher permission to make a telephone call, and he immediately phoned McKellar. A senator who *invariably* took care of his constituents, McKellar got Stahlman released to him, and he took him the next day to an assistant attorney general who gave the major permission to go to Parkersburg to determine if he could find any information that would shed light on the situation. Meanwhile, through a meticulous examination of the naturalization statutes and further consultation with Stahlman, McKellar discerned that the newspaper owner was in fact a citizen because he was under the age of 18 at the time of his stepfather's naturalization. "McKellar Memoirs," 156–61, MPL.

74. Stahlman interview, May 18, 1992.

75. McGill, *The South and the Southerner*, 91.

76. In 1952, the newspaper assumed no public position, although James G. Stahlman assured McKellar privately that he planned to vote for him. "McKellar Memoirs," 163, MPL; and McGill, *The South and the Southerner*, 100.

77. Key, *Southern Politics*, 64–65 (quotes). See also Graham, *Crisis in Print*, 34–35; Corlew, *Tennessee*, chap. 24; and Seigenthaler interview, May 11, 1992.

78. Key, *Southern Politics*, 72–73.

79. Black, "Parsonage to Publisher," unpublished manuscript.

80. Butterfield, "Silliman—He's a Wonder," 92; and Evans interview, May 17, 1992.

81. Perry, *Democracy Begins at Home*, 261, 264–65.

82. Ibid., 272–73.

83. Black, "Parsonage to Publisher," 222.

84. The letter read in part:

If the City of Nashville should ever follow the lead of the progressive City of Memphis and inaugurate a campaign for the extermination of rodents, Silliman Evans . . . will undoubtedly take to the tall timbers.

It was easy for Father Adam to name the hog, snake, elephant, skunk and the hound dog, but when it came to the bubonic rat he evidently had a mental preview of Evans.

(Quoted in Black, "Parsonage to Publisher," 222.)

85. Approved by the Senate Judiciary Committee in April 1945, the subcommittee held an inquest in November of that year. Though not a member of the subcommittee, McKellar participated in the three-day event, grilling Evans, banker Paul Davis, and *Tennessean* attorney Cecil Sims in an attempt to prove that the newspaper was purchased at the behest of Jesse Jones with funds from the Reconstruction Finance Corporation. Butterfield, "Silliman—He's a Wonder"; and Black, "Parsonage to Publisher."

86. Though extreme, McKellar's attack on Evans was not out of character for the senator. In 1939 at the age of 70, he had advanced on Royal Copeland on the floor of the Senate with his fists doubled, inviting the New York senator to fight. A few weeks prior to his encounter with Evans, he had hit and kicked Jack Anderson when the 26-year-old reporter was sent by his boss, Drew Pearson, to talk with him in his office. Then, in a final escapade at the age of 81, Tennessee's senior senator "seized a heavy wooden gavel and apparently . . . prepared to strike [Clarence] Cannon" when the 71-year-old Democratic representative advanced on him in the midst of a heated verbal exchange in a closed House-Senate conference. These episodes were pieced together from newspaper articles in the Clippings File and McKellar Papers, MPL.

87. Crump to McKellar, April 5, 1946, CMC; and Black, "Parsonage to Publisher," 226.

88. E H Crump to Senator Kenneth McKellar, March 27, 1946, CMC; and Gardner, "Political Leadership," 26.

89. E H Crump to Senator Kenneth McKellar, April 15, 1946, July 5, 1946; and Crump to Frank Hobbs [Chairman, State Democratic Executive Committee], July 10, 1946, all in CMC.

90. U.S. Department of Agriculture, BAE, "Veterans' Readjustment to Civilian Life," July 16, 1945, RG 330, NA, 26. In this 1945 survey conducted by BAE, 65 percent of those polled said that government should have more say than business in solving problems like unemployment; 21 percent chose business; while 9 percent opted for the two sharing power equally or neither having any. For a succinct presentation of the argument about Americanism and a summary of much recent literature, see Fones-Wolf, *Selling Free Enterprise*, esp. 1–20; the quotations appeared on 1–2 and 17.

91. Fones-Wolf, *Selling of Free Enterprise*, 20–22. In addition to full employment, other items on labor's agenda included "economic planning and a fuller articulation of the welfare state through an expansion of Social Security and unemployment insurance, and the development of a national health program" (ibid., 21).

92. Crump to McKellar, April 12, 1946, CMC.

93. McKellar to R. H. Routon, copy to Crump, n.d.; Crump to McKellar,

April 12, 1946, with revised copy of Routon letter enclosed; McKellar to Crump, April 12, 1946 [subject: minor revisions to Crump's enclosed, revised letter to Routon]; Will Gerber [Shelby County district attorney] to McKellar, July 9, 1946; and Crump to McKellar, July 7, 1946, all in CMC; and "Americanism vs Communism," "The Democrat," August 1, 1946, both in McKellar Clippings, MPL.

94. The quotations appeared in Bob Kelly to Senator Kenneth McKellar, July 6, 1946; and Crump to McKellar, August 4, 1946. See also Crump to McKellar, August 5 and 6, 1946; telephone message regarding Louis Gordon; and McKellar to Crump, August 6, 1946, all in McKellar Papers, MPL.

95. Crump to McKellar, April 12, 1946; McKellar to Crump, April 12, 1946; "McKellar Liked in the East," October 20, 1946; Ward Hudgins, Secretary to Senator McKellar, to Horace German, April 10, 1946; and McKellar to Honorable A. D. Hughes, March 14, 1946, all in CMC.

96. Stahlman to John H. Sorrells, Publisher, The Commercial-Appeal, July 18, 1946, McKellar Papers, MPL; and *Nashville Banner*, January 8 and July 25, 1946.

97. Stahlman had in fact broken with Roosevelt in 1932 and had been backing Republican candidates since. Thurmond was his only break in this pattern at least through Goldwater.

98. Cartoon by Knox, McKellar Papers, MPL.

99. McKellar had sat beside his candidate and opposite the Senate Judiciary Sub-Committee at Davies's hearing, grilling opposition witnesses and placing supporters on the stand. He had also interrupted debate on Social Security amendments to secure full Senate approval, and he had rushed the decision to the president for his signature before he left town for the funeral of a colleague—and before the chairs of the Judiciary Sub-Committee and of the full Judiciary Committee had time to register the protests they wished to make. Seigenthaler interview, May 11, 1992; *Nashville Banner*, July 6, 12–17, 1939; and *Nashville Tennessean*, July 11–18, 1939.

100. *Nashville Banner*, July 17, 1939.

101. When the possibility of a hearing was under consideration, Davies had informed the U.S. attorney that "he was not in favor of convening a Grand Jury to . . . appease a bunch of radicals and Communists." J. C. Strickland to Mr. Ladd, March 18, 1946, FBI 2.

102. In mid-April, W. D. Hastings, part-owner of the *Herald*, wrote the senator:

I also think I see a great change in the feeling of the people here in Maury county, since it is becoming so evident that Hillman and the left wingers are up solidly behind Carmack. . . . Just let it perculate [*sic*] gradually into the minds of these people that it is the CIO and the communistic element that is at work and you will win in this county.

Hastings to McKellar, April 15, 1946, McKellar Papers, MPL.

103. With SCHW headquarters in Nashville, Dombrowski made an especially convenient target for demonstrating the immediacy of the Communist threat, and the grand jury hearing provided an excellent springboard for a sustained attack on him that lasted throughout the summer. By the fall, plans were underway to move the SCHW's central office to New Orleans, and a major, desperately needed fundraising campaign had begun. For the nature of the attack on Dombrowski, see Adams, *James A. Dombrowski*, 160–62; and *Nashville Banner*, June 12, 1946. The move to New Orleans and the capital campaign are discussed in L. Reed, *Simple Decency*, 41.

104. Hamilton, *The Bench and the Ballot*, 4 (emphasis in original); and Peltason, *58 Lonely Men*, 247.

105. This was not always the case, as Jack Bass demonstrated in his study of four circuit judges who made up the Fifth District Court of Appeals during the heyday of the civil rights movement. The exceptional quality of these individuals is made clear, in Bass's title, *Unlikely Heroes*. Vines quotation is from Peltason, *58 Lonely Men*, 265 (emphasis mine).

106. Peltason describes a similar situation existing in the 1950s, and his description was an important influence on the thoughts expressed here. Peltason, *58 Lonely Men*, 249.

Chapter Seven

1. For the importance of speed in southern trials involving African Americans, see Myrdal, *American Dilemma*, 552.

2. Though Leon Ransom participated in the trial, during this period of his life he was experiencing numerous difficulties. A member of the Howard Law School faculty from 1931 to 1946 and acting dean from 1942 to 1945, Ransom resigned from the school in mid-April just before becoming involved in the Columbia case. Chronically ill, according to his wife, and the father of two sons, both of whom were in college, Ransom was experiencing financial problems, and he and Marshall were constantly at loggerheads over the amount of pay and expenses the attorney should have been receiving. Ransom also missed the Kennedy-Pillow trial because he was allegedly "suffering from temporary amnesia caused by nervous exhaustion" and as a result disappeared from his home for four days during this time. Many memos in the Ransom File of the NAACP Papers attest to Ransom's problems; his frustration over not being chosen dean of Howard Law School and the story of his disappearance and "temporary amnesia" appear in the Ransom Clipping File, Howard University.

3. Initially, the first charge was levied against James Morton, Julius and Saul Blair, Meade Johnson, and James "Popeye" Bellanfante. At the end of the trial, the initial indictment was altered by the prosecution to include only James

Morton and Julius Blair. The others were charged under the second indictment. Charlie Blair was never charged because of a lack of evidence against him, though Attorney General Paul Bumpus firmly believed he was one of the "chief leaders" in the affair, along with his father and older brother.

4. TT, "Closing Arguments," 2311, 2418.

5. No bullets were recovered from his body; no guns were marked as they were confiscated. Perhaps this occurred because the suspects were African Americans and southern authorities were not accustomed to having to build a strong case against blacks whose victims were white. More likely, however, it resulted from the mistakes that minimally trained law officers often commit and that an excited force like Bomar's was sure to make. Even today when most policemen are better trained than in 1946, a study of district attorneys noted that "research consistently proves the impact that the quality of law enforcement has on a case outcome" and that "nationwide, 40 percent of adult felony arrests are either rejected at initial screening or dropped soon afterwards." Galloway to District Attorneys, "Memo on the District Attorney's Roles," February 26, 1988, 10, in author's possession.

6. Auerbach, *Unequal Justice*, 10.

7. Ibid., 9.

8. Bumpus to O'Brien, November 24 and September 29, 1989; Auerbach, *Justice Without Law?*, 120.

9. "Statement of Hon. Tom Clark," April 3, 1947, 16–18, PCCR Papers, TL.

10. TT, "Closing Argument," 2451–53.

11. Bumpus to O'Brien, Sept. 29, 1989; FBI 1:191; and TT, "Closing Argument," 2419.

12. "Transcript of Investigation," 23–24, RG 29, TSLA.

13. Ibid., 30, 54.

14. Ibid., 59, 61.

15. Ibid., 60, 62.

16. Ibid., 22, 63–64.

17. Ibid., 66–67.

18. Bumpus interview, January 30, 1990.

19. "Transcript of Investigation," 70, 73, RG 29, TSLA.

20. FBI 4:2.

21. Ibid., 21, 22.

22. *Berger v. United States*, 295 U.S. 70 (1935), cited in Galloway to District Attorneys, in author's possession.

23. Ibid., 3.

24. Auerbach, *Unequal Justice*, 10.

25. "Law of the State of Tennessee" and "Memorandum, *Attempted Murder*," NAACP Papers, LC.

26. *American Dilemma*, 525; see also 1183–85.

27. FGJ 3:418–19.

28. See especially TT 8:1652–57 for Saul Blair and 1614 for Julius. The elder Blair's financial assistance was reported in the *Nashville Globe*, December 20, 1946.

29. Prior to placing any black Maury Countians on the stand, the attorney general noted that they might be "hostile to the State" and that they would certainly be "reluctant and unwilling witnesses." Not surprisingly, given the circumstances under which the "'Judas' witnesses" appeared, their testimony was less than effective. Several displayed their unhappiness about being there by speaking so softly they could scarcely be heard. No one volunteered information. Some actively evaded the State's questions, while Mamie Fisher reversed herself completely during cross-examination and denied previous testimony outright. Equally damaging for the prosecution, almost all of their black witnesses described physical abuse by police officers at the time of their arrest. Quotations in this paragraph are from TT 4:570 and NAACP Press Release, September 26, 1946, 1, NAACP Papers, LC. For the Mamie Fisher's reversal of her earlier testimony, see TT 5:836–75.

30. George A. Newbern, a graduate of Tennessee Agricultural and Industrial College in Nashville and assistant county extension agent, testified that he and Julius Blair attended the same church, that he saw him there "nearly every Sunday," and that his "general reputation . . . for truth and veracity . . . seemed to be good." Similarly, Reverend Joseph P. Blade, pastor of Mt. Tabor Presbyterian Church in Columbia and a neighbor of Julius, depicted the 76-year-old defendant's reputation "for peace and quietude" as "very good." On his own, Blair also made a very effective witness, as he described his meteoric rise from poverty in the Maury County countryside to East Eighth Street proprietor and property owner, and he had considerable opportunity to amplify to jurors his lynching fears on the 25th. Quotations appear in TT 9:1762 and TT 10:1988.

31. Bradley also reputedly "carried on a losing fight in the jury room" for the freedom of Gentry and McKivins as a result of his negative views of Fisher. Harry Raymond, "Prosecutor's Hitlerism Went Sour," *Daily Worker*, October 7, 1946. The quotations in the paragraph appear in TT, "Closing Argument," 2254–55; Davis interview, July 30, 1989; and Bradley interview, July 30, 1989.

32. The quotations in these paragraphs appear in George Barker, "Man Behind the Move" and "No Place to Hide." Mrs. Grafta Looby Westbrook, Looby's wife for over forty years, shared these news articles. She mentioned his high school graduating class as the last one at Howard in Westbrook interview, May 11, 1992.

33. John Britton, "Z. Alexander Looby Interview," November 29, 1967, 35, CRDP; Westbrook interview; and Barker, "No Place to Hide," 15.

34. In 1910, when the NAACP was founded, black attorneys made up 0.7 percent of all lawyers in the nation (795 out of 114,000); by 1930, this figure had crept up to 0.8 percent, but the number in almost every southern state was declining. Between 1910 and 1940, the number of lawyers in Georgia went

from 18 to 8; in South Carolina from 17 to 5; and in Mississippi from 21 to 3! Meier and Rudwick, "Attorneys Black and White," 915.

35. Barker, "No Place to Hide," 15, 20.

36. Britton, "Looby Interview," 4–5.

37. Auerbach, *Unequal Justice*, 211.

38. Ibid., 211–12.

39. Quoted in ibid., 212.

40. This account of Houston's life and career was pieced together from Auerbach, *Unequal Justice*, 214–15; Greenburg, *Crusaders in the Courts*, 3–6; Hastie, "Charles Hamilton Houston," 364–65, 405–6; McNeil, *Groundwork*, esp. pt. 2; Nieman, *Promises to Keep*; and Williams, "Marshall's Law." The quotations are from Nieman, *Promises*, 114, 115; Williams, "Marshall's Law," 17; and McNeil, *Groundwork*, 84.

41. Auerbach, *Unequal Justice*, 213.

42. McNeil, *Groundwork*, 117.

43. Britton, "Looby Interview," 16, CRDP; McNeil, *Groundwork*, 71; and "Biographical Note," 1, ZALP.

44. Looby's insistence that he was "the first Negro lawyer" to raise the question of Negroes on the jury appeared in Britton, "Looby Interview," 4, CRDP. Looby's work in "the university case, the teacher salary case . . . and the numerous criminal cases all aimed at securing full and complete justice for Negro Americans," are mentioned in Thurgood Marshall to M. G. Ferguson, President, Nashville, Tennessee Branch, December 11, 1946, NAACP Papers, LC, as well as in other sources.

45. Otto McClarrin, "Omega Chapter! Alexander Looby," *The Oracle*, Summer 1973, 14, ZALP; "Z. Alexander Looby. Educator, Lawyer, Activist for Human Rights, 1889[sic]–1972," NAACP Papers, LC; and Dr. Vincent J. Browne, "Interview with C. T. Vivian, Director, Urban Training Center for Christian Missions in Chicago," February 20, 1968, 17–18, CRDP.

46. Auerbach, *Unequal Justice*, 215.

47. Looby's "determination, his capabilities, and his mental astuteness" and his "fearlessness" are invariably mentioned as important aspects of his personality. Interview with Attorney Cecil Branstetter, May 18, 1992; and interview with Judge Adolphus A. Birch, July 25, 1989.

48. Barker, "No Place to Hide," 20; and Auerbach, *Unequal Justice*, 214.

49. McClarrin, "Alexander Looby," 14, ZALP; Britton, "Looby Interview," 22, CRDP; and *Nashville Globe*, December 20, 1946.

50. Birch interview, July 25, 1989.

51. Although Ingram ordered Bumpus's term struck from the record (it appeared in the trial transcript as "this Negro woman"), Looby's interpretation of it is easily inferred, and it is noted specifically in the *Pittsburgh Courier*, October 5, 1946. The quotations in the paragraph are from TT 9:1886; Barker, "No Place to Hide," 14; and the Birch and Davis interviews.

52. Marshall to M. G. Ferguson, President, Nashville Branch, NAACP, December 11, 1946, 2, NAACP Papers, LC.

53. Meier and Rudwick, "Attorneys Black and White," 920.

54. Ibid., 918–21.

55. Kincaid, FGJ 6:792–96; White to Maurice, March 27, 1946, 1; Bradley interview, July 30, 1989; and Looby to Thurgood, March 22, 1947, all in NAACP Papers, LC.

56. White, *A Man Called White*, 310. Unfortunately, the personal attributes that served Weaver so well in the Columbia cases did not serve him so well throughout his life. Although he managed to sustain a vigorous law practice in the wake of his success at Lawrenceburg, he later succumbed to alcoholism and prescription drug addiction. In 1965, the Chattanooga Bar Association began disbarment proceedings, and three years later the Tennessee Court of Appeals upheld the Bar's negative decision. The charges included "failure to pay federal income tax, having an affair with a client's wife, representing opposing parties in a case, absconding with a client's money, and threatening attorneys." Weaver died in 1983 of cirrhosis and emphysema. Ikard, *No More Social Lynchings*, 136–37.

57. Laurent Frantz to O'Brien, January 30, 1991.

58. Auerbach, *Unequal Justice*, 219–20; quotations on 220.

59. Frantz to O'Brien, January 30, 1991; Dixon to Walter White, March 21, 1946; and "Work Report, February 26 To April 19, 1946," 3, all in NAACP Papers, LC.

60. Weaver to Mr. Looby, "State vs. Saul Blair Et Al," NAACP Papers, LC.

61. Kennedy-Pillow TT, 4:959.

62. Marshall himself, however, intervened when Weaver's 19-year-old, pregnant wife, Virginia, rode to the trial with Oliver Harrington and one of Looby's young associates. Worried about the reaction of local whites, he "strongly advised Virginia . . . to ride the Greyhound bus" in the future. Ikard, *No More Social Lynchings*, 80–81.

63. TT, "Closing Argument," 2359.

64. In February 1947, Weaver admitted "less than one year ago I knew nothing at all about the aims, and objectives" of the organization, "but because of the fight it is waging for the protection, and advancement of your oppressed people," he continued, "I am purchasing fifty Jr., memberships, for a group of school children." Peter G. Crawford, Chair, Civic Committee, Inter-denominational Ministerial Alliance of Chattanooga, to Honorable Walter White, February 8, 1947, NAACP Papers, LC.

65. TT, "Closing Argument," 2455, 2394–95, 2354, 2363.

66. TT, "Closing Argument," 2363–64, 2354–55; and Kennedy-Pillow TT, 4:958.

67. Stouffer et al., *American Soldier*, 1:440.

68. This was demonstrated very clearly in the closing months of battle,

when all-volunteer black platoons were integrated into white companies in seven infantry divisions in the European theater.

69. TT, "Closing Argument," 2355.

70. *Chicago Defender*, November 2, 1946.

71. Although in early June the situation in Columbia was described as "so grave that anything may happen at any time" and white spectators called all of the defense counselors "vile, obscene names," it was negative comments about Weaver in particular that Muriel Gravelle, a white woman who "mingled freely with the white people during recess and after adjournment," at this time cited during the change of venue hearing in the Kennedy-Pillow case. Walter White, "Memorandum to Robert Carter, Marian Perry, and Franklin Williams," June 8, 1946, NAACP Papers, LC; and Kennedy-Pillow Trial, 1:45–46.

72. Photographer Roy H. Staggs eventually acknowledged that "to show those men [the police] . . . was the object of the picture" that he took at the behest of Bumpus. Wilsford admitted that African Americans in the Bottom thought a mob was coming; Stofel, that a crowd of whites was following the police as they made their way toward East Eighth Street; and Denton, that he had advised Julius Blair not to remove the Stephensons from jail until later in the day for their own safety.

73. "Sheriff, have you told all you know about this matter?" the Nashville lawyer led off. "I wouldn't think so," Underwood replied. "I thought you hadn't," Looby responded knowingly, and then, relying on Weaver's notes, he elicited from Underwood positive comments about the Blairs, Morton, and the Lockridge brothers; an acknowledgment of the fears the sheriff and black Maury Countians shared about the formation of a white mob; and the admission that many African Americans charged that James Morton and Saul Blair "could have kept down all this trouble" because they were jealous of the two prominent men. TT, 3:427–28 and 498.

74. Looby pressed prosecution witness Mamie Fisher on whether she was drunk on the night of the 25th and cast aspersions on her character, and hence her testimony, in ways that Weaver could not have done. Similarly, in lengthy questioning of Lynn Bomar, Weaver so enraged the Highway Patrol chief that he clearly exhibited his volatile nature, a step a black attorney could not have successfully taken with an all-white jury. TT, 7:1321.

75. Davis, "Reflections," handwritten thoughts composed for author's visit and interview, July 30, 1989.

76. Telegram from Donald Jones to Walter White, filed 3/18/46, and White to Weaver, March 27, 1946, both in NAACP Papers, LC; Westbrook interview, May 11, 1992; Houston to The Secretary, Spingarn Medal Award Committee, October 20, 1946, ZALP; *Chicago Defender*, November 2, 1946; and Peter Crawford to Walter White, February 8, 1947, NAACP Papers, LC.

77. *Charlotte [N.C.] Observer*, July 3, 1946, and *Nashville Tennessean*, July 11, 1946.

78. Black women in Lawrence County who worked outside the home were concentrated overwhelmingly in domestic service, while black men were employed primarily as farm and timber workers. Men also clustered in non-domestic service jobs, though they were farm owners as well. Only a minuscule number of men or women served in professional or semiprofessional capacities, and far fewer than in Columbia were proprietors. U.S. Census Bureau, "Nonwhite Employed Workers 14 Years Old and Over, by Major Occupation Group and Sex, by Counties," *Sixteenth Census: 1940, Population*.

79. "News Stories dictated by O[liver] Harrington," September 19, 1946, NAACP Papers, LC; Davis interview, July 30, 1989; and *Afro-American*, August 24, 1946.

80. In 1860, Lawrence County contained less than half the number of slaves held in Maury County in 1810; the black population of Lawrence in 1940 and 1950 stood at 2 percent, that is, just over 700 souls out of a total population of almost 29,000.

81. In 1946, Lawrenceburg's weekly paper, the *Democrat Union*, was run by Charley and Jim Crawford, brothers whose father had been "a bitter foe of the Ku Klux Klan." A local African American described the newspaper as "not radical"; when asked what he meant, the man responded, "Well, I mean it ain't radical like that fellow Bilbo" (*Chicago Defender*, October 5, 1946). It will also be recalled that it was to the Lawrenceburg jail that white landowner Joel Cheatham initially raced in his attempt to get Cordie Cheek to safety in 1933.

82. In 1950, the average value of the land and buildings on a commercial farm in Maury County was $13,038; the comparable figure for Lawrence County was $4,986. U.S. Bureau of the Census, *Seventeenth Census: 1950, Agriculture*.

83. TT, "Closing Argument," 2203 and 2237 (emphasis mine).

84. *Democrat-Union*, July 12, 1946; and NCJC, "Meeting of the Executive Committee," October 9, 1946, 2, NAACP Papers, LC.

85. Davis interview, July 30, 1989.

86. The quotations in this paragraph appeared in Jamieson, "The German Catholic Settlement in Lawrence County," in "Glimpses of Lawrence County History," 3, TSLA; and Carpenter and Carter, *Our Hometown. Lawrenceburg, Tennessee*, 39, TSLA.

87. *Daily Worker*, September 22, 1946.

88. Carpenter and Carter, *Our Hometown*, 197–98, 204–5, TSLA; and Alice Dickson, "The Amish in Lawrence County," in "Glimpses of Lawrence County History," 4–6, TSLA.

89. Of the 42 black farmers in the county in 1945, 37 were full owners of their land and 1 a part-owner. In contrast, only 5 black men farmed as tenants, though a larger number undoubtedly worked for cash wages (a figure that stood at 18 in 1940). In comparison to the 88 percent of the black farmers who owned their land in 1945, only 63 percent of the white farmers did so. With a

much larger white population than black, this meant that almost 1,300 whites labored as tenants, with 253 of them working as sharecroppers, a category filled by no black Lawrence Countians in 1945.

90. *Pittsburgh Courier*, October 12, 1946; and *Chicago Defender*, October 5, 1946.

91. Higginbotham, *Shades of Freedom*, 131–32.

92. Davis, Gardner, and Gardner, *Deep South*, 50, 52; and Johnson, "Ideology of White Supremacy," 125.

93. Davis, Gardner, and Gardner, *Deep South*, 53.

94. Research Branch, Special Service Division, "Attitudes of Enlisted Men Toward Negroes for Air Force Duty," November 30, 1942, 8–9, RG 330, Army Adjutant General Files, NA. The quotation in the paragraph appeared in "Five Cities Survey," OWI-Alphabetical File, Nash Papers, TL.

95. *Daily Worker*, September 22, 1946; *Chicago Defender*, October 5, 1946; and *Pittsburgh Courier*, October 12, 1946.

96. *Daily Worker*, September 22, 1946.

97. TT, "Closing Argument," 2456, 2460; Davis interview, July 30, 1989; and Sheean, "Lawrenceburg Verdict."

98. Davis interview, July 30, 1989 (emphasis in original).

99. Bradley made a statement to this effect before stepping into the jury box (*Daily Worker*, September 22, 1946) and in a recent interview (Bradley interview, July 30, 1989).

100. Bradley interview, July 30, 1989.

101. Barker, "Man Behind the Move," 20; and Bradley interview, July 30, 1989.

102. Campbell, "World of a Redneck," 113.

103. In a recent chronicle of the pre–civil rights generation in the South, John Egerton concluded that "in retrospect," he had come to see just "how favorable the conditions were for substantive social change in the four or five years right after World War II," though neither Egerton nor the present study suggest that the initiative for change lay with southern leaders. Egerton, *Speak Now Against the Day*, 10.

Conclusion

1. Griffin, Clark, and Sandberg, "Narrative and Event," 31.

2. Estimates by Arthur Raper for the years 1915–32 and by Jesse Daniel Ames for the years 1915–42 put averted lynchings at one-half to two-thirds of all attempted lynchings. Ibid., 26.

3. For an excellent example of this phenomenon, see Adam Fairclough's discussion of the changes in St. Landry Parish by 1952 in *Race and Democracy*, 124–32.

4. Krieger, "Investigation of alleged unwarranted assaults," July 30, 1941; and Lapham and Bonner, "Report of Investigation of alleged 'Dangerous Incident,'" April 27–May 5, 1945, both in RG 407, NA.

5. Not only was one owner outspoken, but also his brother, a co-owner, visited Fort Jackson as part of a committee to complain officially about the treatment of customers in his restaurant. Krieger, "Investigation of alleged unwarranted assaults," 47, 49, RG 407, NA.

6. For the East St. Louis story and the involvement in particular of Dr. LeRoy Bundy—dentist, service station owner, and "super-ward leader" who was "the sort of person that 'the ordinary fellow looks to for guidance'" and who possessed such a "hot-temper" that some African Americans thought it "might get him into trouble with the whites"—see Rudwick, *Race Riot at East St. Louis*. For the participation in the Tulsa affair of John Williams—owner of a service station, confectionery, and movie theater, who defended Greenwood with a 30–30 rifle and a repeating shotgun—see Ellsworth, *Death in a Promised Land*.

7. Resorting to guns and the threat of violence was hardly a restrained action, but in larger political terms it was *defensive* and *reactive* and thereby different from an attempt to integrate a military unit or achieve equal pay or accommodations.

8. Interestingly, Fairclough found doctors, dentists, and pharmacists providing the strongest leadership in NAACP chapters in Louisiana, while branches headed by ministers "tended to be weak ones." Fairclough, *Race and Democracy*, 72.

9. Lockridge interview, July 28, 1989; and Cooper interview, February 3, 1990.

10. Rowan, *South of Freedom*, 42–43.

11. Ibid., 48.

12. Addie Blair Cooper, who continued to work outside the home after her marriage because she "had to," recalled that, while the cab company of black owner Joe Breeden consisted of one car, her husband went "big time" when he opened his operation—he started with two cars. When he died in 1955, he had four—though they were still walking, she added wryly. Cooper interview, February 3, 1990.

13. In 1946, Julius Blair owned eight pieces of property, which carried a tax evaluation of $4,900. James Morton, who had seven pieces of real estate and $2,000 in personal property, had a slightly higher assessment of $6,200. Meade and Sallie Johnson, with fourteen pieces of property and an assessment of $5,300, ranked between the two. On a smaller scale, Saul Blair owned two pieces of property valued at $700. Charlie Blair had one piece worth $150, and Calvin Lockridge owned one worth $300.

14. Chalmers, *Hooded Americanism*, 334.

15. While 62 percent of the black teachers and college students from cities across the South indicated in a 1950 survey that the Klan was active in their

communities, 70 percent said they were not afraid of it. In contrast, only 28 percent from rural areas indicated that the Klan was active in their regions, but 50 percent said they *were* afraid of it. Miller and Hill, "Safety, Security, and the South," SRC Papers, AU.

16. For the centrality of the suffrage issue in the 1940s, see Sullivan, *Days of Hope*, 201–2; and Dittmer, *Local People*, 24–25. For the important role played by veterans in attempts to register, see Sullivan, *Days of Hope*, 197, 207, 218, 251–52; Dittmer, *Local People*, 1–2, 4–6, 7, 9; Egerton, *Speak Now Against the Day*, 397–98; and Payne, *I've Got the Light*, 24–25.

17. Quoted in Gavins, "Black North Carolina, the NAACP, and the Origins of the Civil Rights Movement," 8.

18. For detailed accounts of Moore, Evers, and Henry and their extensive associational activity, see Payne, *I've Got the Light*, 29–66; for Williams's wartime experience and his organizational involvement, see Raines, *My Soul Is Rested*, 426, 435–45.

19. Modell, Goulden, and Magnusson describe the impact of military service on "*individual* ambition, at the expense of more diffuse ambitions focused upon blacks considered as a group," in "World War II in the Lives of Black Americans," 838–48 (quote on 838, emphasis in original).

20. Bolte, "He Fought for Freedom," 71.

21. Constituting 10 percent of the nation's population, African Americans comprised 25 percent of the Army's reenlistments during the first year after the war and prior to the imposition of a ceiling on their numbers. Ibid., 117. For figures on the "whitening" of the southern workforce and the decline of the black population in the South, see Wright, *Old South, New South*, 254–57.

22. On the abysmal job prospects awaiting black migrants by 1950, see Wright, *Old South, New South*, 26–27; on the focus of public policy since 1946 on stabilizing purchasing power rather than achieving full employment and description of the economic expansion in the 1960s that reduced the gap between black and white incomes, see Newman et al., *Protest, Politics, and Prosperity*, 8–10.

23. J. S. Reed, *One South*, 119–26.

24. Bartley, *Rise of Massive Resistance*; Egerton, *Speak Now Against the Day*; and Sullivan, *Days of Hope*.

25. Korstad, "Those Who Were Not Afraid"; and Korstad and Lichtenstein, "Opportunities Found and Lost."

26. According to a Birmingham policeman, even the notorious Eugene "Bull" Connor worried "about what the state troopers might do under Mr. Lingo's direction" (Raines, *My Soul Is Rested*, 174)! The most extensive and vivid account of Lingo's racism and its repercussions, however, appear in D. Carter, *Politics of Rage*.

27. National Minority Advisory Council on Criminal Justice, *Inequality of Justice*, 43.

28. Kennedy, *Race, Crime, and the Law*, 328–31; and Brundage, *Lynching in the New South*, 73, 76–77.

29. "Telephone Conversation," October 5, 1946, NAACP Papers, LC.

30. Sheean, "Lawrenceburg Verdict."

31. Stevenson is quoted in Earley, *Circumstantial Evidence*, 330–31.

32. The distinction between unequal protection and unequal enforcement is made by Kennedy in *Race, Crime, and the Law*; see chaps. 2 and 3.

33. Brown interview, July 28, 1989.

34. Quoted in Singal, *The War Within*, 338.

SOURCES CITED

Manuscripts and Documents

Atlanta, Georgia
    Atlanta University
        Southern Regional Council Papers
            Miller, Alexander F., and Mozell Hill. "Safety, Security, and the
                South" (results of 1950 Atlanta University survey of black college
                teachers and students), SRC pamphlet, 1950.
        Southern Regional Council Office
        Southern Regional Council Papers
Boulder, Colorado
    University of Colorado
        Edward P. Costigan Papers
        Western Federation of Miners Papers
Chapel Hill, North Carolina
    Southern Historical Collection, Wilson Library, University of North
        Carolina at Chapel Hill
        Arthur Raper Papers
        Southern Regional Council Papers, microfilm edition
Columbia, Tennessee
    Maury County Chamber of Commerce
        City Directories, 1933–34, 1942, 1948
    Maury County Public Library
        "The Ku Klux Klan in Maury County," typescript
Independence, Missouri
    Truman Library
        Eleanor Bontecou Papers
        Tom Clark Papers
        Clark M. Clifford Papers

McKinzie, Richard D. "Oral History Interview with Eleanor
    Bontecou," Washington, D.C., June 5, 1973
Philleo Nash Papers
President's Committee on Civil Rights (PCCR) Papers
Harry S. Truman, Official File
Memphis, Tennessee
  Memphis Public Library
    Crump-McKellar Correspondence
    Jim Nance McCord Clipping File
    Kenneth Douglas McKellar Clipping File
    Kenneth Douglas McKellar Papers
    Kenneth Douglas McKellar Personal Correspondence
    "Memoirs of Kenneth Douglas McKellar," Vol. 1, ca. 1955
Nashville, Tennessee
  Fisk University
    Z. Alexander Looby Papers
  Tennessee State Library and Archives (TSLA)
    Carpenter, Viola Hagan, and Marymaud Killen Carter. *Our
      Hometown. Lawrenceburg, Tennessee: The Crossroads of Dixie.*
      Lawrence County: Lino-Litho Printers, 1986.
    Clippings File
    Dwyer, Lynn. "A Study of the Social and Economic History of the Columbia
      Reservoir Area, Volume I: 1807–1890." Submitted to the Tennessee
      Valley Authority in fulfillment of TVA Contract No. TV-60056A.
    "Glimpses of Lawrence County History." Class anthology for American
      History 2121L, Columbia State Community College, 1970.
    Manuscript Division
      Jacob McGavock Dickinson Jr. Papers
      Gov. Jim Nance McCord Papers
      "Transcript of Investigation Taken at Columbia, Tenn. on February
        27th and 28th, 1946, in Regard to Racial Disturbance," RG 29,
        State Historian, Box 29, File 7.
    Shannon, Samuel H. "A Study of the Social and Economic History of
      the Columbia Reservoir Area, Volume II: 1890–1945." Submitted to
      the Tennessee Valley Authority in fulfillment of TVA Contract No.
      TV-60056A.
  Tennessee State Supreme Court
    Lloyd Kennedy v. State of Tennessee. Statement of Case, Assignment of
      Errors, Brief and Argument; Reply Brief for the State. Supreme
      Court of Tennessee at Nashville, December 1946.
    State of Tennessee v. Sol Blair et al., No. 6580. Motion for Severance,
      Plea in Abatement, and Motion for Change of Venue. Circuit Court
      of Maury County, May 1946.

State of Tennessee v. William A. Pillow and Lloyd Kennedy, No. 4720.
   Circuit Court of Maury County. November 15, 1946. 4 vols.
New York, New York
   Columbia University
      Robert Minor Papers
Raleigh, North Carolina
   Author's personal files
      Federal Grand Jury (FGJ) Records: "Columbia, Tennessee,
         Investigation Before the United States District Court Grand Jury of
         Tennessee, Beginning April 8, 1946." 14 vols. [Vols. 12 and 13 missing].
         Obtained from the United States District Court, Middle District of
         Tennessee, via court order dated May 16, 1990. Originals are housed
         in the National Archives, Southeast Region, East Pointe, Ga.
      Letters
         Robert L. Bomar Jr., M.D., to author, January 18, 1990
         Laurent Frantz to author, January 30, 1991
      Tennessee Defense Force History, spiral notebook given to author by
         Brigadier General Harrell E. Webb, Chief of Staff, Headquarters of
         Tennessee State Guard Reserve
      Trial Transcript (TT): *State of Tennessee v. Sol Blair et al.*, No. 6580,
         September 19–October 4, 1946, Circuit Court of Lawrence County.
         10 vols. and Arguments. [aka *State of Tennessee v. Sol Blair*]
Washington, D.C.
   Federal Bureau of Investigation, Headquarters
      FBI Case 44-1366, Sections 1–6, Sub-A
   Howard University
      Civil Rights Documentation Project
      Campbell C. Johnson Papers
      Leon Ransom Clipping File
   Library of Congress
      NAACP Papers
   National Archives
      Army Adjutant General Files: RG 330, RG 407
      Bureau of Agricultural Economics Papers
      William H. Hastie Files, RG 107

Newspapers

The Afro-American   *Daily Worker*
Charlotte [N.C.] Observer   *[Lawrenceburg, Tenn.] Democrat-Union*
Chicago Defender   *Memphis Commercial Appeal*
[Columbia, Tenn.] Daily Herald *Nashville Banner*

Nashville Globe
Nashville Tennessean
New York Herald Tribune
New York Times

Norfolk Journal and Guide
Pittsburgh Courier
Washington Post

Interviews

Barrett, George. May 18, 1992.
Birch, Adolphus A. July 25, 1989.
Bowman, Patricia Martin. February 3, 1990.
Bradley, Jesse. July 30, 1989.
Branstetter, Cecil. May 18, 1992.
Brown, Clarence. July 28, 1989.
Bumpus, Paul F. January 30, 1990.
Cooper, Addie Lou Blair. February 3, 1990.
Davis, James Siegel. July 30, 1989.
Durr, Virginia. November 2, 1990.
Edwards, Clifford. July 28, 1989.
Evans, Amon Carter. May 17, 1992.
Farmer, Fyke. August 2, 1989.
Fleming, Flo. July 29, 1989.
Fleming, John, Jr. July 29, 1989.
Fleming, Peggy Dickinson. May 17, 1992.
Franklin, John Hope. December 2, 1992.
Frantz, Laurent. June 16, 1996.
Gordon, Wallace. July 28, 1989.
Harrington, Penny. May 10, 1992.
Harwell, Avaleen (Mrs. W. A. "Bud"). July 30, 1989.
Hopton, W. E. May 18, 1992.
Hubbard, Maceo. February 27, 1988, and June 8, 1990.
Johnson, Guy. February 22, 1988, and July 12, 1989.
Johnson, Herbert. May 16, 1992.
Jones, Yollette Trigg. May 11, 1992.
Leech, Attorney William M. July 28, 1989.
Lewis, Dwight. February 2, 1990.
Lockridge, Raymond. July 28, 31, 1989, and February 6, 1990.
Matthews, Jimmy. February 5, 1990.
Murray, Milton. February 4, 1990.
Newbern, George A. February 3, 1990.
Noles, E. B. May 11, 1992.
Olker, Genella. May 11, 1992.
O'Rear, Greg. February 14, 1990.

O'Rear, Martha Remslinger. May 16, 1992.
Orr, Web. May 17, 1992.
Ryan, Ronald. February 3, 1990.
Scales, Junius. October 27, 1988, and April 2, 1990.
Seigenthaler, John. May 11, 1992.
Stahlman, Mildred. May 18, 1992.
Stofel, Bernard. July 29, 1989.
Tisby, Ophelia. February 2, 1990.
Underwood, James J., Jr. July 30, 1989.
Westbrook, Grafta Looby. May 11, 1992.
Williams, Avon. July 25, 1989.
Wyatt, Eugene. July 26, 1989

Books

Adams, Frank T. *James A. Dombrowski: An American Heretic, 1897–1983*. Knoxville: University of Tennessee Press, 1992.

Alexander, Virginia W., and Margaret D. Ashton, eds. *Maury County Remembers World War II*. 2 vols. Columbia, Tenn.: Maury County Historical Society, 1991.

Ash, Stephen V. *Middle Tennessee Society Transformed, 1860–1870*. Baton Rouge: Louisiana State University Press, 1988.

Auerbach, Jerold S. *Justice Without Law?* New York: Oxford University Press, 1983.

——. *Unequal Justice: Lawyers and Social Change in Modern America*. New York: Oxford University Press, 1976.

Bartley, Numan V. *The Rise of Massive Resistance: Race and Politics in the South in the 1950s*. Baton Rouge: Louisiana State University Press, 1969.

Bass, Jack. *Unlikely Heroes*. Tuscaloosa: University of Alabama Press, 1981.

Belknap, Michael R. *Federal Law and Southern Order: Racial Violence and Constitutional Conflict in the Post-Brown South*. Athens: University of Georgia Press, 1987.

Bettelheim, Bruno, and Morris Janowitz. *Dynamics of Prejudice*. First published 1950; reprinted in *Social Change and Prejudice*, London: Free Press of Glencoe, 1964.

Black, Earl, and Merle Black. *Politics and Society in the South*. Cambridge: Harvard University Press, 1987.

Brundage, W. Fitzhugh. *Lynching in the New South: Georgia and Virginia, 1880–1930*. Urbana: University of Illinois Press, 1993.

Capeci, Dominic J., Jr., and Martha Wilkerson. *Layered Violence: The Detroit Rioters of 1943*. Jackson: University Press of Mississippi, 1991.

Carr, Robert K. *Federal Protection of Civil Rights: Quest for a Sword*. Ithaca, N.Y.: Cornell University Press, 1947.

Carter, Dan. *The Politics of Rage: George Wallace, the Origins of the New Conservatism, and the Transformation of American Politics*. New York: Simon and Schuster, 1995.

———. *Scottsboro: A Tragedy of the American South*. Rev. ed. Baton Rouge: Louisiana State University Press, 1969.

Cell, John W. *The Highest Stage of White Supremacy: The Origins of Segregation in South Africa and the American South*. Cambridge: Cambridge University Press, 1982.

Chalmers, David. *Hooded Americanism: The History of the Ku Klux Klan*. Durham, N.C.: Duke University Press, 1965.

Chappell, David L. *Inside Agitators: White Southerners in the Civil Rights Movement*. Baltimore: Johns Hopkins University Press, 1994.

Corlew, Robert H. *Tennessee: A Short History*. 2d ed. Knoxville: University of Tennessee Press, 1981.

Dalfiume, Richard M. *Desegregation of the U.S. Armed Forces: Fighting on Two Fronts, 1939–1953*. Columbia: University of Missouri Press, 1969.

Davis, Allison, Burleigh B. Gardner, and Mary R. Gardner. *Deep South: A Social Anthropological Study of Caste and Class*. Chicago: University of Chicago Press, 1941.

Dittmer, John. *Local People: The Struggle for Civil Rights in Mississippi*. Urbana: University of Illinois Press, 1994.

Dower, John W. *War Without Mercy: Race and Power in the Pacific War*. New York: Pantheon, 1986.

Earley, Pete. *Circumstantial Evidence: Death, Life, and Justice in a Southern Town*. New York: Bantam, 1995.

Egerton, John. *Speak Now Against the Day: The Generation Before the Civil Rights Movement in the South*. New York: Alfred A. Knopf, 1994.

Elliff, John Thomas. *The United States Department of Justice and Individual Rights, 1937–1962*. New York: Garland, 1987.

Ellison, Ralph. *Invisible Man*. New York: Random House, 1952.

Ellsworth, Scott. *Death in a Promised Land: The Tulsa Riot of 1921*. Baton Rouge: Louisiana State University Press, 1982.

Fairclough, Adam. *Race and Democracy: The Civil Rights Struggle in Louisiana, 1915–1972*. Athens: University of Georgia Press, 1995.

Finkle, Lee. *Forum for Protest: The Black Press During World War II*. Rutherford, N.J.: Fairleigh Dickinson University Press, 1975.

Fones-Wolf, Elizabeth A. *Selling Free Enterprise: The Business Assault on Labor and Liberalism, 1945–60*. Urbana: University of Illinois Press, 1994.

Gilmore, Glenda A. *Gender and Jim Crow: Women and the Politics of White Supremacy in North Carolina, 1896–1920*. Chapel Hill: University of North Carolina Press, 1996.

Graham, Hugh Davis. *Crisis in Print: Desegregation and the Press in Tennessee*. Nashville: Vanderbilt University Press, 1967.

Greenburg, Jack. *Crusaders in the Courts: How a Dedicated Band of Lawyers Fought for the Civil Rights Revolution*. New York: Basic, 1994.

Hagood, Margaret Jarman. *Mothers of the South: Portraiture of the White Tenant Farm Woman*. First published 1939; reprint, New York: W. W. Norton, 1977.

Hall, Jacquelyn Dowd. *Revolt Against Chivalry: Jessie Daniel Amers and the Women's Campaign Against Lynching*. New York: Columbia University Press, 1979.

Hamilton, Charles V. *The Bench and the Ballot: Southern Federal Judges and Black Voters*. New York: Oxford University Press, 1973.

Higginbotham, A. Leon, Jr. *Shades of Freedom: Racial Politics and Presumptions of the American Legal Process*. New York: Oxford University Press, 1996.

Hirsch, Arnold R. *Making the Second Ghetto: Race and Housing in Chicago, 1940–1960*. Cambridge: Cambridge University Press, 1983.

Honey, Michael. *Southern Labor and Black Civil Rights: Organizing Memphis Workers*. Urbana: University of Illinois Press, 1993.

Ikard, Robert W. *No More Social Lynchings*. Franklin, Tenn.: Hillsboro Press, 1997.

Jackson, Walter A. *Gunnar Myrdal and America's Conscience: Social Engineering and Racial Liberalism, 1938–1987*. Chapel Hill: University of North Carolina Press, 1990.

Kelley, Robin D. G. *Race Rebels: Culture, Politics, and the Black Working Class*. New York: Maxwell Macmillan International, 1994.

Kennedy, Randall. *Race, Crime, and the Law*. New York: Pantheon, 1997.

Kenzer, Robert C. *Kinship and Neighborhood in a Southern Community: Orange County, North Carolina, 1849–1881*. Knoxville: University of Tennessee Press, 1987.

Key, V. O., Jr. *Southern Politics in State and Nation*. New ed. Knoxville: University of Tennessee Press, 1949.

Kirby, Jack Temple. *Rural Worlds Lost: The American South, 1920–1960*. Baton Rouge: Louisiana State University Press, 1987.

Krueger, Thomas A. *And Promises to Keep: The Southern Conference for Human Welfare, 1938–1948*. Nashville: Vanderbilt University Press, 1968.

Kuhn, Cliff M., Harlon E. Joye, and E. Bernard West. *Living Atlanta: An Oral History of the City, 1914–1948*. Athens: University of Georgia Press, 1990.

Lamon, Lester C. *Black Tennesseans, 1900–1930*. Knoxville: University of Tennessee Press, 1976.

Lee, Ulysses. *The Employment of Negro Troops*. Washington, D.C.: Center of Military History, United States Army, 1986.

Lewis, Eugene. *Public Entrepreneurship—Toward a Theory of Bureaucratic*

Political Power: The Organizational Lives of Hyman Rickover, J. Edgar Hoover, and Robert Moses. Bloomington: Indiana University Press, 1980.

McGill, Ralph. *The South and the Southerner*. Athens: University of Georgia Press, 1992.

McNeil, Genna Rae. *Groundwork: Charles Hamilton Houston and the Struggle for Civil Rights*. Philadelphia: University of Pennsylvania Press, 1983.

Mann, Coramae Richey. *Unequal Justice: A Question of Color*. Bloomington: Indiana University Press, 1993.

Minor, Robert. *Lynching and Frame-Up in Tennessee*. New York: New Century, 1946.

Motley, Mary Penick, ed. *The Invisible Soldier: The Experience of the Black Soldier, World War II*. Detroit: Wayne State University, 1975.

Murray, Pauli. *Proud Shoes: The Story of an American Family*. New York: Harper, 1956.

Myrdal, Gunnar. *An American Dilemma: The Negro Problem and* Modern *Democracy*. Vol. 2. New York: Harper, 1944.

Nathans, Sydney. *The Quest for Progress: The Way We Lived in North Carolina, 1870–1920*. Chapel Hill: University of North Carolina, 1983.

National Minority Advisory Council on Criminal Justice. *Inequality of Justice: Report on Crime and the Administration of Justice in the Minority Community*. Washington, D.C.: National Minority Advisory Council on Criminal Justice, 1982.

Newman, Dorothy K., Nancy J. Amidei, Barbara L. Carter, Dawn Day, William J. Kruvant, and Jack S. Russell. *Protest, Politics, and Prosperity: Black Americans and White Institutions, 1940–1975*. New York: Pantheon, 1978.

Nieman, Donald G. *Promises to Keep: African-Americans and the Constitutional Order, 1776 to the Present*. New York: Oxford University Press, 1991.

Odum, Howard W. *Race and Rumors of Race: Challenge to American Crisis*. New York: Negro Universities Press, 1943.

O'Reilly, Kenneth. *Racial Matters: The FBI's Secret File on Black America, 1960–1972*. New York: Free Press, 1989.

Paluadan, Phillip Shaw. *Victims: A True Story of the Civil War*. Knoxville: University of Tennessee Press, 1981.

Payne, Charles M. *I've Got the Light of Freedom: The Organizing Tradition and the Mississippi Freedom Struggle*. Berkeley: University of California Press, 1995.

Peltason, J. W. *58 Lonely Men: Southern Federal Judges and School Desegregation*. Urbana: University of Illinois Press, 1971.

Perry, Jennings. *Democracy Begins at Home: The Tennessee Fight on the Poll Tax*. Philadelphia: J. B. Lippincott, 1944.

Polenberg, Richard. *War and Society: The United States, 1941–1945*. New York: J. P. Lippincott, 1972.

Portelli, Alessandro. *The Death of Luigi Trastulli and Other Stories: Form and Meaning in Oral History*. Albany: State University of New York Press, 1991.

Powers, Richard Gid. *Secrecy and Power: The Life of J. Edgar Hoover*. New York: Free Press, 1987.

Rabinowitz, Howard. *Race Relations in the Urban South, 1865–1890*. Urbana: University of Illinois Press, 1980.

Raines, Howell. *My Soul Is Rested: Movement Days in the Deep South Remembered*. New York: Penguin, 1977.

Raper, Arthur. *The Tragedy of Lynching*. Chapel Hill: University of North Carolina Press, 1933.

Reed, John Shelton. *One South: An Ethnic Approach to Regional Culture*. Baton Rouge: Louisiana State University Press, 1982.

Reed, Linda. *Simple Decency and Common Sense: The Southern Conference Movement, 1938–1963*. Bloomington: Indiana University Press, 1991.

Rowan, Carl. *South of Freedom*. New York: Alfred A. Knopf, 1952.

Rudwick, Elliott. *Race Riot at East St. Louis, July 2, 1917*. Urbana: University of Illinois Press, 1964.

Schott, Fred W., Jr. *Servants . . . Not Lords: A History of the Tennessee Highway Patrol, 1929–1979. Fifty Years of Heritage*. Paducah, Ky.: Taylor Publishing, 1981.

Schuman, Howard, Charlotte Steeh, and Lawrence Bobo. *Racial Attitudes in America: Trends and Interpretations*. Cambridge: Harvard University Press, 1985.

Schweninger, Loren. *Black Property Owners in the South, 1790–1915*. Urbana: University of Illinois Press, 1990.

Singal, Daniel Joseph. *The War Within: From Victorian to Modernist Thought in the South, 1919–1945*. Chapel Hill: University of North Carolina Press, 1982.

Sitkoff, Harvard. *A New Deal for Blacks: The Emergence of Civil Rights as a National Issue. The Depression Decade*. New York: Oxford University Press, 1978.

[Smith, Frank H.]. *Frank H. Smith's History of Maury County, Tennessee*. Columbia: Maury County Historical Society, 1969.

Smith, Graham. *When Jim Crow Met John Bull: Black American Soldiers in World War II Britain*. New York: St. Martin's Press, 1987.

Stouffer, Samuel A., Edward A. Suchman, Leland C. DeVinney, Shirley A. Star, and Robin M. Williams, Jr. *The American Soldier*. 4 vols. Princeton, N.J.: Princeton University Press, 1949.

Sullivan, Patricia. *Days of Hope: Race and Democracy in the New Deal Era*. Chapel Hill: University of North Carolina Press, 1996.

Summers, Anthony. *Official and Confidential: The Secret Life of J. Edgar Hoover*. New York: G. P. Putnam's Sons, 1993.

Tindall, George B. *The Emergence of the New South, 1913–1945*. Baton Rouge: Louisiana State University Press, 1967.

Trelease, Allen W. *White Terror: The Ku Klux Klan Conspiracy and Southern Reconstruction*. New York: Harper and Row, 1971.

Tucker, David M. *Lieutenant Lee of Beale Street*. Nashville: Vanderbilt University Press, 1971.

Turner, William Bruce. *History of Maury County, Tennessee*. Nashville, Tenn.: Parthenon, 1955.

Tuttle, William M. *Race Riot: Chicago in the Red Summer of 1919*. New York: Atheneum, 1974.

U.S. Census Bureau. *Fifteenth Census of the United States: 1930, Population*. Vol. 3, pt. 2. Washington, D.C.: Government Printing Office, 1932.

——. *Ninth Census of the United States: 1870, Population*. Vol. 1. Washington, D.C.: Government Printing Office, 1872.

——. *Seventeenth Census of the United States: 1950, Agriculture*. Vol. 1, pt. 20. Washington, D.C.: Government Printing Office, 1952.

——. *Seventeenth Census of the United States: 1950, Population*. Vol. 2, pt. 42. Washington, D.C.: Government Printing Office, 1952.

——. *Sixteenth Census of the United States: 1940, Agriculture*. Vol. 1, pt. 4. Washington, D.C.: Government Printing Office, 1942.

——. *Sixteenth Census of the United States: 1940, Population*. Vol. 2, pt. 6. Washington, D.C.: Government Printing Office, 1942.

——. *Thirteenth Census of the United States: 1910, Agriculture*. Vol. 7. Washington, D.C.: Government Printing Office, 1913.

——. *United States Census of Agriculture: 1945*. Vol. 1, pt. 20. Washington, D.C.: Government Printing Office, 1946.

Walker, Samuel E. *A Critical History of Police Reform*. Lexington, Mass.: Lexington Books, 1977.

——. *The Police in America: An Introduction*. New York: McGraw-Hill, 1983.

——. *Popular Justice: A History of American Criminal Justice*. New York: Oxford University Press, 1980.

Weare, Walter B. *Black Business in the New South: A Social History of the North Carolina Mutual Life Insurance Company*. Urbana: University of Illinois Press, 1973.

White, Walter. *A Man Called White*. New York: Viking, 1948.

Williams, Hubert, and Patrick V. Murphy. *The Evolving Strategy of Police: A Minority View*. Washington, D.C.: U.S. Department of Justice, 1990.

Wilson, Charles Reagan. *Baptized in Blood: The Religion of the Lost Cause, 1865–1920*. Athens: University of Georgia Press, 1980.

Wilson, James Q. *The Investigators: Managing FBI and Narcotics Agents*. New York: Basic, 1978.

Wright, Gavin. *Old South, New South: Revolutions in the Southern Economy Since the Civil War.* New York: Basic, 1986.

Wyatt-Brown, Bertram. *Honor and Violence in the Old South.* New York: Oxford University Press, 1986.

Zangrando, Robert L. *The NAACP Crusade Against Lynching, 1909–1950.* Philadelphia: Temple University Press, 1980.

Articles and Essays

Barker, George. "Man Behind the Move." *Nashville Tennessean Magazine,* April 16, 1961, 12–3, 22.

——. "No Place to Hide." *Nashville Tennessean Magazine,* April 23, 1961, 14–5, 20.

Beeler, Dorothy. "Race Riot in Columbia, Tennessee, February 25–27, 1946," *Tennessee Historical Quarterly* 39 (Spring 1980): 49–61.

Bolte, Charles G. "He Fought for Freedom." *Survey Graphic* 36 (January 1947): 69–71, 116–17.

Burran, James A. "Urban Racial Violence in the South During World War II: A Comparative Overview." In *From the Old South to the New: Essays on the Transitional South,* edited by Walter J. Fraser Jr. and Winfred B. Moore Jr., 167–77. Westport, Conn.: Greenwood, 1981.

Butterfield, Robert. "Silliman—He's a Wonder." *Saturday Evening Post* 213 (November 23, 1940): 12–13, 86–92.

Campbell, Will D. "The World of a Redneck." *Christianity and Crisis* 34 (May 27, 1974): 111–19.

Capeci, Dominic J., Jr. "The Lynching of Cleo Wright, Federal Protection of Constitutional Rights during World War II." *Journal of American History* 72 (March 1986): 859–87.

Carter, Wilmoth. "Negro Main Street as a Symbol of Discrimination." *Phylon* (Fall 1960): 234–42.

Cooper, Weldon. "The State Police Movement in the South." *Journal of Politics* 1, no. 4 (November 1939): 414–33.

Daniel, Pete. "Going Among Strangers: Southern Reactions to World War II." *Journal of American History* 77, no. 3 (December 1990): 886–911.

Fields, Barbara. "Ideology and Race in American History." In *Region, Race and Reconstruction: Essays in Honor of C. Vann Woodward,* edited by J. Morgan Kousser and James M. McPherson, 143–77. New York: Oxford University Press, 1982.

Griffin, Larry J., Paula Clark, and Joanne C. Sandberg. "Narrative and Event, Lynching and Historical Sociology." In *Under Sentence of Death, Lynching in the South,* edited by W. Fitzhugh Brundage, 24–47. Chapel Hill: University of North Carolina Press, 1997.

Hall, E. T., Jr. "Race Prejudice and Negro-White Relations in the Army." *American Journal of Sociology* 52 (March 1947): 401–9.

Hastie, William H. "Charles Hamilton Houston (1895–1950)." *Crisis*, June 1950.

Honey, Michael. "Industrial Unionism and Racial Justice in Memphis." In *Organized Labor in the Twentieth-Century South*, edited by Robert H. Zieger, 135–57. Knoxville: University of Tennessee Press, 1991.

Hughes, Michael, and David H. Demo. "Self-Perceptions of Black Americans: Self-Esteem and Personal Efficacy." *American Journal of Sociology* 95 (July 1989): 132–57.

Johnson, Guion Griffis. "The Ideology of White Supremacy, 1876–1910." In *Essays in Southern History*, edited by Fletcher M. Green, 124–56. Chapel Hill: University of North Carolina Press, 1949.

Korstad, Robert. "Those Who Were Not Afraid: Winston-Salem, 1943." In *Working Lives: The Southern Exposure History of Labor in the South*, edited by Marc S. Miller, 184–99. New York: Pantheon, 1980.

Korstad, Robert, and Nelson Lichtenstein. "Opportunities Found and Lost: Labor, Radicals, and the Early Civil Rights Movement." *Journal of American History* 75, no. 3 (December 1988): 786–811.

Lawrence, Charles R., Jr. "Race Riots in the United States, 1942–1946." In *Negro Year Book: A Review of Events Affecting Negro Life, 1941–1946*, edited by Jessie Parkhurst Guzman, 232–57. Tuskegee, Ala.: Department of Records and Research, Tuskegee Institute, 1947.

Meier, August, and David Lewis. "History of the Negro Upper Class in Atlanta, Georgia, 1890–1958." *Journal of Negro Education* 28 (1959): 128–39.

Meier, August, and Elliott Rudwick. "Attorneys Black and White: A Case Study of Race Relations within the NAACP." *Journal of American History* 62, no. 4 (March 1976): 913–46.

Modell, John, Marc Goulden, and Sigurdur Magnusson. "World War II in the Lives of Black Americans: Some Findings and an Interpretation." *Journal of American History* 76, no. 3 (December 1989): 838–48.

Prattis, P. L. "The Morale of the Negro in the Armed Services of the United States." *Journal of Negro Education* 12 (Summer 1943): 355–63.

Sheean, Vincent. "Lawrenceburg Verdict." *New Republic*, October 14, 1946, 472–73.

Walker, Samuel E. "The Origins of the American Police-Community Relations Movement: The 1940s." In *Criminal Justice History: An International Annual*, edited by Henry Cohen, 1:225–46. New York: Crime and Justice History Group, Inc. in association with the John Jay Press, 1980.

Weare, Walter B. "Charles Clinton Spaulding: Middle-Class Leadership in the Age of Segregation." In *Black Leaders of the Twentieth Century*, edited by John Hope Franklin and August Meier, 167–90. Urbana: University of Illinois Press, 1982.

Whitt, Wayne. "Long Career Coming to an End." *Tennessean*, June 7, 1970, 5.

Williams, Juan. "Marshall's Law." *Washington Post Magazine*, January 7, 1990, 12–19, 27–29.

Woodruff, Nan Elizabeth. "Mississippi Delta Panters and Debates over Mechanization, Labor, and Civil Rights in the 1940s." *Journal of Southern History* 60, no. 2 (May 1994): 263–84.

York, Max. "A Tall Man with His Feet on the Ground." *Nashville Tennessean Magazine*, Jan. 17, 1971, 4–6.

Dissertations, Theses, and Unpublished Manuscripts

Alcock, Donald Gordon. "A Study in Continuity: Maury County, Tennessee, 1850–1870." Ph.D. diss., University of Southern California, 1985.

Beeler, Dorothy Sue. "Race Riot in Columbia, Tennessee, February 25–27, 1946." M.A. thesis, Vanderbilt University, 1972.

Black, Creed. "Parsonage to Publisher. The Life of Silliman Evans, 1894–1955." Unpublished manuscript in possession of Amon Carter Evans, 1955.

Brundage, W. Fitzhugh. "Southern Black Responses to White Violence, 1880–1930." Paper presented to the Organization of American Historians, Washington, D.C., 1990.

Carter, Wilmoth. "Negro Main Street of a Contemporary Urban Community." Ph.D. diss., University of Chicago, 1959.

Galloway, Patton G., Executive Secretary, Conference of District Attorneys, to District Attorneys, "Memo on the District Attorney's Roles," February 26, 1988.

Gardner, James Bailey. "Political Leadership in a Period of Transition: Frank G. Clement, Albert Gore, Estes Kefauver, and Tennessee Politics, 1948–1956." Ph.D. diss., Vanderbilt University, 1978.

Gavins, Raymond. "Black North Carolina, the NAACP, and the Origins of the Civil Rights Movement: 1945–1955." Paper presented to the 1988 Conference on Civil Rights Studies, Charlottesville, Va., May 5, 1988.

Jones, Yollette Trigg. "The Columbia, Tennessee 'Race Riot' of 1946 and the Legal Aftermath." M.A. thesis, Duke University, 1978.

Parrish, Colonel Noel F. "The Segregation of Negroes in the Army Air Force." M.A. thesis, Air University, Air Command and Staff School of Marshall Field, Ala., 1947.

Ray, Gerda Winston Pettus. "Contested Legitimacy: Creation of the State Police in New York, 1890–1930." Ph.D. diss., University of California at Berkeley, 1990.

——. " 'A Distinctively American Type of Men': The Campaign for the State Police in New York." Paper presented to the Organization of American Historians, 1993.

Smith, Marjorie. "Racial Confrontation in Columbia, Tennessee, 1946." M.A. thesis, Atlanta University, July 1971.

INDEX

middle-class status of, 72–73, 74, 269 (n. 33)

Blair family, 31, 32, 33, 66, 69, 73, 87, 146, 154, 179, 213, 216, 217

Bomar, Lynn, 31, 33, 49, 157, 173, 179, 194, 199; arrival in Columbia, 18–19, 20–21; actions after invasion, 28–29, 33; and jail shootings, 32; and federal grand jury, 36, 39; at Lawrenceburg trial, 45, 265 (n. 107); background and policing methods of, 167–69, 291 (n. 89); and Dickinson, 171–72, 187, 189, 190, 251; ouster of, 174. *See also* Highway Patrol, Tennessee

Bombings, post–World War II, 279 (n. 5)

Bontecou, Eleanor, 36, 37, 141, 171, 187, 192, 201, 202, 209

"The Bottom" (downtown district of Columbia, Tenn.), 11, 12, 14, 17, 59, 151, 179, 232; description of, 65–68, 94, 95, 169. *See also* Mink Slide

Bradley, Jesse, 222, 241, 242–43, 304 (n. 31), 309 (n. 99)

Brown, Clarence, 67, 97, 102, 105, 106, 107, 255–56

Browning, Gordon, 174

Bumpus, Paul F., 31, 37, 39, 41, 42, 149, 151, 236; and Lawrenceburg trial, 45, 48–50, 52, 213–23, 232–33, 237, 241; and legal formalism, 213–14, 219–20; and interrogation of James ("Digger") Johnson, 216–19

Businessmen, black: 3, 149; and Bottom, 68–72; middle-class, 72–73; and whites, 73; and customers, 73–74, 246, 247; multifaceted role of, 74–75; militancy of, 246–47, 310 (n. 6); strategic role of, 248; small size of establishments, 248, 310 (n. 12)

Butler, Hilton, 189, 190

Caldwell, Arthur B., 36, 37, 187, 192, 202, 209

Camp Forrest (Tenn.), 99, 103, 104, 147

Carmack, Edward Ward, Jr. ("Ned"), 204, 206, 208, 210

Carmack, Edward Ward, Sr., 33

Caudle, Lamar, 183, 184, 186, 192, 202, 294 (n. 11)

Cheatham, Joel, 79, 82, 84, 85

Cheek, Cordie. *See* Lynchings: Maury County: Cordie Cheek

Cheek, Fate, 78, 81, 82, 84

Cheek, Rush, 80, 82, 85

Cheek, Tenny, 78, 81, 82

Choate, Henry. *See* Lynchings: Maury County: Henry Choate

CIO. *See* Congress of Industrial Organizations

Civil Rights Section. *See* United States Justice Department

Clark, Edward ("Ed"), 25–26, 28, 261 (n. 61)

Clark, Tom, 34, 36, 183, 192, 199, 200, 209

Claude, Borgie, 19, 36, 283 (n. 73)

Clement, Frank, 174, 292 (n. 99)

Columbia 1946 incident, white mob in: 11, 75; taxi drivers' role in, 11, 13, 19, 130, 283 (n. 71); milling quality of, 11, 15, 109, 132; composition of, 11, 130, 283 (n. 71); Culleoka residents in, 130–31; veterans in, 130–31; imbibing of, 283 (n. 73)

Commission on Interracial Cooperation, 109

Committee of 100, 35

Communist Party, American, 4, 34, 35, 181, 209

Congress of Industrial Organizations (CIO), 30, 94, 174–75, 176, 181, 206, 207–9; Political Action Committee of, 35, 41

Segregation, 3, 68, 102–5, 123, 127, 144, 146, 216, 218, 252–53
Sheean, Vincent, 45, 183, 254
Shelton, Hugh Todd, Sr., 41, 42, 45, 46–47, 52, 213, 236
Slavery, 60, 216
Smith, Ernest F. ("Jack"), 31, 36, 179, 216–19
Smith, Turner, 35, 184, 185, 294 (n. 11)
Soldiers, Confederate, 116, 117
Soldiers, World War II:
—black: 5, 64, 97, 128; broadening experiences of war service, 97–102; discrimination against, 102–5; encounters with Highway Patrol, 165–66; high reenlistment rate of, 250, 311 (n. 21); attitudes toward Army, 277 (n. 46); service commands, 277 (n. 50); collective protests by, 278 (n. 60); complaints from southern, 278 (n. 61)
—white: 16, 88, 133, 134, 250; racial attitudes of, 128–29, 233–34, 283 (n. 68)
Southern Conference for Human Welfare (SCHW), 4, 5, 30, 182; mobilization in behalf of black Columbians, 34, 35, 181, 209; hostility toward, 36, 41, 176, 177, 201, 208
Southern Regional Council (SRC), 4, 28, 34, 35, 97, 177
SRC. See Southern Regional Council
Stahlman, Edward Bushrod, 202–4, 299 (n. 73)
Stahlman, James Geddes, 203, 208
State Guard, Tennessee, 2, 18, 29, 33, 38, 54–55, 141, 143, 189, 201; role in invasion of Bottom, 21–22; pilfering by, 28, 290 (n. 66); structure and members of, 158–62

Stephenson, Gladys, 36, 83, 276 (n. 19); confrontation over radio repair, 7–10; war and personal efficacy, 87–88, 92–94, 108; and sheriff, 149
Stephenson, James, 12, 31, 35, 46, 59, 102, 108, 131, 132; confrontation over radio repair, 7–11, 87, 131; self-defense, 13; departure from Columbia, 15; before federal grand jury, 36–38; as Navy veteran, 88, 93, 98, 105; and law officers, 142, 149; life after Columbia incident, 259 (n. 28)
Stephenson family, 40, 55, 83, 143, 156
Stewart, A. T. ("Tom"), 204, 206, 210
Stewart, Napoleon, 32, 37, 162, 186
Stofel, Bernard O., 97, 128, 144–45, 146, 147, 148
Supreme Court: Tennessee, 53; U.S., 53, 180, 185, 211

Tamm, Edward, 201
Tarpley, Bayard, 177–78
Tennessean. See *Nashville Tennessean*
Tennessee Highway Patrol. *See* Highway Patrol, Tennessee
Tennessee Interracial Commission, 77, 86
Tennessee State Guard. *See* State Guard, Tennessee
Thurmond, Strom, 177, 209, 216
Tilly, Mrs. M. E., 34, 35, 177
Tobias, Channing, 35, 214–15
Trials, state: indictments, 39–40, 302–3 (n. 3). *See also* Kennedy-Pillow trial; Lawrenceburg trial
Truman, Harry S., 183, 209
Tuskegee University, 4, 137
Twitty, W. B., 35, 97